Strategic Market Planning

Problems and
Analytical Approaches

Strategic Market Planning

Problems and Analytical Approaches

DEREK F. ABELL
Associate Professor of Business Administration
Harvard University Graduate School of Business Administration
Boston, Massachusetts 02163

JOHN S. HAMMOND
President
John S. Hammond & Associates
Lincoln, Massachusetts 01773

PRENTICE-HALL, INC. Englewood Cliffs, New Jersey 07632

Library of Congress Cataloging in Publication Data

Abell, Derek F.   (date)
    Strategic Market Planning.

    Includes index.
    1. Marketing management. 2. Marketing
management--Case studies. I. Hammond, John S.,
(date)   Joint author. II. Title.
HF5415.13.A24   658.8   79-12073
ISBN 0-13-851089-X

© 1979 by PRENTICE-HALL, INC., Englewood Cliffs, New Jersey 07632

The copyright on the text portion of this book is held by Derek F. Abell
and John S. Hammond.

The copyright on the Butler & Hammer, Inc. case is held by John S.
Hammond.

The copyright on all other cases in this book is held by the President and
Fellows of Harvard College, and they are published herein by express
permission.

Case material of the Harvard Graduate School of Business Administration
is made possible by the cooperation of business firms who may wish to
remain anonymous by having names, quantities, and other identifying
details disguised while maintaining basic relationships. Cases are prepared
as the basis for class discussion rather than to illustrate either effective
or ineffective handling of administrative situations.

Printed in the United States of America

10 9 8 7 6 5

Cover design by Robin Battino
Book design by Karen Siletti (Walken Graphics)
Manufacturing buyer: John Hall

Prentice-Hall International, Inc., *London*
Prentice-Hall of Australia Pty. Limited, *Sydney*
Prentice-Hall of Canada, Ltd., *Toronto*
Prentice-Hall of India Private Limited, *New Delhi*
Prentice-Hall of Japan, Inc., *Tokyo*
Prentice-Hall of Southeast Asia Pte. Ltd., *Singapore*
Whitehall Books Limited, *Wellington, New Zealand*

Contents

Chapter 3:
COST DYNAMICS: SCALE AND EXPERIENCE EFFECTS **103**

Scale Effect. Experience Effect. Sources of the Experience Effect. Prices and Experience. Strategic Implications. Efficiency vs. Effectiveness: Limitations to Strategies Based on Experience or Scale. Practical Considerations in Using Experience Curves: The Behavior of Costs Over Time. Analyzing Experience on Different Cost Components. Shared Experience. Cost Differences Between Competitors. Measuring Experience From the Right Starting Point. Cost Data. Time Span. Defining the Unit of Analysis. Projecting Future Costs. Steps in Analyzing the Experience Effect. Summary.

Part II:
FORMAL STRATEGIC PLANNING METHODS **171**

Chapter 4:
PORTFOLIO ANALYSIS. **173**

The Growth-Share Matrix. Portfolio Strategy. The Growth-Gain Matrix. Types of Strategies: Building Market Share. Holding Market Share. Harvesting. Withdrawal. Definition of "Product" and "Market". Strategic Analysis of the Product Portfolio: 1. Check for Internal Balance. 2. Look for Trends. 3. Evaluate Competition. 4. Consider Factors Not Captured in the Portfolio Display. 5. Develop Possible "Target" Portfolios. 6. Check Financial Balance. *Limitations. Some Application Considerations. Summary.*

Chapter 5:
MARKET ATTRACTIVENESS—
AND BUSINESS POSITION ASSESSMENT **211**

Market Attractiveness and Business Position. Practical Considerations. Identifying the Relevant Factors. Relating the Factors to Market Attractiveness and Business Position. Weighting the Factors. Constructing the Present Investment Opportunity Chart. Assessing the Future Opportunity: Stage 1: Exploring the Impact of a "No Change" Strategy. Stage 2: The Strategy Decision. Defining the Unit of Analysis. Summary.

Preface

This advanced text and case book on "strategic market planning" (or "business planning" as it is often called) presents important new conceptual ideas that deal with contemporary management problems. It recognizes a distinct trend in business practice: the integration of marketing planning into the strategic planning process. This trend has been accompanied by the evolution of new concepts and analytical techniques presented in detail in this book—techniques which facilitate market analysis and the development of strategic plans. The text and cases represent, to our knowledge, the first published educational material that responds to these developments.

Three major parts to this book correspond to the three legs on which we believe a successful and comprehensive education in planning should rest: *analytical prerequisites for planning,* including ways to analyze customers, competitors, environmental trends, market characteristics, company capabilities, and cost dynamics (in particular scale and experience effects); *formal strategic planning methods* including portfolio analysis, market attractiveness-business assessment, and the PIMS (Profit Impact of Market Strategy) program; and *creative and managerial aspects of planning,* includes ways to creatively define and segment the business, the human side of planning, and ways to actually implement planning and prepare a strategic market plan.

Each of the major analytic approaches described herein has its supporters from consulting firms and research organizations. Consequently, it has been difficult to obtain unbiased material on these approaches until now. A unique feature of this book, we believe, is the balanced way in which each is discussed and a clear presentation of the pros, cons, and *pitfalls* inherent in their application.

This book has a number of important uses. We anticipate that its primary usage will be in advanced marketing management courses having traditional titles such as Marketing Management, Strategic Marketing, Marketing Policy, Marketing Planning, etc., and in a course just now emerging on some campuses, titled Strategic Market Planning. This book is distinct from previous advanced marketing texts in that it presents important new conceptual material rather than covering the same material as in basic texts in more depth. It can be used also in Business Policy courses and in planning courses having titles such as Planning, Planning Methods, Corporate Planning, Strategic Planning, or Corporate Strategic Planning Models.

This book is suitable for courses at the advanced undergraduate, graduate, and executive educational levels as well as for on-the-job use by practicing managers and staff personnel such as planners. In writing for these diverse audiences we have added features for each which we hope enhance the usefulness of this book for *all*. To the undergraduate we have provided ease of understanding and a step-by-step approach; to the graduate, clarity, rigor, and advanced concepts; and to the executive a book which is practical, minimizes the use of academic jargon and is as self-contained as a book on an advanced subject can be.

The case material has been used successfully in various courses at the Harvard Business School, at many other universities and in corporate training programs. Indeed, nearly half of the material has been on the Intercollegiate Case Clearing House's "best sellers" lists.

The Teachers Guide explains in detail how the chapters and cases may be sequenced as well as combined with other readings and cases to meet a wide variety of course needs.

This endeavor has not been accomplished by the authors alone. We have drawn particularly heavily on Sidney Schoeffler and Don Heany at the Strategic Planning Institute; Bruce Henderson and Richard Lockridge at the Boston Consulting Group; Bill Rothschild at the General Electric Company; Ron Frank at Bain and Company; and Bob Buzzell as well as other faculty at the Harvard Business School. Our debt to these friends and colleagues is enormous.

Many of the cases were prepared by research associates working in collaboration with the authors. Their contribution to this book is substantial and is noted on the first page of the cases. In addition revisions to the Electro series were made by Steven C. Wheelwright, Robert L. Banks, and Viveck Talvadkar.

Derek F. Abell
John S. Hammond

Strategic Market Planning

Problems and
Analytical Approaches

Analytical Prerequisites for Planning

The Nature of Strategic Market Planning

A metamorphosis is taking place in planning. Indicative of this is the great number of ways that planning is conducted and the many different terms used to describe it, including: "marketing planning," "market planning," "strategic market planning," "business planning," "strategic planning," and a variety of combinations and permutations thereof. Even for companies using the *same* term, the *process* of planning varies widely—and managers express quite different levels of satisfaction with the results.

Behind this apparent confusion, a new concept of planning is emerging. Planning is becoming more strategic in nature. It is increasingly conducted at the level of the "business unit"—itself an emerging organizational concept. Planning is requiring a "general management" orientation rather than a narrow "functional" orientation and it is depending more and more on market analysis. In this book we shall call the resultant process "strategic market planning" to emphasize these trends, although the less descriptive term "business planning" is also frequently used to describe the same process.

Most firms plan, but few firms have yet mastered strategic market planning. To illustrate what we mean, consider how planning has evolved at International Systems Corporation (ISC) (a disguised name for a real company). As you read the descriptions, think about the strengths and weaknesses of their planning process at each stage of its development.

PLANNING AT ISC IN THE 1960s

ISC had approximately $300 million annual sales in 1960. It was comprised of three major divisions devoted to office equipment, consumer durables, and paper products, as well as several smaller industrial products divisions. Each division was managed virtually autonomously, and each was organized "functionally," usually into manufacturing, engineering, and sales departments.

Planning at ISC was oriented around the annual five-year "long-range" planning and budgeting process. Early each year, a small corporate planning staff issued planning instructions and general economic forecasts to the divisions. Planning instructions required management to fill out a variety of forms stating the major assumptions underlying their sales forecasts, and specific programs for marketing, manufacturing, research and development, and other functions. The instructions also included guidelines on growth and profit expected from each division.

During the spring and early summer, division management compiled a five-year plan. In most cases this effort was spearheaded by divisional controllers working together with sales, manufacturing, research and development, and the general management of each division. The completed plan contained income statements, usually broken down by product line, and balance sheets for five years.

During the late summer, plans were reviewed by the corporate staff. At this point, modifications and refinements were made. In October, each division presented its plan to top corporate management. Following approval, which in most cases was given with only minor modification, the first year of the five-year plan became the basic outline of the budget for the following year.

The procedure followed at ISC was fairly typical of that used by many large companies in the 1960s, and still is practiced by many small companies even today. Unfortunately, many, if not most, managers in such organizations were highly critical of the effectiveness of the five-year plan. At ISC, comments such as the following were made:

> "We filled out the forms mainly to keep corporate management happy—it really didn't help us at all."

> "Once the plan had been approved, we filed it away in a drawer and forgot about it. Operating decisions and capital budgeting decisions were made as if the plan didn't exist."

> "Each year we started all over again. Planning for five years was a waste of time since we only really looked at the first year."

"Our bookkeepers wrote the plans! Management got involved only because some of the forms called for information that the controller's department didn't have."

PLANNING AT ISC IN THE 1970s

A decade later, as a result of a number of major acquisitions and some internal growth, ISC annual sales passed $1 billion. Its 17 divisions ranged in size from $20 million to more than $200 million in annual sales, and spanned areas as diverse as plastics, paints, office equipment, consumer durables, paper products, foods, and industrial supply items. Most divisions were comprised of several related product lines. Overall corporate growth was slow however, and profits were poor. Forty percent of sales and 65 percent of profits came from markets outside the United States. A small percentage of the product lines were growing at rates above 25 percent annually; of the remainder, four major lines were highly profitable although growing slowly; the rest were relatively stable with mediocre profit results.

Organizationally, ISC had also evolved. The most important change was the appointment of product managers responsible for major product lines in each division. Typically, sales departments were now known as "marketing departments" and in the larger divisions a "marketing manager" had overall responsibility for several product managers, sales managers, and a field sales force, and various marketing "services," such as advertising and marketing research.

Planning practices also had changed. Responsibility for planning now was centered in the marketing department of each division. Product managers were each responsible for creating "marketing plans" for their product lines. Although a variety of different formats were used, these marketing plans were based on detailed projections of total market sales and market share for each product, and analyses of customers, competition, and external trends. The marketing plans—dealing mainly with questions of product policy, pricing, channel strategies, advertising and promotion—were used by manufacturing, research and development (R&D), and other functional departments to establish detailed plans and expense budgets for their respective activities.

Marketing plans were written for either one or three years depending on the division involved. Five-year "long-range" planning had generally been dropped because of the difficulty in making long-range sales forecasts and management's belief that the five-year plan was never really utilized. Product managers, however, were supposed to incorporate long-term trends and changes in the market into their marketing plans.

Divisional plans resulted from the aggregation of individual product-line plans. After approval at the divisional level, division managers took their plans to corporate management for approval. In most cases, as long as each division could promise an overall contribution to corporate profitability, these plans were approved as presented.

In spite of these changes, managers still expressed considerable dissatisfaction with the planning process. Among the comments made were the following:

> "Product managers want to protect what they have; they are often reluctant to respond to customer needs if their own product lines might be threatened in the process."

> "Often, product managers and even different divisions are involved in related activities. Yet each operates autonomously and plans nearly independently. We have no way to take a broader view of some of the markets to which several of us sell."

> "The divisions that have opportunities to grow are starved for cash, while others that have cash seem to fritter it away on futile projects. The result is that we don't have enough new products to provide any real growth."

THE DEVELOPMENT OF
STRATEGIC MARKET PLANNING

The brief descriptions of the evolution of ISC and its planning process illustrate some of the differences between long-range forecasting and budgeting, and marketing planning. The former best describes planning at ISC in the 1960s, while the latter might be used to describe planning at ISC in the 1970s. The development of marketing planning has often paralleled the shift from functionally organized companies with narrow product lines to large diversified multiproduct, multimarket companies using product (or market) manager systems.

But a further, important change is now taking place. Over the last decade there has been a growing acceptance of the fact that individual units or subunits within a corporation, e.g., divisions, product departments, or even product lines or market segments, may play different roles in achieving overall corporate objectives. Not all units and subunits need to grow at the same rate; not all units and subunits need to produce the same level of profitability; not all units and subunits must contribute equally to cash flow objectives.

This concept of the organization as a collection of units and subunits having different objectives is at the very root of contemporary approaches to strategic market planning. The term *portfolio* is commonly used to describe such a collection. Differences are expressed in terms of whether the unit is a net source of cash or a user of cash, as well as goals for growth, market share, net income, or return on investment. This is in contrast to practice in the 1960s and earlier that emphasized primarily sales, net income, and return on investment as major measures of performance. Although different divisions or departments were intuitively believed to have different capabilities to meet sales and earnings goals, these differences seldom were made explicit. Instead, each unit was expected to "pull its own weight" in the overall quest for growth and profits.

Part of the metamorphosis in planning is due to the fact that many firms now confront limited cash resources. In the period after World War II, such firms were able to finance growth by some combination of internally generated funds and increased borrowing. In the more competitive markets of the 1960s and 1970s, profit margins have shrunk, decreasing internally generated cash resources. At the same time, debt-to-equity ratios have climbed to levels where further borrowing is difficult. Finally, inflation has increased cash requirements for both fixed capital and working capital needs. This funding limitation forces many companies to be selective in their investments. A key planning question is how to discriminate between those products or businesses that need funding and those that can supply funding. ISC, even in its 1970s planning system, appears not to have incorporated cash flow as a major objective into its planning system nor to have discriminated between different businesses in terms of their role. Consequently, growth opportunities are being starved for cash, while a few isolated businesses appear to be cash-rich.

Increased attention to various measures of financial performance means that planners must be familiar with how such measures are derived. Appendix A to this chapter describes how return on sales (ROS), return on investment (ROI), and in particular, cash flow (CF) are computed.

BUSINESS UNITS AND PROGRAM UNITS

With the recognition that organizational entities may differ in their objectives and roles, a new organizational concept has also emerged. This is the concept of a "business unit." Such a unit is usually regarded by corporate management as a reasonably autonomous profit centre. Normally it has its own general manager. (A *general manager* is a manager with responsibility for the overall operation and health of a business rather than with any particular functional aspect of it.)

But the exact meaning of business unit is difficult to define because managers sometimes use the term to describe very different organizational entities. For example, at General Electric some "Strategic Business Units" (SBU's) encompass several divisions and have annual sales in excess of $500 million. In other companies, business units are defined much more narrowly—either representing a product department or even a product line or major market segment.

One of the major reasons for such differences is that some firms apply the criterion that a business should be self-supporting in terms of manufacturing, sales, R. D., and other functional departments; other firms apply the criterion that a business should have a clear market focus, an identifiable strategy, and an identifiable set of competitors. Application of the first criterion often results in a somewhat broader definition of the business unit than application of the second.

A business unit will usually be comprised of several *program units* as well as functional departments (manufacturing. R&D, sales, etc.). Such organizations are called "matrix" organizations.[1] Program units may represent product lines, geographic market segments, end-user industries to which the company sells, or units defined on the basis of any other relevant segmentation dimension. Many of the same difficulties occur in defining the meaning of a program unit as occur in defining the meaning of a business unit. Firms differ in their designations—some using the term to mean an organizational entity charged with the responsibility for activities in a particular product line or market, while others define programs more narrowly around market segments or subsegments.

Functional departments can be considered as resources—used by program units to implement the programs with which they are charged. In this book we shall often use the term "resources" interchangeably with "functional departments," although strictly speaking the resources are the physical facilities, manpower, technical skills, and capital embodied in such departments.

Although the exact definition of business units and program units may differ from situation to situation, the main point to bear in mind is that the concept of a portfolio exists both in terms of business units within a corporate structure (or substructure such as a group), and in terms of programs within a business. Strategic market plans have to be drawn up for the business unit as a whole, and for programs within the business unit when these represent relatively autonomous activities.

---

[1]See E. Raymond Corey and Steven H. Star, *Organizational Strategy: A Marketing Approach* (Boston: Division of Research, Harvard Business School, 1971), for a detailed description of so-called "matrix" organizations.

In this book we shall use the terms "business" and "program" as well as more common terms such as "product-market," "market segment," "product department," and "division" without being precise as to how their scope is defined on each occasion. In Chapter 8, the subject of business definition will be taken up in detail, since it is a question of strategic and organizational importance. By that time, you will have been exposed to a variety of cases in which definition is an issue and you will have a better grasp of the problems that have to be addressed. At this stage, we will define the term *program manager* to mean a manager charged with responsibility for a program such as a product line or market segment, and the term *resource manager* or *functional manager* to mean a manager charged with responsibility for a particular resource or function such as sales, manufacturing, or R&D.

THE NATURE OF
STRATEGIC MARKET PLANNING

A strategic market plan may be thought of as involving four sets of related decisions:

1. *Defining the Business.*[2] Each manager responsible for an organizational component (business or program) within the corporation must decide "What business am I in?" The definition must state:
   a. product and market *scope:* in particular, which customers are to be served, which customer functions (needs) are to be satisfied, and what ways ("technologies") are to be used to satisfy the functions;
   b. product and market *segmentation:* in particular, whether and how the firm recognizes differences among customers in terms of their needs and the ways they are satisfied.
   The way a business is defined has implications for both customer acceptance and costs. Defining the business is often as much a creative process as a quantitative-scientific one. A creative definition of a business in terms of scope or segmentation often can

---

[2]See Derek F. Abell, "Business Definition as an Element of the Strategic Decision," in *Analytic Frameworks for Product and Market Planning,* A. Shocker, editor. Cambridge, Mass.: Marketing Science Institute, forthcoming. Also, see Derek F. Abell, *Defining the Business: The Starting Point of Strategic Planning.* Prentice-Hall, Inc., Englewood Cliffs, N.J., forthcoming.

produce dramatic results. Strategically, definitions that may be successful at one point in time may be less appropriate at another, as the process of market evolution takes place. Thus business definition is a dynamic, not a static, decision-making process.

2. *Determining the Mission (or Role) of the Business.* Performance expectations in terms of sales growth, market share, return on investment, net income, and cash, must be determined for each business and program. This demands a careful analysis of market opportunities and company capabilities as well as a regard for overall corporate objectives. It often involves making explicit trade-offs among potentially conflicting objectives, especially in the short term when growth, market share gain, profit, and cash cannot all be achieved simultaneously. In this book we shall use the terms *mission* and *role* interchangeably to mean the set of objectives to be pursued. We should point out that the word mission is used by some people as a synonym for business definition. Our meaning, i.e. a set of objectives, is quite different from our meaning of business definition, i.e. scope and segmentation.

3. *Formulating Functional Strategies.* Functional strategies including marketing, manufacturing, research and development, service, physical distribution, etc., can only be formulated in detail after the business has been defined and its mission determined. (Of course, the process is iterative to some extent since questions of business definition and mission require some assumptions about functional strategies and the costs and benefits of various alternatives.) It is at this step that functional managers charged with planning resource strategies interact with general management and program managers charged with planning strategies for each major program of activity.

4. *Budgeting.* Finally, the planning cycle ends with the determination of resource allocations and budgets for carrying out the plans. It is at this stage that specific financial decisions are made, and pro forma income statements, balance sheets, and cash flow statements are projected.

A strategic market plan is *not* the same, therefore, as a marketing plan; it is a plan of *all* aspects of an organization's strategy in the marketplace. A marketing plan, in contrast, deals primarily with the delineation of target segments and the product, communication, channel, and pricing policies for reaching and servicing those segments—the so-called *marketing mix.*

THE ANALYTICAL PREREQUISITES
TO PLANNING

Effective strategic market planning is based on two important analytical ingredients. First, market opportunity has to be analyzed and the company's capability to take advantage of the opportunity has to be assessed. Second, the behavior of costs has to be understood.

Under the first heading, five basic analytical building-blocks are required for planning to be successful:

1. *Customers* must be analyzed to determine how the market can be segmented and the requirements of each segment;
2. *Competitors* must be identified and their individual strategies understood;
3. *Environmental trends* (social, economic, political, technological) affecting the market must be isolated and forecasted;
4. *Market characteristics* in terms of the evolution of supply and demand, and their interaction must be understood; and
5. *Internal company characteristics* must be audited to establish how company strengths and weaknesses relate to market requirements.

Under the second ingredient of cost analysis, two separate phenomena must be considered. These are:

1. *Scale effects* in terms of the impact of absolute size of the operation on costs, and
2. *Experience effects* in terms of the impact of cumulative historical volume ("experience") on costs.

Conducting such analyses is deceptively simple in theory, yet excruciatingly difficult in practice. It requires data, imagination, experience, and good conceptual skills, and must be supported by extensive top-quality staff work. Chapters 2 and 3 suggest how this should be done.

FORMAL PLANNING METHODS

Recently, there has been a vigorous search for new organizing frameworks and concepts to aid the process of analysis and planning. Since the early 1960s, several new analytical approaches have achieved widespread acceptance. Among them, three stand out.

11

1. *Portfolio Analysis.* Two-dimensional displays with a market share measure on one axis and industry growth on the other are prepared to assess the expected cash flow of each product or business unit. This is possible because market share is related to profitability, and industry growth is a predictor of cash required for investment in plant, equipment, and working capital. Such charts may be used to assist the determination of the mission of a business, to track businesses over time, to explore overall cash balance in a portfolio, and to assess competitors' portfolios.

2. *Market Attractiveness—Business Position Assessment.* By analyzing more variables than simply industry growth and market share, an assessment can be made of how "attractive" the market is, and how strong a "position" a business has within that market. When plotted on a two-dimensional display, such measures help to determine the relative overall attractiveness of different business units from an investment point of view.

3. *PIMS (The Profit Impact of Market Strategy).*[3] PIMS is an empirical model that relates a wide range of strategic variables (such as market share, product quality, and vertical integration) and situational variables (such as market growth rate, industry stage of development, and capital intensity) to profitability and cash flow. Simply stated, its purpose is to determine what strategies work best under what market conditions. It is based on an analysis of over 1,000 businesses of more than 150 large and small companies.

Each of these three approaches can play a useful role in the planning process. They are introduced in Chapters 4, 5 and 6 and are compared in Chapter 7.

CREATIVE AND MANAGERIAL ASPECTS OF PLANNING

Planning is not purely a technocratic activity. It is a creative activity, particularly in the way the business is defined in terms of scope

---

[3]See Sidney Schoeffler, Robert D. Buzzell, and Donald F. Heany, "Impact of Strategic Planning on Profit Performance," *Harvard Business Review*, Vol. 52 (March-April 1974), pp. 137–145, and Chapter 6 of this book.

and segmentation, and the way this is reflected in its organizational and functional strategies. This is the subject of Chapter 8.

Planning is undertaken by humans with the occasional aid of computers, not vice versa. It involves people working in business organizations, not in isolation. Some of the inevitable consequences of this "human" involvement in planning are discussed in Chapter 9.

The planning process itself is the subject of the final chapter in this book. Peter Lorange and Richard F. Vancil,[4] after studying the way many companies planned, concluded that planning systems could be classified as "one-cycle," "two-cycle," or "three-cycle" systems in terms of the type of decisions being taken.

A *one-cycle system* constitutes little more than a sales forecasting and budgeting process for the following year, although projections may be made for three or five years (as at ISC in the 1960s). Strategic decisions about the definition and mission of the business are not explicitly dealt with. In a *two-cycle system,* budget preparation is preceded by the preparation of functional plans—in particular, marketing, manufacturing, and research and development plans. On this basis, ISC's planning approach in the 1970s could probably be classified as a two-cycle process. Except for an initial input of objectives from the corporate staff, the focus is on the development of functional plans and budgets. In a *three-cycle system* functional planning and budgeting itself is preceded by "strategic market planning" (or "business planning," as Lorange and Vancil call it). The first step in a three-cycle process involves choices among alternative *definitions* of the business and choices among alternative *missions.*

Figure 1 below compares the three systems in terms of the relative amount of attention given to each phase, as well as the range of choices available at each decision step.

Moving from a two-cycle to a three-cycle system is *not* merely a matter of implementing changes in the *mechanics* of the planning process. It also requires a new frame of mind among executives responsible for planning; they must THINK strategically. This book deals only tangentially with planning mechanics. Its prime mission is to provide you with a working knowledge of strategic market planning problems and analytical approaches that will facilitate *your* strategic thinking. In practice, this is the surest way to guarantee that a three-cycle process actually takes place.

---

[4]Peter Lorange and Richard F. Vancil, *Strategic Planning Systems* (Englewood Cliffs, N.J.: Prentice-Hall, Inc., 1977), Chapter 2.

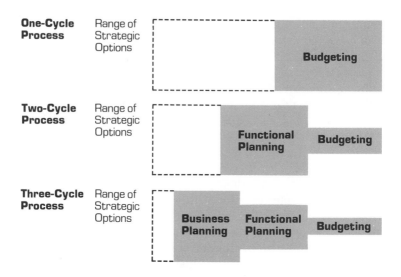

One-Cycle Process	Range of Strategic Options	Budgeting
Two-Cycle Process	Range of Strategic Options	Functional Planning Budgeting
Three-Cycle Process	Range of Strategic Options	Business Planning Functional Planning Budgeting

Time Period Required for Preparing Plans

Figure 1

Examples of One-, Two-, and Three-Cycle
Planning Processes

Source: Peter Lorange and Richard F. Vancil, *Strategic Planning
Systems* (Englewood Cliffs, N.J.: Prentice-Hall, 1977), p. 28.

SUMMARY

Strategic market planning is a natural outgrowth of organizational
evolution in diversified firms and increased concern for the allocation
of limited resources in cash-constrained environments. A consequence
of diversification is that opportunities differ in different markets. A
central concept of strategic market planning is that each business must
be strategically defined to take maximum advantage of such opportunities and that missions must be assigned consistent with the differences
among them.

Strategic market planning describes the process of planning that
(a) is built on sound assessments of market opportunity and company
capability as well as careful cost analysis and (b) involves the development of a firm's total strategic approach to a marketplace. It involves
decisions with respect to how a business should be defined; what its
mission should be; what marketing, manufacturing, research and development, and other functional programs should be undertaken; and
how funds should be budgeted.

A variety of new concepts and approaches to aid strategic market planning now exist. The most important are: portfolio analysis; market attractiveness-business position assessment; and the use of pooled business experience, in particular, PIMS.

There are three distinct cycles in the planning process. In the first cycle, broad strategic alternatives with respect to business definition and mission are identified and analyzed. In the second cycle, the focus turns to functional strategy development consistent with broad strategy choices. In the third cycle, specific short-term plans and budgets are determined.

Planning is a creative as well as a technocratic process. it is conducted by humans working within complex organizations. The key to successful strategic planning is successful strategic *thinking*.

Appendix A

Computing Return on Sales [ROS], Return on Investment [ROI], and Cash Flow [CF]

The three measures of financial performance described here can all be computed from standard balance sheet and income statement data.

RETURN ON SALES [ROS]

ROS is computed by dividing net income (NI) before or after taxes by total revenues. Therefore,

$$ROS = \frac{NI\ (\$)}{Sales\ (\$)} \times 100\%$$

RETURN ON INVESTMENT [ROI]

These are several variants of ROI depending on how investment is measured. The most frequently used bases for measuring investment are (a) total assets, (b) net assets [total assets minus current liabilities] or (c) stockholders' equity. Return is usually measured by net income before or after taxes. Therefore,

$$\text{ROI} = \frac{\text{NI}}{\text{Investment}} \times 100\%$$

$$\text{ROA (Return on Assets)} = \frac{\text{NI}}{\text{Total Assets}} \times 100\%$$

$$\text{RONA (Return on Net Assets)} = \frac{\text{NI}}{\text{Net Assets}} \times 100\%$$

$$\text{ROE (Return on Equity)} = \frac{\text{NI}}{\text{Equity}} \times 100\%$$

Investment can be measured only at a particular point in time. When investment is changing over time, it is usual to compute ROI (or ROA, etc.) on the basis of the *average* investment between two time points, e.g., the beginning and end of the fiscal year.

Return on investment can also be measured as an "internal rate of return" by using a technique known as discounted cash flow analysis. Interested readers should consult any standard financial textbook dealing with this subject (for example: Pearson Hunt, Charles M. Williams, and Gordon Donaldson, *Basic Business Finance*, 5th ed. [Homewood, Illinois: Richard D. Irwin, Inc., 1974]).

CASH FLOW [CF]

Cash flow is not the same as net income for two reasons: (1) "cash flow from operations" is calculated by adding depreciation to net income after taxes; and (2) cash flow also is affected by balance sheet changes, in particular, changes in working capital (WC) and plant and equipment (P&E).

Many students puzzle about the first of these points. Why, they ask, should depreciation, an accounting device anyway, be added to net income to calculate cash flow? The answer is simple. It is not a cash transaction. It is a bookkeeping transaction.

Cash flow then is calculated as follows (using the symbol $\triangle$ to designate "change in"):

$$\text{CF} = (\text{NI} + \text{Depreciation}) - \triangle \text{ P\&E} - \triangle \text{ WC}',$$

where $\triangle$ WC' represents changes in all working capital accounts except cash.

Changes in plant and equipment ($\triangle$ P&E) can be derived easily by comparing balance sheets for two consecutive periods. Changes in non-cash working capital items ($\triangle$ WC') are a little more difficult to calculate, only because changes in each working capital item must be computed separately. Usually,

$$\triangle \text{ WC} = \triangle \text{ Inventory} + \triangle \text{ Accounts Receivable}$$
$$+ \triangle \text{ Other Short-Term Assets} - \triangle \text{ Accounts Payable}$$
$$- \triangle \text{ Other Short-Term Liabilities}$$

You should be aware that in some companies the term "cash flow" is used to mean "cash flow from operations" only, and does not include cash flows due to balance sheet changes.

SPEER INDUSTRIES, INC. (A)[1]

In March 1975, Mr. Paul Berger, President of Speer Industries, Inc. circulated a memorandum to key members of Speer's management. The memorandum announced the formation of a special Task Force to study Speer's longer term approach to the Scientific Instrumentation market. The memo stated, in part:

> Over the last eighteen months, each of the four divisions that do business in the scientific instrumentation area have presented us at headquarters with investment plans for their respective activities. These again raise the question of what our overall long range strategy as a corporation should be in this business area. I am appointing a Task Force to review this matter and to provide us with a set of recommendations for the future. The Task Force will be comprised of Mr. James Young, Executive Vice President, the general managers of each of the four divisions, an outside marketing consultant, and several additional company executives.

> Specifically, the Task Force should:

> 1. Form a summary description of the scientific instrumentation market(s), including a discussion of key business, government, and technology trends, as well as the identification of key growth areas;
> 2. Recommend market areas and types of products Speer should be active in; and
> 3. Determine the major resource committments and organization strategies to gain a significant position in these areas.

COMPANY BACKGROUND

Speer Industries, Inc. of Houston, Texas was founded in 1955 by a small group of university research scientists to manufacture custom designed control and guidance systems for the emerging aerospace industry. Speer's subsequent growth was closely related to the explo-

---

[1]This case was prepared by Derek F. Abell.

sive growth of the whole aerospace market. Twenty years later, aerospace-related activities still remained the core of Speer's business, and accounted for sixty per cent of total 1974 sales of $119 million. Exhibit 1 summarizes Speer's 1974 financial situation.

During the 1960s, growing concern for the future of the aerospace industry led Speer to embark on a substantial program of acquisition and diversification. Heavily dependent on military and government spending, Speer concentrated its efforts on developing new commercial applications for its control and guidance systems technology. In 1961, the Ecko Electronics Company (EEC) located in Newark, New Jersey, was acquired to provide Speer with a competence in radar scanner devices, and sales efforts were concentrated on the growing market for commercial air traffic control devices and systems.

In a further effort to lessen the dependence on the aerospace industry and to provide a more solid foundation for growth, Speer acquired five other businesses between 1962 and 1971. These were:

1962 Reliance Instrumentation Company, Madison, Wisconsin, a leading manufacturer of laboratory electrical meters, potentiometers, analytical balances, fume hoods, blenders, strip chart recorders, and a broad line of other measurement equipment and related hardware and supply items (1974 sales: $23.1 million).

1965 Atherton Company, Chicago, Illinois, a manufacturer of numerical controls for the machine tool industry (1974 sales: $14.8 million).

1966 Brite Instrument Company, Houston, Texas, a small manufacturer of high quality gas chromatographs (1974 sales: $7.2 million).

1971 Intron, Inc., Dallas, Texas, a specialist in custom-built electron microscopes (1974 sales: $1.1 million).

1972 SPD, Inc., Newark, New Jersey, a small manufacturer of advanced technology water pollutant monitoring instruments (1974 sales: $0.4 million).

Following acquisition, each company was treated as a virtually independent and autonomous operating unit. Apart from the regular submission of annual plans and budget data,[2] the general manager of

---

[2]Each of Speer's general managers was required to provide corporate headquarters with a preliminary annual plan and budget in May of each year. In most cases, these plans were phrased in terms of pro-forma sales, cost and profit estimates for each major product line for the upcoming fiscal year. Once these pro-forma plans were approved, detailed plans were drawn up by each division. These detailed plans were generally not reviewed by corporate headquarters.

each division continued to operate in much the same way that they had prior to acquisition. Each general manager reported directly to Mr. Paul Berger.

In the belief that some integration between Speer's various divisions might be possible and desirable, Mr. Berger appointed in mid-1974 a special Task Force on sales and service activities. After six months of deliberation, the final report of the Task Force recommended immediate pooling of sales and service for EEC and the Guidance and Control System Division. As far as other activities were concerned the report stated:

> As a result of various subcommittee enquiries the Task Force was forced to conclude that little or no opportunity exists at present to consolidate sales or service activities for any of these (other) businesses. Nevertheless, several important factors suggest that some form of consolidation might be possible for the scientific instrumentation business. These factors have more to do with *building a future strategy* in the various market sectors than selling and distributing existing products. The attached memorandum (see Appendix A) suggests one possible direction for such future efforts.

In late 1974, Speer took its first step towards integrating and consolidating its aerospace activities. The original Guidance and Control System Division and the Ecko Electronics Company were renamed as the Guidance and Control System Group. The President and General Manager of EEC, Mr. Tom Lipton, was named Group Vice President for the two newly wedded divisions. Although contacts between the divisions were substantially increased, however, each continued to operate virtually independently. In spite of the fact that both divisions shared virtually identical customers (primarily various government agencies and aerospace contractors) each division continued to operate its own direct sales activity, its own R&D and manufacturing, and to develop its own product line.

In addition to organizational changes, Mr. Berger had been giving considerable thought to the question of planning objectives at Speer. In late 1974, he had circulated a memorandum laying down some specific goals for Speer in the years ahead (see Appendix B).

Speer's Scientific Instrumentation Activities

Four Speer divisions, Reliance, Inc., Brite Instrument, Intron, and SPD, Inc. were involved in the manufacture and sale of scientific instrumentation. Each of these businesses is described in more detail below.

Reliance Instrumentation Company was founded in Madison, Wisconsin in 1903 to supply meters and related hardware to laboratories. Over the years Reliance developed a reputation among engineers and physicists as the "Cadillac" of the industry in a broad line of laboratory physical measurement and test equipment. By 1975, the laboratory equipment product line numbered more than 1,500 separate items and accounted for 92 per cent of Reliance's sales.

Reliance's only other line of business, which accounted for $1.8 million of sales in 1975, involved the manufacture and sale of atomic power station instrumentation. In the late 1960's, Reliance had been approached by a major supplier of equipment to the nuclear industry to produce an instrument to their design under license. Further licenses had resulted in several additional new products. These products were sold direct by two sales engineers worldwide. Major customers were utilities, government authorities, and equipment suppliers to the nuclear industry.

The laboratory product line was distributed nationwide via twenty-three distributors who placed Reliance equipment in virtually every school, university, government and industrial laboratory in the United States. Distributor sales efforts were supplemented by a direct sales force of fifteen salesmen. These salesmen were responsible for working with distributors to provide sales and merchandising support, as well as for direct contact with key laboratory accounts. Although the salesmen solicited no orders directly, they attempted to influence purchasers to specify Reliance's equipment in their procurement from distributors. Reliance's sales executives believed that direct contact with the customer played an important role in the customer's selection process. Distributor salesmen sold as many as 10,000 different items from a catalogue and generally did little to influence the customer's choice of a particular brand or product. As one Reliance executive commented: "Dealers don't *sell* meters, they take orders for them."

Virtually all Reliance products were sold as standard off-the-shelf items. Reliance executives regarded their long experience in manufacturing a wide variety of electromechanical equipment as one of the company's major assets. Products were typically produced in runs of 25, 50 or 100, two to three times each year. It was believed that production costs compared very favorably with those of other similar 'broad line' producers of laboratory instrumentation and equipment. Adjacent to the manufacturing plant, Reliance maintained a large warehouse of finished products. Total inventories (including raw materials and work-in-process) in late 1974 exceeded nine million dollars. Reliance deliveries ranged anywhere between six weeks and eighteen months. As one executive put it:

We know our products must be well thought of by the customer. If they are prepared to wait more than a year sometimes to get delivery, they must be superior to those of our competition.

Reliance undertook a modest amount of R&D, mostly in the form of continuing engineering development on its major product lines. Typically a product line was singled out for redesign and improvement every two to three years. Reliance executives believed that, in general, this level of committment was sufficient to maintain Reliance's reputation as a producer of premium products and to allow prices to be set 10–15 per cent above the prices of competitors.

All Reliance products were sold to distributors at full list price less a dealer discount ranging between 35 and 40 per cent. Reliance executives had little idea of the actual prices at which dealers sold to laboratories. In recent years, particularly, some large laboratories had tended to negotiate annual contracts with dealers to give a dollar volume discount on any item in the dealer's catalogue.

New products were added to the line continually. Although Reliance had little direct contact with most of the users of its products, it did receive regularly a listing of new products developed outside the company which might be available for license. This had proved over the years to be a major source of new product ideas. Commenting on the breadth of Reliance's product line Mr. John Wayne, the President commented:

We cannot ignore lower volume items. These give us our "full line" image and more pages in the dealer's catalogue. Some of these items are cases where we have 70–100 per cent of that particular market. Others are cases where we have no significant market share. However, these items represent a tremendous asset. For example, we could bring out a line of such an item and gain immediate acceptance.

Although the entire product line numbered more than 1,500 items, five product lines accounted for nearly 60 percent of sales (see Table 1).

In 1973, warranty card returns were used to compute some basic information regarding the markets to which Reliance products were ultimately being sold (see Exhibits 2 and 3). In addition, using both published data and company sponsored market research studies an attempt was made to estimate market shares for selected Reliance product lines (see Exhibits 4, 5, 6 and 7).

Reliance competed with a variety of different firms in each of its product lines. No firm exactly duplicated another in the breadth or scope of its product offering. Reliance executives identified three

Table 1

1974 Reliance Laboratory Products Sales by Major Product Line

	$ MILLION	%	CUMULATIVE %
Electrical meters	3,101	14.6	14.6
Potentiometers	2,852	13.4	28.0
Analytical balances	2,326	10.9	38.9
Blenders	1,861	8.8	47.7
Strip chart recorders	1,520	7.1	54.8
Parts	1,305	6.1	60.9
Other items	8,342	39.1	100.0
Total	21,307	100.0	

major classes of competitor, however. First, there were a number of firms specializing in a few product areas and selling these products to a wide variety of markets including laboratories. Ellison Electric was regarded as a good example of this first category. Ellison was a major producer of instrumentation for electrical measurement and held a strong position in the market for meters of all types. Sales to laboratories represented only a minor proportion of their total sales volume. Ellison sold direct as well as via distributors and produced highly engineered and customized instruments as well as a range of standard products. They tended to price lower than Reliance and had a sound reputation for quality among users. Dealer margins on indirect sales averaged 25–30 per cent off list.

Secondly, Reliance faced competition from several other "broad line" manufacturers who had concentrated their selling efforts primarily on laboratories. Among those selling a comparable line of physical laboratory instrumentation and equipment, Reliance stood out as a leader in terms of products offered. In this category Reliance viewed Applied Scientific as one of their most aggressive competitors. This company was renowned in the industry for the frequency with which it launched new products. Most of these new products were direct imitations of new products introduced by both American and European competitors. Applied Scientific tended to price below Reliance and to offer considerably better delivery. According to Reliance's sales manager: "Everyone knows that it's Mickey Mouse but they nevertheless get credit for being innovators!"

Finally, Reliance experienced some competition from distributors themselves in selected product lines. Approximately one third of the twenty-three distributors also manufactured products for sale under their own label. In most cases these products were not directly competitive with those supplied by Reliance, but there was always the potential danger that a distributor might decide to offer his own version of a particularly successful product line.

Sales of Reliance's laboratory products are shown in Table 2 below, together with net income for the division.

Table 2

YEAR	LAB PRODUCTS SALES [$000]	AFTER TAX NET INCOME[1] [$000] TOTAL DIVISION[2]
1967	$14,582	714
1968	14,127	826
1969	15,682	930
1970	14,608	325
1971	13,573	(452)
1972	13,982	(835)
1973	16,788	25
1974	21,307	332
1975 est.	22,500	950

[1]Speer levied two annual assessments on each division. The first of these was intended to be a provision for corporate G&A expense and was calculated at 3% of sales. The second represented a "use charge" of 6% on corporate capital employed. In 1974, this capital amounted to approximately 65% of total assets of $23.5 million. Cost of goods sold had averaged about 70% of sales, of which approximately 40% was fixed and 60% variable.

[2]No attempt was made to calculate net income separately for laboratory products and nuclear instrumentation.

It was believed that the recent upturn in volume was due to a variety of factors. Among these, executives listed rising prices, the appointment of a new general manager in late 1972, better manufacturing and inventory controls leading to somewhat improved delivery, the institution of the direct fifteen man sales force to supplement dealer selling efforts, and a small growth in international sales from three percent to eight percent of the total. Although no exact data was available, Reliance executives believed that over the same period, industry sales of comparable laboratory equipment had declined slightly in real terms, but that prices had risen on an average of 10 percent per annum since 1973.

Brite Instrument Company was founded by Mr. Alvin Brite in 1959 to manufacture a very high quality gas chromatograph.[3] The

[3]Chromatography was named in 1906, by Mr. Tswett, a Russian. Gas chromatography, as an analytical method, originated in the early 1950s. Commercial gas chromatographs became available in the mid-1950s. These instruments analyze chemical mixtures in the vapor state by separating them into their individual constituents. Chromatography involves the perpetual absorption of components from a solution during its passage through a column of finely divided solids. The sample is injected into a column packed with a material to which the individual constituents of the sample adhere. The constituents emerge and are detected in a sequence related to their release from the column.

product on which the company was founded was designed by Mr. Brite himself and enjoyed a unique position in the marketplace for more than a decade. The company was acquired by Speer Industries in 1966.

Sensing that the market for the high quality chromatograph was reaching a plateau and that new technologies might soon provide increasing competition, steps were taken in the early 1970s to broaden Brite's base of operation. This eventually resulted in the acquisition in 1974 of a line of lower priced gas chromatographs. Although the product was believed to be superior to existing competitive products, the line had never been actively marketed by its previous owner, the Britton Company. By early 1975, sales of the new line were running at an annual rate of approximately $500,000. The remaining $6.6 million of annual sales were still provided by the original Brite line of high quality chromatographs.

Both the new and old lines of equipment were sold by a seventeen man sales force. Customers for the original line of high quality gas chromatographs tended to be highly qualified research scientists in either university chemistry or physics laboratories, government laboratories, or large industrial research centers. These scientists demanded high specification and performance, and over the years Brite had achieved an outstanding reputation for customizing products for a wide variety of non-routine applications. As one executive put it:

> "We help the customer design his experiment around Brite equipment. We are selling a measurement technology as well as a piece of hardware."

Expenditures on R&D and applications engineering amounted to approximately 10 per cent of sales.

By contrast, the new "G16" line of lower priced chromatographs was believed to have a much broader market potential and to include a wide variety of university chemistry laboratories and government research facilities. Users were expected to be primarily chemists or physicists, and to use the instrument for routine analytical applications. Most of the potential customers for the G16 model were not expected to be familiar with Brite since the total number of high quality chromatograph installations numbered less than 800. As Brite's sales manager stated:

> The biggest problem with this product line is adequate sales coverage and brand identification. Brite has a fine reputation, but only in a small specific market, primarily physics laboratories. The G16 Series market covers medical schools, production lines, chemistry laboratories, etc. In other words, the G16 line is now offered on a routine basis to institutions that have no previous knowledge of Brite. We are, so to speak, an unknown

quantity. As a matter of fact, at present, our salesmen use the name Speer Industries, to lend some feeling of quality and credibility to the G16 product line. This is a real problem at present. The selling price of this instrument makes it very important that we have a relatively low sales expense. Having to justify and prove that Brite is a reputable, worthy company is difficult and expensive. Until we develop a reputation, every sale we make is one "stolen" from another manufacturer.

On several occasions, discussion had arisen at Brite about the possibility of selling the new G16 line via distributors. Most Brite executives believed, however, that because of their technical complexity, chromatographs did not lend themselves to distributor sales. They noted, however, that several other small manufacturers of lower priced chromatographs did use dealers to distribute their products, and that in some cases dealers designated technical specialists to assist in the sale of such product lines.

The market for high quality chromatographs of the type produced by Brite was estimated to be approximately $10 million and to be growing at approximately 5 per cent per annum. The market for lower priced chromatographs comparable to the "G16" model was estimated to be in the neighborhood of $60 million and to be growing only very slowly. Brite had purchased the G16 in the knowledge that it offered the user some very real benefits over any other product existing in the market at that time. Based on a unique but not patented design, they believed that it would be difficult for other competitors to incorporate such features into their own existing equipment.

The high quality Brite line was priced at a premium of about 15 per cent above Brite's nearest competitor. Depending on the particular equipment configuration, prices ranged from $10,000 to $75,000 for a complete instrumentation system. After much discussion, prices for the G16 line were set approximately at a par with existing competitive products. Typically, such instruments sold for between $3,000 and $7,000.

All manufacturing was undertaken at Brite's small but modern Houston plant. Typically, high quality chromatograph instrumentation systems were made-to-order and assembled in ones, twos or threes prior to shipment. Basic components were, however, produced in a small machine shop in lots of up to twenty-five. Since the mid-60s, Brite had shifted increasingly to electronic components to perform certain measurement and recording functions in its instrumentation, and had added a number of electronic engineers to its design and manufacturing staff. Several of its high quality instruments included a built-in mini-computer as part of the overall instrumentation system design.

Competition was quite different in each of the two product markets in which Brite participated. Until the late 1960s, Brite had enjoyed a virtual monopoly in the specific type of high quality chromatographic applications for which its instrument was best suited. Beginning at that time, however, several other small manufacturers entered the market with alternative designs which made them competitive with Brite instruments. As of early 1975, two United States companies and one foreign company were regarded as strong potential competitors.

Substantial competition existed in the lower priced end of the chromatograph market from both U.S. and foreign producers. Brite executives believed that the market was sensitive to price, service and performance. Major competitors included such large companies as Beckman Instruments, Hewlett Packard, Perkin Elmer, Varian and Fisher Scientific. These companies operated with large direct salesforces, extensive branch sales and service organizations, and substantial advertising support for their products. In some cases, their product lines were tailored specifically to the needs of the particular market segments such as industrial process control or clinical laboratories.

Sales of the high quality Brite instrument line together with net income are shown in Table 3 below.

Table 3

YEAR	SALES [$000]	AFTER TAX NET INCOME[1] [$000]
1969	3,910	802
1970	4,852	610
1971	5,678	770
1972	6,011	920
1973	6,817	1292
1974	6,670	1283

[1]After corporate assessment and use charges. Use charges were based on a total corporate capital employed of approximately $2.5 million. Gross margins averaged 50 per cent with variable costs accounting for approximately 65 per cent of cost of goods sold.

Intron, Inc. was the creation of an ex-MIT researcher who had written his Ph.D. thesis in the area of electron microscopy.[4] Aware of the potential future impact of electronics on microscopic techniques,

---

[4]The electron microscope is a type of microscope which is capable of obtaining extremely high magnification, with the upper limit about 500,000 to 1. In the electron microscope the streams of electrons function in essentially the same way that rays of light do in an ordinary optical microscope. Electromagnets produce the lens effect and a high energy source of electrons function as do light rays to produce an image. The electron microscope finds application in medical and biological research, in industrial and scientific research, and also in the metallurgical and chemical fields.

he had, while still at MIT, partly developed a large electron microscope using advanced electronic technology. In 1970 he left MIT to actively market the product. Sales did not materialize and short of cash he was acquired by Speer in 1971. A total of nineteen instruments had been shipped from the Dallas facility by 1975.

Two field salesmen, one of whom also held the position of Manager of Design and Engineering, sold Intron electron microscopes in the field. Intron did little direct canvassing of orders but followed up leads resulting from its participation in trade shows and its limited advertising activity.

The market for electron microscopes was believed to be still at the stage of early growth. Annual industry sales had risen from five million dollars in 1963 to twelve million in 1971 to nearly seventeen million in 1974. Sales were expected to reach between 25 and 30 million dollars by 1980. These gains were expected to result primarily from more diversified applications.

Prices of electron microscopes generally ranged from $40,000 to $75,000. However, some models cost as much as $450,000 including accessories, and the trend was towards higher priced units. Intron's unit with accessories typically sold at around $190,000.

Intron maintained a continuing research and development program, with an annual R&D budget of close to $140,000. Intron's chief executive, Mr. Robert McNaulty, who had replaced the original founder in 1972, believed that Intron's unit was considerably more versatile and of higher performance than nearly any other electron microscope on the market in 1975. For certain applications these performance characteristics could be of considerable advantage to users. Product reliability had also proven to be very high. So far virtually no need for service had arisen on any of the existing nineteen installations.

Intron faced competition from a variety of instrumentation manufacturers and optical manufacturers. These included Perkin Elmer, Applied Research Labs (a Division of Bausch and Lomb), Carl Zeiss, Siemens, Coates and Welters Instruments, and RCA. Many of these companies operated nationwide and even world-wide service networks, in addition to having far more extensive sales coverage than that attempted by Intron. Intron executives believed that their most aggressive competitors were not those selling in the same price range as themselves, but those selling in the $50,000–$75,000 area. In many cases, sales had been lost to a competitor because the customer found it difficult to justify the extra performance characteristics of an Intron unit. When superior performance and versatility were important buying criteria, it was believed that Intron had a reasonable chance of making a sale.

After several years of losses, Intron had become marginally profitable in 1974. Net income after taxes and corporate charges amounted to approximately $39,000 on sales of $1.1 million.

SPD, Inc. was founded in 1965 in Newark, New Jersey by a group of engineers and scientists to work on environmental analysis problems for the government. Initially supported by government research contracts, SPD conducted a number of studies in the area of water pollution and pollution monitoring technology. In the course of this activity, several designs of water pollutant monitoring devices were undertaken. Mindful that contract services to the government would not provide sufficient avenues for long-term growth, the decision was taken in 1971 to actively market these products to federal and local government agencies. By 1975, the contract service activity of SPD had been dropped and all effort was devoted to the sale of the monitoring devices. SPD's major product was a monitoring device for measuring concentrations of pollutants in industrial effluent. SPD expected soon to launch a second monitoring device which could be used to test pollution levels in open bodies of water such as rivers, lakes and other contaminated water areas.

All of SPD's monitoring devices were based on a highly advanced radiation measurement principle. Unlike most other existing water pollutant monitoring devices which required the collection of separate samples for testing and analysis, SPD's instruments produced an immediate read-out of the concentration of pollutants.

The two existing instruments, the WP1000 and WP2000, were designed for use by industrial plant engineers or industrial environmental engineers. The portable WP1000 sold at a price of approximately $3,800. The WP2000, priced at $10,800, was a "stationary" unit which allowed for automatic periodic recording of effluent pollutant levels over a twenty-four hour period.

The new AWP10 unit, while based on the same measurement principles, was designed for use by state and local authorities in testing pollutant concentration in large open bodies of water which might have become contaminated from either industrial or domestic effluent. Both the AWP10 and the WP1000 and WP2000 measured pollutant mass concentration and provided no information as to the identity of the pollutant involved.

Sales of water pollutant monitoring instruments were directly influenced by environmental standards demanded by federal, state and local governments. These standards usually set some absolute limits on the concentration of pollutants in various forms of industrial effluent. Compliance with the standards required regular measurement by industrial plants of effluent concentration. In general, however, the law did not specify the method by which pollutants should be monitored. Most industrial plants collected samples periodically for subsequent chemical analysis. While such measurements satisfied legal requirements, they tended to be time consuming and laborious.

SPD executives believed that their pollutant monitoring instrumentation was unique in that the technology on which it was based allowed immediate read out of pollutant levels. Although it was not mandatory to use such an instrument to meet compliance standards, the instrument appeared to have considerable potential as a replacement for more traditional methods of measuring water pollution. Using SIC data and published information on establishments in various industrial categories, SPD's sales manager had compiled an estimate of the total long run potential for instrumentation of the type offered by SPD (see Exhibit 8).

SPD had initially utilized two direct salesmen and eleven manufacturers agents to sell the SPD effluent monitors. Salesmen concentrated their efforts on selling to government agencies while manufacturers agents called on industrial plant personnel. It was believed that government environmental agencies were particularly important not only as potential customers, but also as "forcing agents" in accelerating the adoption of the instruments by industrial personnel. In mid-1974, following disappointing results, SPD terminated its relationships with all but two of its manufacturers representatives and took over the selling itself. The efforts of the two direct salesmen were supplemented by increases in direct mail, trade journal, advertising, and trade shows. Initial experience in trying to sell the WP1000 and WP2000 had shown that some technical explanation and demonstration to interested plant personnel was important in gaining interest in the new instrument.

As of December 1974, SPD had shipped a total of 182 WP1000 and WP2000 units. Total 1974 sales amounted to $374,000 upon which a net income after taxes and assessments of $22,000 was realized. All of the units were assembled in two rooms contained in a rented facility which also served as office space, R&D laboratory, manufacturing and service facility.[5]

Although the devices which SPD marketed were covered by patents, it was believed that other competitors might enter the market with similar devices if the opportunities appeared attractive. However, SPD executives believed that their experience in dealing with government agencies and the product development work which they had

---

[5]Defective units were returned to Newark by mail for servicing.

already undertaken, ensured them of at least a two-year head start on any direct competition.

Scientific Instrumentation Task Force

The first meeting of the Task Force took place at Corporate Headquarters in Houston, Texas on April 1, 1975. In attendance were:

Mr. James Young (Chairman), Executive Vice President

Mr. John Wayne, President and General Manager, Reliance Instrument Company

Mr. Jack Kingley, Sales Manager, Reliance Instrument Company

Mr. Alvin Brite, President and General Manager, Brite Instrument Company

Mr. Robert McNaulty, President and General Manager, Intron, Inc.

Mr. Otto Poensgen, President and General Manager, SPD, Inc.

Mr. Alan Fayerweather, External Marketing Consultant

Mr. Guy Converse, Manager for New Products, Ecko Electronics Company, and part-time assistant to the President.

Mr. Young opened the meeting with some general comments which then followed by an expression of views from various members of the Task Force. Selected portions of these remarks and the subsequent discussion are transcribed below:

James Young (Chairman)
I thought I might begin this meeting by making a few general comments which will help to place this particular assignment in perspective. This is not the first time that Speer has undertaken some long-range planning activities. I believe we can learn some valuable lessons from our past efforts, so let me talk for 15 or 20 minutes about how I see the history of this particular situation:

Our first step ten to twelve years ago was to make a complete audit of our strengths and weaknesses as a corporation. We had a list as long as your arm as did each operating division. It took us an enormous amount of time and effort to complete; the problem was that once we had completed the lists we never *did* anything with them. The only real use that was made of this work was a definition of four primary business areas where we felt Speer might be able to be successful. These were:

Guidance and Control Systems

Instrumentation

Automation of all types

R&D (in both the profit and non-profit sectors)

This list of areas was used to compile a comprehensive list of acquisition candidates. For each candidate we looked at products, technologies, profits, management, etc. But we compiled the list and selected from it without any clear *plan* in mind. It was just a collection of "random targets" in the general areas of interest. There was no vision of a cohesive whole which would produce a clear thrust or set of activities.

We also reviewed many R&D areas for internal development as opposed to acquisition. Among them were oceanography, meteorology, holography, secondary power, advanced propulsion, sea water conversion, undersea warfare, and others. But we never moved from R&D to action, or conversion into a *business* opportunity. In fact we never did the R&D either.

So these are just some examples to provide some historical perspectives.

John Wayne (Reliance)
Is the title of our Task Force too broad, i.e., "Scientific Instrumentation?"

Jack Kingley (Reliance)
We need to identify the major markets that Speer is currently active in and work from there.

Otto Poensgen (SPD)
What do you mean by market? We sell to literally hundreds of SIC industries; in addition we sell to many different segments within each industry.

Robert McNaulty (Intron)
Let's not get dragged into standard (SIC) categories; but the question is how *should* we segment and identify our markets.

John Wayne
We need to control the way our technology leads us into many unfamiliar markets without rhyme or reason. We can't be everything to all people.

Otto Poensgen
Take care not to start at the market end. It's better to work at the application of the technologies we are in than to look at markets.

Guy Converse (Assistant to the President)
I think we need to do both. But we need to make market extensions which don't require too much change from our core technologies.

Alvin Brite (Brite Instrument Company)
Yes. This at least allows pooled selling in contrast to the other approach.

Otto Poensgen
But its very difficult to define markets. What do you mean by "market"?

Jack Kingley
No its really not. For example, we have only one market really, the laboratory.

Guy Converse
If you stay with a single technological approach you get into lots of small market activities which don't take you anywhere and none of them have any critical mass.

Alvin Brite
Yes, you dissipate yourself. I have been a member of numerous committees which led to nothing. We were buried in our own profundity. We need to establish goals with obtainable results.

Guy Converse
It all depends on your definition. It's OK to start with existing businesses if we don't say "meters" but "ways in which customers solve electrical measurement needs."

Robert McNaulty
What about defining user categories such as basic R&D, applied research, process control, chemical analysis, etc.? That would be a useful way to define markets.

Alvin Brite
Paul (Berger) wants to know "what makes a successful instrumentation company?" My guess is R&D which stays ahead of competitors plus increased productivity to stay ahead of inflation. Its not a matter of market research. We could buy that. The talent round this table shouldn't concern itself with that. The question is "how to be successful."

Jack Kingley
The basic motivation in all business is greed. That means you have to *sell* what you have whether its meters or massage parlors. Its mainly a question of what other products could go through the same marketing structure.

Alvin Brite
Do we need centralized R&D. There is lots of overlap currently. I'll give you an example: we have *four* divisions all working on the micro-processor!

Guy Converse
I don't think we should be limited by what Paul said at all. The goal is to make whatever surveys are needed—not to stay in existing business areas.

Alvin Brite
Inflation is the problem. Its been with us since the Civil War and its a hell of a problem. We need increased productivity in marketing, manufacturing and R&D.

Guy Converse
One way to get increased productivity is to focus on *markets*—it saves a lot of energy that gets dissipated with letting technology take you into unfamiliar market areas.

Alvin Brite
We never even get together to talk about our various technologies. We certainly could gain from each other—there's no question about that.

Guy Converse
The reason that Otto (Poensgen) sees technology as the central thrust is that he sees that as the way to grow *his* business. Whereas Al Brite sees his market as the way to grow his. Maybe each of these is right?

Otto Poensgen
I think we have to: 1) list our technologies, 2) list our markets, 3) list the strengths and weaknesses of Speer in each, and 4) list new opportunities.

Alvin Brite
We shouldn't lose sight of international here because extending some products to new foreign markets is a clear possibility—especially in the high technology area. I don't think the laboratory equipment products really offer that much opportunity there though.

Following this interchange of views, the Chairman called the meeting to order and suggested that each General Manager should talk briefly about how he viewed his business and what areas he saw for future growth. Selected parts of these individual presentations follow.

Mr. John Wayne (Reliance Instrument Company)
We are currently making a major effort to improve our production and inventory control procedures. This should result in considerably improved deliveries with no additional investment in inventories. This will be accomplished primarily through a new computer oriented inventory control and reordering system which is now being installed. I estimate that this will have substantial impact on our sales and profitability over the next few years. Also we have just appointed a "Manager of New Products" to help us identify new opportunities better *and* to prune our product line where necessary.

Aside from these activities, we have two broad strategic alternatives:

a) to offer more general purpose products of the type we already manufacture (e.g., meters, gauges, hardware, etc.)

or

b) to offer more specialized products which require more engineering and a knowledge of end use. These are a higher technology group of products —our effort in the nuclear industry is one example of this approach.

Personally, I feel the future long term growth potential is insufficient in the general purpose product areas. The function of this group is to help select some new future area for Reliance and thus for Speer. For example, we could try to enter the biomedical clinical market, or the market for automation devices.

Mr. Alvin Brite (Brite Instrument Company)

Our future strategy will be to turn our attention increasingly to the lower priced G16 chromatograph line. Our goal is to have a 10–12 per cent share of this business by 1980. The problem is that we present a small company image to customers.

We intend to improve our relations between Research and Marketing for new product concepts and get the maximum amount of cross fertilization between product lines.

One trend we have to be aware of in both our product lines is that many instruments now interface with a computer. Our instrument is often sold as part of a complete measurement system. We have to be able to provide a common interface capability as well as system capability.

Mr. Robert McNaulty (Intron, Inc.)

One possibility we face is to produce a much lower priced electron microscope. This would involve a very substantial expenditure in R&D but would allow us to be competitive in many of the situations where we now lose sales. Also there is a trend away from fundamental research laboratories towards industrial usage. This will require more applications experimentation and development of specific measurement technologies.

If the market for electron microscopes grows as it is predicted, and if we can get our share of it, then I think we can be successful.

Mr. Otto Poensgen, (SPD, Inc.)

Current plans are to expand sales of our existing product lines and add the new AWP10 unit in early 1976. At that time we shall be serving two basic market areas—the industrial market and government. From that base we have a number of different ways to grow in the future (see Exhibit 9). Some of these possible growth directions would require us to develop new technologies (e.g., a capability to chemically analyze the component pollutants in a water sample), others would take us into new markets, e.g., industrial process control or air pollution monitoring.

Based on our current product line, we believe we can reach annual sales of around $3 million by 1980. But if we are to grow we shall eventually need a larger sales group. This will require more than the existing product lines to sustain itself in the long run.

Each presentation was followed by a short period of discussion and questions. At the conclusion of these questions, Mr. James Young turned to the firm's outside marketing consultant, Mr. Alan Fayerweather, and asked him to summarize his views on the day's proceedings, to comment on the various points of view raised, and to suggest what next steps the Task Force should take. Before turning the meeting over to Mr. Fayerweather, he commented:

Let me tell you my bias. I'd creep away into a university library or trade association—find out what the market is—break it down into "globs"—then come back and tell you where the market opportunities lie—then the job would be over. Thats my bias. I'd take the "analytical instrument market"—about $1.5 billion growing at 7 percent, and focus on that.

Exhibit 1
SPEER INDUSTRIES, INC. [A]
Five Year Comparative Summary [$000]

INCOME ITEMS	1974	1973	1972	1971	1970
Net sales	119,980	92,768	63,824	65,124	61,902
Costs and expenses	108,421	83,402	59,303	56,998	56,981
Net interest expense	1,928	610	154	252	365
Federal taxes	4,087	4,265	2,232	4,112	2,213
Net income (after adjustment for extraordinary items)	6,109	4,710	594	3,257	2,620
Depreciation	1,939	1,592	1,798	1,732	1,692
Earnings per share	.93	.71	.09	.49	.38
Current assets	73,729	58,490	41,417	42,972	39,890
Current liabilities	18,152	15,547	15,728	13,410	12,561
Net working capital	55,577	42,943	25,689	29,562	27,329
Plant and equipment (net)	11,685	10,071	10,281	11,126	10,886
Long term debt	20,100	11,900	—	5,950	6,800

Exhibit 2

SPEER INDUSTRIES, INC. [A]

Major Markets by Standard Industrial Classification
Reliance Instrumentation

SIC	Industry		1974 % of Sales
82	EDUCATIONAL SERVICES		27.9
	8221 colleges and universities	27.3	
	8211 elementary and secondary	0.6	
28	CHEMICAL AND ALLIED PRODUCTS		13.7
	2834 pharmaceutical preparations	2.9	
	2818 organic chemicals	2.7	
80	HEALTH SERVICES		9.3
	8061 hospitals	7.0	
	8071 medical laboratories	1.8	
95	ENVIRONMENT QUALITY ADMINISTRATION		6.3
	9511 air, water, solid waste management	5.8	
96	ADMINISTRATION OF ECONOMIC PROGRAMS		4.8
	9641 regulation of agricultural marketing	2.8	
	9621 regulation of transportation	1.1	
20	FOOD AND KINDRED PRODUCTS		4.3
	2082 malt beverages	1.1	
94	ADMINISTRATION OF HUMAN RESOURCES		4.0
	9431 public health administration	3.9	
29	PETROLEUM AND COAL PRODUCTS		3.9
	2911 petroleum refining	3.8	
73	BUSINESS SERVICES		2.9
	7391 R&D laboratories	2.2	
51	WHOLESALE TRADE NON-DURABLE		1.6
	5122 drugs, propriataries, sundries	.5	
	5172 petroleum products	.4	
33	PRIMARY METAL INDUSTRIES		1.5
	3312 blast furnaces and steel mills	.5	
	3357 nonferrous wire products	.5	
All Others			19.8

Source: company data.

Exhibit 3
SPEER INDUSTRIES, INC. [A]
1974 Orders by Area [3 Digit Zip]
Reliance Instrumentation

CALIFORNIA			8.8%
	Los Angeles (900–918)	3.2%	
	Oakland (945–948)	2.2	
		5.4	
TEXAS			7.8
	Galveston (775)	1.6	
	Houston (770)	1.1	
		2.7	
NEW YORK			6.5
	New York (100–104)	4.5	
NEW JERSEY			4.9
	Newark (070–076)	1.5	
	New Brunswick (088–089)	1.0	
		2.5	
PENNSYLVANIA			4.7
	Pittsburgh (150–152)	0.8	
	Philadelphia (191)	1.0	
		1.8	
MICHIGAN			4.1
	Ann Arbor (481)	0.8	
	Detroit (482)	0.7	
	Pontiac (480)	0.6	
		2.1	
ILLINOIS			4.0
	Chicago (600–606)	2.8	
	Champaign (618–619)	1.2	
		4.0	
OHIO			4.0
FLORIDA			3.2
	Ft. Lauderdale (333)	0.5	
	Gainesville (326)	0.4	
	Tampa (335–337)	0.4	
		1.3	
MASSACHUSETTS			3.0
	Boston (017–022)	1.4	
10 States			51.0%

Source: company data.

Exhibit 4
SPEER INDUSTRIES, INC. [A]

Reliance Instrumentation's Share of Market for Laboratory Meters

MANUFACTURER	% OF MARKET BY $	% OF MARKET BY UNITS
Ellison Electric	41.7	39.6
Reliance Instrumentation Co.	20.4	26.4
Ace	5.6	3.5
Englehard	4.7	9.1
Applied Scientific	3.4	4.1
Cetco	3.0	4.4
Brantley	0.4	0.7
Others	20.8	12.2
	100.0	100.0

Source: company data (disguised).

Exhibit 5
SPEER INDUSTRIES, INC. [A]

Reliance Instrumentation: Share of Market for Potentiometers

MANUFACTURER	% OF MARKET BY $	% OF MARKET BY UNITS
Reliance Instrumentation Co.	27.6	23.1
Cetco	15.2	16.1
Applied Scientific	11.3	12.5
Ellison Electric	10.8	10.9
Englehard	8.6	10.1
Ace	8.0	7.2
Wellfleet Instrumentation Company	5.9	4.1
Newsome	5.4	5.7
Others	7.2	10.3
	100.0	100.0

Source: company estimates (disguised).

Exhibit 6

SPEER INDUSTRIES, INC. [A]

Reliance Instrumentation: Share of Market for Analytical Balances

MANUFACTURER	% OF MARKET BY $	% OF MARKET BY UNITS
Baker	38.2	51.0
Kenney	13.2	3.7
GSN	8.5	7.6
Stokely	8.0	1.2
Reliance Instrumentation Co.	7.0	14.0
Catellan	2.9	3.3
Edwards	0.8	0.8
Cetco	0.7	0.7
Leyden	0.3	0.3
Others	20.4	17.4

Source: company estimates (disguised).

Exhibit 7

SPEER INDUSTRIES, INC. [A]

Reliance Instrumentation: Market Share for Blenders

MANUFACTURER	% OF MARKET BY $	% OF MARKET BY UNITS
Hagen	29.1	28.9
Big T	18.2	15.4
Brunswick	6.1	8.3
Brinkmaster	7.0	7.5
Thornton	5.2	7.3
Reliance Instrumentation Co.	5.9	6.0
Worthington	3.1	3.7
Abbey	4.2	3.4
Norris	1.8	1.6
Baxter Equipment	2.1	1.5
Circle	1.9	1.3
Others	15.4	15.1

Source: company estimates (disguised).

Exhibit 8
SPEER INDUSTRIES, INC. [A]
Estimated Total Market Potential for SPD Products
[number of units]

MARKET SEGMENTS	WP1000	WP2000	AWP10
INDUSTRIAL			
Food and kindred products	150	150	0
Textile mill products	132	132	0
Saw mills and planning mills	0	0	0
Paper and allied products	82	82	0
Chemicals and allied products	336	336	0
Stone, clay, glass and concrete products	105	105	0
Primary metals industries	287	287	0
Machinery manufacturing, except electrical	392	1450	0
Electrical equipment, machinery and supplies	61	61	0
Transportation equipment	85	85	0
MINING			
Metal	55	260	0
Coal	0	0	0
Stone	10	10	0
Sand and gravel	12	12	0
Clay and related minerals	0	0	0
Fertilizers	18	110	0
GOVERNMENT AGENCIES			
Federal	225	108	420
State	120	120	810
Municipal	0	0	1600
UTILITY COMPANIES	370	370	0
INSURANCE COMPANIES	25	25	0
R&D AND CONSULTING ORGANIZATIONS	100	100	100
Total Units	2365	3803	2930
Total Dollars	$9,000,000	$41,200,000	$32,000,000

Source: company data.

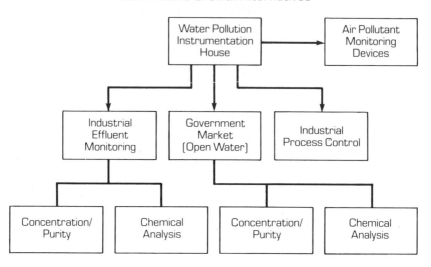

Exhibit 9
SPEER INDUSTRIES, INC. [A]
SPD Future Growth Alternatives

Appendix A

Speer Industries, Inc. [A]

Memorandum

November 15, 1974

Subject: Organizational Alternatives for Non-Aerospace Business

Speer's organizational structure is a product of history. Separate divisions, with widely differing size, have a direct reporting relationship to the President (see Speer Organization Chart on page 43).

This organizational structure has resulted in the development of virtually independent growth strategies on the part of each division. Product lines grow in an uncoordinated and random fashion as new market opportunities are identified. The result is an extremely fragmented approach to many small markets with few opportunities to achieve large scale operations.

Speer Organization Chart—June 1974

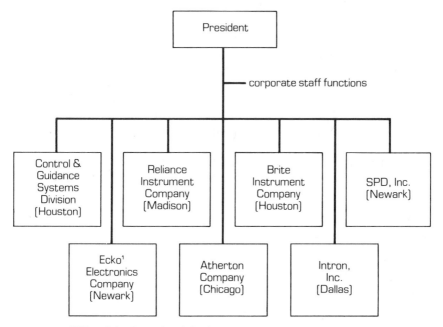

```
                        ┌──────────────┐
                        │  President   │
                        └──────────────┘
                               │
                               ├──── corporate staff functions
                               │
  ┌────────────┬──────────────┼──────────────┬────────────────┐
  │            │              │              │                │
┌────────┐ ┌──────────┐ ┌──────────┐ ┌──────────┐
│Control &│ │Reliance  │ │Brite     │ │SPD, Inc. │
│Guidance │ │Instrument│ │Instrument│ │[Newark]  │
│Systems  │ │Company   │ │Company   │ │          │
│Division │ │[Madison] │ │[Houston] │ │          │
│[Houston]│ │          │ │          │ │          │
└────────┘ └──────────┘ └──────────┘ └──────────┘
     │           │            │
┌──────────┐ ┌──────────┐ ┌──────────┐
│Ecko⁶     │ │Atherton  │ │Intron,   │
│Electronics│ │Company  │ │Inc.      │
│Company   │ │[Chicago] │ │[Dallas]  │
│[Newark]  │ │          │ │          │
└──────────┘ └──────────┘ └──────────┘
```

[6]EEC and the Control and Guidance System Division were consolidated into the "Guidance and Control System Group" in November 1974.

The most obvious example of this problem is the difficulty of establishing a nationwide sales and service network which can rival major competitors such as Beckman, Perkin Elmer and Hewlett Packard in the scientific products area. But similar difficulties arise in manufacturing and R&D. In these areas, divisions such as Intron and SPD appear to be at a disadvantage because of their small size.

The solution to this problem appears to lie in the judicious selection of *new* development opportunities in the future. If, instead of a dozen product lines targeted at a dozen different markets, Speer's growth could be channeled into three or four market areas which several divisions might be able to serve, a "critical mass" could be achieved.

To accomplish this, two major organizational changes are required:

First, each division must be provided with a view of all the other markets in which Speer is active. This could be implemented through the appointment of "market managers" at the corporate (or group) level. The responsibility of a market manager would be to develop Speer business in a particular market, drawing products and technologies from any or all Speer divisions.

Second, product managers must be appointed for each major existing line. The responsibility of these product managers would be to ensure the health of products as opposed to markets.

It is envisioned that the existing divisions would remain the major profit centers of the corporation, with product managers taking responsibility for individual line profitability. But ultimately it is conceivable that market managers might grow important enough to take over as profit centers also. Interaction between product and market managers would be ensured as each sought to exploit his own area of responsibility.

Appendix B
Speer Industries, Inc. [A]
Goals and Objectives

Speer Industries has now reached a size where further growth has to be guided by some explicitly stated goals determined at the corporate level. While the 60's were marked by a program of diversification via acquisition, the 70's have been marked by internal growth and development. The time has now come to channel that growth into paths which fit the overall objectives of the corporation.

This document establishes some overall goals to guide such development. These goals represent fundamental requirements which must be met if we are to strengthen our businesses and provide meaningful opportunities for all Speer employees in the future.

Paul Berger

A. *Sales Objectives*
- total sales have to grow at a compounded growth rate of not less than 15 per cent per annum.

B. *Market Share*
- market shares must be improved.

C. *Profit*
- total per share earnings must grow at not less than 15 per cent per annum.

- total net profits on sales must be increased from 5% to 7% of sales.

D. *Marketing Practices*
  - products must be developed to satisfy a broader spectrum of customer needs.
  - a "sales orientation" must be replaced by a "marketing orientation".
  - pricing policies and practices must be improved.

E. *General*
  - we must develop *large-scale* operations in order to afford adequate manufacturing, marketing and R&D functions.
  - we must develop a competent corporate staff to aid in the management of our broad range of diverse operations.
  - we must establish a continuous system of strategic planning including 3–5 year projections of sales, expenses, profit, balance sheet items, cash flow, and human resource and facilities budgets.
  - we must build a group organizational structure which will carry us into the 1980's.

DISCUSSION QUESTIONS

SPEER INDUSTRIES [A]

1. Compare and contrast the four divisions and their individual product line strategies.
2. What objectives has Mr. Berger set? How appropriate are they for each segment of the overall business?
3. What do The Task Force members seem to believe are the major issues/options?
4. In terms of *next steps*, what should Mr. Fayerweather encourage the Task Force to think about?

Analyzing Market Opportunity and Assessing Company Capability

Defining the business, determining its mission, formulating functional strategies, and setting budgets are complex interrelated decisions requiring considerable analysis. In order to define the business and determine an appropriate mission, market opportunities have to be analyzed and company capabilities have to be assessed to take advantage of the opportunities. In order to formulate functional strategies and set budgets, the specific nature of the opportunities has to be identified and specific ways and means determined to take advantage of them.

This Chapter deals with several of the most important ingredients in this analytical process. These are, on the one hand, how to analyze customers, competitors, market characteristics, and environmental trends to assess market opportunity, and on the other hand how to analyze a company's strengths and weaknesses to determine whether and how the opportunities may be exploited. The analysis of customers serves to identify the range of existing opportunities and possibilities for segmentation. The analysis of competitors identifies how the market is currently served and potential gaps which might be exploited; the analysis of market characteristics in terms of the evolution of supply and demand and analysis of environmental trends produces a dynamic perspective. Finally, the assessment of company strengths and weaknesses against the backdrop of evolving opportunities results in a determination of the company's "fitness" to fill these opportunities, their relative attractiveness, and ways and means of taking advantage of them.

The contemporary planning tools described in Part II of this book, i.e., portfolio analysis, market attractiveness-business position assessment, and PIMS, formalize and quantify certain parts of this analytical process, and highlight certain factors that appear to be related to financial performance. They are, however, only aids to planning. None completely replaces the need for the qualitative analysis with which this chapter deals. In most cases qualitative analysis is used to augment the planning aids; in some cases, particularly in the assessment of market attractiveness and business position, it is an essential ingredient to a more formalized approach.

It is impossible in a single chapter to adequately encompass all the concepts and procedures that analysis of customers, competitors, market characteristics, environmental trends, and company capabilities entails. A good marketing text can provide a reasonable foundation for this task.[1] This chapter will simply highlight the kinds of analyses and concepts that may be useful.

CUSTOMER ANALYSIS AND SEGMENTATION

Why do we undertake customer analysis? We do so because not all customers have the same needs for a product or service. This leads automatically to the strategic implication that businesses may choose to serve different customer segments. Customer *segmentation* is defined as the division of a market into groups of customers having similar needs. Needs must be interpreted very broadly, in terms far broader than only product characteristics. Customers may differ also in their needs for information, reassurance, technical support, service, distribution, and a host of other "non-product" benefits that are part of their purchase. They may also differ in their willingness or ability to pay for these benefits.

Some examples will illustrate how different products in the same industry serve different needs. Revlon and Avon both sell cosmetics, yet Avon customers purchase a far different "package of benefits" through door-to-door "in-home" demonstrations than customers of heavily advertised Revlon products sold in stores. IBM and so called "plug compatible" computer peripheral manufacturers both sell tape drives; yet IBM sells its drives as part of a complete computer system,

---

[1]See, for example, Kotler, Philip, *Marketing Management: Analysis, Planning and Control.* Third Edition (Englewood Cliffs, N.J., Prentice-Hall, Inc. 1976) or Robert D. Buzzell and Robert E. M. Nourse, *Marketing: A Contemporary Analysis.* Second Edition. (New York, McGraw Hill, 1972). See also, Rothschild, William, *Putting it All Together: A Guide to Strategic Thinking.* New York, Amacom 1976, Chapters 3–7.

while its plug-compatible competitors sell drives separately, primarily on the basis of price. Familiar examples of segmentation abound: regular and charter airlines, branded and private-label grocery products, Texas Instrument and Hewlett Packard hand calculators, the *New York Times* and the *New York Daily News.*

Market segmentation is certainly one of the most important aspects of strategic market planning, and it may be the most difficult. When it is well done, it seems obvious. It often requires as much creativity as it does science. Effective segmentation divides the market into pieces that are identifiable, accessible to specialized marketing approaches, substantial enough to be profitable, and above all, defensible against competition.

Segments are described either by differences in the benefits sought,[2] including physical product differences as well as non-product benefits; or by the identity or characteristics of the occupants of the segment. We can say, for example, that the segment that travels with charter airlines seeks lower prices, vacation packages, and is willing to forego firm departure and arrival times (the benefits) or we can say that they tend to be under 40, and travel for pleasure rather than business (the identity). In order to target the occupants of segments with our marketing programs, we would like to be able to relate differences in the benefits sought to identifiable customer characteristics.

The most advantageous way to segment a market may change over time. These changes in segmentation directly result from the continual struggle for competitive advantage. This forces competitors to look for new creative ways to segment their markets and put their particular skills to work. Competitors who react rather than initiate with respect to segmentation often are left at a disadvantage because changes in segmentation change the requirements for doing business.

What kind of analysis is required for creative segmentation to result? A good, practical approach to *identifying differences among customers* is to ask yourself questions such as:

WHAT
- benefits does the customer seek?
- factors influence demand?
- functions does the product perform for the customer?
- are important buying criteria?

---

[2]See Daniel Yankekovitch, "New Criteria for Market Segmentation," *Harvard Business Review,* March/April 1964 and Russell I. Haley, "Benefit Segmentation: A Decision Oriented Research Tool," in Engle, Fiorillo, and Cayley, *Market Segmentation: Concepts and Applications.* New York. Holt, Rinehart and Winston, Inc., 1972, pp. 196–205.

- is the basis of comparison with other products?
- risks does the customer perceive?
- services do customers expect?

HOW
- do customers buy?
- long does the buying process last?
- do various elements of the marketing program influence customers at each stage of the process?
- do customers use the product?
- does the product fit into their life style or operation?
- much are they willing to spend?
- much do they buy?

WHERE
- is the decision made to buy?
- do customers seek information about the product?
- do customers buy the product?

WHEN
- is the first decision to buy made?
- is the product repurchased?

WHY
- do customers buy?
- do customers choose one brand as opposed to another?

WHO
- are the occupants of segments identified by previous questions?
- buys our product, and why?
- buys our competitors' products, and why?

Several points should be kept firmly in mind when using questions such as these to facilitate segmentation. First, the list of questions is only *suggestive*; in any given situation some questions will be more important than others or questions not contained in this list might be profitably asked. Second, *data* is usually needed to supply the answers. This data can come from marketing research designed specifically to answer such questions. Third, the answers themselves have to be related to the decision at hand. It is not enough to ask "WHERE does the consumer buy this product?" Instead the question must be "WHERE does the consumer buy this product and what is the significance of the answer?" For example, "What does it mean for channel strategy? Advertising strategy? Packaging strategy? Physical distribution strategy, etc?"

COMPETITOR ANALYSIS

An evaluation of each competitor is useful for two reasons. First, it reinforces the analysis of customers, just described. Understanding a competitor's strategy helps us to understand the buying behavior and identify the particular class of customer to whom that strategy appeals. Second, it is useful in its own right as the basis for identifying areas of relative strength and weakness and hence potential market opportunity. In this respect it may suggest, also, how a competitor might react to threat or opportunity in a future competitive situation.

Competitor analysis breaks down into two classes of questions. First, *WHO* are the present competitors and potential new entrants? Secondly, *HOW* do they compete?

Identifying Present Competitors and New Entrants

Present competitors fall into two classes. First, there are those competitors who define their activities similarly to you. This means they serve approximately the same customer groups, they seek to perform the same customer functions, they utilize similar technologies, and they exhibit similar degrees of vertical integration. For instance, General Foods would identify Nestle as a similar competitor in the coffee business.

Second, there may be competitors who define their activities differently than you. These differences may appear as differences in the customer groups served, the customer functions served, the technologies used to serve the functions, the degree of vertical integration, or any combination of these. As an example of *customer group* differences, Kimberly Clarke sells paper products extensively in the consumer market while the lesser-known Fort Howard Company sells similar products extensively to the institutional market. Yet the companies compete for some specific applications. In terms of *functions,* some smaller scientific instrument manufacturers, selling only a physical measuring device, find themselves competing with companies like Hewlett Packard and Beckmann Instruments who sell complete "systems" of equipment including measuring devices, analytical devices, mini-computers and display and recording capabilities. Or, the *technology* on which the product is based may differ. Manufacturers of engineered plastics compete with metal producers; synthetic fiber manufacturers compete with natural fiber producers; and refrigerated foods processors compete with fresh and frozen food processors. In terms of differences in vertical integration, "independent" gasoline retainers stand in sharp contrast to the large vertically integrated branded oil companies. Therefore, it is important to identify not only those competitors who reflect your particular approach to the market, but also all the others who "intersect" you in a market, but approach the market from a different perspective.

Potential new entrants to the market should also be identified. Newcomers may enter your market from any one of several starting points:

- they already sell to your customers, but expand their participation to include new customer functions which you currently satisfy (e.g., they initially sell a component of a computer system and expand into other system components which you supply.)
- they already satisfy customer functions which you satisfy but expand their participation into your customer market from activities in other customer markets (e.g., they initially sell pumps for oil exploration only and then expand into the marine pump business where you are active.)
- they already operate in an "upstream" or "downstream" business (e.g., Texas Instruments entered calculators from its position as a semi-conductor manufacturer, while some calculator manufacturers have integrated backwards into the manufacture of semi-conductors.)
- they enter as a result of "unrelated" diversification.

It is important to keep a watch out for entry from each of these vantage points and to continually assess the likelihood, and potential consequences, of such an event.

Analyzing How They Compete

An evaluation of how competitors compete falls into four parts.

1. What is their current strategy?
2. How are they performing?
3. What are their strengths and weaknesses?
4. What actions can be expected from them in the future?

It is essential that each major competitor should be analyzed *separately*. Analyzing competition "generally," while better than nothing, tells you very little about potential threats, or opportunities that can be exploited.

Competitor Strategies. A strategy is very difficult to describe since it involves so many different dimensions. A useful checklist for thinking about competitors' strategies can be based upon the steps in the strategic decision process outlined at the beginning of this chapter:

- How is the competitor defining the business in terms of customer groups, customer functions, and technologies, and how vertically integrated is he? And at a lower level of aggregation, how is he segmenting the market and which segments are being pursued?
- What mission does this business have in his overall portfolio of businesses? Is it being managed for sales? growth? market share? net income? ROI? cash? What goals does he appear to have for each major segment of the business?
- What is his marketing mix, manufacturing policy, R&D policy, purchasing policy, physical distribution policy, etc.?
- What size are his budgets and how are they allocated?

Competitor Performance. Actual performance should be ascertained as closely as possible in terms of sales, growth, market share, profits, margins, net income, return-on-investment and cash flow.

Competitor Strengths and Weaknesses. An analysis of competitive strengths and weaknesses should include a comparative assessment of such factors as:

- products and product quality
- dealers and distribution channels
- marketing and selling capabilities
- operations and physical distribution
- financial capabilities
- management and human resources
- costs and how they are changing with time

Competitive Reactions. Finally, an analysis of a competitor should take account of how he might act *in the future.* This has two components. First, how is he likely to respond to changes going on in the external environment and in the marketplace; second, how is he likely to respond to specific competitive moves that my company or other competitors might initiate? Where is he most vulnerable? Where is he strongest? Where is he likely to be provoked and how? Where is the most appropriate battleground to fight him on and how?

The data for this analysis of competitors comes from a wide variety of sources. Apart from the obvious sources such as published financial reports, 10K reports to the Securities and Exchange Commission (which augment the information contained in company annual reports), company brochures; advertisements and bulletins, industry association data, the trade press, and newspaper and magazine clippings, there are many less obvious sources. Competitors' speeches and public statements should be scrutinized; security analysts reports should be studied; technical people should be quizzed about competitors' products; patent files should be searched; suppliers and customers should be used as information sources; and management and sales people should be trained to collect competitive intelligence. By piecing together information from a variety of different sources, answers to most, if not all, of the above questions can be found.

ANALYZING ENVIRONMENTAL TRENDS

Environmental analysis involves the careful study of economic, social, political, and technological changes. It is important because these changes continually reshape customer behavior and competitive strategies. Environmental analysis was defined in one major corporation as "a scan of markets and technology far enough in the future so that actions can be taken ... rather than reactions."[3]

Economic Changes derive from broad secular movements in various underlying economic factors, as well as changes due to business cycles. Among the most important factors to consider are gross national product, personal income, number of people holding jobs, number of households and household formations, government spending, capital spending, capital availability and interest rates, and sectoral growth patterns.

Social Changes are difficult to classify into any exhaustive list. Among the factors that might have been considered in the decade of the 70s are changes in the status of women and minorities, changes in family life styles, shifts to less work and more leisure, improved living standards, and apparent declines in traditional values.

Political Changes include those on a global, national, state, and municipal level. At a global level, political changes influence trade between nations, foreign investment, defense spending, and the functioning of multinational corporations. At a national level, regulatory policies, antitrust policies, fiscal and monetary policies, industrial policies, consumer policies, regional policies, labor policies, and envi-

---

[3]Coca-Cola Company.

ronmental policies all affect the functioning of markets. At a state and local level, taxation, employment issues, community development policies, and local regulatory policies are important.

Technological Changes proceed constantly and show little recognition of the boundaries that traditionally divide industries. In fact, most of the important technological changes that effect an industry originate outside it. Semiconductor technology, for example, has had an impact on an enormous variety of industries including computers, process control, the watch industry, scientific instrumentation, calculators, radio and television, appliances, telecommunications, etc. The list is extremely long. Technological change not only leads to improved products but also to new substitute ways to meet customer needs. Further, it often leads to the identification and exploitation of previously unfilled needs. Air transportation, synthetic food protein for developing countries, high-performance plastics, office copying, automated office equipment, television satellites for world-wide communication, and hand calculators, are all examples.

Sensitivity to all these environmental influences is essential to strategic market planning. The process of analyzing the environment must identify key changes, in particular those that could "make or break" the business, e.g., as electronics and miniaturization "broke" the mechanical desk-top calculator business. It must result in a determination of the range of strategic alternatives open to your firm and its competitors for anticipating and continually adapting to the new conditions.

ANALYZING MARKET CHARACTERISTICS

There are certain characteristics of the market that cannot be gained from a study of customers, competitors, or environmental trends alone. They deal with the character of demand on the one hand and of supply on the other, and the dynamic interaction between the two.

Demand

An analysis of the demand side of the market should include:

1. a delineation of *market boundaries* and how they are changing.
2. assessments of present and future *buyer concentration.*
3. *projections of demand* for the total market and for major segments.

Market boundaries. Usually it is not possible to define market boundaries precisely. Theoretically a market is defined as being bounded by all the closely substitutable products that may be sold to satisfy a given customer need. But here the problem of precise definition begins. What is "closely" substitutable? How broadly should the customer "need" be defined? How many customers should be included in the market definition when different offerings are made to different grour of customers?

Boundaries ideally should be defined so that only "close" technological substitutes in the consumer's eyes are included in the definition (e.g., alternative brands of decaffeinated coffee); only customer needs that are served with related marketing programs are included in the definition (e.g., car battery and accessory purchases); and only customers with "similar" needs are included in the definition (e.g., male and female buyers of toothpaste). Plainly, judgment is needed in all these issues. The question becomes particularly pertinent when market share is being considered. The question becomes, share of what? We shall deal with these problems in depth in Chapter 8.

Here, the assumption will be made that judgment can be sensibly applied. As planners we are interested not only in how the market is currently defined, but how it may be redefined by competitive initiative as the market evolves. Market redefinition can occur in any one of three ways.

First, a market may be extended by the application of a particular product technology to new customer groups. This usually occurs in the normal process of "diffusion" of an innovation. For example, nylon was originally developed for military use; later the nylon market was extended to hosiery, rugs, tires, bearings, and a host of other applications.

Second, a market may be redefined by the inclusion or exclusion of related customer functions. The combination of individual scientific instruments with mini-computers is an example of the extension of a market from a component to a system; the sale of individual "plug compatible" peripheral devices in place of devices previously included in an IBM computer system is an example of a "systems" market being redefined as a components market.

Third, market redefinition can occur through the substitution of new technologies. The watch market was redefined by the entry of digital watches; the foods market has been progressively redefined by the development of dry packaged foods, then of refrigerated and frozen foods; the photographic products market has been redefined by the invention of "instant" photography.

Buyer concentration is a measure of how many buyers exist in the market and how sales are distributed among them. It is an important indicator of the balance of power between suppliers and buyers. Where a few buyers account for a large proportion of purchases, they may be able to exert considerable influence over suppliers, as do automobile manufacturers, for example, over parts suppliers in the U.S. automobile industry.

Demand projections can be expressed in either units or dollars. If there are price changes, it is useful to examine both. In periods of general price inflation, growth should be measured in both "current" and "constant" dollars (using a price deflator). An analysis of demand should include an estimate of both overall growth and the growth of different market segments.

Supply

An analysis of the supply side of the market should include:

1. assessments of present and future *supply structure* (in terms of supply concentration, product differentiation, and entry barriers.)
2. a description of the *character of competition* both present and projected.
3. an analysis of *cost structure and cost behavior.*

Supply structure involves three major elements: first, how many firms supply the market and how are sales distributed between them? We call this supply concentration. Second, how "differentiated" (different from each other) are the products offered? We refer both to differences among the offerings of competing suppliers (e.g., Ford versus GM) and to differences in the offerings of any single supplier across market segments (e.g., Chevrolet versus Cadillac). As markets develop, it is common to see product differentiation among competing suppliers diminish due to imitation, while product differentiation across segments increases as customer needs are satisfied more precisely. Third, what "barriers" exist to either entry to the market by new firms, or exit from the market by incumbent competitors? Entry barriers take many forms, including financial requirements, technological requirements, and manufacturing scale or marketing scale requirements. Exit barriers usually derive from difficulties of liquidating plant and equipment or working capital without incurring substantial losses. Government regulation may also impede exit; for example, regulatory barriers have prevented the railroads from dropping some passenger service.

The Character of Competition. Competition in a market is highly dependent on the nature of customer behavior. Since customer behavior varies with the type of product and buying situation, as well as with time as new markets develop, the character of competition can take many forms. One good way to assess the character of competition is through an analysis of changes in the composition of value added by competing firms. *Value added* is the amount by which selling price exceeds the cost of purchased goods and services. In this way the relative importance of such factors as product development, process development, advertising, selling, technical assistance, channel services, and price can be assessed. Figure 2 compares typical value-added structures for a high-technology product such as an engineered plastic with a lower-grade commodity plastic, at early and later life cycle stages.

The character of competition is also measurable in terms of whether competitors are trying to develop new total industry demand (primary demand) or compete for existing demand with other firms (selective demand). When primary demand stimulation is the objective, the emphasis is on identifying and entering new customer segments ahead of competition. When selective demand stimulation is the objective, the emphasis is on satisfying the needs of particular segments better than any other competitor. This may be done through any element of the marketing program including the product itself, advertising, promotion, channels of distribution, or price.

Cost Structure and Cost Behavior. Cost *structure,* usually defined as the ratio of variable to fixed costs, is an extremely important supply factor mainly because it is an important determinant of the character of competition. In businesses exhibiting high fixed costs, as in the paper industry, profits are very sensitive to volume. Consequently it is usual to see competition directed at ways to fill capacity and keep plants operating. In some cases where customer demand is sensitive to price this can result in vicious price cutting. In businesses exhibiting high variable costs as in canned specialty foods, profits are very sensitive to prices and margin improvement; thus ways are sought to differentiate products and raise prices as a way to improve margins and profits.

The strategic implications of cost *behavior* are also very important. Chapter 3 is devoted to this topic; in particular how costs fall as cumulative volume increases—so-called learning or experience effects; and how costs vary with the size of the operation—or so-called scale effects.

High Technology Plastic ¢/Unit

25¢	Profit [before tax]
12¢	Marketing
12¢	Technical
6¢	Administrative
12¢	Fixed Manufacturing
10¢	Variable Manufacturing

20¢	Profit [before tax]
8¢	Marketing
8¢	Technical
6¢	Administrative
10¢	Fixed Manufacturing
9¢	Variable Manufacturing

Commodity Plastic ¢/Unit

10¢	Profit
3¢	Marketing
3¢	Technical
3¢	Administrative
10¢	Fixed Manufacturing
8¢	Variable Manufacturing

5¢	Profit
2¢	Marketing
2¢	Technical
3¢	Administrative
9¢	Fixed Manufacturing
8¢	Variable Manufacturing

Figure 2

Comparison of Value-Added Components in the Early and Late Stages of the Product Life Cycles for Two Types of Plastics

Demand and Supply Dynamics. Market evolution continually changes the characteristics of both demand and supply. Evolution results from the dual influence of external environmental trends and the relatively more systematic influence of "life cycles." The life cycle phenomenon is usually described in terms of the evolution of individual products or brands through four stages: development, growth, maturity, and decline. An idealized life cycle pattern is shown in Figure 3.

Although few products exactly obey this pattern of sales development, the product life cycle does provide some indication of what may be expected to happen. It may help in forecasting sales; it also may help in anticipating changes in the "character of competition." Typically, in the early stages of the life cycle, advertising and promotional expenditures are high and prices are high enough to support these expenditures. Later, as maturity approaches, and as customer needs for information and reassurance decline, advertising and promotional expenditures fall and so do prices.[4] In the decline stages, outright price competition may set in.

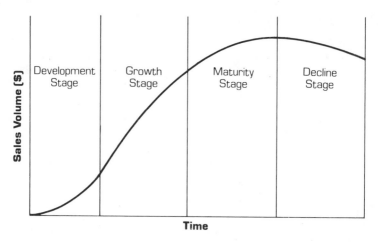

Figure 3
An Idealized Product Life Cycle

The concept of "stages of development" is one that may also be applied at higher levels of aggregation than individual products or brands. For example, the appliance "industry" is relatively mature even though some new products such as trash compactors are still in their growth stage. The difficulty in applying the concept at higher levels of aggregation is that stages often last for much longer time periods, making their beginning and end harder to identify. As yet there are only a few partial theories which can be applied to the evolution of

---

[4]See Robert D. Buzzell, "Competitive Behavior and Product Life Cycles," in *New Ideas for Successful Marketing*, J. S. Wright and J. L. Goldstrucker (Eds.), *Proceedings* of the 1966 World Congress, American Marketing Association.

whole industries or "markets".[5] This is one of the major areas where new theoretical work valuable to planners is likely to take place in the next decade.[6]

A short example will now be used to illustrate how the four elements of analysis required to assess market opportunity—analysis of customers, competitors, environmental trends, and market characteristics—can be combined to produce strategic insights. This example is provided by the experience of a British potato-chip manufacturer in the mid-1960s.

During the early 1960s Smith's Potato Crisps Ltd. held approximately 60 percent of the U.K. market for potato chips (known as "crisps" in Great Britain)[7]. Crisps were manufactured in fifteen regionally located "batch processing" plants and distributed to small grocery stores and licensed bars ("pubs") for on-premise consumption. They were packaged in semi-opaque bags with relatively short shelf life. Daily deliveries by a large fleet of small pick-up trucks ensured freshness (and crispness!).

In the mid-1960s the Golden Wonder Company, a subsidiary of Imperial Tobacco having extensive supermarket distribution, introduced a new brand of potato crisp, packaged in transparent bags, with substantially longer shelf life. Manufacturing was concentrated in two large plants with large-scale continuous processing capabilities. The advent of supermarket distribution rapidly expanded the "at home" consumption of potato crisps, and most of this new segment was captured by Golden Wonder. In five years, total sales of crisps almost doubled. Golden Wonder's sales increased several fold while Smith's increased only slightly as a result. Smith's share declined to about 35 percent of the total market. Remarkably, more than a year after Golden Wonder's entry, Smith's management announced to its stockholders that the company was experiencing "one of its best years ever". (This is a graphic example of the danger of concentrating on sales and not market share as a measure of performance.)

With the development of "at home" consumption, the character of competition changed dramatically. Previously crisps were "PUSHED" to the trade by retail delivery salesmen; subsequent to Golden Won-

---

[5]See Derek F. Abell, "Competitive Market Strategy: Some Generalizations and Hypotheses," *Marketing Science Institute Report*, No. 75–107, 1975.

[6]In our opinion, major advances are likely to come from the integration of concepts from "industrial organization economics" and those of marketing planning, and business strategy.

[7]Alan Bevan, "The U.K. Potato Crisp Industry: 1960–72," A Study of New Entry Competition, *Journal of Industrial Economics*, June 1974.

der's entry, crisps began to be heavily advertised and "PULLED" through supermarket channels of distribution. What had once appeared to be a fairly mature market became a rapid growth market.

In this example we can see how customer segmentation changed (with the opening up of a whole new segment of primary demand); how the needs of this new "at home" segment were quite different than those of the "pub" buyers (in terms of the need for shelf life, convenient distribution, advertising, and brand reassurance, see-through packaging, etc.); how a new competitor with supermarket and mass-merchandising skill appeared using marketing techniques similar to those required for tobacco merchandising; and how two technological changes (packaging and continuous manufacturing processes) completely transformed the character of manufacture, physical distribution, and marketing. Forecasting such patterns of evolution *before* they occur is an essential ingredient to strategic market planning.

We may still ask, however, whether Smith would have been in a position to take advantage of the opportunity that Golden Wonder pioneered even if its management had been more far-sighted. These are the questions to which we now turn.

INTERNAL COMPANY SELF-ASSESSMENT

The analysis of customers, competitors, environmental trends, and market characteristics have as their objective the assessment of *opportunity*. The analysis of the company itself, aims at assessing whether our company is equipped to *seize* the opportunity.

Such assessment parallels that suggested under the heading of competitor analysis. It involves an analysis of historical strategy, performance, strengths and weaknesses, and possible response patterns. In addition it asks whether company resources are relevant to and adequate for an identified opportunity, and if not, what can be done to obtain the necessary resources.

Each business should identify its particular "distinctive competence." What is it about its mode of doing business, its resources, or the value system of management and employees, that distinguishes it from other competitors in the market? Timex, for example, developed a distinctive competence in mass distribution, low-cost production based on standardized products, and international marketing. Polaroid developed a distinctive technological capability coupled with mass marketing. Proctor and Gamble prides itself on its superior products and its marketing and merchandising skills, as did Imperial Tobacco in the example of the British potato-chip market.

A firm's ability to cope with continual market change varies with the severity of the change. When change is relatively small it may adapt by modifying marketing or other functional programs to reflect the emergent requirements of the marketplace. Frequently however, when change is severe, the competence of the firm to continue competing effectively can be questioned. This may happen when new, unfamiliar segments of primary demand develop; as market definition changes along functional lines; or as new technologies emerge. Smith's Potato Crisps Ltd., described earlier, faced this problem as marketing requirements shifted from specialty-outlet, "PUSH" marketing to mass-distribution and "PULL" marketing.

The term *strategic window*[8] is used to describe the fact that there are often only limited periods when the "fit" between the "key requirements" of a market and the particular competences of a firm competing in that market are at an optimum. Investment in a product line or market area has to be timed to coincide with periods in which a strategic window is open, i.e., where a close fit exists. Disinvestment should be considered if, during the course of the market's evolution, changes in market requirements outstrip the firm's capability to adapt itself to the new circumstances.

The strategic window concept can be useful to incumbent competitors as well as to would-be entrants into a market. For the former it provides a way of relating future strategic moves to market evolution and of assessing how resources should be allocated to existing activities. For the latter it provides a framework for diversification and new entry. Smith's Ltd. saw a strategic window closing because it had failed to assemble the resources or develop the skills for effective mass production, supermarket distribution, and mass merchandising. Imperial Tobacco saw a potential strategic window in the potato-chip business where its distinctive competence could be profitably applied.

Relating market opportunities with company capabilities is a prerequisite to defining the business, determining what an appropriate "mission" should be, and what functional strategies and budgets are necessary. Golden Wonder defined itself as a supermarket merchandiser of packaged goods while Smith's Ltd. defined itself as a manufacturer of potato chips. Golden Wonder saw the potato-chip line as an opportunity for substantial marketing investments in advertising and promotion, and apparently set high goals for sales growth and market share gain. While Smith's Ltd. was content with historical levels of sales improvement and continued with manufacturing, distribution, and marketing arrangements suitable to "on premise" buyers, Golden

---

[8]Derek F. Abell, "Strategic Windows," *Journal of Marketing,* July 1978.

Wonder streamlined manufacturing, distribution, and marketing to meet the needs of "at home" consumers buying in supermarkets.

Effective strategic market planning might have forewarned Smith's Ltd. of what was to happen and allowed them to prepare themselves much earlier; or it might have stimulated a search for other opportunities, for example, additions to their line of products going to licensed outlets.

SUMMARY

Analyzing market opportunity requires careful analysis of customers and customer segmentation, competitors (both present and potential new entrants), environmental trends, and market characteristics. Matching opportunities with internal company capabilities is at the heart of effective strategic market planning. The process is a dynamic one; as markets evolve, new opportunities continually present themselves and existing opportunities decline. Thus you must plan in order to anticipate such opportunities and to assemble ahead of time the resources and skills required to take advantage of them.

DOCUTEL CORPORATION[1]

Docutel Corporation lost $649,000 in 1974, but for the first half of 1975 expected profits before tax of $208,000. With this turnaround behind him, Mr. B. J. Meredith, President, believed it was time to ponder his long-range strategy:

> We have spent most of the last eighteen months just trying to survive. Now we are beyond the 1973–1974 crisis and can look at the future. Eight years ago, we were the first company to market Automated Teller Machines (ATMs) to banks. We still have the major share of that market, but there is a great deal of uncertainty about its future direction, and major competitors are becoming active. The question for us is—what should our objectives and strategy be?

COMPANY BACKGROUND

Docutel Corporation was founded in May 1967 by Recognition Equipment, Inc., a pioneer in the development and marketing of Optical Character Recognition (OCR) equipment.[2] REI founded Docutel as a way to show short-term returns from two technologies that were spun off from the major developmental activities of the company. These were automated baggage handling equipment for airline terminals, and Automated Teller Machines (ATMs) for banks. Sales of the baggage handling equipment were slow, mainly due to the airlines' financial troubles in 1969–70. Eventually, this business was sold to the Boeing Company. ATM sales were more encouraging, but faced with the need for continued infusions of cash to support the business, REI sold Docutel to Information Processing Corporation of Dallas (IPC) in 1970.

---

[1]This case was prepared originally by Joseph D'Cruz in collaboration with Derek F. Abell. It was condensed by Ralph Biggadike in conjunction with the original authors.

[2]OCRs are electronic data processing peripherals which can optically "read" a printed character on a document and convert this information into electronic signals.

Docutel's Automated Teller, called the Docuteller® [3], allowed a bank customer to withdraw funds at any hour of the day or night simply by entering the appropriate instructions on the externally mounted keyboard. Upon takeover, Mr. Meredith discovered that none of the 30 installed machines were working, apparently because of service problems. Furthermore, the Docuteller itself needed updating. A modified machine was designed with a small computer to perform the logic and control functions and do some limited data processing. IPC invested more than $1 million in the company in the first year after its acquisition for service and machine improvements.

Product and market development continued throughout the early 1970s. In 1971, Docutel introduced the Total Teller, a machine that could not only dispense cash but could also handle customers' deposits and transfer cash from one account to another. In 1972, a prototype automatic fuel dispensing system was developed which offered a way to dispense fuel, provide credit card authorization, and handle billing at gasoline filling stations. Although Atlantic Richfield purchased five pilot installations, the remaining oil companies took a "wait and see" attitude towards adoption. Docutel executives decided to restrict this activity, apart from a small research project funded by Atlantic Richfield.

In early 1973, Docutel began to explore markets for ATMs in Europe. While domestic acceptance was encouraging, foreign business failed to materialize. This was attributed in part to the fact that European banks were mostly extremely large multiple branch organizations, with highly centralized purchasing arrangements.

In total, Docutel's sales grew rapidly through 1973. (See Exhibits 1, 2, and 3 for selected financial data on the company.) However, in September 1973, sales began to drop off and backlogs to slip. In describing this period, Mr. Meredith said:

> I think we misread the signs and made some major mistakes in this period. Banks faced severe economic conditions with the recession, the energy crisis, and Watergate. But we did not foresee the turndown. Instead, buoyed by early 1973 results, we decided to substantially increase our selling effort. I just didn't know what the size of the market was for this product. So we worked backwards. We decided how much money we wanted to make and then worked out how much we had to sell. That became our target.

---

[3]Docuteller, Total Teller, and Table Top Teller (T4) are trademarks of Docutel Corporation.

We had seventeen salesmen in the field, but our vice president often had to go in and close the sales personally. Eventually we brought in Bob Heckman as Vice President of Financial Systems Marketing. Bob had spent ten years at IBM in several marketing, new product development, and management positions and had excellent contacts with sales people in the field. I told him that we wanted him to have fifty salespeople in the field by January 1974. I didn't think he could do it, but he had the contacts, and come January 1, there were my fifty people ready to go.

Optimism was soon replaced by a more sober attitude. Sales ran below forecast and expenses were high. According to Mr. Meredith:

In May 1974 we realized that we needed to "back down." We had no idea how to go about it. All our experience was in planning for growth.

By the end of 1974 Mr. Meredith felt that the company had managed to survive a period of general reverses in the economy and a crisis in the company's operations. Docutel remained the market leader with a majority of the installations as well as the largest sales of ATMs.

THE U.S. MARKET FOR FINANCIAL TRANSACTIONS SYSTEMS EQUIPMENT

In the early 1960s banking executives began to look with concern at the growth in the volume of transactions and the number of accounts. One analyst estimated that in 1969 the average U.S. family had as many as five different bank accounts. Two major problems were foremost in bankers' minds. One concerned the sheer volume of paper and the costs of processing each transaction. The other problem involved what bankers called "float"—the amount of money tied up in transactions under processing.

The banking system looked to electronics and automation as a possible solution to these problems. Bankers began to experiment with Electronic Funds Transfer Systems (EFTS) which would replace paper with telecommunications and bring in the "cashless society." Such a system would provide the ability to make deposits and withdrawals from remote locations (for example: a retail store, apartment complex, or gas station). These remote locations would be connected to customer account files in banks and credit card companies by telecommunications. These files showed the status of the customer's account; whether, for example, the checking account had sufficient funds to cover the transaction or whether the customer had exceeded a limit on a credit card account. In addition to extensive computer hardware and software, each location in an EFT System required an electronic machine that accepted commands from the user. Typically three distinct, but related, machines might be included in such a system.

1. Automatic Teller Machine (ATM): a machine that enables the customer to perform banking transactions without communicating with a human being.
2. Point-of-Sale Machine (POS): an ATM located in a retail store; these machines could be programmed to perform additional functions such as inventory control and sales accounting.
3. On-Line Teller Terminal (OLTT): a machine that provides the bank teller with immediate access to a customer's file.

A full EFTS could consist of these three types of machines in many different locations, connected together by telecommunications to customers' files in a variety of financial institutions. In 1975, financial transactions in the U.S. were not conducted by anything approaching this comprehensive a system. But these machines were in use, either as stand-alone components or as machines in what might be termed partial systems. The rate at which the nation would approach a full EFTS, and what would happen to stand-alone components sales and their manufacturers, were among the crucial strategic questions facing executives at Docutel.

These three machines and their uses are explained below:

Automatic Teller Machines

Docutel pioneered the development of ATMs in the late 1960s. Originally, these machines were merely cash dispensers which allowed the customer to withdraw a limited amount of cash from an account without the help of a human teller. Later, the functions of these machines were extended to allow deposits and transfers from one account to another. These machines could be placed within a bank lobby, which would make them available only within banking hours; on an outside wall, which would make them available on a twenty-four hour, seven-day-a-week basis; or in a remote location. Most early machines were off-line, stand-alone types which required that the bank reprocess all transactions later in a batch mode. Later machines were developed which could be connected on-line to a real-time system of account processing.

The bank customer activated an ATM by inserting a plastic card embossed with a magnetic stripe. The stripe represented a coded identification number which the machine checked against an identification number entered by the customer on the keyboard. When the two numbers matched, the machine allowed the customer to commence bank transactions on his or her account. Transaction time ranged from 15 to 35 seconds. See Exhibit 4 for an explanation of how an ATM works.

ATM prices varied from $24,000 to $35,000; installation costs were extra and could amount to an additional $10,000 if installation involved bricks, mortar, and lighting. Most ATM manufacturers also charged a monthly service fee, ranging from $130 to $350. Additional costs for supplies and internal processing if the machine was not on-line could be $800 per month; if on-line, these costs amounted to about $300. In contrast, the average wage of a teller in urban areas could be around $900 with an additional 50 percent for employee benefits.

By the middle of 1975, over 3,000 of these terminals had been installed in some 500 or so banks, in all the states and Canada. Over 80 percent of these machines had been supplied by Docutel. Industry estimates of future ATM sales ranged, according to one Docutel executive, "all the way from modest growth to Boomsville, U.S.A." One set of estimates which Mr. Meredith considered as reliable as any he had seen are shown in Table 1.

Table 1
ESTIMATED ATM MARKET 1976–1980

YEAR	UNITS	$ MILLION
1976	1,500	$52
1977	1,700	60
1978	2,000	72
1979	2,100	76
1980	2,200	80

Source: Docutel estimates.

Point-of-Sale Machines

POS machines were used to provide automated banking facilities in the retail store. Several different types of POS devices were envisaged, ranging from a single credit authorization function ("bike") to a multi-function device that recorded the customer's purchases, immediately debited the customer's bank account, and provided the store with inventory control and sales accounting ("Bentley").

Price estimates of a single function POS machine were in the $1,500–$2,000 range, although one recent contract was rumored to be at a price of $1,200. One forecast estimated demand at 800,000 units by 1980.

Savings and loan banks had taken the lead in experimenting with POS. One widely publicized experiment was conducted by the First Federal Savings and Loan Association of Lincoln, Nebraska. This bank placed Remote Service Units in two Hinky Dinky Stores, offering its customers seven-day, ninety-hour-a-week access to their savings accounts.

During the first forty-seven days of operation, First Federal acquired $664,000 in new deposits, half of it from new customers. Despite attempts by combinations of commercial bankers, some S&Ls, and the Attorney General of Nebraska to obtain court injunctions against the system, it survived. First Federal decided to conduct future operations through a subsidiary, employing a switching system that would permit other banks to join in the use of the system.

NCR was reported to have a large share of the POS system business, with IBM and other computer manufacturers vying to develop strong positions.

On-Line Teller Terminals

These machines were used to access customer files in those financial institutions which had put their internal operations on to an on-line, real-time system. One industry observer noted that "to date only the mutual savings banks and S&Ls have thoroughly exploited on-line systems. Commercial banks have been reluctant to commit themselves even though they see this as the wave of the future."

Industry estimates placed the number of teller-operated terminals in use in the United States in mid-1975 at between 55,000 and 65,000 and saw an eventual market for 250,000 if all the human tellers were to be supplied with terminals. Docutel executives believed that the major suppliers of such machines were Burroughs, IBM, and NCR which together accounted for over 75 percent of the total market.

FACTORS INFLUENCING ADOPTION OF EFTS

In 1975, it was not clear how fast ATMs, POSs, or OLTTs, or combinations of these in complete EFT Systems would be introduced by the financial institutions. There were two major types of institutions in the U.S.—commercial banks and thrift institutions; see Exhibit 5 for the number and assets of each type of institution. An important motivation for considering EFTS was to find ways of lowering the costs of banking. But many other factors would influence adoption, notably—regulation, competition between commercial banks and the thrifts, and consumer habits.

REGULATION

Regulation influenced adoption of EFTS machines because of its impact on branching—one method by which banks competed to offer improved customer service. A remote ATM was, in effect, another branch. A POS machine in a store handling customer deposits and withdrawals could also be considered a branch. But, viewing EFTS machines in this way raised two regulatory problems. First, regulation did not permit all commercial banks to branch wherever they wished. Some states did not permit branching at all. Exhibit 6 shows a classification of states by type of bank branching permitted. Exhibit 7 shows the frequency of branches for various types of financial institutions.

The second regulatory problem was whether or not EFTS machines should even be viewed as the legal equivalents of branches. In 1974, the Comptroller of the Currency ruled that these machines "could be established by national commercial banks without geographic limits, and do not constitute branches if they are not located on the premises of a bank." In 1975, under pressure from the states—worried that national banks would now branch more widely than state banks—the Comptroller reversed his decision. Nevertheless, there was a widespread view that commercial banks would be allowed to place EFTS machines at remote locations in the near future through legislative changes in Congress and the states.

In states where branching was restricted and remote EFTS machines were regarded as branches, provision of deposit and withdrawal services was restricted to the exterior of a bank building. Usage of remote machines was restricted to the single function of guaranteeing customer checks. For example, City National in Columbus, Ohio had installed check-guarantee terminals in sixty-eight supermarkets. These machines were IBM devices on-line to the bank's central files, with the deposit and withdrawal functions made inoperative.

Thrift institutions were less restricted in adding branches. In fact, commercial banks opposed the spread of EFTS by the savings & loans because federally chartered S&Ls can branch in any state, whereas commercial banks cannot. Federally chartered S&Ls were also permitted to establish mobile branches which visited a community on a regular schedule. In 1972, they were also permitted to open "satellites"—branches in locations operated by another business, such as retail stores. They could be manned by tellers or completely automated.

Branching was permitted for the mutual savings banks in most of the seventeen states where they operated. Though the total number of mutual savings banks was small, their average size was larger than the average size of both commercial banks and S&Ls.

BANK COMPETITION

Competition between commercial banks and S&Ls had become severe throughout the early 1970s. Unprecedented rate wars between the two occurred and massive shifts in deposits took place, causing severe problems for the S&Ls. They responded by expanding the type of services they could offer their customers. As each type of bank expanded its services, the distinction between the various types of institutions from the consumer's point of view diminished.

In general, competition between the two types of banking organizations augured well for innovations that represented significant improvements in consumer service. S&Ls appeared to view ATMs and POSs as marketing tools to break into the commercial banks' business. Indeed, one analyst remarked: "S&L marketers viewed ATMs as a symbol of their new aggressiveness against the commercial banks."

CONSUMER HABITS

Some observers believed that consumers would be loath to accept EFTS. The debiting of consumers' accounts at the time of purchase was not necessarily attractive for the purchaser. Some consumer groups had expressed concern that EFT Systems could lead to further "invasion of privacy." Other obstacles included consumers' misapprehensions about service by machine, and computer errors. It was also possible that consumers would feel a loss of control over their money—cancelled checks provided a record of their transactions.

On the other hand, there was the added convenience of 24-hour access to the customer's money. Also, it was quicker to cash a check at an ATM than at a human teller inside a bank. Most attractive of all, perhaps, was the prospect of cheaper credit if EFTS machines helped banks lower processing costs.

DOCUTEL'S AUTOMATIC TELLER MACHINE BUSINESS

The President, Mr. Jack Meredith, personally directed marketing activities and was closely involved with all major policy decisions. Exhibit 8 shows a company organization chart.

Product Line

Docutel offered a series of products for automatic customer-activated terminal banking systems. These are described briefly in Table 2.

Docutel claimed that its machines were capable of being used either on-line or off-line; however, some specialized software was needed to link the Docutel machines with the on-line system of a particular bank. Over 1,000 of the installed Docutel ATMs were on-line.

Table 2
DOCUTEL'S PRODUCT LINE

PRODUCT	FUNCTIONS	REMARKS	1975 % OF SALES
Docuteller*	Cash dispenser	Launched in 1969. 389 machines installed by 1974.	9%
Total Teller*	Cash dispenser and depository. Performs 12 transitions.	Launched in 1971. 1,740 machines installed by 1974.	56
Table-Top Teller		Table-top version of Total Teller.	21
Docucoder	Input-output type writer and unit for encoding plastic cards.	Launched in 1971. 101 machines installed by mid-1975.	14
Other/			14
On-Line			100%

*Both the Docuteller and the Total Teller were available either as outdoor wall-mounted units or as drive-up units, designated as Model 1 and Model 5 respectively.

Docutel ATMs had been installed by 508 commercial banks, thirty S&Ls, sixteen mutual savings banks, and five credit unions at more than two thousand locations in forty states, Puerto Rico, and Canada. Of these, ten banks accounted for about 17 percent of the machines installed, but no single customer had accounted for more than 5 percent of Docutel's sales. Fifty-nine machines were installed in locations remote from the banks. See Exhibit 9 for details of the geographic location and distribution of Docutel customers. Currently, approximately 70 percent of Docutel's sales were to banks that had already purchased ATMs from Docutel previously.

Prices

The installed price for the Total Teller was $32,500; additional costs for options brought the average price of machines to $35,000. This did not include the cost of the masonry and carpentry work which was the responsibility of the customer. The prices for other machines and accessories are shown in Exhibit 10. For those customers who did not wish to buy the machines outright, Docutel offered a lease plan. Leased machines were sold by Docutel to Ford Motor Credit Corporation, who in turn leased the machine to the customer. The standard lease was for seven years, and the monthly rental was calculated at 1.82 percent of the sales price of the machine. At the end of the lease, the customer had the right to purchase the equipment at 10 percent of the original price. Docutel required that all leased machines be covered by a service contract.

Sales and Marketing Activities

The field sales organization operated out of 24 offices and consisted of 37 salesmen, 85 percent of whom had a college education. Each field sales office was managed by one of the salesmen acting as a field sales manager. Salesmen were paid a fixed salary plus a commission amounting to 2 percent of sales. Sales areas and offices are shown in Exhibit 11.

In describing the sales operations of the company, Mr. Heckman said:

> Up to 1974 most of our selling effort was directed at the marketing department of the bank. They were interested in methods of gaining market share, and they saw the Docutel machines as a way of differentiating the product of their bank. This "soft dollars" approach could be used by us in two ways. We went to the pioneer bank in an area and tried to sell them on the idea of being the first in their market with ATMs. This gave us a chance to talk to them about the possibility of increasing their share of market. Then, when they were sold on the idea, we could go to the other banks in the area and tell them that if they, too, did not install these machines, they ran the risk of losing market share.

An example of this type of marketing was the introduction of ATMs into Atlanta. Citizens and Southern (C&S)—the largest bank—introduced ATMs first as an offensive measure. The other three major banks' moves were in reaction to C&S's move. Some bankers thought that the best campaign for this new service was conducted by the last bank to install ATMs—First National. With their "Tillie the Teller" campaign they had a lot of success in personalizing the machines, so that people would not be reluctant to use them. At the time First National made the decision to install ATMs, they were faced with an eroding market share position and needed a major effort to effect a reversal of this trend. They saw ATMs as the tool they needed.

Another contrasting example was provided by the Cleveland market. Cleveland was generally characterized by a lack of vigorous competition and innovation among the major banks, with one bank, Cleveland Trust, holding nearly 50 percent market share. In this environment some observers believed it might be small S&Ls who would take the lead in adopting ATMs. In yet other markets, smaller commercial banks had adopted ATMs in response to S&Ls' developing POS installations in supermarkets and other remote locations.

Mr. Heckman emphasized that this "soft dollars" exposure to marketing was proving less effective, however. He continued:

> Banks are now talking "hard dollars." Since 1974, they want to be convinced that they will be able to save money by installing our machines. Also, many banks are beginning to worry about how they will integrate these machines into on-line systems. The Docutel machines look like the decorations on a Christmas tree for these banks. They are pretty and attractive, but the banks are worried more about the tree than the decorations. As time goes on, our salesmen have to get more and more into system selling. They have to learn to talk about time sharing and computer interfaces, and things that they have never had to worry about before. If this trend continues, and we are sure that it will, we will either have to organize a massive retraining program, or we will have to get out and find ourselves a new sales force.

Mr. Norton Stuart, Vice President, agreed with these views and added:

> We are now talking to the operations people in the banks, not the marketing people. These people are systems-oriented and talk in terms of bits and bytes. We need to do a great deal of software developmental work if we are to continue to sell these machines in the large systems.

According to Mr. Meredith, the company's salesmen had excellent access to bank management because bankers wanted to stay informed about ATMs and they thought Docutel knew the market.

Docutel made some efforts to assist its customers in developing advertising and promotion campaigns for their ATM installations. Mr. Robert Heckman was convinced that the ultimate success of the ATM depended very much on whether or not it was used by the customers of the bank. He tried, therefore, to get banks to promote the machines among their customers. At one installation, to encourage initial use of the machines, he had managed to get the bank to offer its customers free hamburgers at McDonald's.

For 1975, the company planned to keep marketing expenses at approximately 16 percent of sales. For the first six months of 1975, total marketing expenses amounted to $1,746,000. Table 3 shows the breakdown of these expenses.

Table 3
Details of Docutel's Marketing Expenses
[$000s]

	FIRST SIX MONTHS 1975	FULL YEAR 1974
Selling	$ 813	$2,118
Commissions	255	592
Travel	262	685
Office	173	470
Other (advertising, etc.)	243	869
	$1,746	$4,734

Field Service

Most customers were extremely concerned about the reliability and service of ATMs since they operated at the interface between the bank and its customers. Some banks insisted on a guaranteed amount of uptime when they bought the machines, and most banks wanted a guarantee that a service man would be available around the clock.

Docutel offered its customers maintenance contracts for regular maintenance, as well as repair and emergency service for its machines. Most customers chose to have the maintenance carried out by Docutel field engineers. In some cases, the Docutel contract included a guarantee of up to 98 percent uptime. Docutel executives believed that no other supplier of ATMs had been able to equal this record of service performance.

About half of Docutel's 720 employees worked in the Field Service organization: Field engineers numbered 300. These field engineers were trained to maintain and repair the automatic teller machines and to ensure that where the tellers were part of a larger system, Docutel components functioned properly. The company maintained a large stock of parts and service equipment in the field which, in 1975, was valued at about $11.5 million.

As the number of machines in operation grew, service revenues as a percent of total revenues had increased steadily, as shown in Table 4.

Table 4
GROWTH OF SERVICE REVENUES

YEAR	SERVICE REVENUES AS A PERCENT OF TOTAL REVENUES
1970	1.8%
1971	4.0
1972	4.6
1973	9.0
1974	14.1
1975	27.0 (est.)

Maintenance contract prices are shown in Exhibit 10. Typically, service revenues ran between 93 percent and 94 percent of total service costs.[1] Commenting on these figures, Mr. Washburn stated: "Field engineering is an essential part of the package we sell our customers. Some bankers pay as much as $20,000 per month for service. They would be very upset if we raised our prices any higher. On the other hand, we cannot sell our machines without servicing them."

Manufacturing

Manufacturing was the responsibility of Mr. C. T. Fuqua, Vice President. He managed a manufacturing department of 136 people and an engineering staff of over ninety people. In describing the manufacturing operations, Mr. Fuqua said:

I have plotted our manufacturing costs against cumulative volume on log paper, and we came out right on the 90 percent line. We do not even have to take inflation into account: I have used current figures for purchases, which have not risen too much because we have long-term purchase contracts.

Approximately 65 percent of Docutel's cost of manufacturing was spent on purchased parts and components. The remaining 35 percent was split about 75 percent for fixed overhead and 25 percent for direct

---

[1] For purposes of estimating total service costs, Docutel estimated labor as 68 percent, parts and parts repair as 6 percent, travel at 10 percent, and overhead and parts handling as 16 percent of the total.

labor. The cost of manufacture also varied from machine to machine, as shown in Table 5.

Table 5
STANDARD COST OF MANUFACTURE OF SELECTED PRODUCTS
JUNE 15, 1975

	COST OF MANUFACTURE AS % OF SALES PRICE
Total Teller (Model 1)	54.3
Drive-up Teller (Model 5)	42.8
Table Top Teller (T4)	86.3
Ducocoders	52.9
Average, all products	49.9%
Variances	(4.6)
Actual, 1st 6 months	54.5%

The manufacturing process was not highly capital intensive. Mr. Meredith estimated that production could be at least doubled without any substantial additions to either plant or equipment.

Product Development and Engineering

Docutel's engineering staff was engaged in three types of activities—continuing engineering, development projects, and funded projects. A breakdown of engineering and R&D expenses for 1974 is shown below:

Table 6
BREAKDOWN OF ENGINEERING AND R&D EXPENSES—1974
[$000s]

Continuation engineering	$ 417
On-line systems development	250
Table Top Teller—T4	427
ARCO terminal (gasoline dispensing system)	115
Total Teller	78
Datalog	151
Other, miscellaneous, project overhead	407
Total	$1,845

On several past occasions, customers had asked Docutel to supply them with estimates for either POS machines or OLTTs. In one case the customer required a simple POS machine which would be capable of making an account verification check and printing out the verification data and time. Docutel estimated that this machine would cost about $250 thousand for research and development and that the company would be able to market the machine in the $1,500 to $2,000 price range. A similar estimate for a simple teller-operated terminal placed the development costs at $1 million, and the sales price in the $7,000 range. By comparison, Docutel had spent about $5 million on the development of the Docuteller and about $1.5 million on the development of the Total Teller.

Planning

Mr. Meredith had strong views about the type of planning that a small company could do successfully.

> One of the greatest disservices you people at the Harvard Business School have done for small business is to publicize your theories about planning. They may be useful for IBM and for Xerox, but they just do not work in my company. I cannot get anyone to tell me what the size of our market should be this year, let alone five years from now. The Harvard Business School should help small companies—if small business does not prosper in the United States, capitalism will die.

In describing the details of the planning process at Docutel, the Treasurer, Mr. Washburn, said that the company was trying to work towards a target of a 12 percent pretax return on equity by 1978 and to set intermediate goals for the periods in between, based on the current performance of the company. He explained that since the company did not have any firm figures for the size of the market and the share that Docutel could expect to get of this market, the planning process tended to work backwards from profit targets to sales targets.

For the 1976 plan, Mr. Washburn was working with six alternative sets of figures; the variables being considered were sales, engineering expenses, and marketing expenses. Figures for other expenses were taken from the ratios of the current experience of the company, modified in some cases by expectations of changes. The six alternatives which Mr. Washburn was considering are shown in Table 7.

Table 7
SIX ALTERNATIVE BUDGETS FOR 1976
[$000s]

	A	B	C	D	E	F
ATMs						
Sales	$22,000	$23,000	$24,000	$24,000	$25,000	$26,000
Cost of Goods Sold	12,100	12,535	12,960	12,960	13,375	13,780
Gross Profit	$ 9,900	$10,465	$11,040	$11,040	$11,625	$12,220
MAINTENANCE						
Sales	$ 9,400	$ 9,500	$ 9,600	$ 9,600	$ 9,650	$ 9,700
Cost of Goods Sold	9,800	9,950	10,100	10,100	10,150	10,200
Gross Loss	$ - 400	$ 450	$ 500	$ 500	$ 500	$ 500
Total Contribution	$ 9,500	$10,015	$10,540	$10,540	$11,125	$11,720
Less:						
Marketing	3,680	3,840	4,000	3,750	4,160	4,320
Engineering, R&D	2,000	2,100	2,500	2,200	2,400	2,500
General & Admin-						
istrative	2,100	2,200	2,200	2,200	2,200	2,300
Net Profit before						
Tax	$ 1,720	$ 1,875	$ 1,840	$ 2,390	$ 2,365	$ 2,600

These summary plans were to be submitted to the Board for them to select one for further planning for 1976. After obtaining basic approval of the Board for the summary plan, the figures would be sent to the manager in charge of each cost center. These managers would then be asked to prepare detailed budgets for expenses, head count, inventory levels, and capital expenditure. These projections would come back to Mr. Washburn in early December, and he would use them in preparing the final budget for 1976. In addition to this formal process, there was frequent informal contact among members of management.

Competition

While Docutel executives realized that the company's early lead had enabled it to capture a large share of the ATM market, they foresaw considerably increased competition in the future. Its 10-K report of December 1974, stated:

There are several other firms which produce, are developing or have announced plans to develop systems similar to the DOCUTELLER or TOTAL TELLER. Some of these firms have historic relationships with the banking industry as suppliers of automated equipment and have substantially greater research and developmental efforts and financial resources than our company. The company expects to encounter vigorous competition.

Evidence of this trend was apparent both from reports from field salesmen, as well as from published industry statistics, as shown in Exhibit 12.

Docutel faced competition from three major firms in the computer industry: IBM, Burroughs, and NCR; two firms in the bank vault and security equipment business: Diebold and Mosler; and several smaller firms. Comparative product line information for each of these competitors is shown in Exhibit 13.

According to the information available to Docutel, the company's competitors were selling to the same customers and market segments as Docutel. It was felt that the smaller competitors like Diebold tended to concentrate on customers who bought one unit at a time, whereas competitors like IBM tended to make more efforts with customers who had the potential of buying several machines at a time. There was, however, no breakdown of competitor sales by customer type for Docutel to make an accurate comparison.

Mr. Robert Heckman believed that the smaller competitors such as Mosler and Diebold tended to compete mainly on the features of their machines in comparison with Docutel. By 1975 each company offered some features that Docutel machines did not have. On the other hand, the larger companies such as IBM, Burroughs, and NCR tended to stress their overall systems capabilities and the existence of a highly trained field organization for customer training and service support. He said, "We need to fight a features battle with the small companies, and at the same time, we are concerned about winning the systems war with the majors."

One group of consultants commissioned by Docutel questioned whether overall ATM sales would be large enough to attract IBM.[5] They concluded "IBM will enter the market as a systems supplier and develop terminals that help to sell their computers ... but will probably not become the dominant supplier in the ATM market." On NCR, the consultants commented "NCR has not been considered an ATM competitor but has a strong position in the POS market. As with IBM and Burroughs, they have strong sales and service support, computer expertise, and proven ability with the financial community."

---

[5]This conclusion was based on the following assumptions:

Total installed ATM units 1980 = 30,000 machines

Dollar value of installed units 1980 = 30,000 × $35,000 = $1,050 million

IBM installed value, assuming 30% MS = 3 × $1,050 = $350 million

Average sales for year (1975–1980) = $\frac{350}{6}$ = $58 million

In forecasting the future structure of the ATM market, observers were divided as to whether it would be concentrated or fragmented. Some observers pointed to the OLTT market where IBM, NCR, and Burroughs predominated and concluded that the ATM market would be similarly concentrated. Other observers disagreed—arguing that ATMs would be viewed as "add-on" components, not as integral components of the systems marketed by these three companies.

MANAGEMENT VIEWS ABOUT THE FUTURE

Mr. Meredith felt fairly confident about Docutel's ability to tackle the problems it would face in the near future, and he anticipated profits in 1975 and perhaps 1976. However, he was concerned about the long-range future of the company.

As part of the effort to define a set of long-range plans, Docutel commissioned a group of business school students to study the various opportunities open to them. As a first step, the students conducted interviews with customers. The students' report stated:

> Externally, Docutel's financial image is poor. Several sources were concerned that Docutel's capitalization would not permit the R&D investment needed to perfect current machines or to meet future EFTS requirements with new products. Others stated that doubts about Docutel's financial condition represented an incentive to postpone purchases until larger competitors develop their equipment. Perceived cutbacks in marketing support, advertising, users' conferences, and sales staffs, reinforced their opinions.

The report posed two major alternatives for Docutel:

1. Continue to develop the market for ATMs and enter the market for POS devices as well.
2. Remain in the ATM market only.

After the students analyzed these two major options, they came to the conclusion that the POS market would not, in fact, prove profitable to Docutel. They felt that the POS market would be dominated by large firms supplying retail and banking systems which already had a substantial lead over Docutel. They did not believe that Docutel had the resources necessary to make up this lead. Therefore, they recommended that Docutel concentrate on the ATM market.

While Mr. Meredith agreed with the students that Docutel could not afford to devote the resources needed to develop new machines for the POS market, he was not at all sure that the company could not find another way to enter the market. In discussing this option, he said:

> There is a lot of confusion in the market about what POS will actually be. Sure, if you think that these machines are combination cash registers, Universal Product Code Readers, and teller machines, all hooked up to a central computer which can communicate with the bank's computer, we are not in that market and cannot afford the R&D to get in. But it may be that all you need in a supermarket is a machine which the customer can go up to to draw cash from her bank account. This is what she now does anyway with a check cashed in the service section of a supermarket. In that case, all we need do is set up one of our Total Tellers in the store, hook it up to the bank's computer, and we have a POS machine.

Mr. Washburn looked at the options available to Docutel in another way. His projections showed that the company would continue to throw off cash up to the end of 1976, and he estimated that at the end of that year, the company would have over $6 million in cash and certificates of deposit. He felt that these funds could be taken out of the business without lowering the current level of sales and profits, and be reinvested in preferred stock in other companies for 9 to 10 percent return without much risk.

Docutel management had also considered other possibilities. Mr. Meredith and Mr. Fuqua had looked at the possibility of the company acquiring another company with a related line of business but had not found any suitable prospects. Management had also considered trying to get Docutel acquired by a major computer firm to combine Docutel's technology with the larger firm's resources. So far, however, no buyer had appeared on the scene. The company had also been in negotiation with a large business machine firm for an arrangement whereby Docutel would supply ATMs on an OEM basis. These negotiations continued for over a year, but finally, the company decided not to pursue the matter and, instead, launched its own line of ATMs.

Docutel had continued to investigate international sales and had very recently signed its first international contract with Nordisk Scandata, a consortium of Swedish data centers. This contract involved the development and manufacture of 360 special-purpose cash dispensers for $4.4 million. The company was also on the verge of reaching an agreement with Data Saab, the world's fourth largest manufacturer of minicomputers. Data Saab manufactured its own line of teller terminals for the banking industry and under the proposed contract would sell Docutel's ATMs exclusively in the Scandinavian countries, and on a nonexclusive basis in the rest of Europe. As of mid-1975, the company was not planning to expand its international staff, and hoped to rely on agents such as Data Saab for international sales.

In parallel with these explorations of a variety of broad strategic alternatives open to Docutel, top management, and particularly Mr. Heckman and Mr. Stuart, were concerned about Docutel's future approach to the ATM market. The student report had outlined three broad options for Docutel to consider (see Exhibit 14):

1. A "dominate" strategy;
2. A "mini-dominate" strategy;
3. A "maintenance" strategy.

The "Dominate" Strategy

The dominate strategy called for Docutel to maintain its leadership position in the ATM market. Among the provisions of this strategy were:

1. Concentration of selling effort on (a) large commercial banks or bank holding companies (in particular, 500 banks with assets over 100 million dollars) and (b) consortia of thrift institutions.
2. Establishment of six key-account marketing teams, one for each region, to call on high potential accounts.
3. Concentration of selling effort on the T4 in-lobby machines. This was seen as a way to introduce the bank's customers to ATM use, to permit cost justification of the purchase, and finally, to enhance Docutel's image as a firm having state-of-the-art equipment.
4. R&D effort directed at the development of a drive-up version of the Total Teller, a "weather protected" glass vestibule enclosure, programmable display screen, single bill dispensers, and machines with faster transaction time (currently 40 seconds).
5. Upgrading of field service by:
   a. training programs for field engineers,
   b. the addition of "operational coordinators" to visit accounts periodically and handle customer relations *ahead of complaint,*
   c. provision of user assistance by training bank staff in simple maintenance procedures.
6. The establishment of a "crack on-line team" to help banks get ATMs on-line and to "establish Docutel as a leader in on-line systems."
7. Development of "marketing support packages" consisting of (a) education of potential buyers in advertising techniques for new ATMs, (b) providing advice on consumer education and location

strategy, and (c) working with banks to ensure that the marketing end of the users' effort was a success.

8. Quantity discounts for multiple sales to large accounts.
9. Pricing of service to break even.
10. Advertising with two major objectives:
    (1) to strengthen the image of ATMs as an integral part of EFTS;
    (2) strengthening Docutel's position as the market leader among ATM suppliers.

A tentative annual budget (exclusive of direct service expenses) for these activities was estimated as follows:

	[$000s]
Field office expenses (5 × $75)	$ 375
Operational coordinators (19 × $24)	455
On-line specialists (19 × $30)	570
Trainees (6 × $22)	130
Salesmen (25 × $30)	750
Sales managers (6 × $40)	240
Sales and service training	400
Advertising & promotion (trade shows, etc.)	680
Key account marketing teams	500
Marketing support programs	500
Travel and overhead	1,050
	5,650
R&D & engineering	3,050
Total marketing and technical expense	$8,700

The "Mini-Dominate" Strategy

The report described the mini-dominate strategy as:

A mini version of the dominate strategy. Emphasis will be placed on conserving corporate resources by concentrating sales efforts on only a few selected geographic areas at one time, and developing them completely before moving on to other areas. With the exception of sales force structure, key elements of the marketing mix are the same as in the dominate strategy. It cannot be emphasized enough that service is critical. Not only must it be at least a breakeven operation, but it must be efficient enough to act as an entry barrier to competition.

Sales would be the responsibility of three small regional teams (initially in the Northeast, South, and West), supported by a Dallas-based sales staff. A tentative budget was estimated as:

	[$000s]
Field office expenses (3 × $75)	$ 225
Operations coordinators (6 × $30)	180
On-line specialists (3 × $40)	120
Regional salesmen (3 × $35)	105
Regional managers (3 × $40)	120
Dallas-based sales team (10 × $50)	500
Sales and service training	200
Advertising and promotion	450
Marketing support programs	350
Travel and overhead	700
	2,950
R&D and engineering	3,050
Total marketing and technical expense	$6,000

The "Maintenance" Strategy

According to the report, this alternative called for maintaining a "small but profitable company by segmenting the ATM market on a geographic basis, as well as by targeting a specific customer." The key provisions of this approach were:

1. To target medium-sized institutions ($25–100 million in deposits). These institutions were judged to be either "defensive" buyers of ATMs, i.e., institutions seeking protection against the encroachments of big banks, or banks buying to enhance their image.
2. Sales effort spearheaded by a Dallas-based sales team, together with twelve "area coordinators."
3. Elimination of all major new product development; the adoption of a "me-too" policy to allow competition to bear the costs of R&D.
4. In conformance with the "me-too" policy, continuing engineering would be reduced to "debugging" only.
5. Maintenance of the field service staff at existing levels, but no retraining, etc.
6. Increases in service prices to yield a 20 percent gross margin.
7. Pricing ATMs at discount levels where necessary to remain competitive; establishment of quantity discount schedules.
8. Consolidation and reduction of corporate overheads.

A tentative budget for this approach was established as:

	[$000s]
Field office expenses (3 × $75)	$ 225
Area salesmen/coordinators (12 × $20)	240
Dallas-based sales team (10 × $50)	500
Advertising and promotion	450
Marketing support programs	250
Travel and overhead	400
	2,065
R&D and engineering	900
Total marketing and technical expense	$2,965

As Mr. Meredith reviewed these specific alternatives, he wondered how consistent they were with Docutel's current direction, and what course Docutel should now embark on.

Exhibit 1

DOCUTEL CORPORATION

Operating Results (excluding baggage, handling equipment) and Stock Prices 1968–1974

YEAR ENDED	NET SALES	PRE-TAX INCOME (LOSS)	DOCUTEL'S STOCK PRICE $	
	[$000s]		HIGH	LOW
October 31, 1968	—	$ (386)	52	19
October 31, 1969	—	(785)	42	22
October 31, 1970	$ 1,176	(2,072)	28	3 1/4
December 31, 1971	4,452	(2,733)	23	5
December 31, 1972	19,381	4,300	45	20
December 31, 1973	29,449	6,507	57 1/4	7 1/8
December 31, 1974	25,147	(649)	11 7/8	2

Source: Company records.

Exhibit 2
DOCUTEL CORPORATION
Consolidated Balance Sheet
[$ Millions—rounded]

DECEMBER 31	1974	1973
ASSETS		
Current assets:		
Cash	$ 1.6	$ 1.1
Certificates of deposit	.8	3.6
Accounts receivable (Note 4)	5.4	5.9
Inventories (Note 3)	10.7	10.1
Net assets related to division to be discontinued (Note 2)	1.2	.7
Prepaid expenses	.3	.1
Total current assets	20.0	21.5
Property and equipment, at cost:		
Furniture and fixtures	.6	.4
Machinery and equipment	1.5	1.2
Leasehold improvements	.6	.6
	2.7	2.2
Less accumulated depreciation and amortization	1.2	.8
	1.5	1.4
Licenses	.4	—
Other assets (including $367,286 deferred income tax in 1973)	.2	.6
Total assets	$22.1	$23.5
LIABILITIES AND STOCKHOLDERS' EQUITY		
Current liabilities—accounts payable and accrued liabilities	$ 2.4	$ 2.8
Promissory note payable November 1, 1976 (Note 4)	2.2	2.2
Commitments (Note 9)		
Stockholders' equity (Note 6):		
Common stock, $.10 par value, 6,000,000 shares authorized, 2,561,537 shares outstanding (Note 5)	.3	.3
Capital in excess of par value	20.6	20.6
Deficit	(3.4)	(2.4)
	17.5	18.5
Total liabilities and stockholders' equity	$22.1	$23.5

Exhibit 3

DOCUTEL CORPORATION

Consolidated Statement of Operations
[$ Millions—rounded]

YEARS ENDED DECEMBER 31	1973	1974	1ST HALF 1975[1]
Net Sales and Services	$29.5	$25.2	$12.3
Cost and expenses:			
Cost of sales and services	17.1	16.7	8.6
Other operating expenses (principally engineering and research and development costs)	1.4	1.9	.8
Selling, general, and administrative	4.6	7.1	2.7
Other (income) expense, principally interest, net	(0.1)	.2	—
	23.0	25.9	12.1
Income (loss) from continuing operations before income tax and extraordinary credit	6.5	(0.7)	0.2
Provision for income tax (Note 7)	3.2	—	
Income (loss) from continuing operations before extraordinary credit	3.3	(0.3)	
Other (losses) or credits	.8	(0.3)	
Net Income (loss)	$ 4.1	$ (1.0)	$ 0.2
Weighted average common and common equivalent shares outstanding	2.5	2.6	2.6

[1]Unaudited.

Exhibit 4
DOCUTEL CORPORATION
Description of the Use of a Docutel Total Teller

1 The customer inserts the magnetically encoded card into the automated customer terminal to initiate any of the thrift transactions.

2 Then, customer enters a secret security code that verifies the card and identifies the customer.

3 The customer then selects the type of transaction . . . the customer can make a deposit by cash or check to the desired account, transfer funds from one account to another, make a loan payment or a cash withdrawal . . . any one of the eleven transactions shown on the keyboard.

4 The transaction amount is then entered to update passbook or statement records and to verify an amount deposited.

5 In this deposit transaction, the deposit is inserted into the depository where the deposit envelope is time-stamped and sequentially numbered to match the transaction record.

6 Verification and updating of records begins in the customer terminal, or is done by your computer if the terminal is on-line. Two receipts are then printed, one for the customer and one for you to provide an audit trail.

7 For the last step, the terminal gives your customer the confidence of a printed receipt that shows the type, time, and amount of the transaction, other pertinent information, and even a message from your institution.

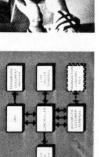

8 The result is . . . customers that participate with you in managing their money **AT THEIR CONVENIENCE** and an enhanced image for you. Customers know your institution as a total service thrift institution that serves its customers better.

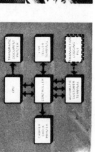

total service

Exhibit 5

DOCUTEL CORPORATION

Number, Total Assets and Average of Selected Types of Financial Institutions,

Selected Years, 1900–1974

[In Millions of Dollars]

	MUTUAL SAVINGS BANKS			COMMERCIAL BANKS			SAVINGS AND LOAN ASSOCIATIONS		
YEAR	NUMBER	TOTAL ASSETS	AVERAGE ASSETS	NUMBER	TOTAL ASSETS	AVERAGE ASSETS	NUMBER	TOTAL ASSETS	AVERAGE ASSETS
1900	626	2,328	3.7	12,427	9,059	.7	5,356	571	.1
1910	637	3,598	5.6	24,514	19,324	.8	5,869	932	.2
1920	618	5,586	9.0	30,291	47,509	1.6	8,633	2,520	.3
1930	592	10,496	17.7	23,679	64,125	2.7	11,777	8,829	.7
1940	540	11,919	22.1	14,534	67,804	4.7	7,521	5,733	.8
1945	532	17,013	32.0	14,011	160,312	11.4	6,149	8,747	1.4
1950	529	22,446	42.4	14,121	168,932	12.0	5,992	16,846	2.8
1955	528	31,346	59.4	13,716	210,734	15.4	6,071	37,533	6.2
1960	515	40,571	78.8	13,472	257,552	19.1	6,276	71,314	11.4
1965	506	58,232	115.1	13,804	377,264	27.3	6,185	129,580	21.0
1970	494	78,995	159.9	13,686	576,242	42.1	5,669	176,183	31.1
1971	490	89,581	182.8	13,783	640,255	46.5	5,474	206,023	37.6
1972	486	100,593	207.0	13,927	739,033	53.1	5,298	243,127	45.9
1973	482	106,650	221.3	14,171	835,224	58.9	5,170	271,905	52.6
1974	480	109,550	228.2	14,457	916,320	63.4	5,102	295,616	57.9

Source: Board of Governors of the Federal Reserve System. Federal Home Loan Bank Board and National Association of Mutual Savings Banks.

Note: Data are as of end of year for savings and loan associations, mutual savings banks beginning 1930, and commercial banks beginning 1945; mid-year for mutual savings banks prior to 1930 and commercial banks prior to 1945. Data on total assets of mutual savings banks for 1930, 1940 and 1945, and on the number of savings banks for 1945, differ somewhat from Tables 1 and 7 which are compiled from other sources.

Exhibit 6
DOCUTEL CORPORATION
Classification of States According to Types of Branching Prevalent

STATEWIDE BRANCH BANKING PREVALENT	LIMITED BRANCH BANKING PREVALENT	UNIT BANKING PREVALENT
Alaska	Alabama	Arkansas
Arizona	Georgia	Colorado
California	Indiana	Florida
Connecticut	Kentucky	Illinois
Delaware	Louisiana	Iowa
Hawaii	Maine	Kansas
Idaho	Massachusetts	Minnesota
Maryland	Michigan	Missouri
Nevada	Mississippi	Montana
North Carolina	New Hampshire	Nebraska
Oregon	New Jersey	North Dakota
Rhode Island	New Mexico	Oklahoma
South Carolina	New York	Texas
South Dakota	Ohio	West Virginia
Utah	Pennsylvania	Wyoming
Vermont	Tennessee	
Washington	Virginia	
	Wisconsin	

Source: A Profile of State Chartered Banking, Conference of State Bank Supervisors, Washington, D.C., December 1971, p. 65.

This classification is made for the purpose of discussing changes in the banking structure and is based on the type of banking seemingly prevalent in each State and not necessarily on the current status of legal provisions. The classification of some States in this list depends on the interpretation of the key words Prevalent, Limited, Severely Limited, and Prohibited and this classification may differ in respect to a few States from similar classification made for other purposes.

Exhibit 7
DOCUTEL CORPORATION
Number of Offices of Selected Types of Financial Institutions
Selected Year End Dates 1965–1974

END OF YEAR	NUMBER OF INSTITUTIONS	NUMBER HAVING BRANCHES	NUMBER OF BRANCHES	TOTAL OFFICES
MUTUAL SAVINGS BANKS				
1945	542	85	143	685
1950	529	113	213	742
1960	515	195	487	1,002
1970	494	300	1,087	1,581
1973	482	341	1,492	1,974
1974	480	354	1,642	2,122
COMMERCIAL BANKS				
1945	14,183	1,138	4,025	18,208
1950	14,164	1,301	4,945	19,109
1960	13,484	2,409	10,619	24,103
1970	13,705	4,016	21,880	35,585
1973	14,194	4,799	26,718	40,912
1974	14,481	5,186	28,705	43,186
SAVINGS & LOAN ASSOCIATIONS				
1945	6,149	n.a.	n.a.	n.a.
1950	5,992	n.a.	n.a.	n.a.
1960	6,275	826	1,611	7,886
1970	5,738	n.a.	4,337	10,075
1973	5,170	n.a.	7,036	12,206
1974	5,102	n.a.	8,820	13,922

Source: Federal Deposit Insutance Corporation and United States League of Savings Associations.

n.a.—not available.

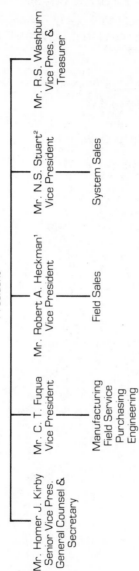

Exhibit 8

DOCUTEL CORPORATION

Extract from the Organization Chart of Docutel Corporation
July 1975

Mr. Jack Meredith
President

Mr. Homer J. Kirby
Senior Vice Pres.
General Counsel &
Secretary

Mr. C. T. Fuqua
Vice President

Manufacturing
Field Service
Purchasing
Engineering

Mr. Robert A. Heckman[1]
Vice President

Field Sales

Mr. N. S. Stuart[2]
Vice President

System Sales

Mr. R.S. Washburn
Vice Pres. &
Treasurer

Headcount

General and Administration	50
Field Engineering	368
Manufacturing	130
Engineering	90
Marketing	82
Total	720

[1] Mr. Heckman was responsible for the field sales force and supervised sales to smaller banks.

[2] Mr. Stuart was responsible for marketing activities directed at the major banks.

Exhibit 9
DOCUTEL CORPORATION
Location of Installed Docutel ATMs

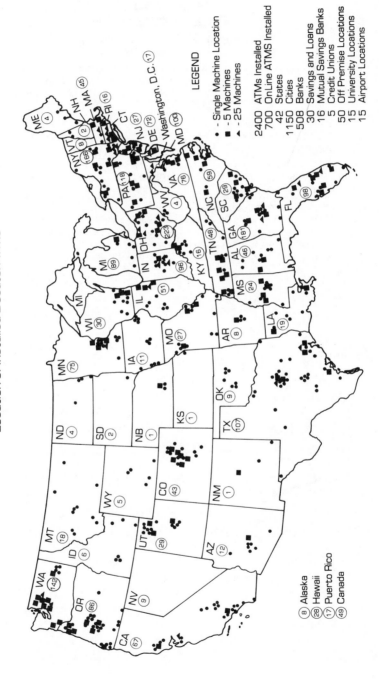

LEGEND

• - Single Machine Location
■ - 5 Machines
▲ - 25 Machines

2400	ATMs Installed
700	OnLine ATMS Installed
42	States
1150	Cities
508	Banks
30	Savings and Loans
16	Mutual Savings Banks
5	Credit Unions
50	Off Premise Locations
15	University Locations
15	Airport Locations

ⓈAlaska
㉘Hawaii
⑰Puerto Rico
㊾Canada

Exhibit 10

DOCUTEL CORPORATION

Extracts from Docutel's Price List
1975

PRODUCT	PURCHASE PRICE[1]	MONTHLY MAINTENANCE[2]
Docuteller	$19,000	$212.00
Total Teller[4] Model 1	32,500	331.00
Total Teller Model 5	36,000	331.00
Table Top Total Teller	17,900	305.00
Additional Terminals		
for Above	10,000	125.00
Docucoder	12,000	120.00

Notes: 1. All prices are FOB, Dallas, Texas.

2. Maintenance prices include 24 hour emergency service. Lower rates apply for 8 and 12 hour emergency service. Quantity discounts are offered on maintenance.

3. The monthly lease option is 1.82% of the price shown above.

4. Model 1 is an outdoor wall-mounted unit; Model 5 is the drive-up unit.

Exhibit 11

DOCUTEL CORPORATION

Sales Areas and Regions

REGION	AREA OFFICE	STATE[S]	% OF U.S. HOUSEHOLDS	NO. OF DOCUTEL ATM LOCATIONS
Southern	Charlotte	Virginia/Carolinas	5.5%	161
	Tampa	Florida	3.6	94
	Atlanta	Georgia/Alabama	3.8	136
	Nashville	Tennessee/Mississippi	2.9 15.8%	64 22.3%
Mid-western	St. Louis	Missouri	2.4%	25
	Minneapolis*	Minnesota/Iowa	3.2	75
	Chicago	Wisconsin/Illinois	7.6 13.2%	68 8.2%
Central	Detroit	Indiana/Michigan	6.7%	158
	Columbus*	Ohio	5.2	187
	Buffalo	Western Pa./Western New York	4.7 16.6%	100 16.9%
Northeast	Hartford	Connecticut/Mass.	4.3%	158
	New York*	N.Y. City/New Jersey	8.5	159
	Philadelphia	Delaware/Maryland Dist. of Columbia/ East Pa.	7.9 20.7%	248 20.4%
South-western	Dallas*	Texas	5.4%	98
	Denver	Colorado	1.1	31
	Salt Lake City	Utah	.5 7%	26 19.7%
Western	Los Angeles	So. California		13
	San Francisco*	No. California/So. Ore.		83
	Portland	No. Ore./Washington	13.2% 12.5%	160
	TOTAL		86.5%	100 %

*region centers.

97

Exhibit 12
DOCUTEL CORPORATION
Market Share, August 1974 Installed to Date

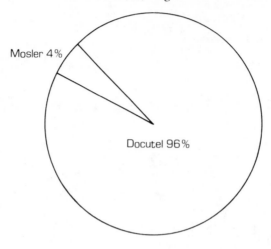

Mosler 4%

Docutel 96%

Share of Backorders, August 1974

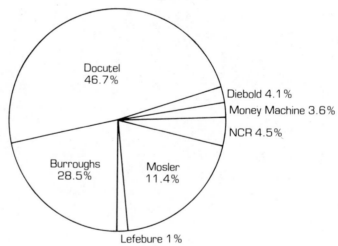

Docutel
46.7%

Diebold 4.1%

Money Machine 3.6%

NCR 4.5%

Burroughs
28.5%

Mosler
11.4%

Lefebure 1%

Source: Linda Fenner Zimmer in "Bank Administration," August 1974.

Exhibit 13

DOCUTEL CORPORATION COMPETITIVE ATM ANALYSIS

VENDOR	PRICE	RENTAL	MONTHLY MAINTENANCE	READER	DISPLAY	DISPENSER	PRINTER	TRANSACTION CAPABILITY
BURROUGHS 4500 on-line ATM Vandal Guard	31,700 795 32,495	1,043 25 1,068	118 10 128	ABA + Track 3 secure properties in card	Backlighted panels	Plastic Clips 352 capacity 8 bills per clip	Check Size 2-part, pin feed	W/D, Dep., trans. paym'ts, bal. inquiry
DIEBOLD Tabs 550 on-line Off-line	38,000 500 38,500	Not available	8 hr. 197 24 hr. 265	ABA + Track 3	Programmable display 16 lines 32 char./line	Single bill dual denom.	500 2-part receipts	W/D, Dep., trans. bal. inquiry
DOCUTEL Total teller On-line 200 bad accounts	32,500 2,250 2,100 36,850	671	8 hr. 229 16 hr. 288 24 hr. 331	ABA + Track 3 + Docu-	Rotating Drum	Prepackaged currency	400 2-part receipts	W/D, Dep., trans. paym'ts, bal. inquiry
IBM		Rental includes maintenance if purchased 8 hr.	24 hr.	ABA only	44 character gas dischg.	Single bill single denom. 2000 new bills 3000 old bills	3" × 3" customer copy only can be selective for certain transaction	W/D, Dep., trans. paymt's, bal. inquiry
3614 outdoor unit	21,200	672	119					
Depository	2,545	87	10					
Printer	3,500	119	21					
Accessory group	4,500	50	15					
Logo panel	80	50	15					
Interface with 3601	1,728	62	5					
Additional storage for 3601	2,545	520	70					
3601 controller	20,140 56,238	1,510	240					

Exhibit 13 [cont.]
DOCUTEL CORPORATION
COMPETITIVE ATM ANALYSIS

VENDOR	PRICE	RENTAL	MONTHLY MAINTENANCE	READER	DISPLAY	DISPENSER	PRINTER	TRANSACTION CAPABILITY
LEFEBURE Model 724 Act On-line/Off-line	38,000		190	Track III lefebure format	Backlighted panels	Single bill denom. 1000 bills	600 2-part pin feed	W/D Dep., trans. paymt's, inquiry
MONEY MACHINE Model 802 On-line/Off-line Paper tape punch Receipt printer	32,000 2,500 1,750 36,250	752 59 42 853	180 14 10 204	ABA + Track III + money	32 character gas dischg.	Prepackaged currency capacity 625	3½" paper roll to customer only	Full ATM
MOSLER ON-LINE Teller matic 5000 Interchange	36,000 250 36,250		8 hr. 150 15 hr. 240	ABA + Track III	Backlighted panels	Single bill single denom. capacity 1,000	2-part receipt	Full ATM
MOSLER ON-LINE 770-302 ATM Time of day clock Hot card file Modern Safe	28,150 400 850 500 2,000 31,900		130	ABA + Track III	105 millimeter backlighted film strip	Single bill dual denom.	2-part receipt	W/D Dep., trans. paymt's, bal. inquiry

Exhibit 14
DOCUTEL CORPORATION
Analysis of Options in Student Report
Comparative Income Statements
[$000s]

	DOMINATE	MINI-DOMINATE	MAINTENANCE
ATMs			
Sales	$20,000	$15,000	$12,000
CGS	10,000	7,500	6,000
Gross Profit	$10,000	$ 7,500	$ 6,000
MAINTENANCE			
Sales	$ 7,000	$ 7,000	$ 8,400
CGS	7,000	7,000	7,000
	$ 0	$ 0	$ 1,400
Contribution	$10,000	$ 7,500	$ 7,400
Less:			
Marketing	5,650	2,950	2,065
Engineering	3,050	3,050	900
G&A	1,500	1,200	1,000
Net Profit Before Tax	$ (200)	$ 300	$ 3,435
Estimated cash-on-hand at end of year 1	$ 2,100	$ 3,500	$ 6,500

DISCUSSION QUESTIONS

DOCUTEL CORPORATION

1. What is Docutel's current position in the marketplace?
2. What is Docutel's current strategy? Strengths? Weaknesses?
3. What major changes are taking place in the marketplace and what are the major determinants of future market size and character?
4. What market projections should Docutel's strategy be based on?
5. How is/will this market be segmented?
6. Appraise Docutel's competitors—present and future?
7. What are the overall economics of: 1) sales; 2) service in this industry?
8. What broad strategic alternatives do *you* believe Docutel faces?
9. What course of action would you recommend?

10. What marketing mix, R.D., etc. decisions are consistent with the chosen strategy?

11. What 1976 annual budgets should be set consistent with long-term plans?

Cost Dynamics: Scale and Experience Effects

Market share is one of the primary determinants of business profitability; other things being equal, businesses with a larger share of a market are more profitable than their smaller-share competitors. For instance, a study by the PIMS Program[1] (the subject of Chapter 6) found that, on average, a difference of 10 percentage points in market share is accompanied by a difference of about 5 points in pretax ROI ("pretax operating profits" divided by "long-term debt plus equity"). Additional evidence is that companies having large market shares in their primary product markets—such as General Motors, IBM, Gillette, Eastman Kodak and Xerox—tend to be highly profitable.

An important reason for the increase in profitability with market share is that large-share firms usually have *lower costs*.[2] The lower costs are due in part to economies of scale; for instance, very large plants cost less per unit of production to build and are often more efficient than smaller plants. Lower costs are also due in part to the so-

---

[1]Robert D. Buzzell, Bradley T. Gale, and Ralph G.M. Sultan, "Market Share—a Key to Profitability," *Harvard Business Review*, 53, no. 1 (January-February 1975), pp. 97–106.

[2]Another important reason is that large share businesses often achieve significantly higher prices for their products. Some experts—especially economists involved in antitrust work—argue that the market power arising from their size allows large share businesses to charge these higher prices. The PIMS data indicate an additional explanation; firms with the high shares tend to have products of higher quality and to spend much more on R&D than smaller share firms. Thus they receive higher prices for distinctive, high-quality, and often innovative products. IBM, Eastman Kodak, and Proctor & Gamble are three firms that have done so repeatedly.

called *experience effect,* whereby the cost of many (if not most) products declines by 10–30 percent each time a company's experience at producing and selling them doubles. In this context *experience* has a precise meaning: it is the cumulative number of units produced to date. Since at any point in time, businesses with large market shares typically (but not always) have more experience than their smaller-share competitors, they would be expected to have lower costs.

This chapter is designed to help you understand why and how cost advantages can be obtained from scale and/or experience in a given situation. Such analyses require strategic market planners to study how their own firm's costs decline with scale and experience for each product, and to attempt to infer the same for their competitors. Not only are these analyses important for strategy formulation for individual products, but they are also crucial for allocating scarce financial and marketing resources *among* products. For instance, as we will show later, they may imply that strategies aiming for a relatively small number of "winners" are likely to be more profitable than those seeking a larger number of "also-rans."

This chapter considers how costs decline due to scale and to experience, practical problems in analyzing the experience effect, strategic implications of scale and experience, and limitations of strategies based on cost reduction. It is oriented primarily to decisions on *individual* products or businesses; Chapter 4 addresses the allocation of resources *among* products and businesses.

Relatively more attention is paid to experience than scale for several reasons. Scale effect is well-known and discussed in many other places,[3] whereas the experience effect is a newer, less widely understood concept. Also, the portfolio concepts introduced in Chapter 4 require a sound understanding of the experience effect. In fact the two effects are very closely related and often difficult to distinguish.

SCALE EFFECT

As mentioned earlier, scale effect refers to the fact that large businesses have the potential to operate at lower unit costs than their smaller counterparts. The increased efficiency due to size is often referred to as "economy of scale"; it could equally be called "economy of size."

---

[3]See, for example, Joe S. Bain, *Price Theory* (New York: Holt Reinhart and Winston, 1952), p. 112, or Edwin Mansfield, *Microeconomics: Theory and Applications,* (New York: W.W. Norton, 1975).

Most people think of economy of scale as a manufacturing phenomenon because large manufacturing facilities can be constructed at a lower cost per unit of capacity and can be operated more efficiently than smaller ones. In the process industries, such as petroleum and chemicals for example, as a rule of thumb, capital cost increases by the six-tenths power of capacity. For instance a 90 million-ton oil refinery costs only $(90/45)^{0.6}$ = 1.5 times as much as a 45 million-ton refinery. Thus doubling the size of a plant reduces the cost per unit of capacity by about 25 percent. This, of course, translates into lower depreciation charges per unit of output.

Just as they cost less to build, large-scale plants have lower *operating* costs per unit of output. For instance it takes less than twice as many workers to run the 90 million-ton refinery as the 45 million-ton one. Also, as scale increases, efficiency-increasing features (such as more accurate process controls) can be added to the design of a facility; these features would be uneconomic on a smaller scale.

While substantial in manufacturing, scale effect is also significant in other cost elements, such as marketing, sales, distribution, administration, R&D, and service. For instance, a chain with 30 supermarkets in a metropolitan area needs much less than three times as much advertising as a chain with 10 stores. Likewise greater automation is possible with large clerical operations than small ones; the same is true with large warehouses compared to smaller ones. In addition, larger operations provide greater opportunity for specialization of tasks, with resultant efficiencies.

The cost elements listed above are value-added cost elements; they are costs of operations provided by the business for itself and its customers. Economies of scale are also achieved with purchased items such as raw material and shipping. Examples include volume discounts and discounts for shipping in carload lots; these are available in greater measure to large businesses than small ones.

On value-added items there exist both long-run and short-run economies of scale.[4] The examples cited so far, such as building larger and more efficient plants, are long run. Short-run economies of scale derive from a fuller utilization of existing capacity whether it be a plant, a sales force, or service force. Thus, in the short run, scale economy comes from fully utilizing fixed-cost resources.

Although scale economies potentially exist in all cost elements of a business in both the short and long run, large size alone doesn't assure the benefits of scale. It is evident from the above illustrations that

---

[4]These correspond to what economists refer to as long-run and short-run cost curves; see, for instance, Joe S. Bain, *Price Theory*, pp. 117–120, or Edwin Mansfield, *Microeconomics*.

size provides an *opportunity* for scale economies; to achieve them requires strategies and actions consciously designed to seize the opportunity, especially with operating costs. For example, focusing expansion of a supermarket chain in a few metropolitan areas is preferable to scattering an equal number of new stores among many cities, *only* if potential economies in purchasing, distribution, and advertising are taken advantage of.

EXPERIENCE EFFECT

The experience effect, whereby costs fall with cumulative production, is measurable and predictable; it has been observed in a wide range of products including automobiles, semiconductors, petrochemicals, long-distance telephone calls, synthetic fibers, airline transportation, the cost of administering life insurance, and crushed limestone, to mention a few. Note that this list ranges from high technology to low technology products, service to manufacturing industries, consumer to industrial products, new to mature products, and process to assembly oriented products, indicating the wide range of applicability.

The phenomenon is age-old. For example, in the eighteenth century U.S. clockmaking was by and large a handcraft, and its products could only be afforded by the wealthy. But about 1800 it began to change; as experience increased, producers found better designs and more efficient means of manufacture. In Boston, Simon Willard produced shelf clocks that were similar and less expensive than the tall case clocks of the eighteenth century. In Connecticut, Eli Terry began to use waterpowered machinery to make wooden works for clocks and use assembly-line methods and unskilled labor to assemble them. In the 1830s inexpensive parts enabled Connecticut clockworkers to mass produce brass shelf clocks with simple mechanisms. With their extremely low prices, they quickly dominated the international market. By 1840, what had formerly been a luxury had become accessible to a large number of American families. In 1860, Chauncy Jerome,[5] a pioneer clock manufacturer, wrote, "The business of manufacture of them has become so systematized of late that it has brought the prices exceedingly low and it has long been the astonishment of the whole world how they could be made so cheap and yet be good."

However, it is only comparatively recently that this phenomenon has been carefully measured and quantified; at first it was thought to apply only to the *labor* portion of *manufacturing* costs. Perhaps the

---

[5]Chauncy Jerome, *History of the American Clock Business for the Past Sixty Years: Life of Chauncy Jerome Written by Himself* (New Haven: F. C. Dayton, Jr., 1860).

earliest quantification was in 1925, when the commander of the Wright-Patterson Air Force Base observed that the number of direct labor hours required to assemble a plane decreased as the total number of aircraft assembled increased. The relationship between labor costs and cumulative production became an important quantitative planning tool, known as the *learning curve.*

In the 1960s evidence mounted that the phenomenon was broader. Personnel from the Boston Consulting Group and others showed that each time cumulative volume of a product doubled, total value-added costs—including administration, sales, marketing, distribution, etc. in addition to manufacturing—fell by a constant and predictable percentage. In addition, the costs of purchased items usually fell as suppliers reduced prices as *their* costs fell, due also to the experience effect. The relationship between costs and experience was called the *experience curve.*[6]

An experience curve is plotted with the cumulative units produced on the horizontal axis, and cost per unit on the vertical axis. An "85 percent" experience curve is shown in Figure 1. The "85 percent" means that every time experience doubles, costs per unit drop to 85 percent of the original level. It is known as the *learning rate.* Stated differently, costs per unit decrease 15 percent for every doubling of

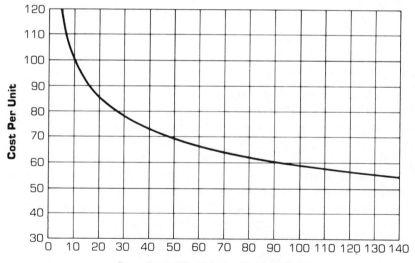

Experience (Cumulative Units of Production)

Figure 1

A Typical Experience Curve [85%]

---

[6]Staff of the Boston Consulting Group, *Perspectives on Experience* (Boston, Mass.: Boston Consulting Group, Inc., 1972).

cumulative production. For example, the cost of the 20th unit produced is about 85 percent of the cost of the 10th unit.

The formula for the experience curve is

$$C_q = C_n \left(\frac{q}{n}\right)^{-b}$$

where:

q = the experience (cumulative production) to date,
n = the experience (cumulative production) at an earlier date,
C_q = the cost of unit q (adjusted for inflation),
C_n = the cost of unit n (adjusted for inflation), and
b = a constant that depends on the learning rate; see Table 1.

Table 1
VALUE OF EXPONENT FOR VARIOUS EXPERIENCE CURVES

EXPERIENCE CURVE	b
100%	0.000
95	.074
90	.152
85	.235
80	.322
75	.415
70	.515
65	.623
60	.738

In other words, the *ratio* of experience at one point of time to that at another point in time, (q/n), is the key to reducing costs; doubling experience from one million units to two million units has the same percentage impact on costs as moving from 1,000 to 2,000 units. Table 2 shows how costs fall with experience for various learning rates and ratios of experience.

An experience curve appears as a straight line when plotted on a double log paper (logarithmic scale for both the horizontal and vertical axes). Figure 2 shows the "85 percent" experience curve from Figure 1 on the double logarithmic scale. (To determine the learning rate of an experience curve check the ratio of costs for any two points having a ratio of experience of 2 to 1. For example, in Figure 2 costs are 72 at 40 units and 61 at 80 units, yielding a learning rate of 61/72 = .85.)

As previously noted, the experience effect has been observed for a very wide range of products in a wide range of industries; Figure 3 provides illustrations for eight different products.

Table 2
SAMPLE COST REDUCTIONS DUE TO
INCREASED EXPERIENCE

RATIO OF OLD EXPERIENCE TO NEW EXPERIENCE	EXPERIENCE CURVE					
	70%	75%	80%	85%	90%	95%
1.1	5%	4%	3%	2%	1%	1%
1.25	11	9	7	5	4	2
1.5	19	15	12	9	6	3
1.75	25	21	16	12	8	4
2.0	30	25	20	15	10	5
2.5	38	32	26	19	13	7
3.0	43	37	30	23	15	8
4.0	51	44	36	28	19	10
6.0	60	52	44	34	24	12
8.0	66	58	49	39	27	14
16.0	76	68	59	48	34	19

Example:
If experience is quadrupled and the product is on an 85 percent experience curve, then costs will be reduced by 28 percent.

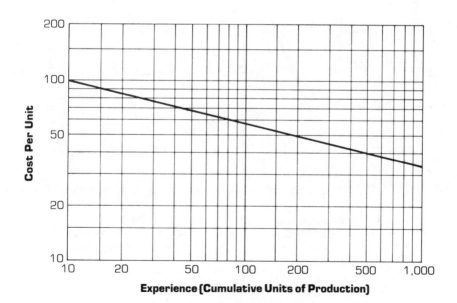

Figure 2
An 85% Experience Curve Displayed on Log-Log Scales

Figure 3
Some Sample Experience Curves

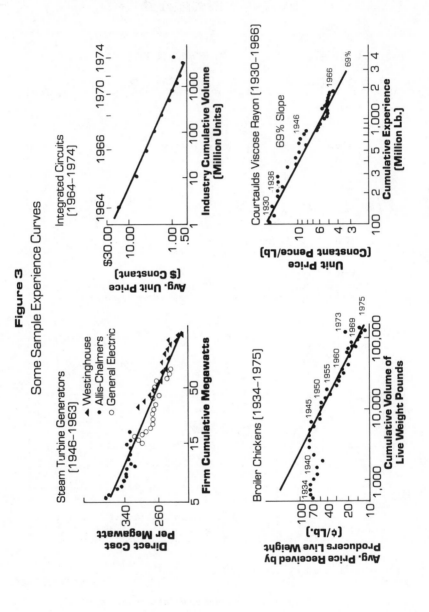

Figure 3 [cont.]

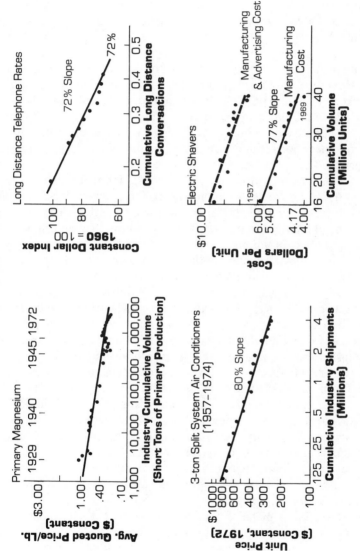

Source: The Boston Consulting Group.

Note: Technically an experience curve shows the relationship between cost and experience. However, cost figures are seldom publicly available; therefore most of the above experience curves show industry price (in constant dollars) vs. experience.

SOURCES OF THE EXPERIENCE EFFECT

The experience effect has a variety of sources; to capitalize on it requires knowledge of why it occurs. Sources of the experience effect are outlined below:

1. *Labor efficiency.* Labor's contribution to the experience effect, portrayed by the learning curve, has already been mentioned. As workers repeat a particular production task, they become more dextrous and learn improvements and shortcuts which increase their collective efficiency. The greater the number of worker-paced operations, the greater the amount of learning which can accrue with experience.

     This learning effect goes beyond the labor directly involved in manufacturing. Maintenance personnel, supervisors, and persons in other line and staff manufacturing positions also increase their productivity, as do people in marketing, sales, administration, and other functions.

2. *Work specialization and methods improvements.* Specialization increases worker proficiency at a given task. Consider what happens when two workers, who formerly did both parts of a two-stage operation, each specialize in a single stage. Each worker now handles twice as many items and accumulates experience twice as fast on the more specialized task. Redesign of work operations (methods) can also result in greater efficiency.

3. *New production processes.* Process innovations and improvements can be an important source of cost reductions, especially in capital-intensive industries. The low-labor-content semiconductor industry, for instance, achieves experience curves of 70 percent to 80 percent from improved production technology by devoting a large percentage of its research and development to process improvements. Similar process improvements have been observed in refineries, nuclear power plants, and steel mills, to mention a few.

4. *Getting better performance from production equipment.* When first designed, a piece of production equipment may have a conservatively rated output. Experience may reveal innovative ways of increasing its output. For instance, capacity of a fluid catalytic cracking unit typically "grows" by about 50 percent over a 10-year period.[7]

5. *Changes in the resource mix.* As experience accumulates, a producer can often incorporate different or less expensive resources

---

[7]Winfred B. Hirschmann, "Profit from the Learning Curve," *Harvard Business Review,* 42, no. 1 (January-February 1964), p. 125.

in the operation. For instance, less skilled workers can replace skilled workers or automation can replace labor.

6. *Product standardization.* Standardization allows the replication of tasks necessary for worker learning. Production of the Ford Model T, for example, followed a strategy of deliberate standardization; as a result, from 1909 to 1923 its price was repeatedly reduced, following an 85 pecent experience curve.[8] Even when flexibility and/or a wider product line are important marketing considerations, standardization can be achieved by modularization. For example, by making just a few types of engines, transmissions, chassis, seats, body styles, etc., an auto manufacturer can achieve experience effects due to specialization in each part. These in turn can be assembled into a wide variety of models.

7. *Product redesign.* As experience is gained with a product, both the manufacturer and customers gain a clearer understanding of its performance requirements. This understanding allows the product to be redesigned to conserve material, allows greater efficiency in manufacture, and substitutes less costly materials and resources, while at the same time improving performance on relevant dimensions. The change from wooden to brass works of clocks in the early 1800s is a good example; so are the new designs and substitution of plastic, synthetic fiber, and rubber for leather in ski boots.

The above list of sources dramatizes the observation that cost reductions due to experience don't occur by natural inclination; they are the result of substantial, concerted effort and pressure to lower costs. In fact, left unmanaged, costs rise. Thus, experience does not *cause* reductions[9] but rather provides an opportunity that alert managements can exploit. Consequently strategies resulting from market planning should explicitly address *how* cost reductions are to be achieved.

Gaining full efficiency benefits from experience requires high quality and stability in the work force. Otherwise, productivity gains are diminished from slow learning by marginal workers, and as new workers are brought up to proficiency. The compensation plan[10] of the firm and employee relations policies can also have an important influence on its experience curves.

The list of reasons for the experience effect raises perplexing questions on the difference between experience and scale effects. For

---

[8]William J. Abernathy and Kenneth Wayne, "Limits of the Learning Curve," *Harvard Business Review*, 52, no. 5 (September-October 1974), pp. 109–119.

[9]The experience effect can be thought of as making an equivalent product for less cost, a product of greater value for the same cost, or a combination of the two.

[10]N. Baloff, "Startup Management," *IEEE Transactions in Engineering Management*, EM–7, no. 4 (November 1970).

instance, isn't it true that work specialization and project standardization, mentioned in the experience list, become possible because of the *size* of an operation? Therefore, aren't they each really scale effects? The answer is that they are probably both.

The confusion arises because growth in experience usually coincides with growth in size of an operation. We consider the experience effect to arise primarily due to ingenuity, cleverness, skill, and dexterity derived from experience as embodied in the adages "practice makes perfect" or "experience is the best teacher." On the other hand, scale effect comes from capitalizing on the size of an operation. The chicken broiler experience curve in Figure 3 is a good example. By the 1930s egg-laying chicken-raising had been separated from meat raising. Since then, intensive cross-breeding and raising in close confinement has reduced the amount of feed needed for a given weight gain. (A three-pound chicken can be raised on six pounds of high-quality feed vs. 15 pounds in the 1930s). Furthermore the fattening up process takes only about half the time it once did.[11] These are experience effects. At the same time scale of operations has increased enormously.[12] By 1970 approximately 20 percent of broilers were produced in operations having over 100,000 chickens each. The largest operation in the 1920s had only 2,000 chickens.

There are those who would include scale as part of, or as a reason for, the experience effect.[13] But there are important examples where firms with low experience use scale to achieve significant cost advantages over firms with far greater experience. The Japanese steel industry has done so to its more experienced U.S. counterpart. So scale effect can exist independently of experience effect. Likewise experience effect can exist independently of scale effect; for example, you tie your shoes much faster now than when you were younger.

Usually the overlap between the two effects is so great that it is difficult (and not too important) to separate them. This is the practice we will adopt from here on (while remaining alert for those exceptions where scale effect can be achieved alone, such as in high fixed-cost, capital-intensive industries.)

---

[11] "Fresh Chicken," *Consumer Reports*, 43, no. 5 (May 1978), p. 255.

[12] "Optical Distortion, Inc.," Harvard Business School Case, 9-575-072 (Boston, Mass.: Intercollegiate Case Clearing House, 1975).

[13] And there are those who would include experience as a part of scale effect. For instance, Pessemier refers to what we have called scale effect as static scale effect (since it is achieved at isolated points in time) experience is a dynamic scale effect (since it is achieved over time). See Edgar A. Pessemier, *Product Management: Strategy and Organization* (New York: John Wiley & Sons, 1977), pp. 51–99.

PRICES AND EXPERIENCE

In stable competitive markets, one would expect that as costs decrease due to experience, prices will decrease similarly. (The price-experience curves in Figure 3 are examples of prices falling with experience.) If profit margins remain at a constant percentage of price, average industry costs and prices should follow identically sloped experience curves (on double logarithmic scales). The constant gap separating them will equal the profit margin percentage; Figure 4 illustrates such an idealized situation.

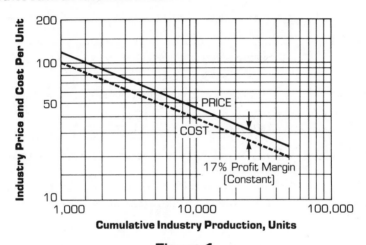

Figure 4

An Idealized Price-Cost Relationship
When Profit Margin is Constant

In many cases, however, prices and costs exhibit a relationship similar to the one shown in Figure 5, where prices start briefly below cost, then cost reductions exceed price reductions until prices suddenly tumble. Ultimately the price and cost curves parallel, as they do in Figure 4. Specifically, in the development phase, new product prices are below average industry costs due to pricing based on anticipated costs. In the price umbrella phase, when demand exceeds supply, prices remain firm under a price umbrella supported by the market leader. This is unstable. At some point a shakeout phase starts; one producer will almost certainly reduce prices to gain share. If this does not precipitate a price decline, the high profit margins will attract enough new entrants to produce temporary overcapacity, causing prices to tumble faster than costs, and marginal producers to be forced

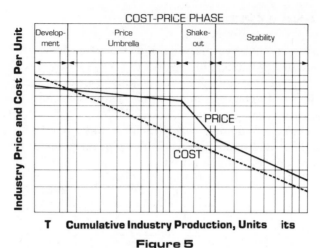

Figure 5
Typical Price-Cost Relationship

Source: Adapted from *Perspectives on Experience* (Boston: The Boston Consulting Group, 1972), p.21.

out of the market. The stability phase starts when profit margins return to normal levels and prices begin to follow industry costs down the experience curve. For instance, both the prices of silicon transistors and polyvinyl-chloride exhibited the characteristics[14] shown in Figure 5.

STRATEGIC IMPLICATIONS

In industries where a significant portion of total cost can be reduced due to scale or experience, important cost advantages can usually be achieved by pursuing a strategy geared to accumulating experience faster than competitors. (Such a strategy will ultimately require that the firm acquire the largest market share relative to competition.)

To see this, consider a three-firm industry where each competitor is moving down the same experience curve and firm A leads firm B which in turn leads firm C in experience. This situation is shown in Figure 6. Firm A has a significant cost advantage over B and a major edge on C. The difference in cost can spell the difference between profit and loss; if industry price is falling with experience, as assumed in Figure 6, then A will have a substantial profit, B a much smaller profit, and C a loss. In the extreme, if firm A pursued an aggressive

---

[14]Staff of the Boston Consulting Group, *Perspectives in Experience* (Boston: The Boston Consulting Group, 1972), pp. 71, 85.

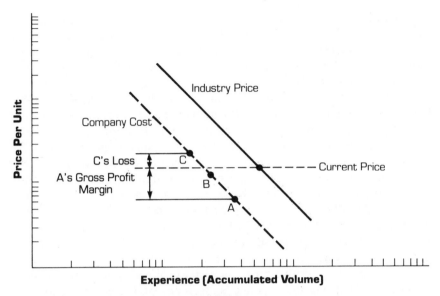

Figure 6

Profitability Advantages of Greater Experience
[Market Share]

Source: Adapted from "The Experience Curve-Reviewed: I. The
Concept" (Boston: The Boston Consulting Group, 1973), *Perspectives*,
No. 124.

strategy, cutting prices in proportion to cost reductions, it could easily
drive out smaller, inefficient competitors such as C. Or, it could reduce
its prices more slowly to improve its own margin, but it will thereby
improve the margin of its competitors, too. This will improve their financial health and may encourage them to improve their own performance by increasing their experience (and consequently market share),
relative to the leader.

The dominant producer can greatly influence industry profitability. The rate of decline of competitors' costs must at least keep pace
with the leader if they are to maintain profitability. If their costs decrease more slowly, either because they are pursuing cost reductions
less aggressively or are growing more slowly than the leader, then
their profits will eventually disappear, thus eliminating them from the
market.

In situations such as the foregoing ones, the advantage of being
the leader is obvious. Leadership is usually best seized at the start
when experience doubles quickly (e.g. experience increases tenfold as
you move from the 20th to the 2,000th unit, but only doubles as you
move from the 2,000th to the 4,000th unit.) Then a firm can build an un-
assailable cost advantage and at the same time gain price leadership.

The best course of action for a product depends on a number of factors, one of the most important being the market growth rate. In fast-growing markets, experience can be gained by taking a disproportionate share of new sales, thereby avoiding taking sales away from competitors (which would be vigorously resisted). Therefore, with high rates of growth, aggressive action may be called for. But, share-gaining tactics are usually costly in the short run, due to reduced margins from lower prices, added advertising and marketing expense, new product development costs, and the like. This means that if it lacks the resources (product, financial, and other) for leadership and in particular if it is opposed by a very aggressive competitor, a firm may find it wise to abandon the market entirely or focus on a segment it can dominate. On the other hand, in no-growth or slowly growing markets it is hard to take share from competitors and the time it takes to acquire superior experience is usually too long and the cost too great to favor aggressive strategies.

In stable competitive markets, usually the firm with the largest share of market has the greatest experience and it is often the case that each firm's experience is roughly proportional to market share. A notable exception occurs when a late entrant to a market quickly obtains a commanding market share. It may have less experience than some early entrants.

Before embarking on any experience-based strategy, especially a share-increasing one, it is essential to calculate explicitly the required time and investment to see whether the target is feasible and desirable. These pro forma projections must extend over many years. For instance, consider a firm with 6 percent of a market that is growing at an 8 percent real growth rate and whose leader has a 24 percent share.

To catch up with the leader's share, our firm would have to grow at a 26 percent growth rate for nine years, if the leader held its share by growing at the 8 percent industry rate. That means expanding at over three times the industry rate for nine years, and that sales and capacity would have to expand by 640 percent.

These numbers raise important questions, some of which are: Can the expansion be financed? What strategy will achieve such a large share gain? From which competitor(s) will the share come? Will the smaller ones be squeezed out by an aggressive strategy? What competitive reactions can be expected? Will the market be worth leading nine years from now?

The importance of doing these calculations and heeding their implications was underscored by the withdrawal of RCA, Xerox, and GE from the main-frame computer business; all three firms experienced multi-million dollar losses in computers.[15] An appropriate set of calculations, done at the outset, might have dissuaded these companies from even entering this market.

The example also shows that good information about the market, its growth, market shares, and competitors' experience or costs is essential. Without knowledge of how fast a market is actually growing, a firm may be unaware that competitors are rapidly gaining share. Or it may be in a poor position to assess the probable effects of proposed market actions. On the other hand, a fully informed company is equipped to make successful strategic decisions at the expense of less-informed competitors.

It is clear that when experience and scale are significant cost factors, being the leader is advantageous and being a distant follower is a serious handicap. However, since no firm has the resources to lead in all markets, it must decide which market to attempt to lead, in which to hold a viable non-leadership share (as firm B does in Figure 6), and which to abandon. Techniques for making these decisions are covered in Chapter 4.

EFFICIENCY VS. EFFECTIVENESS: LIMITATIONS TO STRATEGIES BASED ON EXPERIENCE OR SCALE

The selection of a competitive strategy based on cost reduction due to experience or scale often involves a fundamental choice. It is the selection of cost-price *efficiency* over non cost-price marketing *effectiveness*. However, when the market is more concerned with product and service features and up-to-date technology, a firm pursuing efficiency can find itself offering a low-priced product that few customers want. Thus two basic questions arise: 1) when to use an efficiency strategy and 2) if so, how far to push it before running into dangers of losing effectiveness. For instance, Hewlett-Packard (HP)[16] has been outstandingly profitable using an "effectiveness" strategy against successful "efficiency"-oriented companies such as Texas Instruments (TI) in calculators and Digital Equipment Corporation in small computers. These companies have aggressively used "experience curve pricing" to achieve an early market share and a subsequent strong

---

[15]William E. Fruhan, "Pyrrhic Victories in Fights for Market Share," *Harvard Business Review*, 50, no. 5 (September-October 1972), pp. 100–107.

[16]"Hewlett-Packard: Where Slower Growth is Smarter Management," *Business Week*, June 9, 1975, pp. 50–58.

competitive cost position. In contrast, HP maintains its prices, concentrating on developing products so advanced that customers are willing to pay a premium for them. The low-share, high-quality strategy works well for it.[17]

Whether to pursue an efficiency strategy depends on answers to questions such as:

1. Does the industry offer significant cost advantages from experience or scale (as in semiconductors or chemicals)?
2. Are there significant market segments that will reward competitors with low prices?
3. Is the firm well equipped (financially, managerially, technologically, etc.) for or already geared up for strategies relying heavily on having the lowest cost (as TI was in the above example)?

If the answer is "yes" to all these questions, then "efficiency" strategies should probably be pursued.

Once it decided to pursue an "efficiency" strategy a firm must guard against going so far that it loses effectiveness, primarily through inability to respond to changes. For instance, experience-based strategies frequently require a highly specialized work force, facilities and organization, making it difficult to respond to changes in consumer demand, to respond to competitors' innovations, or to initiate them. In addition, large-scale plants are vulnerable to changes in process technology, and the heavy cost of operation below capacity.

For example, Ford's Model T automobile ultimately suffered the consequences of inflexibility due to overemphasizing "efficiency."[18] Ford followed a classic experience-based strategy; over time it slashed its product line to a single model (the model T), built modern plants, pushed division of labor, introduced the continuous assembly line, obtained economies in purchased parts through high volume, backward integrated, increased mechanization, and cut prices as costs fell. The lower prices increased Ford's share of a growing market to a high of 55.4 percent by 1921.

In the meantime, consumer demand began shifting to heavier, closed-body cars and to more comfort. Ford's chief rival, General Motors, had the flexibility to respond quickly with new designs. Ford

---

[17]One can also argue that HP is in a different market segment (high quality and performance) than TI and DEC and thus is not a direct competitor of either. Further, HP's experience in its segment is far greater than its competition's; it dominates its segment and thus has the greatest profitability as the experience curve model suggests.

[18]William J. Abernathy and Kenneth Wayne, "Limits of the Learning Curve," *Harvard Business Review*, 50, no. 5 (September-October 1974), p. 109.

responded by adding features to its existing standard design. While the features softened the inroads of GM, the basic Model T design, upon which Ford's "efficiency" strategy was based, inadequately met the market's new performance standards. To make matters worse, the turmoil in production due to constant design changes slowed experience-based efficiency gains. Finally Ford was forced, at enormous cost, to close for a whole year beginning May 1927 while it retooled to introduce its Model A. Hence experience or scale-based *efficiency* was carried too far and thus it ultimately limited *effectiveness* to meet consumer needs, to innovate, and to respond.

Thus the challenge is to decide when to emphasize efficiency and when to emphasize effectiveness, and further to design efficiency strategies that maintain effectiveness and vice versa.

PRACTICAL CONSIDERATIONS IN USING EXPERIENCE CURVES

The experience effect, while a simple concept, requires dealing with a number of practical issues in its application to a given product. Considerable judgment is required and great care is needed to avoid misinterpretations and erroneous conclusions. Some of the more important considerations are outlined below.

The Behavior of Costs over Time

Many managers, especially of mature products, doubt that the experience curve applies to their product, because they observe little if any annual decrease in costs. In some instances, increases in cost are observed over time. Their conclusions usually turn out to be erroneous for two reasons:

1. They are looking at cost data that is not corrected for inflation. A good example is the price data for crushed limestone, shown in Figure 7. The unadjusted data shows a price increase, whereas adjusted data follows an 80 percent experience curve.
2. Even if corrected for inflation, they are looking at cost data plotted against *time* as opposed to data plotted against *experience*, the relevant variable. The confusion arises because experience accumulates at a slower and slower rate with respect to time, when annual volume is growing at a constant rate. This gives the impression that cost reduction has slowed down; it has, with respect to time, but not with respect to experience. For instance, at

a constant 15 percent annual growth rate of volume and a 75 percent experience curve, experience more than doubles the second
year, resulting in a 27 percent cost decrease. In the tenth year
experience increases only by about 18 percent, resulting in only
a 7 percent cost decrease. (The latter decrease could easily be
hidden by inflation.)

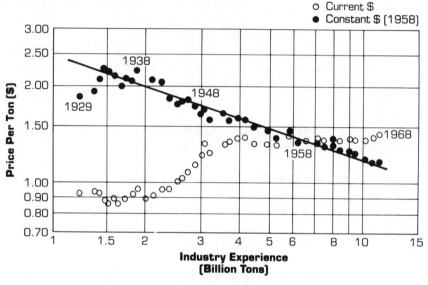

Figure 7

The U.S. Price Per Ton of Crushed and Broken Lime-
stone, Uncorrected and Corrected for Inflation vs.
Experience
Source: The Boston Consulting Group.

The uninitiated analyst often underestimates the rate that experience accumulates with respect to time and is confused about the relationship between growth in annual volume and growth in experience.
For all but very large values of annual volume growth rate (greater
than about 20 percent a year), experience grows at a faster rate than
volume for at least the first ten years of a product's life. Figure 8 illustrates this for an annual volume growth rate of 10 percent. While it
takes just over eight years for annual volume to double, experience has
doubled well over three times. Table 3 shows how quickly experience
accumulates for various annual growth rates, using the first year's volume as a base point.

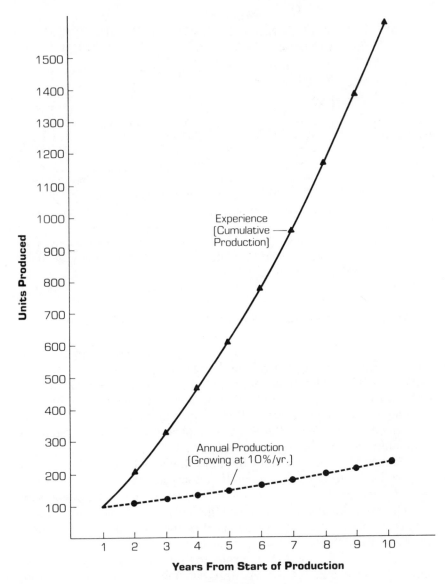

Figure 8

Example of How Cumulative Production Grows Faster
than Annual Production [for annual production growing
at 10% per year; production in first year = 100]

Table 3

WHEN DOUBLING OF CUMULATIVE PRODUCTION WILL OCCUR
AT VARIOUS GROWTH RATES OF ANNUAL PRODUCTION

TIME FROM START OF PRODUCTION TO:	GROWTH RATE IN ANNUAL PRODUCTION				
	0%	5%	10%	15%	20%
First doubling	2 yrs.	1.95 yrs.	1.92 yrs.	1.88 yrs.	1.89 yrs.
Second doubling	4 yrs.	3.75 yrs.	3.54 yrs.	3.36 yrs.	3.22 yrs.
Third doubling	8 yrs.	6.9 yrs.	6.2 yrs.	5.65 yrs.	5.23 yrs.
Fourth doubling	16 yrs.	12.1 yrs.	10.4 yrs.	8.75 yrs.	7.85 yrs.

Source: "Experience and Cost: Some Implications for Manufacturing Policy", Harvard Business School note, 9-675-228. (Boston, Ma.: Intercollegiate Case Clearing House, 1975), p. 21.

Time is measured from the *start* of production; doubling is measured with production of first year counted as "1".

Example: If annual production is growing at 15 percent per year, cumulative production will reach eight times that at the end of the first year (third doubling) in 5.65 years.

Analyzing Experience on Different Cost Components

The cost of an individual product falls because of the experience effect on the cost components (metal stamping, moulded parts, assembly, packaging, distribution, service, etc.) that combine to make up the product. However, the amounts of experience accumulated in individual components might be very different, as might be the slopes of their experience curves. Thus the relative importance of each component may change as experience is accumulated.

To illustrate this, consider the following hypothetical situation: A new product consisting of one each of components A and B, and two each of component C has just entered production. The company has no previous experience with A (a new, high-technology item) which is on a 75 percent curve; it has produced 10,000 units of B on an 80 percent curve and 1,000,000 units of C on an 80 percent curve.

The cost of the product is projected for various cumulative production quantities in Table 4. At first, component A is the major cost, but it doubles experience rapidly until its contribution to the cost per unit falls below B at 10,000 units of production. Ultimately C becomes the major cost component at 1,000,000 units. Notice that B starts at 20 percent of cost, rises to 44.2 percent, and then falls to 34.6 percent. The overall experience curve showing total cost of the product plotted against experience for the product will not follow the "classic" straight line on log-log paper; its slope will initially be 83 percent, later level to 90 percent, and then ultimately steepen towards 80 percent. This shows that an experience curve for a product is the result of the complex interaction of the experience curves of its cost components.

Thus it is essential to consider each major cost component separately in a refined experience curve analysis. Not only is detailed analysis important to get reliable cost projections, but it also has important competitive implications. In the above example, a naive, short-range experience curve analysis of total cost will be dominated by the cost contribution of A, hiding the fact that C will ultimately become the most significant cost. If a major competitor has vastly more experience on component C, it could have an ultimate competitive advantage. This in turn could change a seemingly profitable product into an unprofitable one. The example also illustrates that the main challenge in cost reduction may shift from one cost component to another as a product grows in experience. Thus the fact that cost components behave differently with experience has analytical, stratetgic, and managerial significance.

Shared Experience

Additional complications and strategic opportunities arise when there is shared experience. *Shared experience* can occur when two or more products share a common resource or activity in a similar manner. For instance, the same assembly operation may produce high-torque motors for oil exploration and low-torque motors for conveyors. Or tape drives and disk drives may share the same computer marketing organization. Or foam and cellulose insulation may be sold through the same distribution channel. The key is that they use the common resource or activity in a similar manner so that any economies learned from dealing with one product can be applied to the rest. (This was the case with component C in the example in Table 4.) Thus shared experience is important because costs of one product are reduced additionally due to experience accumulated in dealing with the other products.

One of the most common manifestations of shared experience occurs when two or more products share a common component, as when several automobile models use the same transmission or several petrochemical products derive from the same intermediate product. However, it can occur when the products serve different customer groups (the motor example), customer functions (the computer example), or use different technologies (the insulation example).

Opportunities for shared experience must be carefully sought, analyzed, and exploited to gain cost advantage over competition, especially in diversified companies. By focusing new product efforts where shared experience plays a major role, a firm can build diversity into a strength. Likewise, the impact of reducing shared experience

Table 4
AN EXAMPLE SHOWING HOW THE RELATIVE CONTRIBUTION OF VARIOUS COST COMPONENTS CHANGES WITH EXPERIENCE

EXPERIENCE WITH THE PRODUCT	COST COMPONENT									TOTAL UNIT COST
	A [75% CURVE; 1 ITEM PER UNIT]			B [80% CURVE; 1 ITEM PER UNIT]			C [80% CURVE; 2 ITEMS PER UNIT]			
	COMPONENT EXPERIENCE	COST PER UNIT	% OF TOTAL UNIT COST	COMPONENT EXPERIENCE	COST PER UNIT	% OF TOTAL UNIT COST	COMPONENT EXPERIENCE	COST PER UNIT	% OF TOTAL UNIT COST	
100 units	100	$70.00	70.0%	10,100	$20.00	20.0%	1,000,200	$10.00	10.0%	$100.00
1,000 units	1,000	26.92	47.8	11,000	19.46	34.5	1,002,000	9.99	17.7	56.37
10,000 units	10,000	10.35	28.4	20,000	16.05	44.2	1,020,000	9.94	27.4	36.34
100,000 units	100,000	3.98	17.5	110,000	9.27	40.9	1,200,000	9.43	41.6	22.68
1,000,000 units	1,000,000	1.53	11.7	1,010,000	4.53	34.6	3,000,000	7.02	53.7	13.08

when a product is dropped must also be analyzed. Shared experience is an important special case of the need to analyze cost components separately—but one providing significant strategic opportunities.

Cost Differences Between Competitors

The difference in cost between two competitors is important to know, yet difficult to determine for reasons that are not obvious at first. The temptation is to assume that competitors are moving down similar experience curves, beginning at the same starting points. Therefore, if Competitor A has twice the experience of Competitor B and an 80 percent curve applies, then A's costs should be 20 percent less than B's. In fact, such conclusions often overstate the cost differences.

The problem is that the erroneous conclusions are based on over-simplified premises:[19]

1. Competitors don't necessarily start from the same point; for instance, if B is a late entrant, it can sometimes start at costs lower than A's initial costs.
   a. Firm B may benefit from knowledge on how A is doing business at the time of entry.
   b. Firm B may benefit from advances in the technology of production equipment purchased from common suppliers.
   c. Firm B may benefit from the decline in cost of goods and services purchased for the product from common suppliers due to the supplier's experience.
2. Firm B may be able to exploit shared experience that A can't.
3. Firm B might have a higher proportion of value added in its product than firm A (because for example it is more backward or forward integrated.)
4. Firm B may later acquire and use knowledge of how A is doing business thereby accelerating B's learning. (This can occur, for instance, if B hires some of A's management.)

Considerations such as these must be carefully taken into account when analyzing cost differences.

Measuring Experience from the Right Starting Point

Many analysts mistakenly use the wrong starting point to measure experience on a cost component. For instance, a product planner

---

[19]Bruce D. Henderson, "Cross Sectional Experience Curves," (Boston: The Boston Consulting Group, 1978), Perspectives No. 208.

may be debating whether to have 100,000 or 200,000 high-tolerance electrical components manufactured outside, and may assume that the 200,000 order would double the supplier's experience. In fact, the manufacturer may have made hundreds of millions of similar components and neither size would add even 0.1 percent to its experience. Such errors—underestimating previous experience—are common and result in over-optimistic cost projections.

Other starting point judgments are more subtle, as, for example, determination of the proper starting point for the assembly operation of a new-model light aircraft by a long-time light aircraft manufacturer. On one hand, the fact that there is a great deal to be learned about how to assemble this model efficiently argues that the starting point is the first aircraft of this model. On the other hand, the organization has vast experience in assembling light aircraft generally, much of which will be applicable to the new model. This would argue that the starting point was thousands of aircraft ago. If so, experience will double less frequently and costs will come down more slowly. Actually, it is likely that cost reductions will at first be dominated by learning on this model, behaving in the short run as if the recent starting point applied. Later they will behave as though the starting point was earlier.

Cost Data

Cost data may be unavailable in the form required: costs may have been gathered on a time (e.g., per week or per month) or departmental (e.g., marketing department) basis rather than tied to the units of a particular product handled. Joint costs[20] may be allocated in a manner not reflecting "true" production circumstances; for instance, R&D might be allocated on the basis of percentage of sales, even though a disproportionate amount of R&D might be related to a given product. The data may contain abrupt shifts due to accounting changes, major production changes, product modifications, or external circumstances, such as commodity price breaks or price controls. Thus developing cost history as a function of total units produced is often difficult, costly, and tedious. But great care is important to avoid serious distortions.

Another issue is what to use as a unit of production for cost analysis. The answer isn't necessarily obvious. For instance, consider a basic product whose design is changing somewhat each year, such as an automobile. Cost per pound may more accurately measure the expe-

---

[20]Joint costs are costs of shared resources such as R&D.

rience effect than cost per automobile, if design modifications significantly change weight. The appropriate costs to use are short-run average costs measured over a small portion of total production such as a "batch" or over a month's or year's production.

Time Span

Some of the factors which influence the experience effect may fluctuate considerably in the short run as, for example, a sudden assembly cost drop due to new equipment or a rise due to increased wage rates. Only after many doublings of experience can the underlying pattern or trend be distinguished. This requires making cost observations often enough and over a long enough time to render these fluctuations insignificant. Also it means that in most situations experience curves cannot be used reliably for short-range operating controls or decision making.

Defining the Unit of Analysis

An important decision that is a prerequisite for good experience curve analysis is determining its purview. This we call defining the unit of analysis. Should costs be analyzed for a market segment? For individual products? For a product line? For a business as a whole? The answer is particularly important if market share is being used to make judgments about experience relative to competitors. A company may have a large share of a small market segment, yet have considerably less experience than a larger competitor who has a smaller overall share of a much broader market.

There are risks both of defining the unit of analysis too broadly and too narrowly. If it is defined too broadly, then important *specialized* experience advantages might be missed. For instance the grinding wheel industry produces hundreds of thousands of different types of wheels, each particularly suited for certain industrial applications. Production of a *given type* of wheel requires development and control of a "recipe" consisting of quantity, type and size of abrasives, bonding agents, fillers, wetting agents, and so forth; the timing of adding these to the "mix;" baking times and temperatures; finishing techniques; and so on. Likewise, a firm can gain important experience advantages in the selling and servicing of wheels for a particular application or a particular industry. Experience advantages on a given type of wheel can yield important cost advantages. Here the unit of analysis should be the type of wheel or the application; if it were simply "grinding wheels," significant cost advantages due to specialization would be missed. Important supporting evidence is that while the U.S. grinding industry is dominated by three producers, many small, specialized companies are very successful.

In other situations, defining the unit of analysis too narrowly can cause problems, such as missing important shared experience. Related to this is the difficulty of isolating costs applicable to the unit of analysis, when a resource (such as a sales force or R&D) is shared with other potential units of analysis.

Thus, flexibility and art are required to balance conflicting needs in defining the unit of analysis. Sometimes it is wise to repeat a cost analysis using several different definitions; sometimes it is wise to use a different unit of analysis for estimating a competitor's costs than that used to estimate your own. (This is particularly true when one competitor pursues a "specialized" strategy and another challenges you on much broader market.)

And sometimes it is wise to analyze experience effects for different resources separately, as a prelude to defining the unit of analysis. This will be especially true when resources are shared by several products. A manufacturing plant may, for example, make pumps for oil drilling and for marine applications; at the same time, one sales force may sell pumps and motors to oil companies, while another sells pumps, motors, and controls to marine buyers. In such a case, costs must be estimated for selling and manufacturing separately, taking into account the fact that two types of pumps share the manufacturing resource, while some pumps, motors, and controls share the sales resource. This analysis will reveal the potential for experience gains in each resource and the relative contribution of each resource to the cost of each product. This information in turn can often be used to group products into units of analysis.

Projecting Future Costs

Once the slope of an experience curve has been determined by plotting historical costs at various points in time and fitting a line through various points, costs can be projected for various future amounts of experience directly from the graph. Alternatively, the slope can be used to determine the appropriate exponent from Table 1, and the formula for the experience curve can be used on a computer or on a calculator having an exponent function. Or the graph in Figure 9 can be used, given a slope, to project costs starting from any base amount of experience and base cost.

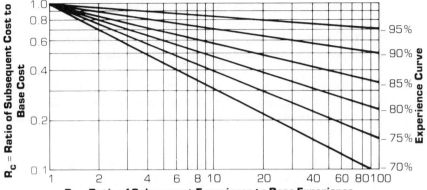

Figure 9

Graph for Projecting Costs at Various Learning Rates

Example: Current experience is 15,000 units and cost is $5.75 per unit. If an 85% experience curve applies, what will unit cost be at 150,000 units?

$$R_e = \frac{150,000}{15,000} = 10.$$

From graph, using 85 percent experience curve, R_c = .58.

Therefore, cost at 150,000 units will be

$$.58 \times \$5.75 = \$3.34 \text{ per unit}$$

Steps in Analyzing the Experience Effect

The basic steps in a careful experience curve analysis are:

1. Determine the unit of analysis.
2. Gather relevant historical cost data for the various cost components over a time period covering many doublings of experience.
3. Determine which of these costs should be actually allocated to the unit of analysis.
4. Group cost components which will be likely to behave similarly with respect to experience, isolating those that have significantly different amounts of prior experience, and different learning rates or shared experience.

5. For each group determine and plot (on double log paper) short-run average unit costs at various points in time.
6. Fit a line through the plotted points, judiciously selecting a slope which appears to be most representative of how future costs will behave.
7. Use the fitted line to project future costs of each cost component allowing for shared experience with other units of analysis.
8. Combine the projections of the separate cost components using a format similar to Table 4.

When a careful breakdown of costs into components (as assumed above) is unnecessary or impossible due to inadequate data, then aggregate data will be used. Steps 4 and 8 can be omitted, and steps 5–7 will be performed on the aggregate data.

SUMMARY

The fact that most value-added cost components of a product decline steadily with experience (cumulative production to date) and can be reduced as the scale of an operation increases has profound implications for strategy. When these effects have a pronounced impact on total costs, significant cost advantages over competition can usually be obtained by acquiring greater experience. Since experience and size are closely related to market share, being the market leader or having a large share is usually advantageous in such circumstances. However, resources for accomplishing this are usually limited, which suggests aiming for a dominant positon in each of a few carefully selected markets, rather than a weaker presence in a larger number of markets. It also suggests that for attractive new products, aggressive entry aimed at a leadership position is a preferred strategy, if resources for doing so are available. For existing markets the best strategy depends on current market position and whether the market itself is growing, static, or declining.

Cost-based "efficiency" strategies of the sort described in the previous paragraph are appropriate when experience and scale effects are significant, when the market rewards low price, and when the firm has the resources to implement them. In some market segments and for some companies it may be more advantageous to use "effectiveness" strategies aimed at producing difficult-to-copy products of great value to the buyer, for which price is a secondary consideration. In most cases, strategies will mix elements of effectiveness and efficiency. It is particularly important to design efficiency strategies that maintain many virtues of effectiveness, especially flexibility, and vice versa.

While experience curve concepts are straightforward, their application often requires considerable ingenuity. Products and markets must be defined carefully with difficult tradeoffs between narrow and broad definitions and between market versus production-oriented definitions. Cost data are frequently difficult to obtain from the accounting system, and correction must be made for inflation. Each major component of cost must be analyzed separately when components have different learning rates and amounts of experience. The cost behavior of the product is the complex interaction of these component costs. Opportunities for shared experience must be sought out, analyzed, and exploited. Data must cover a sufficient time period to overcome the effects of short-run cost fluctuations. The costs and potential benefits of strategic alternatives must be carefully weighed, often years into the future. Similar analyses of competitors' costs and market positions will be needed, but competitive data will be even more difficult to acquire than internal data. In all cases, incomplete data is better than none, but considerable effort to collect, refine, and check data is usually justified.

Increased experience and scale provide an opportunity for cost reduction rather than *causing* costs to fall. Therefore, any experience- or scale-based strategy requires the implementation of explicit, well-thought-out cost reduction efforts.

This chapter has stressed that a strong market position is important for success, for many individual products. However, attaining that position requires considerable resources. Since these are usually limited, a firm must wisely allocate its resources among its products. A framework dealing with this problem is the subject of Chapter 4.

ELECTRO INDUSTRIES, INC. (A)[1]

Early in January 1975, David Warner, President of the MOStronics Division of Electro Industries, Inc., faced the most difficult decision of his career. By January 30, he had to decide whether or not MOStronics should continue to produce hand-held calculators, a product line which represented more than half of MOStronic's 1974 sales and had been a major factor in the company's growth. Due to severe price competition from large, integrated calculator producers, MOStronics had recently incurred heavy losses in its calculator line and Electro management had requested that Mr. Warner develop a plan to return MOStronics to profitability. Electro management had further suggested that Mr. Warner really had only two alternatives: prove he could reduce costs and remain competitive in the calculator industry, or write off calculator production and return to the basic semiconductor component production which had remained profitable for MOStronics.

MOStronics had been one of the most successful acquisitions made by Electro (1974 sales: $875 million) immediately following the 1969–1970 recession. Under Mr. Warner's direction, MOStronics had grown from an unprofitable $7 million producer of specialized semiconductor components to a highly profitable manufacturer of electronic calculators which had earned $5.9 million on sales of $22.8 million in 1973 (see financial statements, Exhibits 1 and 2). However, in 1974, industry giants like Texas Instruments, Inc., and other firms had experienced severe price erosion as they jockeyed for increasing shares of the booming personal calculator market. In little more than a year, average retail prices for hand-held calculators had plummeted 50 percent; by the end of 1974 MOStronics had shown a loss of $1.9 million despite sales of more than $43 million. More losses seemed inevitable for the early months of 1975.

Mr. Warner believed strongly that MOStronics could compete successfully in the calculator industry. He had directed MOStronics' aggressive entry into the business in 1970 and, armed with only one prototype and no firm orders, had achieved spectacular success. He felt much of 1974's losses were attributable not to the competition, but to footdragging on the part of Electro management which had hindered

---

[1]This case was prepared by Gerald B. Allan in collaboration with John S. Hammond.

MOStronics' ability to react in the rapidly changing calculator market. He was certain that his able production team could reduce costs to a competitive level. Despite his strong personal conviction about the strategy, Mr. Warner had consulted Electro's vice president for corporate planning, who, on the other hand, presented a strong case for dropping calculators.

MOSTRONICS' HISTORY

Like several other companies in the industry, MOStronics had been the creation of a Fairchild Semiconductor alumnus. David Warner, an electronics engineer by training, had worked for Fairchild since shortly after its founding in 1957. Warner, along with several fellow engineers, had left the company in 1969 to form MOStronics to exploit the newly developing MOS (Metal Oxide Semiconductor) integrated circuit[2] technology.

By late 1971, however, MOStronics had been on the verge of failure. Underfinanced and struggling with poor component yields,[3] MOStronics had rapidly consumed both its founders' capital and several investments made by a local venture capital firm. In desperation, Mr. Warner had used remaining funds on a crash program to develop a low-priced entry for the personal calculator market. Concurrently, he had begun searching for a merger partner which could inject badly needed capital.

MOStronics had become profitable in the third quarter of 1972, and sales for that year had reached $11.5 million. Late in 1972 the company had added two new eight-digit calculator models and had constructed a 38,000 square-foot assembly plant next to MOStronics' original 30,000 square-foot plant. Production yields on integrated circuits had improved substantially and MOStronics had developed expertise in newer CMOS[4] technology which was a key to longer calculator battery life. By early 1973, all IC production had been shifted to CMOS circuits.

---

[2]Integrated circuits (ICs) were of two basic types: bipolar, the original transistor type, and the MOS type, developed in the early 1960s. Although much slower in calculating speed than the bipolar type, MOS integrated circuits were much simpler to make and offered a 10:1 price-per-function advantage over bipolars.

[3]Yield—the percentage of good components from each production batch—was the key to profitability in semiconductor manufacture. Yield problems, which could drop yield by 80 percent from one batch to the next, could generate monumental production overloads and skyrocketing costs.

[4]CMOS (Complementary-MOS) circuits were formed by combining two types of MOS transistors into a single device having extremely low power consumption and other characteristics ideally suited both for demanding industrial applications and for many consumer products.

MOSTRONICS PRODUCTS AND PRODUCTION

MOStronics in 1974 had produced three major product lines: (1) digital logic (MOS) integrated circuits, (2) random access memory (RAM) semiconductor components, and (3) calculators.

MOStronics forte since its inception had been in custom-designed medium- and large-scale integrated circuits, though the company had shifted emphasis to more standard production items in the last two years. MOStronics possessed a highly developed MOS production expertise and supplied digital logic circuits to both end users (including the military) and original equipment manufacturers (OEMs) for use in a variety of consumer and industrial products. The company had become an important second source[5] for especially difficult-to-manufacture ICs as well.

MOStronics in 1973 had begun producing random access memory (RAM) components on a limited-scale mass production basis; prior to that time RAM production had been performed on a custom basis, usually as part of a development or testing contract for an equipment manufacturer. Random access memory chips performed the same function in a computer as did ferrite core memories.

In 1974, the market for RAMs was estimated to be 4 million units worth $100 million, with Texas Instruments and Intel each claiming a 40 percent market share. This market was expected to grow to 30 million units in 1978, an annual growth rate of 160 percent over the next four years. Mr. Warner and his research director, therefore, felt that these MOS memories would be the semiconductor growth market of the '70s. MOStronics had been researching RAM components for three years and were as far down the learning curve as anyone, according to Mr. Warner. The learning curve represents the phenomenon of an item's manufacturing cost decreasing in a regular way as the number of items produced increased.[6] Moreover, since RAM chips were based on MOS and CMOS components, MOStronics could profit from shared production experience. This is to say that when a product is made from a number of components, the experience already gained in the production of those components helps bring down the cost of the product.

MOStronics had quickly gained a strong reputation as a RAM component maker, and RAM sales had increased to almost $8 million in

---

[5] Many large manufacturers utilized two or more sources for components to minimize risk if one supplier could not complete a contract. A large supply contract might, for example, be divided 60–40 between first and second sources.

[6] See the text of Chapter 3 for a discussion on the learning curve and shared production experience.

1974. However, RAM production had not been trouble-free. Start-up costs on the RAM line had greatly exceeded revenues and production growth had been slowed to try to resolve some persistent manufacturing problems. Additionally, there had been some industry concern that RAM components would undergo the same type of price cutting as had calculators. For one thing, RAM components would soon be mass-produced by the same large companies which produce calculator semiconductor components. For another, even before most producers had marketable RAM components, announced prices had plummeted from an initial $30 per unit to $11 [Texas Instruments (TI) latest preproduction price estimate].

Calculator production had accounted for the bulk of MOStronics manufacturing activities in 1974. Two-thirds of MOStronics' production space had been devoted to the production of ICs and LEDs for calculators and to the assembly of the machines. MOStronics had attempted to achieve economies as quickly as possible in both component and calculator production: Carroll Bennett, MOStronics production manager, insisted that only high-volume-potential, standard products be accepted for production. To reduce costs he had hired two of the industry's best production engineers and their combined efforts had begun to visibly affect costs in mid-1972. Generally, MOStronics had been able to reduce production costs continuously since then.

MOStronics had recently expanded its facilities to 188,000 square feet of space. In early 1973, with both its California plants operating near capacity, MOStronics had found itself losing potential sales of the high-margin RAM and digital logic MOS chips. In an attempt to expand both component and calculator production, Mr. Warner had proposed to Electro the addition of a 40,000 square foot assembly plant in California and an 80,000 square foot plant in Taiwan. After considerable foot-dragging, approval for the construction of these plants had been granted in December 1973. Production had commenced at both plants in July 1974. MOStronics had allocated 25 percent of the California addition to the production of RAM components.

With the company's focus on calculator production, deliveries of noncalculator components had been deliberately stretched as far as customers would accept without contract cancellation. While this situation had not pleased MOStronics' customers, no contracts had yet been cancelled as growing shortages of semiconductor components throughout the industry had made extended deliveries more common.

MOStronics' calculators were sold mainly to a small number of mass merchandisers under private label arrangements. A "house brand" line was also being sold through several manufacturers' representatives who distributed the machines to small retail electronics outlets and to other retailers as promotional items. Mr. Warner and Mr. Bennett had handled all of MOStronics' calculator marketing, a task which consumed relatively little time once major contracts had been signed. Mr. Warner closely monitored cash flow and contribution to profits of each product line (see Exhibit 3) and held monthly meetings to review the cash generating abilities of the various lines.

THE CALCULATOR MARKET

A major technological advance in the electronics industry—the development of integrated circuits—had set the stage for the introduction of electronic calculators in the early '60s. Using American ICs, the Japanese had introduced the first electronic desk-top calculators in 1966. Several firms, such as Sharp, Canon, Casio, and Busicom, had invaded the U.S. business calculator market and caught the entrenched U.S. manufacturers of electro-mechanical machines like SCM, Victor Comptometer, Friden and Monroe completely by surprise. By 1971 Japanese producers had cornered 85 percent of the U.S. market for larger electronic calculators.

A secondary technological advance—the development of Large Scale Integrated circuits (LSIs)—allowed the production of small hand-held calculators. LSIs utilized metal oxide semiconductor (MOS) technology to achieve both the compactness and low-power requirements of small machines.

Most personal calculators provided four or five functions (four arithmetic functions and percentage) with a floating decimal point and an eight-digit display. More expensive models contained a memory while the least expensive types had only four functions, a six-digit display and a fixed decimal point. "Scientific" machines, containing up to 15 engineering and mathematical functions and 12-digit displays, along with the Hewlett-Packard business calculators, formed the upper segment of the calculator market.

The earliest hand-held calculators had retailed for $400, but in 1971 the Bowmar Instrument Corp. had introduced mass-produced pocket calculators in the U.S. with a four-function machine selling for $240. By late summer 1971, three other producers—Rapid Data Systems & Equipment, Ltd., of Toronto, Texas Instruments, and Commodore Business Machines, Inc.—had followed Bowmar's lead and introduced competing machines. Subsequently many other firms had entered the business, but Bowmar had held its dominant market position through 1972. In 1973 Bowmar had been overtaken by Texas

Instruments as the leading marketer of calculators, though Bowmar still held second place as of early 1975.[7] Although TI in 1974 commanded 41 percent of the U.S. market, Mr. Warner felt that due to antitrust implications, TI would be unlikely to attempt to increase its share significantly in the future.

The growth in the personal calculator market had been very rapid. Total industry sales had gone from zero in 1970 to 12 million units in 1974 in the U.S. and Canada, and 25 million units worldwide. In three short years calculators had become a billion-dollar market despite continuous and intense price competition. The growth in industry sales was expected to continue through 1978 at an annual rate of 25 percent to 30 percent. Eventual saturation of the world market had been projected at 160 million units which, with a four- to five-year replacement cycle, would generate an annual replacement market of 40 million units. Industry data on personal calculator sales has been provided in Exhibit 4.

THE MARKET EXPERIENCE CURVE

Two phenomena characterized the personal calculator market: continual price erosion as manufacturers worked their way down the experience curve and rapid obsolescence due to the introduction of new models.

Calculator prices began their downward trend with Rapid Data's "under $100" unit in mid-1972. TI's entry into the market with its TI-2500 at $149 retail, $30 less than a competitive Bowmar model, gave greater impetus to the price decline as Bowmar responded with an equivalent cut. TI thereupon dropped its price another $30. Similar competitive behavior over the subsequent two years resulted in a late 1974 price of $44.95 for the TI-2500, a price which Bowmar continued to match in equivalent models. Prices had fallen 12 percent to 30 percent on some models between June and September of 1974 alone.

Retail margins, once in excess of 50 percent of the retail price, had declined substantially as mass merchandisers came to dominate

---

[7]Bowmar's unaudited preliminary report for the year ending September 30, 1974, had shown a loss of $13 million (after tax) on sales of $83 million; there had been some industry speculation that Bowmar would be forced into bankruptcy by the end of 1974. Bowmar had filed a $240 million suit against Texas Instruments, charging TI with "deceitful misrepresentation, conversion of trade secrets and fraudulent patent practices" and claiming that TI was given certain chip manufacturing information on the understanding that TI would not become a competitor. Texas Instruments' 41 percent share of the U.S. market (virtually all of TI's calculator production was marketed in the U.S.) was attacked by Bowmar as allegedly resulting from discriminatory pricing practices and a monopoly position in the market in violation of antitrust laws.

calculator retailing. Although large quantity discounts from manufacturers rarely exceeded 3 percent for lots of 10,000 machines, many large discounters were able to sell popular minicalculator models profitably at margins as low as 15 percent to 20 percent. Smaller retail outlets and wholesalers, requiring margins in the range of 25 percent to 35 percent to survive, were finding calculator sales only marginally profitable as manufacturers' discounts decreased to the 30 percent range.

New models were being introduced almost monthly, often accompanied by a new, lower price. Dealers, protected against price changes for only 30 days in most cases, became increasingly reluctant to hold more than a 30-day inventory in the face of short model lives and frequent price decreases. Inventory management had become especially difficult as a seasonal buying pattern developed during 1974. One New England dealer estimated that at least 60 percent of his calculator sales occurred in the Christmas, back-to-school, and tax-time seasons.

In the earliest electronic calculators, selling for about $400, the semiconductor components had cost about $170. In 1974, the same functions were performed by an LSI chip costing $3.50. Assembly time for simpler machines was only a few minutes while even the most complex minicalculators could be assembled in less than a half-hour. Labor and manufacturing overhead had been driven down so far in fact that semiconductor components—the chips and display—now represented 70 percent to 80 percent of unit cost in a typical machine. *Business Week* had recently quoted Robert F. Wickham of Creative Strategies Inc., Palo Alto, California, a market research organization, as saying that an integrated manufacturer with a volume output could save up to $1 on the $3 IC chip in each calculator, a significant saving on a $30 calculator which wholesaled for $15.

Texas Instruments, the market leader among some 50 or more calculator makers in 1974 with an estimated $225 million in calculator sales, relied upon experience curve pricing as its main marketing strategy under a sharply focused corporate objective of becoming the dominant producer in each product field it entered. In its April 18, 1973, report to stockholders, TI outlined four elements of this strategy: aggressive pricing[8] to follow experience curve reductions in cost (25 percent to 30 percent for each doubling of accumulated production); continuing efforts to improve products and reduce costs; building on shared experience; and keeping capacity growing ahead of demand. Targets were high-growth markets which would allow both rapid increases in cumulated volume and increases in market share which did not seri-

---

[8]TI generally set its factory selling price at two times its manufacturing cost per unit.

ously affect competitors' growth. A large New England calculator dealer claimed that TI had several times reduced retail prices on machines that had been ordered long before but had not yet been shipped from the factory. He understood that TI's price changes were made from a predetermined schedule on the basis of a cost curve and accumulated production volume without reference to current market conditions, excess demand or competitive conditions.

Since early 1973, an estimated 25 to 30 North American and Japanese producers had dropped out of the minicalculator business. Of the remaining firms, less than a dozen had been expected to survive through the end of 1975. Many firms were actively considering in-house IC production, if they did not already have it, as product reliability and manufacturing costs had become increasingly dependent on IC technology. Bowmar, for example, had completed a $7 million semiconductor facility in Arizona late in 1974 and several other firms appeared likely to follow in 1975. However, not all felt this was the proper course. Jack Tramiel, President of Commodore Business Machines (Canada) Ltd., had decided not to produce ICs in-house, reportedly noting that the ability to move in and out of a technology easily was to him worth more than the $1 saving on a chip. An additional problem in entering semiconductor production had been an over-capacity situation in the semiconductor industry, which had become apparent in 1974, and which increased the probability of plunging semiconductor prices in 1975.

RELATIONS WITH ELECTRO

Through mid-1973, Electro had remained a virtual observer of MOStronics. Electro required only that MOStronics send it monthly income and cash flow statements, monthly balance sheets, and quarterly operating budgets. Electro had agreed in the beginning to finance fixed assets and MOStronics had been obliged to finance all of its working capital needs internally, with the exception of a $2 million cash infusion made by Electro at the time of purchase. This arrangement had provided MOStronics with greater financial leverage than it could have obtained as an independent firm, and Mr. Warner had been quite satisfied with it since MOStronics' most urgent early needs had been for equipment. (Electro had agreed to provide needed expansion capital in the form of long-term debt, privately placed and guaranteed by Electro, up to a limit of two times net worth.)

In 1973, however, Electro management had begun to wonder whether Mr. Warner's attempt to gain a large share of the personal calculator market was the best course for MOStronics. When Mr. Warner had come to Electro in July with his request for the additional 120,000 square feet of production space at a total cost of $5.3 million, Electro's corporate planning department had decided to conduct a detailed study of the calculator market and of the asset structures of competing producers. Electro's reasoning had been that a number of economists and members of the financial community had been predicting a deepening recession through 1974 and 1975, and Electro didn't want MOStronics to be overextended, thereby placing Electro in a position which it had managed to avoid in the 1970–1971 period. Moreover, losses being experienced by some of Electro's other divisions had strained Electro's financial resources.

With the demand for calculators increasing rapidly, Mr. Warner had been forced to move quickly to mitigate problems caused by the unexpected delay in approval of the proposed production facilities by subcontracting calculator assembly to a plant in Singapore. This had allowed the California plants to continue MOS chip production for both calculators and other products. In December 1973, Electro had finally approved the construction of the new California and Taiwan plants. Both had come on-stream in July 1974 but plant costs had escalated to $8.5 million as a consequence of inflation and the crash construction program.

FINANCIAL STRAINS

By September 1974 MOStronics' financial strains had become acute. The company's long-term debt capacity was near maximum and credit lines had been fully extended. Working capital needs associated with the rapid expansion of production continued to increase, and there had been a price for the immediate commencement of high volume production at the new plants: MOS chip yields, always unpredictable, had fallen sharply in August, for reasons which could not immediately be explained, and they had not moved back into the acceptable range of 50 percent to 60 percent until late in October.

In early November, Mr. Warner had been obliged to transfer ownership of MOStronics' new Taiwan assembly plant to Electro on a sale and leaseback arrangement in order to remain solvent through the year. Electro had agreed to the deal as a temporary relief measure, reluctantly admitting its contribution to the cost overrun and MOStronics' current cash bind.

In a few days Mr. Warner had to make a final decision on how to deal with MOStronics' current profit problems. He believed strongly that MOStronics could reduce costs and remain competitive in the calculator industry, a position he supported with a learning curve analysis shown in Exhibit 5. On the other hand, a well-known consultant, to whom he had sent this analysis for an opinion, had recommended a quick withdrawal from the calculator market (Exhibit 6). Electro's vice president for corporate planning was also strongly in favor of dropping calculators. He had based his opinion on an extensive report conducted by his office, which he had summarized for Mr. Warner (Exhibit 7).

Mr. Warner planned to carefully and objectively review all of the arguments concerning calculator production. Although he felt confident of MOStronics' ability to compete successfully against other integrated producers, he knew that convincing the Electro Executive Committee would not be an easy task.

Exhibit 1
ELECTRO INDUSTRIES, INC. [A]
MOStronics Division
Balance Sheet Summary
[dollar amounts in thousands]

	DEC. 31 1971	DEC. 31 1972	DEC. 31 1973	DEC. 31 1974**
ASSETS				
Current Assets:				
Cash and Equivalents	$ 96	$ 446	$ 4,372	$ 1,274
Accounts Receivable	1,408	2,934	5,774	9,038
Inventories:				
Material	256	612	2,344	3,342
Work-in-process	864	2,102	2,844	5,182
Finished Goods	12	76	996	2,696
Prepaid Expenses	148	242	368	472
Total Current Assets	$2,784	$6,412	$16,698	$22,004
Plant, Property, and Equipment:				
Land and Buildings	44	182	380	3,034
Machinery, Tools, and Equipment	1,082	2,172	4,176	10,456
Leasehold Improvements	120	330	550	992
Less: Accumulated Depreciation	(456)	(526)	(836)	(1,342)
Net Fixed Assets	790	2,158	4,270	13,140
Total Assets	$3,574	$8,570	$20,968	$35,144
LIABILITIES				
Current Liabilities:				
Accounts Payable	$2,286	$3,634	$ 4,722	$11,944
Accruals	410	690	1,420	2,462
Notes Payable*	500	984	856	5,702
Total Current Liabilities	$3,196	$5,308	$ 6,998	$20,108
Long-term Debt, Noncurrent	—	—	4,766	7,756
Net Worth:				
Common Stock	2,460	2,460	2,460	2,460
Retained Earnings	(2,082)	802	6,744	4,820
Total Net Worth	$ 378	$3,262	$ 9,204	$ 7,280
Total Liabilities	$3,574	$8,570	$20,968	$35,144

*Includes current installments on long-term debt.

**Unaudited.

Exhibit 2

ELECTRO INDUSTRIES, INC. [A]

MOStronics Division
Income Statement Summary
[dollar amounts in thousands]

| | YEAR ENDING DECEMBER 31 | | | |
	1971*	1972	1973	1974**
Net Sales	$7,024	$11,478	$22,824	$43,166
Cost of Goods Sold:				
Materials	4,318	4,584	8,710	25,348
Direct Labor	1,602	1,748	1,722	12,658
Overhead	632	712	1,036	2,696
Total	$6,552	$7,044	$11,468	$40,702
Gross Profit	472	4,434	11,356	2,464
Interest Expense	56	106	616	1,456
Total S&GA Expense	1,130	1,286	1,844	2,932
Net Profit before Taxes	$ (714)	$ 3,042	$ 8,896	$(1,924)
Income Tax	—	158	2,954	—
Net Profit after Taxes	$ (714)	$ 2,884	$ 5,942	$(1,924)

*MOStronics was acquired by Electro Industries, Inc., on November 30, 1971.
**Unaudited.

Exhibit 3
ELECTRO INDUSTRIES, INC. [A]

MOStronics Division
Sales and Contribution by Product Line

MOStronics' Sales By Product
[millions of dollars]

PRODUCT GROUP	1971	1972	1973	1974
Digital Logic:				
Standard Products	1.2	0.8	1.2	3.4
Custom Products	5.4	1.2	1.8	8.4
Semiconductor Memory (RAM)	0.4	1.0	1.4	7.6
Calculators	—	8.4	18.4	23.7
Total Sales	7.0	11.4	22.8	43.1

Contributions to Gross Profit of Each Product Group
[thousands of dollars]

PRODUCT GROUP	1973	1974
Digital Logic:		
Standard Products	525	700
Custom Products	1,042	4,940
Semiconductor Memory (RAM)	(640)	1,184
Calculators	10,429	(4,360)
Gross Profit	11,356	2,464

Exhibit 4
ELECTRO INDUSTRIES, INC. [A]
Industry Data
Personal Calculator Sales

	CORPORATE TOTAL SALES [$ MILLIONS]	WORLDWIDE CALCULATOR SALES [THOUSANDS OF UNITS]	
REPRESENTATIVE PRODUCERS	*1973*	*1973*	*ESTIMATED 1974 (RANGE)*
Semiconductor Manufacturers:			
Texas Instruments	1,290	2,000	4,500–5,000
Rockwell International	3,179	820	1,500–1,700
Electro (MOStronics)	850	264	810 (actual)
National Semiconductor	99	160	800–1,500
Mostek	42	100	300– 500
Assemblers:			
Bowmar Instrument	65	1,200	1,800–2,200
Commodore Business Machines	33	950	1,200–1,300
Litronix	27	180	800–1,000
Summit International	n.a.	400	600– 700
APF	12	200	400– 600
Hewlett-Packard	661	250	330– 350

Source: Business Week, August 24, 1974, p. 34.

Personal Calculator Prices [Factory Price]

TYPE	SEPT. 1971	SEPT. 1972	SEPT. 1973	SEPT. 1974
Six-Digit, 4 Function	$240	$100	$40	$20
Eight-Digit, 4 & 5 Function	400	150–225	80–150	40– 60
Twelve-Digit Scientific	—	400	120–500	70–745

Source: Ralph Stoddard, President of General Business Machines, Inc., Boston, Massachusetts.

Personal Calculator Market Estimates

	UNIT SALES		FACTORY DOLLAR SALES	
	U.S. [MILLIONS]	WORLDWIDE [MILLIONS]	U.S. [MILLIONS]	WORLDWIDE [MILLIONS]
1971	0.5	n.a.	n.a.	n.a.
1972	2.5	n.a.	$150	n.a.
1973	7.0	6.5–7.5	420	n.a.
1974	12.0	25.0	500	$1,500
1978	20.0	40.0	n.a.	n.a.

Source: Various industry publications.
(n.a. = not available)

Exhibit 5
ELECTRO INDUSTRIES, INC. [A]

MOStronics Division

Mr. Warner's Statement of His Preferred Strategy and Outline of Supporting Analysis

My basic position is this: MOStronics' present difficulties have arisen in my opinion solely from our reluctance to market aggressively and build volume as TI and Bowmar have done. Bowmar, which has only recently begun to gain CMOS expertise and to produce its own ICs, has grown in sales from $13 million in 1971 to around $90 million in 1974 and has been very profitable in doing so (until the last few months, at least). Our technological advantage is being completely offset by Bowmar's superior marketing effort.

The industry's current, general lack of profitability is due more to a short-term flattening of sales growth and to inventory write-downs than to any long-range weakness in the consumer calculator market. This will shake out many marginal assemblers but it should not give a financially well-supported firm like MOStronics more than temporary profit problems.

I strongly favor remaining in the calculator business over the long haul. We have a good, if somewhat limited, position in the market, one which we gained as the result of an enormous effort and a superior product. Building volume through aggressive marketing—lots of advertising, competitive pricing, nationwide distribution, and special pricing deals for very large orders—will eventually put MOStronics into the cost range of the majors. They are highly profitable now and we will be too—but only if we make the necessary commitment. It must be large and it must be made immediately.

To be specific, I make the following proposal. First, we must upgrade our product line slightly so that we no longer compete in the ruinous, $20–$50 (retail) low-priced segment but in the higher-margin middle range ($50–$100). With only minor changes, mostly of a styling nature, we can become directly competitive with TI's 2500, 3500, 2550, and 4000 models now retailing at between $49 and $79. Our present line, which is technically competitive with these TI models, has been retailing recently at about $30 to $40, requiring a factory price of as low as $18. This has been a major contributor to our present losses in calculator products.

Until our volume moves into the $75 million range, we must become a follower rather than a leader in new product develop-

Exhibit 5 [cont.]
ELECTRO INDUSTRIES, INC. [A]

ment. Our entire engineering effort should be directed toward better component yields, increased production automation and fewer parts per unit. We must begin national brand advertising and distribution. I favor depending partly upon advertising done by large retailers and partly upon a substantial advertising budget—perhaps $5 million in 1975. And finally, I propose that we offer very attractive pricing on orders of 10,000 units or more to broaden our distribution among the country's mass merchandisers. I estimate the cash cost of this proposal to be $7 million beyond our internal cash generation capability for next year, an amount that seems feasible if Electro will provide assistance in enlarging our bank lines of credit from $5 to $12 million.

I will outline the analysis on which this proposal is based. The $50–$80 market segment, dominated by TI and Bowmar, is growing at about 20 percent a year now, considerably slower than the low-priced segment. With a concerted effort to gain market share, I am confident that we can double our unit sales in 1975 without difficulty. At our current learning rate (74 percent), our costs are declining faster *with time* than are those of competitors like TI, whose total production is now so large that at least two years will be needed to achieve a production doubling (against our one year). Consequently, we can catch up to prices in the middle segment rather quickly if momentum is not lost. Calculators should begin making a positive contribution to profits within six to eight months. We cannot do this in the low end where many smaller producers will be growing at rates comparable to our own.

The chart below illustrates this reasoning. In Figure 1, our costs have been plotted together with a weighted-average price line for our present product line. Costs have followed a 74 percent experience curve (except in 1974 when our "learning" was delayed by plant start-up problems) indicating that we have been able to reduce costs as effectively as anyone else in the industry. We should be able to continue this rate of reduction indefinitely. Prices have been plotted each time we reduced price in response to competitive pressures. A rough curve through these price points shows prices falling much faster than our costs, a consequence of the fact that the market leaders have been growing much faster than MOStronics in unit volume. This allows them to reduce prices faster than we can and still maintain acceptable profit margins. When their growth rate slows to match MOStronics', prices should decline roughly parallel to our costs—that is,

Exhibit 5 (cont.)
ELECTRO INDUSTRIES, INC. [A]

at the 70 percent–75 percent experience-based rate. By then, however, prices will be substantially below MOStronics' costs and, unless we can reverse the process and grow faster than the dominant producers, MOStronics' costs will never drop below prices in the low-priced market segment.

On the chart I have included a weighted average price line for medium-priced calculators in Figure 2, which I derived from industry prices and our prices (if we upgrade) projected for the future. Our average costs remain pretty much as before since the product line upgrading can be accomplished at an insignificant cost. But, as our growth rate increases beyond the growth rates of TI and Bowmar, price lines in the medium-priced segment will flatten when plotted against our production base. The margin increase I anticipate shows up clearly here. While we may never achieve the profit margins of TI, we should be able to reach a satisfactory contribution level within a year or so in this segment.

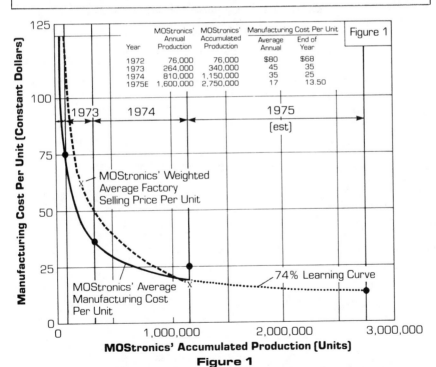

Year	MOStronics' Annual Production	MOStronics' Accumulated Production	Manufacturing Cost Per Unit Average Annual	Manufacturing Cost Per Unit End of Year
1972	76,000	76,000	$80	$68
1973	264,000	340,000	45	35
1974	810,000	1,150,000	35	25
1975E	1,600,000	2,750,000	17	13.50

Figure 1

Plot of MOStronics' Manufacturing Costs vs. Accumulated Production

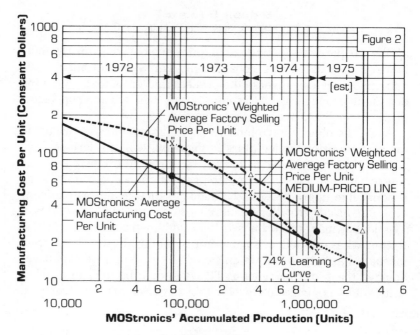

Figure 2

Same Plot as Above on Log-Log Paper

Exhibit 6

ELECTRO INDUSTRIES, INC. [A]

MOStronics Division

Report from the Consultant to Mr. Warner

In a letter to Mr. Warner, the consultant recommended withdrawal from the calculator market. A summarization of his letter is reproduced below:

Mr. David Warner
President
MOStronics Division
Electro Industries, Inc.
12752 El Monte Avenue
Mountain View, California 94040

Dear Mr. Warner:

I am delighted you thought of asking our assistance in your strategy problem. As I promised, I will give you the best advice I can, given the information available. It is always risky to venture an opinion on such short notice with so little information. Given your understanding of that caveat, however, I will be what help I can.

As you have described your situation to me, you are currently devoting most of MOStronics' resources to the manufacture and marketing of hand-held calculators. The competition has increased to the point where you are now incurring substantial losses in that business. I recommend that you withdraw from the calculator business. Let me explain my position.

The battle for market position in the calculator business is effectively over. Texas Instruments clearly commands the market. Despite the remaining high growth in demand, MOStronics will not catch up to Texas Instruments. You will therefore never achieve a cost position allowing reasonable profits in the business.

Your 1974 U.S. market share appears to be about 5 percent. This is not only small absolutely, but also relative to Texas Instruments' market share of approximately 40 percent. If the 74 percent experience curve used in your analysis prevails among competitors as well as over time, this ten times relative market share for TI translates into costs of about $9.50 per unit—only a third of your costs of $28 a unit in 1974! Even if there is a great deal of

Exhibit 6 (cont.)
ELECTRO INDUSTRIES, INC. [A]

shared experience in the industry, an 85 percent curve still gives TI costs of about $16 a unit. Given these cost figures and the highly competitive environment of this market, it is not surprising that prices have declined below your costs.

You recognize in your analysis that achieving overall parity with TI is too great a task. Considering the lack of aggressive support on the part of your parent organization as you described in your note, this is especially true. I do not think, however, your proposed strategy to focus on only the high-priced segment has a much greater chance of success. It depends on two important assumptions with which I must take issue.

First, you assume this segment is so unique in its characteristics that it has its own price curve. With this assumption you translate the lower growth rate in the high-price segment into less price attrition over time. Second, you assume you will continue down your historic cost curve despite the change in your product mix. The two assumptions are mutually exclusive.

There is probably a great deal of common costs and therefore shared experience between models. This is especially true of displays, key boards, batteries, and cases. For the integrated circuits themselves, it is probably also true between calculator chips and other MOS devices, and perhaps between MOS and bipolar as well. This supports your assumption that you will continue down your historic cost slope—adjusted slightly upward for the added cost of the added features you plan to offer in your new mix.

Unfortunately, this will also be true of the competition—especially TI and Bowmar who hold particularly commanding positions in the higher price/higher feature end of the market. Therefore, their relative cost advantage vis-à-vis MOStronics will remain unchanged. To the extent that a price umbrella exists in the high end of the market, continued competition in the low end will force others to seek refuge in the high-priced end of the market. This in turn will force continued erosion of prices in these models and/or continued introduction of higher featured models (with added costs accordingly) at the current price levels.

All this argues that market prices will remain below MOStronics' cost regardless of mix unless your basic market position is improved. I doubt this can be improved. Therefore, I think the battle is lost. You should abandon the business as rapidly as possible to cut your losses.

Exhibit 6 (cont.)
ELECTRO INDUSTRIES, INC. [A]

   This recommendation is made with all the caveats mentioned in the opening paragraph of this letter. There is much to be resolved before one could be confident he had made the right choice. This is particularly true regarding the uniqueness of the businesses and segments, the degree of shared experience between businesses, and the proper experience bases for each. All this will affect the forecast of future costs and prices.

   There may be more strategy options available to MOStronics than the ones you are presently considering. Perhaps most importantly, the competitors' strategies and probable reactions to moves by MOStronics are really undefined. Right now you are in the best position to address each of these remaining questions. My associates and I are presently investigating a number of businesses which MOStronics could profitably exploit. When I call you next week for your reaction to my letter, I will let you know the results of the investigation. In the meantime, if I can be of any further help, do not hesitate to give me a call.

   Sincerely,

Exhibit 7
ELECTRO INDUSTRIES, INC. [A]
MOStronics Division

Report Summary from Electro Industries' Corporate
Planning Group to Mr. Warner

Electro Industries' Vice President of Corporate Planning recommended a retrenchment into CMOS integrated circuit production in order to minimize risk and to align the division more closely with corporate objectives calling for more fully integrated production. Several points were made in his argument for this approach:

1. Another shakeout similar to that of 1970, which may turn out to be even more severe and of longer duration, has begun. Semiconductor markets have softened substantially since mid-year and layoffs and plant closings have been announced by nearly everyone in the industry. MOStronics represents Electro Industries' sole internal source of MOS and CMOS technology and production. As you will recall, this was our primary reason for acquiring your firm. Under these circumstances, it seems prudent to focus the division's entire effort on maintaining, or even improving, its position in MOS production. I feel strongly that attempting to survive this recessionary period in *both* calculators and semiconductors entails extreme risk.

2. We suggest that the calculator game is lost. Prices set by the dominant producers are now below your average cost and there is no indication that prices will stabilize any time within the next two to three years. Losses which you would incur in order to remain in the business until prices stabilize seem unwarranted, particularly in view of Electro's present financial constraints. More important, these losses will grow exponentially with time since continued sales growth at the market rate of 20 percent to 30 percent, or more, will be needed to establish MOStronics ultimately as one of the industry's major calculator producers. You should cut your losses quickly while they are still relatively small and concentrate on an area where your costs now are fully competitive.

3. So far as we can determine, MOStronics' competitive position as a MOS producer seems very strong both technologically and from a unit cost standpoint. The division's high margins on

Exhibit 7 [cont.]
ELECTRO INDUSTRIES, INC. [A]

MOS and CMOS component sales supports this finding. A very rough analysis of MOStronics' position in MOS semiconductor production indicates that, while you are now competitive with other major producers, an enormous commitment will be required to retain your share of market over the next five years. There would appear to be no realistic means of supporting both the calculator growth and the MOS component growth. A choice must be made at this point.

4. Of particularly great interest to Electro from a longer-range viewpoint is the encouraging progress you have been making on RAM (random-access-memory) circuits and contracts. As we have discussed many times, RAM promises to do for small-scale computing applications what LSI technology did for calculators. It should ultimately make obsolete the ferrite core memory and open vast new markets for computers whose largest cost right now is in the memory. The opportunity here for MOStronics is tremendous since this market is still in its infancy and your market position, costs, and experience are on a par with the leading producers.

5. MOS memory sales have a forecast growth rate of about 30 percent a year (compounded). In order to stay even with industry growth, MOStronics' sales in MOS components must double, or better, in the next three years. More to the point, your sales must grow at the same *rate* as sales of the major producers if you are to keep up with their cost decreases. This probably means sales increases in the range of 50 percent to 150 percent —clearly a formidable task but one which seems achievable if the division's attention is not diverted by end product manufacture.

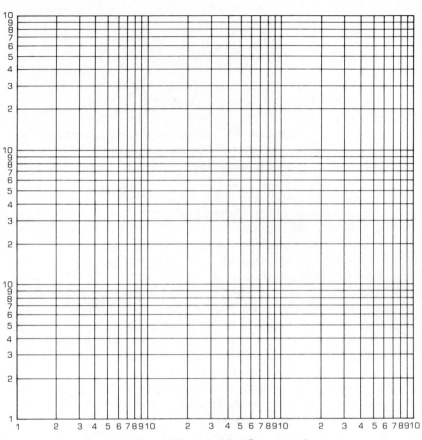

Log-Log Paper Provided for Computations

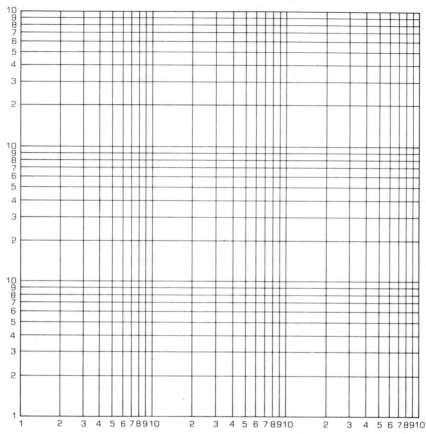

Log-Log Paper Provided for Computations

DISCUSSION QUESTIONS

ELECTRO INDUSTRIES, INC. [A]

1. What is the present situation at the MOStronics Division? Why has it occurred?

2. What do you think of Mr. Warner's proposed strategy? The consultant's? The corporate planning department's? Which do you favor? Do you have one of your own that you prefer? Why?

3. In particular, what do you recommend that the division do about its calculator line? (Do a thorough analysis to support your recommendation).

4. How would you implement your chosen strategy? (For example, if you plan to expand to challenge TI, how will you do it? If you plan to withdraw, how?)

ELECTRO INDUSTRIES, INC. (B)[1]

In mid-January 1975, Mr. Warner, President of the MOStronics division of Electro Industries, Inc., was examining the status report on the division's year-old development and testing program for digital watches. It was clear from the report that MOStronics could introduce a digital watch into the market as early as mid-1975. Mr. Warner was, therefore, giving serious consideration to the idea of moving quickly into high-volume production of digital watches. Such a step, of course, would mean getting out of calculators [see Electro Industries, Inc. (A) for background on this]. A few days later, the consultant who had advised Mr. Warner to abandon the calculator market, called with a strong recommendation to enter the digital watch market. The consultant's advice reinforced Mr. Warner's own arguments to pursue such a strategy.

Besides appealing to his entrepreneurial instincts, this strategy provided an opportunity to exploit MOStronics' semiconductor production know-how at a very early stage in the digital watch product growth cycle. He felt that MOStronics was on a relatively even footing with competing watch producers and that it would be able to maintain its cost position as the market grew. Mr. Warner knew that entering the digital watch market was a risky proposition and felt he needed more information on the market and the manufacturing techniques before he could make the final decision.

THE ELECTRONIC DIGITAL WATCH

The electronic digital watch was made up of five main components: a quartz crystal; an integrated circuit; a digital time display; a silver oxide battery cell; and a watch case. (See Exhibit 1 for a typical watch layout and production cost estimates.) The quartz crystal, stimulated by the battery, oscillated at more than 32,000 times per second. These impulses were then fed into the integrated circuit which converted the vibration into seconds, minutes, and hours.

---

[1]This case was prepared by Gerald B. Allan in collaboration with John S. Hammond.

Despite the relatively large variety of digital watches being offered, consumer acceptance seemed to be lagging as a consequence of both product difficulties and recessionary conditions present in late 1974. Styling was an especially difficult problem for the watchmakers: In a market where thinness was associated with high quality and fine craftsmanship, the digitals suffered from inherent bulkiness and high weight. Receiving major attention still was reduction in size of components—a problem that, until very recently, had prevented introduction of women's models.

Time displays were another serious concern. The display devices were currently of two types, light emitting diode displays (LED) and liquid crystal displays (LCD). The difference between the two was that LCDs reflected light whereas LEDs emitted their own light. The LEDs were more common and had the advantages of being readable in the dark and aesthetically attractive. On the other hand, they were hard to read in direct sunlight and had to be activated by pushing a button. LCDs could rarely be read in poor light but had a continuous time display. Time setting on digital watches was a laborious process for both types of displays. Reliability problems had been reported by a number of users.

THE DIGITAL WATCH MARKET

Unlike the personal electronic calculator market, which created an entirely new market, the digital watch was a novel innovation in an old and established watch market. Worldwide watch sales, which had grown steadily at 6 percent to 10 percent annually for over 20 years, were expected to increase from 205 million units ($4 billion at retail) in 1974 to 290 million units ($6 billion at retail) in 1980. Watches priced under $50, the likely range of mass-produced digital watches, accounted for 90 percent of the units sold.

Digital watch sales estimates for 1974 varied over an extremely wide range. *Electronics* estimated sales as low as 150,000 units and *Business Week* as high as 1.2 million units. A Wall Street research firm had come up with an estimate of 700,000 watches sold in 1974 at an average retail price of $140.

The future for digital watches seemed particularly bright in 1974 even though the economic outlook was gloomy and uncertain due to the worldwide recession and inflation. Though future estimates of sales varied considerably, one reputable industry research firm estimated digital watch sales would reach 53.0 million units in 1980 with an average retail price of $40. Table 1 below shows its estimate of worldwide unit watch sales through 1980.

Table 1
FORECAST FOR DIGITAL WATCH SALES
BY INDUSTRY RESEARCH FIRM

ESTIMATED WATCH SALES	1974	1975	1976	1980
Worldwide (million)	205	220	230	290
Digital (million)	0.7	2.5	4.5	53.0
Digitals as % of Total	0.3%	1.1%	2.0%	18.3%

It was clear from the market figures that digital watches were now just scratching the surface of the watch market. Since the growth of watch sales was approximately 6 percent, the explosive growth of digital watches would be at the expense of the mechanical watches. This would significantly benefit the U.S. since it was the leader in semiconductor technology, the heart of the digital watch. In 1974, the U.S. accounted for less than 12 percent of worldwide watch production in comparison to 41 percent for Switzerland. However, if digital watches became popular, this relationship could substantially change. (See Exhibit 2 for information on the world watch industry and Exhibit 3 for data on world production and export of watches.)

John Bergey, President of Pulsar Time Computer Inc., was among those who expected the digital watch to revolutionize the marketing and distribution of watches. Servicing, for example, was expected to move from the jeweler to electronics outlets, and the solid-state watches' inherent ruggedness would tend to eliminate the $25 periodic cleaning required for most conventional watches. Although digital watches were presently sold in the high-priced end of the watch market, distribution markups of 100 percent at each stage of distribution did not appear consistent with a mass-produced, mass-merchandised consumer product. Distribution seemed likely to split between traditional channels for the low volume, high-priced models (over $300), and the large retailers, discounters, and drugstores for the high volume, low-priced models.

The high semiconductor content of digital watches made domination by large semiconductor manufacturers very likely, especially in view of current developments in the calculator markets. *Electronics* reported that a digital watch entry from Texas Instruments was expected soon. National Semiconductor had already made its appearance with a $125 retail LED watch. National Semiconductor's Novus Division, for example, had recently completed distribution arrangements with 17 large jewelry outlets and 12 department store chains and had established a service center in Santa Clara, California, with plans for a second in the east in 1975.

Although the circuitry of the digital watch was similar to that of the electronic calculator (which could mean costs and prices dropping sharply as volume increased) there were a number of important differences. Since the electronic calculator had created an entirely new market, all the participants in that market had an equal chance at establishing brand identity. In the watch market, however, the traditional watchmakers had established lines of distribution, consumer identity, and were familiar with styling, service, and advertising which were particularly crucial in watch sales.

Digital watch prices were expected to drop to the mass market price of under $50 within two years. Many retailers and distributors, already scarred by the massive calculator price cuts, were fearing similar rapid price cuts in digital watches. Another important aspect that differentiated the digital watch market from the calculator field was styling. Unlike the calculator, which had become a utilitarian product after its novelty value wore off, the digital watch was a personal item. Even in the established watch business, low-end, mass market watches were made with stylistic considerations. Nevertheless, as with calculators, only firms fully integrated through distribution were expected to survive the eventual price erosion in the lower price (under $50) watch markets.

DIGITAL WATCH MANUFACTURERS

Digital watch manufacturers could be classified into five groups on the basis of their relative strengths in watch styling and marketing and in solid-state watch technology. At one extreme were the traditional watchmakers who were obliged to purchase the solid-state watch technology needed to complement their commanding positions in styling and distribution. At the other extreme were semiconductor manufacturers like Hughes Semiconductor, American Microsystems, Optel, RCA, and Texas Instruments, who were supplying watch assemblers and marketers with both components and watch assemblies. Reaching out from either extreme were watchmakers integrating backward into semiconductor production[2] and semiconductor producers integrating forward into end products having a high semiconductor content. The Novus Division of National Semiconductor was the first of this latter group to reach the market, introducing a line of six LED watches in the fall of 1974. Referred to as "hybrids," the fifth type of watch manufacturer was a fully integrated electronic watchmaking

---

[2]Bulova, together with three other nonconflicting manufacturers, had recently purchased controlling interest in Synertek, a new, smaller producer of CMOS integrated circuits.

organization, combining semiconductor production, watch assembly, and marketing in a single firm. Microma, a subsidiary of Intel, and Pulsar, a subsidiary of HMW Industries, Inc. (formerly the Hamilton Watch Company), were representative of the "hybrid" manufacturers. At this time, none of the five groups had yet gained a dominant position. Traditional watchmakers were weak technologically, semiconductor manufacturers lacked styling expertise (but were rapidly developing consumer marketing know-how as the result of calculator experience), and the hybrids were still relatively small and inexperienced.

Key to mass production of the digital watch was the efficient integration of chips, crystal, displays, and other components into a low-cost, compact watch package. Advances in technology were expected to decrease physical size and manufacturing complexity considerably and to reduce power requirements by a factor of 10, greatly extending battery life.

Apart from semiconductor and packaging technology developments, the other main technological battle centered on the time display itself. LEDs, introduced in 1969 by Monsanto, glow red when a current is passed through their semiconducting material. More costly versions emitted green and yellow light. Large quantity prices for LEDs in 1974 had moved into the range of $1.00 per digit, as compared to $1.50 to $3.00 early in 1973, and $2.50 to $4.00 in 1972. Chief producers of LED displays for calculators and watches were Fairchild's Discrete Products Division, Litronix, Inc., and Monsanto's Electronics Special Products Division. Offsetting the LEDs advantages of high-reliability, low-voltage requirements and a wide operating-temperature range was the relatively high-cost raw material and high power consumption (which prevented the watch display from being lit continuously).

LCDs, newer and unlike the LEDs, did not generate light but reflected room light when a voltage was applied to the crystal. This characteristic made them hard to read in dim light. However, several developments, such as the field-effect LCD in which dark digits appear against a white, lighted background, seemed capable of overcoming this deficiency to some extent. Although operating at a somewhat higher voltage than LEDs, the LCD consumed only 0.01 percent of the power, allowing LCD timepieces to display time continuously. LCDs still suffered in low temperatures, becoming inoperative below freezing, and from a limited (2-year) life. Producers of LCDs included Princeton Material Sciences Corp., Optel Corp., Microma (an Intel subsidiary), American Microsystems International, Rockwell International, Ilixco, Hughes' Microelectronics Division, and Motorola's Semiconductor Products Division.

A watch industry expert was quoted as predicting a 50:50 split between LCD and LED watches despite the significant cost difference.

LCD watches in 1973 could be made for about $40.00 while LED types cost upwards to $80.00. Until some new technological breakthrough in displays shifted the balance toward one type or another, the LCD appeared destined for low-priced watches while the LED seemed practical only in higher priced lines.

The Japanese—Seiko, Citizens, and Orient—all had LCD models either on sale or planned for introduction in late 1974. Seiko obtained its MOS watch circuits from a variety of sources—internal, other Japanese IC producers and American firms—while Citizen bought MOS chips from Mitsubishi Electric Corp. and Orient, from Sharp. Unlike the aggressive Japanese producers, the Swiss firms remained largely uncommitted by late 1974. *Electronics* reported only a single, Swiss-made entry to Nepro which utilized American circuitry and a Swiss, field-effect LCD display. Volume was estimated at a miniscule 5,000 units for 1975.

THE DECISION

The MOStronics' digital watch, styled by a leading Swiss watch designer, used extremely sophisticated and reliable circuitry and the latest liquid crystal display. It was designed to sell at $99.00 retail ($49.50 factory selling price).

Making an early entry into the digital watch business looked extremely attractive. It was a new business with potential for high growth and a fluid competitive situation. At present, MOStronics had a relative advantage in the manufacture of CMOS chips, thus establishing an equal footing with regard to the costs of the chips. Although Mr. Warner had no data to confirm this, it appeared that the cost curve for digital watches would be quite unique to that business. This meant that leadership in the digital watch field would result in lower costs relative to the competition, and therefore, higher returns. Since the business was so new, no competitor had an insuperable cost advantage, as was the case in calculators. Everyone's experience base was small and no firm had gained a dominant position. MOStronics' total lack of experience in digital watch assembly was, therefore, less important.

Mr. Warner was also aware that the digital watch market would become extremely competitive in the years to come. He would, therefore, require the prompt and continued support from Electro if his division was to be successful in this market. Otherwise it would be a repeat performance of the calculator problem.

During the next few days Mr. Warner would have to choose from three alternatives to return his division to profitability: prove he could reduce costs and remain competitive in the calculator industry, write off calculator production and return to the basic semiconductor component production, or abandon the calculator business and move quickly into high-volume production of electronic digital watches.

His decision, to be presented to Electro's executive committee on January 30, would not only influence MOStronics' fortune but also his own. Mr. Warner realized that he had to review each of the three alternatives thoroughly to make a decision on which he would be prepared to stake his fortune.

Exhibit 1
ELECTRO INDUSTRIES, INC. [B]
Manufacture of a Digital Watch

[A] INTERNAL LAYOUT OF A TYPICAL LCD DIGITAL WATCH

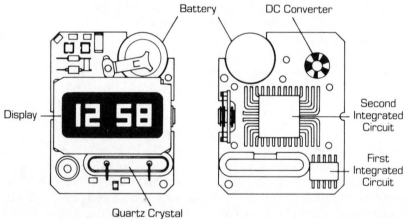

Source: American Express Company mail-order advertisement for its Quartz Segtronic timepiece.

[B] ESTIMATED MANUFACTURING COSTS

	1972	1975
Size of production run (units)	10,000	100,000
Quartz Crystal	$ 3.00	$ 1.50
Integrated Circuit	10.00	2.50
Digital Display (LCD)	3.00	1.00
Battery	0.80	0.50
Watch Case	4.00	2.00
Other Hardware	7.50	2.00
Labor	5.00	1.00
Total Manufacturing Cost	$33.30	$10.50
Probable Retail Price	$185–$250	$40–$50

Source: Business Week, April 22, 1972, p. 62.

Exhibit 2
ELECTRO INDUSTRIES, INC. [B]

A Note on the Watch Industry

Watch production in Western nations amounted to approximately 145 million units in 1970, representing about $1.1 billion in sales at factory prices and $3.2 billion at retail levels. Market growth had ranged between 7 percent and 11 percent per annum over the preceding decade and there was no strong evidence of saturation being approached.

THE SWISS

Traditionally dominant in the industry, the Swiss accounted for just over 50 percent of this production, split about evenly between the more expensive, jeweled-lever watch types and the inexpensive, pin-lever types. Industry concentration increased rapidly during the late 1960s and early 1970s in response to international competitive pressures: from a highly fragmented industry of some 2,000 watchmaking enterprises in 1960, three-quarters of the Swiss output in 1971 was accounted for by only eight producers. However, many problems still faced the larger firms as a result of this merger activity, among which were eliminating duplicate product lines, combining production facilities and streamlining management systems. As a further move to strengthen their position in the large U.S. market, Swiss firms made investments in such U.S. watchmakers as Waltham Watch Company (100 percent Swiss-owned), Elgin (16 percent), Gruen (20 percent) and Hamilton (51 percent, ultimately). Swiss watchmakers handled both promotion and R&D on an industry-wide basis. Campaigns by organizations such as the Federation of Swiss watchmakers stressed "Swiss-made" quality and reputation instead of specific brands. Only a few major watchmakers promoted individual brands like Rolex and Omega but a shift toward brand and company promotion became apparent in the early 1970s. Industry R&D activities were focused on the electronic watch, although at the comparatively low level of about 1½ percent of sales. Efforts were concentrated on the development of integrated circuits to end Swiss dependency on U.S.-made circuitry and on the development of quartz crystal timing devices.

Exhibit 2 (cont.)
ELECTRO INDUSTRIES, INC. (B)

THE JAPANESE

Japan in 1970 accounted for about 17 percent of Western watch production, making it the second largest watch-producing country. Unlike the Swiss, who exported all but a tiny percentage of their production, Japanese firms exported slightly less than 60 percent. Industry concentration had been high from the start: In 1970, two firms, K. Hattori & Co. (Seiko Group watches) and the Citizen Watch Co., produced nearly 90 percent of Japan's watches and movements. Hattori, as sales arm for the Seiko Group, sold over twice as many watches as Citizen. The Japanese firms concentrated on jeweled-lever type watches, mainly for the medium-priced market segments, and kept out of the luxury watch market since it was not compatible with their basic competitive strength in mass production. Although they did not compete directly in the low-priced segment, Japanese producers supplied inexpensive jeweled-lever movements to U.S. firms such as Benrus and Elgin, who used Seiko movements, and Bulova, who bought movements and parts from Citizen. This allowed these U.S. firms to compete directly with Timex in the low-priced end of the market. A combination of low-wage rates, automated production, vertical integration and mass production of standardized movements and models gave Japanese manufacturers unmatched cost advantages. Together with Japan's large domestic market, these advantages gave Japanese watchmakers the ability to undercut Swiss prices from 15 percent fo 45 percent in U.S. markets. Both Seiko and Citizen, as manufacturers of electronic calculators and related electronic products, were in an excellent technological position from which to enter the electronic watch market. Seiko in fact introduced the first quartz crystal regulated timepiece in 1970 which, due to problems with temperature effects, led to its temporary withdrawal from the market.

THE AMERICANS

Absorbing 45 million watches in 1970 with a retail volume of roughly $1 billion, the U.S. offered the world's largest market for watches. About 40 percent of the watches were of domestic manufacture but only two firms were involved: Timex and Bulova.

Exhibit 2 (cont.)
ELECTRO INDUSTRIES, INC. [B]

Price competition started by Timex in the 1950s and joined by the Swiss and the Japanese during the 1960s, together with a mass-merchandising revolution that disrupted traditional distribution through jewelers and fine department stores, led to the withdrawal from domestic production of one U.S. firm after another until only two remained by 1970. The others shifted production to foreign plants or began to market under their own labels watches made by Swiss and Japanese firms. Of the main U.S. watch companies, including Benrus, Bulova, Elgin, Gruen, Hamilton, Longines-Wittnauer, Timex, and Waltham, most did not manufacture in the U.S., most were unprofitable in the early 1970s, several had sold out to companies like Westinghouse (Longines) or to Swiss interests, and many were heavily in debt. Only Timex and Bulova were strong both competitively and financially.

Bulova's position developed from a decision in the 1960s to become multinational in both production and marketing and to compete aggressively in all market segments. To compete with Timex in the under-$30 range, Bulova introduced its "Caravelle" line built around Citizen's inexpensive jeweled-lever movement. This highly successful line was followed by Bulova's traditional middle market strength, the $30 to $100 range. Bulova's tuning-fork regulated watch, the "Accutron," quickly dominated the over-$100 category after its introduction in 1960. Competitive pricing was supported heavily by enormous advertising expenditures and distribution efforts. Low-cost manufacturing in Switzerland and elsewhere around the world provided broad flexibility in production and contributed to Bulova's becoming the world's largest watch seller (in dollar sales).

Timex, from a standing start in 1950, built a world-wide manufacturing and marketing organizations matching Bulova's by 1970. Relying upon a mass-produced, simplified pin-lever movement, Timex used extensive advertising and distribution through drugstores and mass merchandisers to dominate the low-priced market segment. During the 1960s, its product line was broadened to include electric and jeweled-lever models. Timex, with estimated sales in excess of $200 million, was privately owned.

Brand names were heavily promoted by both Bulova and Timex, a key factor to their success in a watch market offering over 800 different watch models from which consumers might choose. Both placed major emphasis on R&D work outside their

Exhibit 2 (cont.)
ELECTRO INDUSTRIES, INC. [B]

traditional areas. Bulova produced a broad array of electronic and electromechanical devices for the defense industry in which miniature electronics played a major role. Gyroscopes and electronic timing devices were developed and manufactured by Timex.

THE ELECTRONIC WATCH

Swiss, Japanese, and American watchmakers had lined up for the battle over the U.S. electronic watch market by the mid-1960s. Seiko was first, temporarily at least, with a quartz crystal analog[3] watch in 1970, followed closely by Bulova's $1,350 analog Accuquartz and several others. Late in 1971, Hamilton introduced its digital Pulsar at $2,000 retail and others began to offer analog and digital quartz crystal watches at between $300 and $400. By April 1972, the Swiss brought to market full lines of both varieties at retail prices of $300 and below. A $125 analog quartz crystal watch was introduced about that time by Timex but no sooner had this taken place when Benrus announced a $99 retail analog quartz watch, the "Techniquartz," to be marketed through the full range of distribution channels.

The completely solid-state, low-priced digital watch became a reality shortly afterward with the announcements by Waltham Watch Company of a $200 retail, liquid crystal display watch and by Gruen of its comparable, $150 retail, Teletime watch. Considered of even greater importance was the announcement by Microma Universal, a small California manufacturer of integrated circuits and liquid crystal displays, of its intention to manufacture analog and digital electronic watches to sell at retail levels of $79.50 and $149.50 respectively, and to market those both under its own brand name and as a private label supplier to Sears, Roebuck. Thus, the entry of electronics manufacturers into watchmaking began.

Source: "Note on the Watch Industries in Switzerland, Japan, and the United States," Harvard Business School Case (9–373–090). Revision 10/72.

---

[3]An "analog" electronic watch is one with a regular dial face and hands, distinguishing it from digital watches having only a four- or six-digit time display on the face. Both are driven by solid-state electronic timing circuits.

Exhibit 3
ELECTRO INDUSTRIES, INC. [B]
World Production and Exports of Watches

	WORLD PRODUCTION [MILLION UNITS]*					
	1969	1970	1971	1972	1973	1974
Switzerland	71.6	73.6	72.3	78.2	85.2	88.8
Japan	21.3	23.8	24.3	25.4	28.0	32.4
USSR	20.5	21.7	23.3	24.5	25.0	25.5
U.S.	17.7	19.4	21.5	21.8	22.1	23.7
France	10.6	10.9	12.5	14.1	15.8	16.7
W. Germany	8.3	8.4	7.9	9.2	9.7	8.7
E. Germany	3.3	3.5	3.5	3.4	3.5	4.0
China	—	—	—	—	5.7	6.7
Italy	2.5	2.6	2.6	2.3	2.5	2.5
Portugal	—	—	—	1.3	1.8	2.0
Total World	164.7	173.6	179.0	197.0	215.8	229.6

	EXPORTS [MILLION UNITS]					
	1969	1970	1971	1972	1973	1974
Switzerland	69.5	71.4	70.2	75.8	81.8	84.4
Japan	9.4	11.4	13.3	15.3	16.5	18.7
USSR	9.4	10.7	11.2	12.0	13.3	14.0
W. Germany	4.8	4.0	3.8	3.6	3.8	4.0
France	3.8	5.0	6.5	7.1	8.4	8.8
E. Germany	1.9	2.1	1.8	1.8	1.9	2.3
Portugal	—	—	—	1.1	1.8	1.9
U.K.	1.0	0.9	0.8	0.7	0.8	2.1
Italy	0.4	0.6	0.6	0.6	0.6	0.55
U.S.	0.15	0.15	0.16	0.2	0.5	0.5
Total World	100.4	106.4	108.4	118.2	129.3	137.5

Source: *Financial Times*

*Estimates for watches and watch movements.

DISCUSSION QUESTIONS

ELECTRO INDUSTRIES [B]

Please refer to the Electro Industries (A) case as necessary in preparing this assignment.

1. How does the digital watch market compare with the calculator market?

2. What factors are critical to success in the watch market? To what extent does MOStronics have them?
3. What are the strategies of the major competitors in the watch market?
4. What are the possible ways of entering the digital watch market?
5. Should MOStronics enter the watch market?
6. What should be the MOStronics Division's strategy?

Formal Strategic Planning Methods

Portfolio Analysis

As indicated in Chapter 1, strategic market planning for multi-product, multimarket companies is a particularly complex problem. A firm may have tens or hundreds of products serving similar numbers of markets with widely differing potentials. Some of these products may be in a strong position relative to competitors and others may be in a weaker position. Each will have its own strategy. The competing organizations may be numerous, as will be the strategies for their competing products. Some products may need cash to finance growth or competitive battles, while others may be generating more cash than they need. Somehow the organization must deploy its limited financial resources among these products so as to achieve the best performance possible.

Many companies—such as ISC (described in Chapter 1)—manage this complexity by breaking their organization into decentralized profit centers, each of which is then treated as if it was an independent business. Strategies for such "business units" are then assembled into a corporate-wide plan and adjusted independently from one another to meet corporate financial performance targets and constraints.

This decentralized approach is inherently suboptimizing for the corporation as a whole. Its sole advantage is the financial strength and stability arising from diversification. As Bruce Henderson, President of The Boston Consulting Group (BCG), has written:

> A multidivision company without an overall strategy is not even as good as the sum of its parts. It is merely a portfolio of nonliquid, nontradeable

173

investments which has added overhead and constraints. Such closed-end investments properly sell at a discount from the sum of the parts.[1]

A multidivisional, multiproduct company has an important advantage over undiversified firms because of its ability to channel its considerable resources into the most productive units. Instead of the decentralized approach, a number of such companies conduct integrated strategic planning at the corporate or division level to match product potential with resources and to establish the sequence and timing of resource transfers. For example, a diversified conglomerate may decide to slow down the growth of its paper-board division so that it will throw off cash for the expansion of its light aircraft division. Such integrated planning may deliberately suboptimize a division's activities to optimize corporate performance.

The product portfolio approach, which is the topic of this chapter, differs from most other integrative planning techniques in that strategic roles for each product are assigned on the basis of the product's market growth rate and market share relative to competition. These individual roles are then integrated into a strategy for the whole "portfolio" of products, taking account of the product portfolios of significant competitors. The differences in growth potential, relative market share, and hence cash flow potential—unique to each product—determine which products represent investment opportunities, which should supply investment funds, and which should be candidates for elimination from the portfolio. The objective is to get the best overall performance from the portfolio, while keeping cash flow in balance.

Several ways have been devised[2] to display relevant information about the firm's portfolio while at the same time reducing the inherent complexity of the problem to somewhat more manageable proportions. It is the creation and interpretation of these displays—for the firm and its competitors—that forms the heart of portfolio analysis. The key displays are the growth-share matrix and the growth-gain matrix.

THE GROWTH-SHARE MATRIX

The most prominent display is the so-called *growth-share matrix* (see Figure 1 for an example), that shows a firm's whole portfolio by giving for each product:

---

[1]Henderson, Bruce, "Intuitive Strategy" (Boston: The Boston Consulting Group, 1970), Perspectives No. 96.

[2]These displays and the associated portfolio concept originated with the Boston Consulting Group. See Bruce D. Henderson, "The Experience Curve—Reviewed. IV. The Growth Share Matrix of The Product Portfolio" (Boston: The Boston Consulting Group, 1973), Perspectives No. 135. Also: "The Product Portfolio" (Boston: The Boston Consulting Group, 1970), Perspectives No. 66.

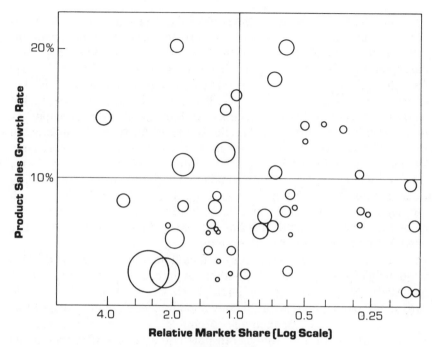

Figure 1

A Typical Product Portfolio Chart (Growth-Share Matrix) of a Comparatively Strong and Diversified Company

Source: Bruce D. Henderson, "The Experience Curve Reviewed: IV. The Growth Share Matrix of The Product Portfolio" (Boston: The Boston Consulting Group, 1973), Perspectives No. 135.

1. Its *dollar sales* (represented by the area[3] of the circle representing it on the matrix).
2. Its *market share* relative to the firm's largest competitor (by the horizontal position of the circle on the chart).
3. The *growth rate of the market* (corrected for inflation) in which the product competes (by the position of the circle in the vertical direction).

---

[3]Note that some practitioners represent sales by the diameter of the circle rather than by the area. (See for example George S. Day "Diagnosing the Product Portfolio," *Journal of Marketing,* 41, No. 2 (April 1977), pp. 29–38.) However, we favor area because the visual impact of a circle relates more to area than to diameter. To see this, look at Exhibit 8 of the Electro Industries (C) case (which appears at the end of this chapter), where diameter is used to represent sales. TI's sales of calculators are only 2.5 times those of Bowmar and yet one gets the visual impression that they are about six times as large.

Relative market share is the ratio of the firm's unit sales of a product to the unit sales of the same product by the firm's largest competitor, which is the same as the ratio of the two companies market shares. For example, if Product A's annual sales were 3.1 million units for the firm and 10 million units for the market leader, the firm's relative market share for Product A would be 0.31. The firm will have relative market shares of more than 1.0 for markets in which it is the largest competitor and of less than 1.0 for markets it doesn't lead. A ratio of 1.0 means the firm is tied for the lead. (Relative share is used instead of simply market share, since it captures well the relationship to the leader's share; for instance, a 10 percent market share has quite a different meaning if the leader has a 12 percent share than if the leader's share is 45 percent. Because relative share is so closely related to relative experience, relative share is indicative of relative cost.) A log scale is normally used for the relative market share axis.

A series of charts made for various points in time will provide a trajectory of each product that indicates both its direction and rate of movement. Superimposing two such charts can dramatize movements over time. Similar charts can be developed for each major competitor.

While we have spoken of "products" (e.g., cross-country ski bindings) as the unit of analysis in portfolio analysis, it is sometimes appropriate to have the unit of analysis be a "business" (e.g., skiing equipment) or even a division (e.g., recreational products). The choice of the appropriate unit of analysis is dealt with more fully later in this chapter and in Chapter 8. In the meantime the word "product" should be interpreted to mean "appropriate unit of analysis."

PORTFOLIO STRATEGY

Product growth is usually separated into "high" and "low" growth areas by an arbitrary, 10 percent growth line.[4] Similarly, relative market share is usually divided at a relative market share of 1.0, so that "high" share signifies market leadership. There is nothing sacred about either of these dividing lines. The point is to place the lines so that, if they just hold share, most products in the lower left corner of the chart would be cash generators, those in the upper right are cash users, and those in the upper left and lower right are roughly in cash balance—neither using nor throwing off significant amounts of cash.

---

[4]Note that market growth rate is a rough proxy for stage in the product life cycle; products above the line can be thought of as in the growth phase, whereas those below can be considered mature.

Interpretation of the matrix is based on the following observations:

1. Margins and cash generated increase with relative market share, due to the experience and scale effects described in Chapter 3.
2. Sales growth requires cash input to finance added capacity and working capital. Thus, if market share is maintained, cash input requirements increase with market growth rate.
3. In addition to the above-mentioned cash input to keep pace with market growth, an increase in market share usually requires cash input to support increased advertising expenditures, lower prices and other share-gaining tactics. On the other hand, a decrease in share may make cash available.
4. Growth in each market will ultimately slow as the product approaches maturity. Without losing market position, cash generated as growth slows can be reinvested in other products that are still growing.

Thus, products to the left of the market share dividing line have strong cash flows from operations due to their good margins and those to the right will have weaker or negative cash flows from operations. Products below the market growth dividing line will need relatively little investment to hold share, whereas those above will need significant investment of cash to keep pace with market growth.

This leads to classification of products into four categories, based on their cash flow characteristics (see Figure 2).

"**Cash Cows**" (indicated by "$" in the lower left quarter of the chart where they are usually found) are products that characteristically generate large amounts of cash, far more than they can profitably invest. Typically they have a dominant share of slowly growing markets. They are the products that provide the cash to pay interest on corporate debt, pay dividends, cover corporate overhead, finance R&D, and help other products to grow.

"**Dogs**" (indicated by an "x" in the lower right) are products with low share of slowly growing markets. They neither generate nor require significant amounts of cash. Maintaining share usually requires reinvestment of their modest cash flow from operations, as well as modest amounts of additional capital. Because of low share their profitability is poor and they are unlikely to ever be a significant source of cash; therefore they are often called "cash traps."

"**Problem Children**" or "question marks" (indicated by a "?" in the upper right) are products with low share of fast-growing markets.

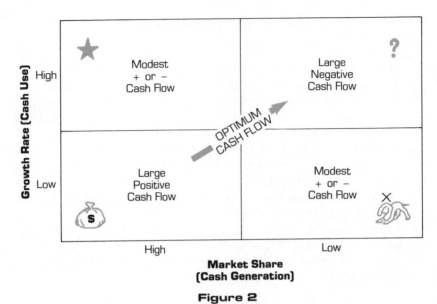

Figure 2

Product Categories in the Product Portfolio Chart

Source: Adapted from "The Product Portfolio" (Boston: The Boston Consulting Group, 1970), Perspectives No. 66.

Their low share often means low profits and weak cash flow from operations; at the same time because they are in rapidly growing markets, they require large amounts of cash to maintain market share, and still larger amounts to gain share. Hence their name; market growth is attractive, yet large amounts of cash will be required if they will ever gain sufficient share to be strong members of the product portfolio.

"**Stars**" (indicated by a "*" in the upper left) are high-growth, high-share products which may or may not be self-sufficient in cash flow. This depends on whether their strong cash flow from operations is sufficient to finance rapid growth. Their present, modest cash needs or throw off will change to a large cash throw off in the future, when the growth rate of their market slows.

The location of products on a portfolio chart is indicative of the current health of a portfolio; over time products will move due to market dynamics and to strategy decisions. The object is to analyze the current state and natural dynamics of the portfolio so that decisions yielding a strong portfolio in the future will result.

Movements in the vertical direction, i.e., changes in the rate of market growth, are largely beyond the firm's control (except when their policies influence primary demand as Black and Decker did; see p. 182

and must be anticipated when developing strategic moves. For example, given only a share-maintaining investment, all products will eventually fall vertically to become either "cash cows" or "dogs," depending upon relative market share held prior to the slowing of market growth and product maturity. "Problem children" ultimately become "dogs" unless enough investment is made during the growth phase to shift the product into the "star" area. "Stars" assure the future in that they will become "cash cows" as growth slows and investment needs diminish.

With market growth largely noncontrollable in most instances, portfolio analysis reduces to determining a market share strategy for each product. The foundation of a sound long-term strategy is to use cash generated by "cash cows" to finance market share increases for "problem children" products in which the company has a strong competitive footing (see arrow in Figure 2). If successful, this strategy produces new "stars" which will in turn become "cash cows" of the future. This "success sequence" is shown in Figure 3. The "problem child" product with a weak competitive position is a liability and should be allowed to remain in the portfolio only on a "no cash input" basis, a strategy that will cause it to become a "dog" eventually. "Dogs" should be retained only as long as they contribute some positive cash flow and provided they don't tie up capital that can be used more profitably elsewhere. At some point, many "dogs" become candidates for elimination from the product portfolio. There are many "disaster sequences," for example: allowing a "star's" share to erode to that of a "question mark" and ultimately to a "dog" or allowing the share of a "cash cow" to erode to that of a "dog." Figure 3 illustrates these basic sequences.

Unfortunately many managements pursue strategies other than the success strategies described in the previous paragraph; they over-invest in seemingly safe "cows" and "dogs." They invest less than needed in "question marks," and instead of becoming "stars," these "question marks" ultimately tumble into "dogs." They spread their resources too thinly among products rather than focusing to achieve outstanding performance from a smaller number, even though that smaller number still provides sufficient diversification from a risk reducing standpoint.

Given these remarks about portfolio strategies, it is easy to see why the portfolio shown in Figure 1 was termed strong and diversified. A large percentage of products are share leaders (relative share greater than 1.0), promising excellent cost positions. Furthermore, these profitable products are among the largest. There are a large number of cash cows to feed the problem children; many of the problem children have good relative market positions; most of the dogs have viable shares; and there are many stars.

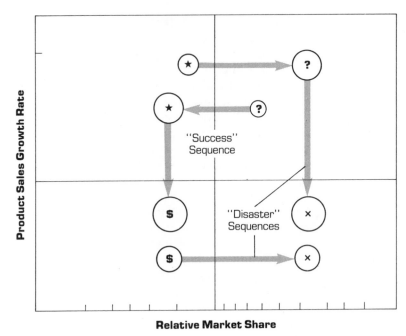

Relative Market Share

Figure 3

Product Dynamics in the Portfolio Chart

Source: "The Product Portfolio" (Boston: The Boston Consulting Group, 1970). Perspectives No. 66.

THE GROWTH-GAIN MATRIX

A second very useful portfolio display is the *growth-gain matrix*, that indicates the degree to which the growth of each product is keeping pace with market growth. The growth rate of a product (or of its capacity) is plotted on the horizontal axis, and the growth rate of its market on the vertical axis, as shown in Figure 4. (As before, the area of a circle representing a product is proportional to its sales.) Products whose growth just matches market growth are located along the diagonal; they are holding share. Share gainers are below the diagonal and share losers are above.

The ideal location of products on the matrix is shown in Figure 4b. "Dogs" should be concentrated near the market growth axis indicating zero capacity growth. "Cash cows" should be clustered along the diagonal, indicating that market share is being held on the average. "Stars" should appear in the high growth region, near or below the

180

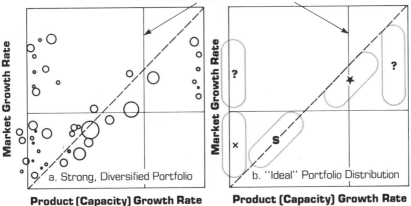

Figure 4

Portfolio Strategy and Maximum Sustainable Growth

Source: The Boston Consulting Group.

diagonal since they are holding or gaining market share. "Question marks" are ideally in two clusters: a group presently receiving little growth capital (on the left) and a group being supported heavily (on the right). Note that the strong, diversified portfolio in Figure 4a has many of the ideal characteristics.

An important consideration for interpreting the growth-gain matrix is the firm's *maximum sustainable growth*,[5] defined as:

$$G = \frac{D}{E}(R - i)p + Rp,$$

where

G   = maximum sustainable long-term asset growth rate,
D/E = debt-equity ratio,[6]
R   = after-tax return on assets (adjusted for inflation),
p   = earnings retention rate (= 1 – dividend payout ratio), and
i   = after-tax current cost of debt.

(All of the terms in this formula are decimals except debt and equity.)

---

[5]Alan Zakon, "Growth and Financial Strategies" (Boston: The Boston Consulting Group, 1971); this formula assumes that no equity funds are raised from outside.

[6]When this ratio changes over time, use incremental debt divided by incremental equity for the period considered.

The value of maximum sustainable growth is plotted as a solid vertical line on the matrix, as shown in Figure 4. (Although the formula is for asset growth, capacity growth rate is often used as a surrogate, since the two are very closely related.)

The weighted average growth rate of the products cannot exceed the maximum sustainable growth rate; in other words, the "center of gravity" of the spots on the chart cannot be to the right of the vertical line. To the extent it is to the left, the firm can support additional growth. (At a glance it appears that the firm shown in Figure 4 can support more growth, but the existence of balance must be determined by calculation rather than by visual means.)

If adjustments are needed, products can be repositioned by strategy changes. For instance, a "dog" near the maximum growth-rate line can be moved near to the "ideal" zero growth-rate axis by slowing its growth. Clearly, plotting growth-gain matrices for key competitors and highlighting key competitive products can yield significant insights into where competitors are placing their emphasis.

TYPES OF STRATEGIES

There are four basic strategies that can be pursued with a given product: building share, holding share, harvesting, or withdrawal. Which is appropriate depends on such factors as a product's present market and cost position, the product's life cycle stage (market growth rate), the firm's resources relative to competitors, its time horizon, its other products, and likely actions and reactions by competitors. The four basic strategies and when each might be appropriate will now be described.

Building Market Share

Sometimes building share is an offensive strategy; firms with a viable share will build share to increase their profitability. Black and Decker's expansion in the hand-held electric tool market by reducing prices as costs fell with experience is an example; the reduced prices not only helped share, but also increased primary demand by putting "more products in reach of more incomes."[7] Sometimes it is defensive; in most industries a minimum relative market share is needed for long-run viability. Firms without this critical share are in an untenable

---

[7]Black and Decker, "First Quarter Report: Three Months Ended December 24, 1972."

position; they must increase share, or withdraw. (Often the critical share is of the order of ¼ of the leader's share.)

The appropriateness of share building depends in part on market growth rate.[8] Unless share leaders are competitively asleep, gaining share in slowly growing, static, or declining markets is difficult and uneconomic. On the other hand, when experience or scale effects are pronounced, when the firm has competitive strength in a product, and when it has the resources to do so, market dominance is the appropriate objective for products in high-growth markets. Market share is usually less expensive to achieve during the rapid growth phase in a product's life cycle because purchase patterns and distribution channels are fluid, and—most importantly—share gains don't have to come from reducing competitor's sales. Instead they can come from capturing a disproportionate share of incremental sales and through sales to new users of the product.

But large share increases are seldom built quickly and they sacrifice short-range profits for profits later. Thus share building is difficult to sell in organizations emphasizing short-run earnings. At the same time, share building is easier to carry out against competitors unwilling to sacrifice short-run profits to hold on to their share.

Share building can be accomplished by price reduction; by improved delivery, quality or product support; or by concentrating on a market segment, isolated in terms of experience, where dominance can be achieved. An example of the latter is the Digital Equipment Corporation's strong performance in the small computer segment of the computer industry, even though IBM dominates the industry as a whole.

Holding Market Share

Holding share is appropriate for mature businesses with leading or strong shares; it is preservation of a desirable status quo. Strongly established products have the advantage of greater experience and consequent lower costs and higher profitability than their rivals with lower shares. Holding share is appropriate for such products, because building share is very costly and time consuming in slowly growing markets. Since increased share must come at the expense of other competitor's sales, it will be resisted strenuously. Furthermore distribution patterns and purchasing relationships are usually stable and difficult to change.

---

[8]It also depends on antitrust considerations which are beyond the scope of this text. See, for example, Paul Bloom and Philp Kotler, "Strategies for High Market Share Companies," *Harvard Business Review*, 53, No. 6 (November-December 1975), pp. 63-72.

Harvesting

The harvesting strategy purposely allows share to decline to maximize short-term earnings and cash flow (both from operations and freed up working capital). It is especially appropriate for products with poor positions in declining markets. It also may be selected for "problem children" products that have a poor competitive position. The cash generated from harvesting can be used to nurture more promising, growing products. For instance, pharmaceutical companies will often pursue harvesting strategies for proprietary drugs on which patents have expired, allowing producers of generic drugs to gain share. The harvested cash is then invested in R&D and in expanding promising new drugs.

Withdrawal

When a product has less than the critical share for viability—or, in other words, competition is so far ahead in costs that overwhelming short-run sacrifices would be required to catch up—then withdrawal is appropriate. For instance, in the early 1970s, RCA, General Electric and Xerox each realized they had an uneconomic share of the computer market and that they lacked the resources to build share.[9] Each opted for withdrawal.

Selection from among these four basic strategies requires much judgment and analysis. How selection might depend on a firm's current market position and the product's life cycle phase is shown in Table 1. But Table 1 is an oversimplification, meant to convey promising strategies for further investigation; many other factors, beyond the information on the portfolio charts, must be considered before a decision is reached. (For instance, a follower with a growing product might opt not to invest to increase share if it was too far behind or lacked sufficient resources to achieve a viable share.) These other factors are considered in detail in Chapters 5 and 6.

DEFINITION OF "PRODUCT" AND "MARKET"

A crucial prerequisite for this analysis is a careful definition of products and markets. This is as much an art as a science. Consider the following example of a coffee manufacturer serving the New England

---

[9]William E. Fruhan, "Pyrrhic Victories in Fights for Market Share," *Harvard Business Review*, 50, No. 5 (September-October 1972), pp. 100–107.

Table 1

BASIC STRATEGIES APPROPRIATE FOR VARIOUS LIFE CYCLE STAGES
AND COMPETITIVE POSITIONS

COMPETITIVE POSITION	PRODUCT LIFE STAGE		
	GROWTH	MATURITY	DECLINE
LEADER (HIGH SHARE)	Build share by reducing prices to discourage new competitive capacity. Utilize own capacity fully, adding in anticipation of needs.	Hold share by improving quality, increasing sales effort, and advertising.	Harvest: maximize cash flow by reducing investment and advertising, development, etc., (market share will decline).
FOLLOWER (LOW SHARE)	Invest to increase share. Concentrate on a segment which can be dominated.	Withdraw, or hold share by keeping prices and costs below the market leaders.	Withdraw from the market.

region, which is wondering how to analyze its instant coffee offerings on a portfolio display. Possible product-market definitions include:

1. New England region: a. decaffeinated instant
                        b. regular instant
2. New England region: all instant
3. Nationwide: all instant

The choice between the first and second alternatives is one of *level*; in other words, how much segmentation is desirable for analytical purposes? Should the two different types of instant coffee be shown as separate products or a single product? The choice between the second and third alternatives is between *"served market"* or *"total market,"* as the basis for measuring share. In this case the company's served market is New England, but many of its competitors may serve the national market. Whenever the company's "served market" is less than the "total market" (either on geographic or other segmentation dimensions), this question will arise.

The choice of level and the choice between served versus total market requires addressing two considerations. First, the definition must be such that relative market share bears some relationship to relative costs. Otherwise the underlying cash flow relationships in which the displays are based become meaningless. Practically speaking this means that the level should be selected in a way that takes account of shared experience or economies of scale arising from shared production or marketing activities on the part of you or your competitors. Usually this consideration pushes you to a broader definition of the market. It can occasionally indicate a narrower definition, especially when there are unique economies of scale or experience in serving a particular market segment.

Second, the definition should separate markets which are essentially different in terms of competitors, strategies, growth rates, and share achieved. In the coffee situation, for example, it would probably not make sense to aggregate instant and regular coffee nationwide since these markets are distinct. Even though share measured on this basis may provide some indication of relative costs, strategy choices must be articulated for each major segment of the business and are meaningless when considered in aggregate.

Usually product and market definition reflects a compromise between these two considerations. The need to relate share to costs often argues for a relatively broad definition; the need to deal with strategically meaningful market segments argues for a relatively narrow definition. When these two considerations lead to sharply differing definitions, it is advisable to repeat the portfolio analysis with several alternative definitions. If the results of the analysis differ significantly, appropriate qualifications of the results of the selected approach should be made.

Particularly challenging definitional problems are posed by businesses that are strongly integrated vertically. An upstream or downstream component may not really be a separate "business" from an analytic standpoint, since it is so interrelated with the rest.

STRATEGIC ANALYSIS OF THE PRODUCT PORTFOLIO

A six-step strategic analysis can be carried out using the growth-share and the growth-gain matrices.

1. Check for Internal Balance

The growth-share matrix should be checked to see if products are properly distributed among the four quadrants. Products with the largest sales (largest circles) should be either "stars" or "cash cows."

Few products should be in the "question marks" quadrant, because of the heavy cash commitment required to transform them into "stars." Also, they can be major losers if something goes wrong. The majority of sales should be from market-leading "cash cows," to provide cash to underwrite the remaining products. Few products should appear as "dogs." [The balance just described is an ideal which a small number of strong firms achieve. Remember that only one product in each market can be the leader; therefore, the average firm will have many more products to the right of the relative share dividing line ("question marks" and "dogs") than to the left.] Tentative ideas for improving balance should result from this analysis.

2. Look for Trends

An equivalent growth-share display should be developed for a period three to five years earlier. It can then be superimposed on the the current chart to reveal the direction and rate of travel of each product. When major shifts have occurred in the interval between these two charts, annual plots for the products affected may be needed to accurately determine the current movement vector. The corresponding growth-gain matrix should be checked carefully to confirm identified trends. A third growth-share matrix should project where each product would be in the forthcoming five-year period if present policies were maintained. Some tentative ideas for improving upon the current trends in the portfolio should result from this analysis.

3. Evaluate Competition

For this step, the two types of displays are developed for each of the firm's major competitors. Although these charts will not be as reliable as those for one's own firm, they will usefully display the best information available about competitors.

The first step in competitive analysis is careful study of each competitor's chart to determine what each is doing. Are their strategies coherent? Which are their "cash cows," "stars," and so forth? How close are they to their sustainable growth rates? Interesting insights and potential weaknesses of competition can be revealed. For instance, it might appear that a competitor is so concerned with one product that it is unlikely to have resources to hold off a market share-gaining strategy by you on another.

Next, the charts of competitors should be compared with yours, taking one competing product type at a time to evaluate competitive strength. This is particularly important when share increase is contemplated. In low growth segments, for example, share gain should only be attempted where the firm has share roughly on par with the dominant firms, where it has clear leadership in product characteristics, where it has strong leftward momentum (as evidenced by the trend charts), or where competitors appear not to be investing. Attention should be focused on products close to the 1.0 relative share line and in a market of sufficient size to warrant a battle with the leader. It should also be focused on "question marks" with significant leftward momentum. Likewise, products that appear to be doing poorly relative to competition—especially those where competitors appear to be aggressively expanding strong competing products—can be identified and tentatively earmarked for possible harvesting or divestment.

Competitive analysis is crucial for sound strategy development, yet it is often the weakest link. It is difficult and highly speculative, and as a result many analysts retreat to analysis of easier internal issues. Much of the problem is lack of data, but it is surprising what imaginative analysis of data from sources mentioned in Chapter 2 can reveal.

4. Consider Factors Not Captured in the Portfolio Display

The portfolio displays address three of the key characteristics of products relevant to planning: relative market share (and through it, presumably profitability), size, and market growth (which is usually strongly related to the product life cycle stage and market attractiveness). In addition the location of products on the charts usually indicates their cash characteristics. This information about a firm's and its competitor's portfolios, properly employed, can usually carry the planning process a long way.

However, there is a great deal of additional information that must be weighed before deciding on basic strategies for each product (gaining share, harvesting, etc.), and how (acquisition, pricing, etc.) to implement the strategies. The added information includes such important factors[10] as: barriers to entry; technological changes; social, legal, political, and environmental pressures; unions and related human factors; management capabilities; cyclicality of sales; the rate of capacity utilization; responsiveness of sales to changes in prices, promotion, service levels, etc.; the extent of "captive" business; production and process opportunities (including off-shore manufacture); etc. Thus, for example, a small chemical plant might be located near supply sources and pipe most of its product directly to a nearby customer. It would

---

[10]George S. Day, "Diagnosing the Product Portfolio," *Journal of Marketing,* 41, No. 2 (April 1977), pp. 29–38.

have a small market share, but enjoy a captive relationship with its customer if the nearest alternate source is distant. Thus profits and cash flow would greatly exceed what its "dog" status might indicate. Likewise changes in technology either by a firm or its competition might tip the competitive balance in ways not captured in the portfolio displays.

In addition, separate account must be taken of such considerations as the need for investment to assure continuity of critical supplies of raw material or the need for diversification among economic sectors or markets to reduce year-to-year volatility.[11] Although these factors cannot be represented on the portfolio displays, they must nonetheless be considered in assessing strategic moves. To a large extent, the techniques described in Chapter 5 are designed to take into account such considerations.

5. Develop Possible "Target" Portfolios

By combining the results of the previous four steps of checking for balance, studying trends, studying competition, and considering factors not shown on the portfolio displays, a series of potential "target" portfolios indicating desired portfolio arrangements can be developed along with associated strategies for achieving them. Typical strategies[12] for various types of products are:

"Cash Cows" Normally strategies are to maintain market dominance and the strong cash flows these products generate. These include maintaining product, technological, and price leadership, while at the same time guarding against over-investment in product proliferation and market expansion that would sap the strong cash flow. (Exceptions would include expansion to exploit a competitor's weaknesses, and new, hard-to-copy product innovation, or increases in primary demand.) Generally, once the strong position of the product is assured, excess cash should be channeled elsewhere.

---

[11]Indeed the term "portfolio analysis" is used among financial analysts to refer to the appropriate diversification among investment securities to achieve a desired balance between risk and return. The reasoning lying behind *financial* portfolio analysis applies equally to *product* portfolio analysis although its formal application is difficult in the product setting. See Harry M. Markowitz, *Portfolio Selection: Efficient Diversification of Investments* (New Haven: Yale University Press, 1975); and William F. Sharpe, *Portfolio Theory and Capital Markets* (New York: McGraw-Hill, Inc., 1970).

---

[12]See George S. Day, "Diagnosing the Product Portfolio," *Journal of Marketing* 41, No. 2 (April 1977), pp. 29–38.

"Dogs" Products near the "cash cow" category can often be treated as such. However, the lower the relative share and slower the growth the greater the need for decisive action. Alternatives include abandonment, divestment, harvesting or a focusing strategy.

"Problem Children" Because of the poor margins and large cash demands associated with having a small share of a fast-growing market, these products are usually in an untenable position. The choices will be to expand a few into "stars," focus the strategies of others, and get out of the rest. Expansion can come from gaining a disproportionate share of new sales or acquisition of competitors. Focus can come through identifying a segment where a firm has the resources to achieve dominance. Getting out can come through divestment of the business as a growing concern, harvesting, or abandonment.

"Stars" Once again the appropriate strategy is usually to hold the dominant share, and in some instances to build share. As mentioned earlier, share increases are often easier in fast growing markets; building share can come from gaining a large portion of new users or applications, while holding share can come through price reductions, product improvements, increased production efficiency, better market coverage and the like. Most "stars" will end up roughly self-sufficient in cash or requiring modest infusions.

6. Check Financial Balance

In this final step, qualitative strategy selections are revised and firmed up on the basis of detailed pro forma cash flow projections. Cash flow needs or throw offs are projected for all products in accordance with the tentative strategies developed in previous steps: A few "dogs" and "question marks" slated for harvesting and divestment produce some cash, and "cash cows" and some "stars" produce the remainder of the internally generated funds. "Question marks" targeted for share gains and certain "stars" will be the only cash users.

Estimates of externally generated cash will be used finally to balance cash flows. If external cash is insufficient, some products will have to be reclassified; more "dogs" and "question marks" may have to be abandoned or harvested. Or some share gaining plans will have to be foregone. Making a comparable cash flow tabulation for major competitors may reveal the growth constraints which will ultimately shape their portfolio strategies. It seems unlikely, for instance, that any computer manufacturer, other than perhaps IBM, could support major growth efforts in more than a few segments of the computer market.

The end result of the foregoing steps is a target portfolio, balanced with respect to cash, with associated strategies to move from the current to the new position. Figure 5 shows how one company (actually a composite of a number of situations) upgraded its portfolio following an analysis of the sort just described. It represents the following strategic decisions:

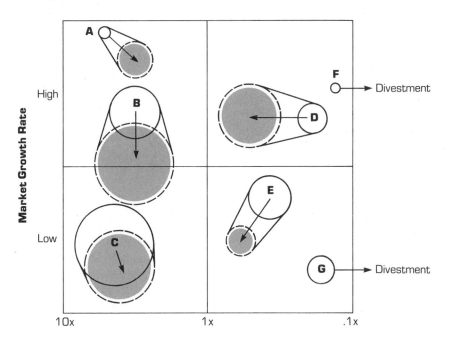

Relative Market Share
(Share Relative to Largest Competitor)

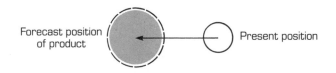

Figure 5

Example of Forecasted Positions of a Portfolio After a Strategic Analysis

Source: Adapted from George S. Day, "Diagnosing the Product Portfolio," *Journal of Marketing,* April 1977, p. 34.

1. Aggressively support the newly introduced product A, to ensure dominance (but anticipate share declines due to new competitive entries).
2. Continue present strategies of products B and C to ensure maintenance of market share.
3. Gain share of market for product D by investing in acquisitions.
4. Narrow and modify the range of models of product E to focus on one segment.
5. Divest products F and G.

It is obvious from this description that strategy development is very much a "cut and try" process, involving frequent returns to earlier steps and a great deal of imagination, intuition, and persistence. To accomplish it requires high quality, skillful staff analysis, and creative display of data. The effort required to deal well with these complex problems is great indeed, but so are the stakes and ultimate rewards.

LIMITATIONS

As previously indicated, two key assumptions of portfolio analysis are: (1) cash flow from operations of products with high relative market shares will be stronger than those with smaller shares and (2) cash needs for products in rapidly growing markets will be greater than for those in slower growing ones. Actual cash flow patterns can deviate from these assumptions for a variety of reasons:

1. The supposed relationship between relative market share and cash flow may be weak. This can occur when:
   - experience or scale effects are small;
   - value added is relatively low;
   - a competitor has a low-cost source of purchased materials unrelated to relative share position;
   - low share competitors are on steeper experience curves than high share competitors by virtue of superior production technology;
   - differences in experience have little impact on costs because innovations in production technology are quickly adopted by all suppliers;
   - capacity utilization rates differ;
   - strategic factors other than relative share affect profit margins, e.g., product quality or other forms of competitive differentiation.

2. The supposed relationship between industry growth rate and cash flow may be weak. This can occur when:

- capital intensity is low;
- entry barriers are high so that even in rapid growth, margins are large enough to finance growth and produce positive cash flow;
- price competition depresses margins in maturity so that even though financing needs decline, cash flow deteriorates;
- legal/regulatory intervention holds down profits in maturity, with the same result as above;
- seasonal or cyclical factors produce short-run, supply-demand imbalances which affect profit and cash flow.

When one or more of the above exceptions applies, it must be taken into account in the "off-the-chart" analyses of step 5 of the analytical process.

SOME APPLICATION CONSIDERATIONS

Like most management systems, portfolio analysis is subject to manipulation by managers who are eager to gain a share of corporate resources for their own products, and further their own careers. Market share figures can be made more favorable by manipulating product-market boundaries, especially when they are ambiguous in the first place. Likewise growth rate figures can be stretched. Alert planners at higher levels must challenge such distortions, but unfortunately they are often at a disadvantage, since the suppliers of the information know their markets better than the corporate planners do.

The source of these distortions is often an evaluation system that rewards managers of "stars," gives mediocre marks to managers of "cash cows" and "problem children," and punishes managers of "dogs." Instead, the system must reward results consistent with the mission of the business, which will be different for different businesses.

Equally, the right *type* of manager must be put in charge of a given type of business. For instance, "cash cows" require efficiency whereas "problem children" earmarked to become "stars" require aggressive marketing, flexibility, and imagination. This is essential not only for performance, but also morale. A manager with the characteristics to run a "star" might be utterly frustrated running a "dog" and vice versa.

The long-range outlook of the product portfolio approach should be underscored. A five-year horizon seems minimal except for markets in which five years represents a large part or all of a product's life cycle.

This relates to the high degree of long-term commitment that managements must make to chosen strategies, especially share-gaining ones. To be worthwhile, share gain objectives must be *achieved* and held, otherwise, considerable expense will have to be incurred for no ultimate benefits in relative costs. Managements who are "hot and cold" on a strategy—who pursue it, let up, then pursue it again—will often be disappointed in the outcome. Indeed, even with properly pursued strategies they must be prepared for mediocre short-run financial results, in many instances, while the ultimate goal is being achieved. If these dips in earnings are likely to dissuade them, then they are usually better advised not to embark on the strategy in the first place.

SUMMARY

The allocation of resources among a diverse portfolio of products is a difficult, complex task involving the weighing of large amounts of internal and competitive information. The portfolio approach deals with this problem through analyzing the growth-share and growth-gain matrices for the firm and its competition, other data, and pro forma cash projections.

The underlying basis of the analysis is maximizing benefits of the experience and scale effect to achieve a strong portfolio of high market-share products, while achieving cash balance. Rapid growth takes considerable cash input, whereas products with high share, in slowly growing markets—"cash cows"—generate cash due to their favorable cost position. The object is to use cash to turn a few well-selected "question marks" into "stars." These will ultimately become "cash cows" that generate cash to support other "stars" and future "question marks." "Dogs" and other "question marks" are harvested, divested, focused, or maintained on a no-cash-input basis.

Doing portfolio analysis is a "cut and try" process involving:

1. Checking the status of the current portfolio,
2. Studying trends,
3. Analyzing competition,
4. Considering information not included in portfolio displays,
5. Determining "target" portfolios, and
6. Achieving cash balance.

This process frequently requires returning to earlier steps to ask new questions raised as a result of analysis in later steps. It is simplified and greatly improved by using growth-share and growth-gain matrices as a guide—not substitute—for strategic thinking.

ELECTRO INDUSTRIES, INC. [C][1]

Electro Industries, a large diversified manufacturer of computer systems, industrial electronics, electronic components, and consumer electronics and a supplier of a broad range of services, had suffered its first loss in more than 15 years. Preliminary results for 1974 indicated a net loss of $5.7 million on sales of $875 million despite sales growth of almost 20 percent during the year.

Electro, a $35 million manufacturer of industrial electronic equipment in 1968, had grown to its present size by buying small undercapitalized, high-growth firms for cash. By introducing a significant amount of debt into its traditionally conservative financial structure, Electro grew extremely rapidly between 1968 and 1972, even though its stock price remained relatively depressed for almost the entire period. The years 1972 and 1973 had resulted in high profits as the acquired firms began to benefit from Electro's capital infusion.

By early 1974, however, it had become clear that the corporation could no longer carry its present debt service and still maintain a reasonable level of profitability. The majority of its debt load was short and medium term, reflecting the company's basic reluctance to commit itself to long-term borrowings and its considerable optimism concerning the future of the electronics industry. Rising interest rates had been largely responsible for Electro's first operating loss. Somewhat shocked, Electro management reacted quickly by undertaking an immediate and comprehensive assessment of the company's current position and its long-term strategic outlook.

Each division president had been asked to draw up an assessment of his own position and to prepare a detailed presentation of his plans for one- and five-year periods. These plans were due to be discussed at a week-long meeting of Electro's executive committee beginning January 30, 1975. At that meeting, a tentative decision would be made on the future of each division. Several divestment decisions were probable as management attempted to bring Electro's debt service into line with its currently depressed earnings.

---

[1]This case was prepared by Gerald B. Allan, in collaboration with John S. Hammond.

The problem facing Charles Whitman, Electro's chairman and chief executive, was to develop some sort of comprehensive framework for evaluating these divisional plans. He recognized that much of Electro's underlying strength lay in its diversity and degree of integration and that this strength must be preserved in any reorganization plan. Present competitive pressures in the electronics industry generally were such that only the strongest firms in each segment were expected to survive.

ORGANIZATION

Electro Industries began its growth phase with the merger of Jackson Instruments Corp., a southwestern manufacturer of process control instrumentation and computer systems, and Electro, then an aggressive producer of OEM electronic packages for large industrial and defense manufacturers. Following this, more than two dozen acquisitions were completed between 1968 and 1974. Although none of the acquisitions later proved fundamentally unsound, nearly all took somewhat longer to turn around than Mr. Whitman had anticipated. Earnings for the corporation, as a result, remained at relatively low levels until 1972. Summary financial information for Electro is given in Exhibits 1 and 2.

As each new unit was brought into the company, it was accorded divisional status and placed into one of the seven main product groups. The divisions, as wholly owned subsidiaries, were managed in most cases by their former chief executives. A few executives, however, were removed by Electro within one or two years of the purchase under the terms of the acquisition agreement. Division presidents reported either to a group vice president or directly to Mr. Whitman. In this latter category at present were the large and very profitable Jackson Instruments Division and the MOStronics Division, bought in late 1971.

The MOStronics Division, the initial unit in what was to become a semiconductor products group, had become Electro's fastest growing division in terms of percentage of sales. Its strong technological base, highly innovative product development group, and aggressive, capable leadership held the promise of generating a semiconductor products unit rivalling Jackson Instruments in sales and profitability by 1980. Of particular interest to Mr. Whitman was the opportunity to gain a foothold in the consumer electronics market via MOStronics' line of inexpensive personal calculators. With a steady stream of new consumer products from MOStronics' development laboratory, he envisioned building a marketing organization that would someday be of the calibre of those in IBM and Texas Instruments.

CORPORATE OPERATIONS

The seven product groups of Electro Industries operated essentially as autonomous, wholly owned subsidiaries. Following approval of their annual budgets and profit plans, the division presidents were free to decide how best to meet their objectives. Only when a division gave evidence of serious trouble, and nearly always at the request of its senior executive, would the corporate officers take an active part in the division's management.

Corporate operations at Electro were concerned mainly with monitoring divisional performance, corporate financing, long-range planning and acquisitions. A small, high-level staff group carried on these activities with the close direction and involvement of Mr. Whitman. While he left divisional operations almost completely under the purview of division management, no detail of the work at corporate headquarters escaped him. All decisions of any consequence were made either by Mr. Whitman or with his full, prior knowledge and concurrence.

Over the years, this management style had filtered out a corporate staff core consisting of highly skilled professionals who were fiercely loyal to Mr. Whitman and his goals. High turnover characterized the remainder of the corporate group, many of whom ultimately found more compatible circumstances at high levels within Electro's divisions. One important consequence of this turnover was a constant influx of new analytic techniques, different points of view, and fresh ideas. Staff members were recruited as much for their ability to broaden Electro's analytic, MIS, and planning capabilities as for specific industry or functional knowledge.

PRODUCT PORTFOLIO ANALYSIS

One such analytic technique which appeared to offer potentially valuable insights into Electro's problem of profit center coordination was introduced by a recent addition to the staff, James Weatherby. He had become familiar with the technique, which he referred to as "product portfolio analysis," while working for several years as assistant to the vice president of Corporate Planning in a large computer manufacturer. Portfolio analysis had been used by the company's consultants to develop a comprehensive, long-range corporate strategy for the firm's diverse product line.[2]

Having joined Electro early in 1974, just as its profitability began to falter, Mr. Weatherby's initial assignment was to help develop a plan to decide which of the company's twenty-six operating divisions should be divested. Mr. Whitman was convinced that each division had great potential but that even Electro's considerable resources would not be adequate to develop this potential fully for all divisions. The time had come to concentrate the firm's resources in fewer areas.

It was clear that a decision could not be made simply on the basis of current profitability (ROI) or even on a five-year trend. Several divisions presently reporting losses seemed to hold some of the firm's greatest potential for growth. Others, principally those in low-growth markets, while offering relatively little future growth in existing product lines, had been massive contributors of cash to the corporation. The Jackson Instruments group contained three such divisions. Still others were largely self-supporting even though their growth rate was unspectacular. Some divisions, particularly like MOStronics, had become major cash consumers despite every effort to keep them basically self-financing (except for major capacity additions). In almost every case, these divisions held a vital piece of technology that was crucial to Electro's long-term effort to vertically integrate in its main product areas. Selecting divestment candidates from among these businesses seemed almost impossible on any consciously rational basis.

Mr. Weatherby nevertheless began to assemble data for a rough analysis of the company's product portfolio. He decided to carry out the analysis at two levels: first, he considered the corporation as a portfolio of twenty-six divisions corresponding to the official set of profit centers. Because Electro was organized along market lines, with buyer needs in each market providing the fundamental segmentation, he was confident that the profit centers would adequately represent a product as required for the "product portfolio analysis," at least as an initial cut. His next step was to develop a similar portfolio analysis within each of the twenty-six profit centers, moving one level lower in product aggregation.

Based on the data shown in Exhibit 3, Mr. Weatherby developed a corporate portfolio chart for the years 1973 and 1974 (based on current projections) as shown in Exhibit 4. Using similar charts for the firm's main competitors (not shown), he reached a set of tentative con-

---

[2]This technique is described in the text portion of Chapter 4.

clusions regarding a portfolio strategy for the corporation as a whole. Highlights of these conclusions are listed in Exhibit 5.

MOSTRONICS DIVISION[3]

The "level 1" corporate portfolio analysis had taken several months to complete. Mr. Weatherby, on Mr. Whitman's request, presented his initial findings to the board of directors at its October meeting. His presentation was received enthusiastically by most board members, the consensus being that the analysis had provided considerable insight into Electro's rather perplexing situation and that the second-level analysis should be pursued with the utmost dispatch. Mr. Whitman, however, remained somewhat unconvinced and persuaded the board to look first at a single second-level analysis before committing itself to the relatively massive and costly analysis on a corporate-wide basis. MOStronics Division's current problems seemed to offer an ideal test for such a single second-level analysis. Subsequent discussion resulted in a decision by the board to retain the division and to support its growth fully.

A few days after the board meeting, Mr. Whitman met with Mr. Weatherby to outline his assessment of MOStronics' position. It was his feeling that the division had overextended itself in calculator manufacture, losing efficiency and ignoring distribution in the process. He believed that digital watches such as the prototype unit he had been shown on a recent visit to MOStronics' California headquarters had tremendous potential if approached soundly and methodically. He regarded marketing as the key to success in digital watches. But he was concerned above all with preserving MOStronics' technological position in MOS semiconductors: the division's MOS component output had begun to supply several of the most profitable Jackson Instrument product lines in which the MOS technology had become a key selling feature. He was, however, becoming increasingly reluctant to consider making the massive commitment that would be needed to compete effectively in the semiconductor memory market. Present indications were that 4K RAM memories would become the next major battleground of the semiconductor giants: Significant price erosion to well below costs had occurred, under Texas Instruments' leadership, even before most producers had begun to manufacture the memory circuits in volume. He thus favored attempting to remain in calculators, be-

---

[3]Details of the MOStronics Division are contained in Electro Industries, Inc. (A), Chapter 3.

coming a MOS component supplier mainly to other Electro divisions, and proceeding cautiously into digital watches, probably as a joint venture with an established marketer. Nevertheless, he was very eager to consider other alternatives which might be proposed since he was not at all sure of the appropriate strategy for MOStronics.

He then asked Mr. Weatherby to develop his own analysis of MOStronics' situation using the product portfolio concept and to be prepared to present that analysis at the January 30 meeting of Electro's executive committee.[4] This meeting was part of the week-long series of executive committee meetings organized for the purpose of deciding which divisions of the company would be pruned in order to improve Electro's long-range profit potential. The entire day had been set aside for MOStronics since it was the largest contributor to Electro's current losses as well as the greatest potential contributor to Electro's near-term growth. Mr. Warner had been advised of the board's earlier decision to retain MOStronics and its tentative agreement to provide adequate funding for its growth. Just how best to realize its potential was, therefore, to be the focal issue of the meeting.

Mr. Weatherby immediately set about the task of gathering data to use in his analysis. Summaries of the data he collected are given in Exhibits 6 and 7. Exhibit 8 contains a product portfolio chart of the type he intended to use to display MOStronics' position in semiconductors, calculators, and watches vis-á-vis its three major competitors: Texas Instruments, Bowmar, and Rockwell International. While Mr. Weatherby used the 10 percent market growth rate to separate the high- and low-growth areas on the corporate product portfolio chart, Mr. Warner thought that 15 percent was a more appropriate number for MOStronics' portfolio chart. Mr. Warner's argument for this higher number was that MOStronics' products were in a high-growth, high-technology area, compared to the rest of Electro's portfolio.

---

[4]The executive committee consisted of Mr. Whitman, his financial vice president, and presidents of the four largest divisions (who were corporate group vice presidents).

Exhibit 1

ELECTRO INDUSTRIES, INC. [C]

Consolidated Balance Sheet Summary
[millions of dollars]

	AS OF DECEMBER 31				
	1970	1971	1972	1973	1974*
ASSETS					
Current assets:					
Cash and equivalents	2.3	3.8	9.8	28.6	25.3
Accounts receivable	20.2	34.7	58.2	85.0	117.4
Inventories	23.5	37.5	90.5	118.3	143.4
Other current assets	0.7	1.1	1.2	3.9	5.8
Total current assets	46.7	77.1	159.7	235.8	291.9
Plant, property and equipment	48.6	77.4	119.6	216.6	337.0
Less accumulated depreciation	23.0	26.8	34.3	47.2	67.8
Net fixed assets	25.6	50.6	85.3	169.4	269.2
Total assets	72.3	127.7	245.0	405.2	561.1
LIABILITIES					
Current liabilities:					
Accounts payable	8.9	17.2	45.3	70.1	121.5
Accruals	1.6	4.9	8.7	15.0	28.6
Notes payable	4.1	4.7	11.5	34.3	44.0
Total current liabilities	14.6	26.8	65.5	119.4	194.1
Long-term debt, noncurrent	11.9	22.6	50.3	95.2	140.1
Net worth:					
Common stock	2.5	2.6	7.7	10.4	16.4
Capital surplus	17.2	17.9	45.6	60.8	96.8
Preferred stock (5%)	0.0	27.3	27.3	27.3	27.3
Retained earnings	26.1	30.5	48.6	92.1	86.4
Total net worth	45.8	78.3	129.2	190.6	226.9
Total liabilities and net worth	72.3	127.7	245.0	405.2	561.1

*Preliminary.

Exhibit 2
ELECTRO INDUSTRIES, INC. [C]
Consolidated Income Statement Summary
[millions of dollars]

| | YEAR ENDING DECEMBER 31 | | | | |
	1970	1971	1972	1973	1974*
Net sales	204.0	337.6	523.4	721.3	875.5
Cost of sales	160.6	257.9	365.7	457.6	679.0
Gross profit	43.4	79.7	157.7	263.7	196.5
Selling, general, and administrative expenses	36.6	67.4	114.3	150.1	177.2
Operating profit	6.8	12.3	43.4	113.6	19.3
Interest expense	1.1	2.1	4.8	19.0	32.0
Income before taxes	5.7	10.2	38.6	94.6	(12.7)
Income taxes	(3.2)	(5.6)	(20.5)	(51.1)	7.0
Net income	2.5	4.6	18.1	43.5	(5.7)
Earnings per common share	$0.62	$1.12	$2.98	$5.71	$(0.66)

*Preliminary.

ELECTRO INDUSTRIES, INC. [C]

Corporate Portfolio Analysis: Summary Data
[dollar figures in millions]

	SALES		CASH FLOW*		1974 LONG-TERM MARKET GROWTH RATE	RELATIVE MARKET SHARE		QUADRANT**
	1973	1974	1973	1974		1973	1974	1974
JACKSON INSTRUMENTS GROUP								
Division A	$ 90.6	$108.1	$13.9	$ 6.3	7.5%	1.25	1.31	$
Division B	49.7	57.2	4.1	1.2	7.3	0.38	0.48	X
Division C	35.0	35.2	0.5	0.3	3.5	0.17	0.15	X
Division D	21.5	22.6	1.9	1.0	2.8	1.02	1.00	$/X
Division E	21.4	20.8	2.4	0.4	9.8	1.60	1.45	$/*
AEROSPACE/DEFENSE PRODUCTS GROUP								
Division F	$ 34.5	$ 37.9	$ 4.7	$ 0.6	4.3%	1.00	1.10	$/X
Division G	32.7	40.9	1.5	0.7	18.2	1.80	1.70	*
Division H	22.3	24.5	1.8	0.1	6.0	0.11	0.095	X
Division I	17.6	18.1	1.2	0.2	2.8	0.42	0.40	X
Division J	11.1	15.0	0.6	(1.3)	15.5	0.24	0.31	?
Division K	10.7	15.2	(0.1)	0.2	17.6	0.41	0.59	?
INDUSTRIAL PRODUCTS GROUP								
Division L	$ 51.8	$ 62.9	$ 8.8	$ 3.7	2.8%	1.85	2.10	$
Division M	34.4	31.9	1.9	(1.4)	6.0	1.25	1.15	$
Division N	33.6	43.7	0.8	1.3	12.0	1.03	1.11	*
Division O	28.4	34.5	1.2	0.9	10.6	0.16	0.23	?
Division P	26.3	30.5	4.4	1.9	9.5	2.60	2.70	$
Division Q	24.7	33.9	(0.2)	0.4	21.7	1.25	1.15	*
Division R	21.5	26.5	2.0	0.9	11.5	0.35	0.33	?
Division S	17.2	21.9	1.5	1.0	12.7	0.23	0.25	?

Exhibit 3 [cont.]
ELECTRO INDUSTRIES, INC. [C]

| | SALES | | CASH FLOW* | | 1974 LONG-TERM MARKET GROWTH RATE | RELATIVE MARKET SHARE | | QUADRANT** |
	1973	1974	1973	1974		1973	1974	1974
DATA SERVICES GROUP								
Division T	$ 37.1	$ 47.5	$ 0.2	$ 0.3	9.3%	0.13	0.20	X
Division U	28.0	37.8	(1.2)	(1.5)	14.0	0.16	0.17	?
Division V	6.4	9.6	(1.5)	(1.2)	20.2	0.19	0.25	?
FINANCIAL SERVICES GROUP								
Division W	$ 26.2	$ 34.6	$ (0.8)	$ 0.6	16.4%	0.095	0.105	?
Division X	6.4	8.3	0.4	0.7	6.5	0.20	0.25	X
MOSTRONICS DIVISION								
Division Y	$ 22.8	$ 43.2	$ 6.3	$ (1.4)	30.0%	0.21	0.15	?
AZTEC PROPERTIES DIVISION								
Division Z	$ 9.4	$ 13.2	$ 4.2	$ (1.0)	8.7%	0.060	0.090	X
Totals	$721.3	$875.5	$60.5	$14.9	10.6%	0.82	0.86	
						—Weighted Averages—		

*Cash flow = earnings + depreciation.
**key: * = Star
    X = Dog
    $ = Cash Cow
    ? = Problem Child
    (See Exhibit 4 for positioning of these divisions.)

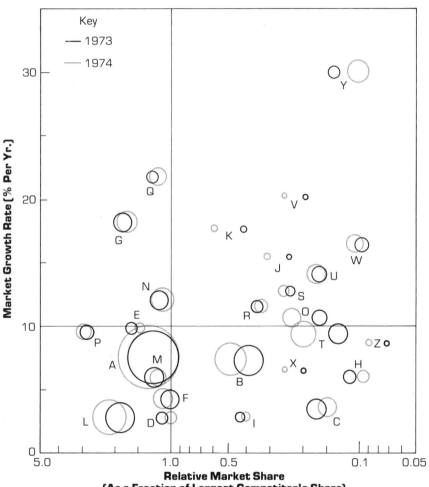

Exhibit 4

ELECTRO INDUSTRIES, INC. [C]

Corporate Portfolio Chart for 1973 and 1974

Exhibit 5

ELECTRO INDUSTRIES, INC. (C)

Summary of Mr. Weatherby's Corporate Portfolio Strategy Recommendations

1. It would appear that some of Electro's 1974 loss may be the result of costly efforts to gain market share in low-growth markets (Divisions A, B, F, L, P, T, X and Z). Share building strategies might better be limited to our high-growth divisions. This would suggest that:

   (a) We invest only as necessary to maintain present market share for Divisions A, D, E, F, L, M, and P.

   (b) Divisions B, C, H, I, T, and Z be operated under a "harvesting" strategy with investments limited to funds generated by each division (net of corporate charges).

2. Electro seems to be supporting a rather large number of high-growth divisions relative to its resources. Concentrating our investments in fewer divisions might produce more attractive increases in market share. Specifically:

   (a) Unless Divisions G, N, and Q are in a position to gain additional market share quite cheaply, we might set investment flows to these divisions at share maintaining levels. Since each is losing share now, an increase in capital budget allocations seems warranted.

   (b) Of the remaining nine high-growth divisions, it appears unlikely that Electro can support more than three or four under a market dominance strategy. Looking at the competitive position of each in some detail (using information provided by the management of these divisions), Divisions K, U, and W appear to be strongest relative to competitors. These divisions should be supported to the maximum amount of capital that they can absorb.

   (c) MOStronics is in a unique position. Considering the value of its technology and the immense growth potential of its three markets (including digital watches), abandoning the division would probably be short-sighted. Full support seems justified *except*, perhaps, in the semiconductor memory area which is already coming under solid control of several-billion-dollar corporations.

   (d) The disposition of Divisions J, O, R, S, and V should be considered. Meanwhile, if feasible from a morale standpoint, these divisions should be kept on a "no cash input" basis to conserve funds for the divisions selected for growth.

Exhibit 6
ELECTRO INDUSTRIES, INC. [C]
Market Share Data

	MARKET SHARE
A. PERSONAL CALCULATORS (1974)	
Texas Instruments	33%
Bowmar Instruments	13
Rockwell International	11
Commodore Business Machines	9
MOStronics	4.75
National Semiconductor	4
	74.75%
B. MOS INTEGRATED CIRCUITS (1973)	
Intel	25%
American Microsystems	22 .
Mostek	16
Texas Instruments	15
Rockwell International	13
National Semiconductor	6
MOStronics	1
	98%

Source: The Boston Consulting Group.

Note: Motorola Inc., was scheduled to have a 300,000 square foot MOS facility in production by mid-1975. Output, estimated to be in the range of $100 million annually, was intended for digital watch, automotive, and 4K memory applications.

Exhibit 7
ELECTRO INDUSTRIES, INC. [C]
Competitor's Financial Profiles [1973]

	NET SALES (MILLIONS)	AFTER-TAX PROFIT (MILLIONS)	TOTAL DEBT TO NET WORTH	TOTAL ASSETS (MILLIONS)
American Microsystems	$ 55.1	$ 4.8	86%	$ 48.7
Bowmar Instruments	64.8	7.6	232	48.8
Commodore Business Machines	32.8	2.5	184	25.6
Intel	65.6	9.2	82	50.6
Mostek	41.9	6.6	67	28.7
National Semiconductor	99.4	3.7	96	53.4
Rockwell International	3,179.0	131.0	106	2,014.2
Texas Instruments	1,287.3	83.2	77	828.0

Sources: Moody's Industrial Manual, 1974.

Exhibit 8
ELECTRO INDUSTRIES, INC. [C]
Product Portfolio Chart for MOStronics' Main Product Lines

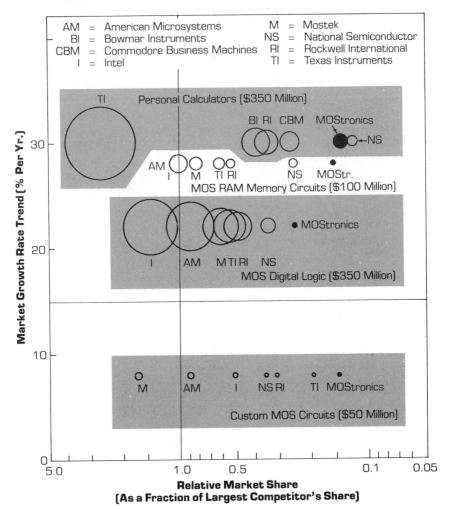

Note: Annual sales are represented by the diameter of circles.

DISCUSSION QUESTIONS

ELECTRO INDUSTRIES, INC. [C]

1. What problems do you think are confronting Electro?
2. What is the corporate cash flow situation?
3. What can we learn from Exhibits 3, 4, and 5?
4. What can we learn from Exhibits 6, 7, and 8?
5. What recommendations would you make as a member of the Board:
   a) in terms of further analysis?
   b) in terms of specifications?

Market Attractiveness— Business Position Assessment

A critical step in the formulation of a strategic market plan is the determination of an appropriate mission for each business. When a business can be subdivided into parts according to differences in strategic approach or market opportunity, a mission must be determined for each part. Should the business unit or subunit receive investment funds? What goals should be set for sales growth, market share, profitability, and cash flow? These decisions provide a context within which marketing, manufacturing, research and development, and other functional policies can be formulated.

The portfolio charts described in Chapter 4 provide management with a visual check on several important strategic relationships, including internal cash flow balance, and market share and growth trajectories vis-à-vis competitors. Users of product portfolio charts recognize, however, that these insights, while necessary and useful, are in most cases insufficient by themselves to make investment decisions affecting the mission of a business. Critics point to three major shortcomings:

1. In many circumstances, factors other than simply relative market share and industry growth play a significant role in influencing cash flow.
2. Cash flow may be viewed as less important than ROI as a basis for comparing the attractiveness of investing in one business unit as opposed to another.

3. Portfolio charts provide little direct insight into how one business unit might be compared with another in terms of investment opportunity. Is every "star," for example, necessarily better than a "cash cow"? How should one "question mark" be compared to another in terms of whether it should be built into a "star" or allowed to decline?

Concern for these issues has resulted in the development of an approach that we shall call "market attractiveness-business position assessment." As with portfolio analysis, two-dimensional displays are used to portray the situation of a particular business unit or subunit and each business is represented on the chart by a circle whose area is proportional to sales. Instead of industry growth rate and relative market share, however, the axes are labelled "market attractiveness" and "business position." In large part, this approach provides a formal way of reporting and displaying the kinds of analyses described in Chapters 2 and 3.

MARKET ATTRACTIVENESS
AND BUSINESS POSITION

Two major sets of factors appear to influence the relative attractiveness of investing in a business unit. First, how attractive is the market in which the business is located? For example, is it growing? Are profit margins high? Is it regulated? Second, how well-equipped and how well-positioned is the business to take advantage of opportunities within the market? For example, does it have technological leadership? Low manufacturing costs? High market share? (For now we shall use the word "business" without specifying how it may be defined or at what level of aggregation the analysis should be carried out. As in earlier chapters a "business" could conceivably be defined as narrowly as an individual product or market segment or as broadly as a division.)

The portfolio displays described in Chapter 4 may thus be viewed as a special case of a more general theory relating market and company variables to performance. In the special case of the portfolio approach performance is measured in terms of cash flow, growth is the only market variable considered to affect performance, and relative market share is the only company variable considered to affect performance.

In the more general case, where some *composite* measures of market attractiveness and business position are plotted on a two-dimensional display, some conclusions may be drawn about overall investment opportunity, according to where a business is located on the chart. Sometimes such charts are divided into three "bands" as shown in Figure 1. A business with high overall attractiveness, for example would then be plotted in the top left part of the chart.

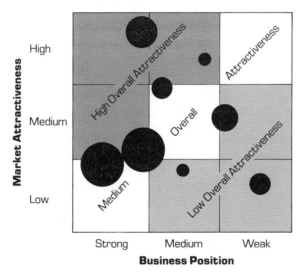

Figure 1
3 × 3 Chart Depicting Relative Investment Opportunity

What makes a market "attractive" or a business position in a market "strong?" Experience has shown that the factors listed in Table 1 below are among the most important.[1] These factors are usually grouped under five major headings: market factors, competition, financial and economic factors, technological factors, and socio-political factors. Note that this requires some rearrangement of the data that might be produced from the analyses suggested in Chapters 2 and 3.

---

[1]For a much more detailed description of the ways to assess "market attractiveness" and "business position," see William E. Rothschild, *Putting It All Together: A Guide to Strategic Thinking,* New York Amacon, 1976. See also Peter Lorange, "Divisional Planning: Setting Effective Direction," *Sloan Management Review,* Fall 1975, pp. 77–91.

Table 1
FACTORS CONTRIBUTING TO MARKET
ATTRACTIVENESS AND BUSINESS POSITION

ATTRACTIVENESS OF YOUR MARKET	STATUS/POSITION OF YOUR BUSINESS
MARKET FACTORS	
Size (dollars, units or both)	Your share (in equivalent terms)
Size of key segments	Your share of key segments
Growth rate per year:	Your annual growth rate:
Total	Total
Segments	Segments
Diversity of market	Diversity of your participation
Sensitivity to price, service features, and external factors	Your influence on the market
Cyclicality	Lags or leads in your sales
Seasonality	
Bargaining Power of Upstream Suppliers	Bargaining power of your suppliers
Bargaining Power of Downstream Suppliers	Bargaining power of your customers
COMPETITION	
Types of competitors	Where you fit, how you compare in terms
Degree of concentration	of products, marketing capability,
Changes in type and mix	service, production strength, financial
	strength, management
Entries and exits	Segments you have entered or left
Changes in share	Your relative share change
Substitution by new technology	Your vulnerability to new technology
Degrees and types of integration	Your own level of integration
FINANCIAL AND ECONOMIC FACTORS	
Contribution margins	Your margins
Leveraging factors, such as economies of scale and experience	Your scale and experience
Barriers to entry or exit (both financial and non-financial)	Barriers to your entry or exit (both financial and non-financial)
Capacity utilization	Your capacity utilization
TECHNOLOGICAL FACTORS	
Maturity and volatility	Your ability to cope with change
Complexity	Depths of your skills
Differentiation	Types of your technological skills
Patents and copyrights	Your patent protection
Manufacturing process technology required	Your manufacturing technology
SOCIO-POLITICAL FACTORS	
IN YOUR ENVIRONMENT	
Social attitudes and trends	Your company's responsiveness and flexibility
Laws and government agency regulations	Your company's ability to cope
Influence with pressure groups and government representatives	Your company's aggressiveness
Human factors, such as unionization and community acceptance	Your company's relationships

Table 1 is intended to be suggestive only. It should be used as a starting point. Some items will be deleted and others added depending on the situation, as described later in this chapter.

The actual analyses required to develop such specific summary measures require considerable skill. Sometimes "prose" statements about the various characteristics are more revealing than plain numerical estimates. Table 2 shows such an analysis of just two of the five major sets of variables that contribute to market attractiveness, namely market factors and competition. This hypothetical analysis of the color television market shows the amount of detail that may be needed to build up a careful assessment of a market and a company's position in it. Such analyses are constructed from a detailed examination of customers, competitors, market characteristics, the external environment, and the company itself as outlined in Chapter 2.

Table 2

EXCERPT FROM A SAMPLE ANALYSIS OF THE
NORTH AMERICAN COLOR TELEVISION SET MARKET

MARKET ATTRACTIVENESS

MARKET

- Large market: at least 7.6 million sets sold in 1975, approximately $3 billion sales.
- Growth erratic, correlates to GNP, and personal disposable income (PDI).

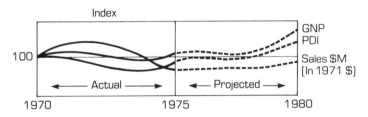

— Compound annual growth
     1971–75   x %
     1976–80:
        most likely y %
        highest y_1
        lowest y_2
— Saturation may deflate growth by 1980.
- Mix changing toward more table models, fewer consoles; therefore downward pressure on average price/set.
- Customer segments are not likely to change significantly as percent of total.
- New related product segments won't be significant through 1980:
    — Video player $x million by 1980
    — Large screen $y
    — Video $z

Table 2 [cont.]
EXCERPT FROM A SAMPLE ANALYSIS OF THE
NORTH AMERICAN COLOR TELEVISION SET MARKET

COMPETITION
- Relatively concentrated:

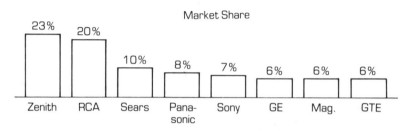

Market Share

50% of market held by 3 suppliers

- GE may drop out.
- Magnavox (Philips) expected to become more aggressive.
- Apparent strategies vary:
  - Zenith
  - RCA
  - Sears
  - Panasonic
  - Sony
  - GE
  - Magnavox
  - GTE Sylvania
- Focus of leaders seems to be on performance:
  - Quality of picture.
  - Frequency of repair.
  - Features that differentiate short-term, e.g., Zenith's zoom.
- Leaders advertise heavily—estimates:
  - Zenith $x
  - RCA $y
  - GTE $z

PRACTICAL CONSIDERATIONS

Unfortunately there are three very distinct problems in making assessments of either market attractiveness or business position:

- The relevant list of contributing factors in any given situation has to be identified.

- The direction and form of the relationships have to be determined.
- Each of the contributing factors has to be weighted in any composite measure of "attractiveness" or "position," depending on its relative importance.

The resolution of all three of the above issues depends heavily on whether the financial criterion for measuring the performance of business is return-on-investment (ROI) or cash flow. Since the point of this analysis is to assess *investment* opportunity, ROI is usually considered more appropriate. This means that a display of high market attractiveness and strong business position is not necessarily indicative of high cash flows. This is especially true in a high growth industry where high ROI may be associated with negative cash flow. In the remainder of this chapter, it will be assumed that ROI is the criterion being used. This, of course, contrasts with the cash flow criterion used in portfolio analysis.

Each of the three issues will now be taken up in turn.

IDENTIFYING THE RELEVANT FACTORS

Each industry is likely to be somewhat different in terms of what factors are important, depending primarily on the nature of the product and customer behavior. With highly differentiated products, for example, for which the customer seeks technical innovation or other special benefits, relative technological position may be a key to a strong business position, and patent protection may be a major factor determining market attractiveness. For commodity products, low manufacturing costs and entry barriers may be prime contributors to business position and industry attractiveness, respectively. Analysts using this approach must rely heavily on management judgment and experience and avoid easy generalizations about what particular factors are relevant. For the same reason, upper-level management, when called on to approve recommendations for investment based on such analysis, must take care to understand why certain factors are included in the analysis and why others have been excluded.

RELATING THE FACTORS TO MARKET
ATTRACTIVENESS AND BUSINESS POSITION

Each factor may increase or decrease market attractiveness or business position. Usually the relationship is not a simple one. Supposing, for example, that supplier concentration was considered to be a possible variable affecting market attractiveness. Does high concentration enhance attractiveness? Under all circumstances? Is a two-company industry twice as attractive as one with four major competitors? Usually few clear guidelines are possible since the answers to such questions often depend on the particular company and its markets. As before, management judgment is required. As an example, Table 3 summarizes the judgments of executives in one major industrial company about what makes a market environment "attractive." We should be quick to point out that another company in a different market environment may, quite appropriately, come up with a different list.

Table 3

ISSUE: WHAT IS AN ATTRACTIVE ENVIRONMENT?
EXECUTIVE PREFERENCES IN ONE MAJOR CORPORATION

	HIGH	MEDIUM	LOW
MARKET CHARACTERISTICS			
Size	Over $500 million	$250–500	Under $250 million
Growth	Over 15% / year	10–15%	Under 10%
Cyclicality	Counter cyclical		Cyclical
COMPETITION			
Type	U.S. domination	U.S./some imports	Foreign domination
Concentration	Top three with 75% (One who is recognized leader)	Top 5–75% (Two who alternate as leader)	Fragmented (No leader)
FINANCIAL			
Capital Intensity (plant and equipment)	High	Medium	Low
TECHNOLOGY			
Maturity	Evolving and chance to differentiate	Stable	Revolutionary
Protectability	Patent protectable	Process protectable	Easy to follow
SOCIO/POLITICAL			
	Many reinforcing positive trends	Many/some conflicting	Few or negative trends

WEIGHTING THE FACTORS

A procedure now has to be devised to translate the assessments of the various contributory factors, such as growth rate and maturity, into summary measures of market attractiveness and business position respectively. This can take one of two forms: either an overall summary measure is judgmentally assessed from the various "high," "medium," and "low" factor scores, or scores are given to each factor, these are then weighted and combined.

Tables 4 & 5 show a scheme by which management can assign weights to the various factors depending on their relative importance. (Many of the factors listed in Table 1 have simply been ignored in this illustration.) As always, what should be included or excluded, and how it should be scored and weighted, is purely a matter of managerial judgment and experience.

Table 4
MARKET ATTRACTIVENESS

FACTOR	SCORE*	WEIGHTING	RANKING
1. Market size	.5	15	7.5
2. Volume growth (units)	0	15	0
3. Concentration	1.0	30	30.0
4. Financial	.5	25	12.5
5. Technology	.5	15	7.5
		100	57.5

* High = 1.0
  Medium = 0.5
  Low = 0.0

Table 5
BUSINESS POSITION

FACTOR	SCORE*	WEIGHTING	RANKING
1. Product technology			
—Current quality	0	20	0
—New technology	.5	20	10
2. Manufacturing			
—Scale	.5	10	5
—Efficiency	.5	10	5
—Physical distribution	.5	10	5
3. Marketing			
—Expertise	0	10	0
—Sales	.5	10	5
—Service	.5	10	5
		100	35

* High = 1.0
  Medium = 0.5
  Low = 0.0

CONSTRUCTING THE PRESENT
INVESTMENT OPPORTUNITY CHART

Assessment of each factor leads finally to some overall judgments about the position of a business unit (or subunit) on each axis of a two-dimensional display. Normally, as in portfolio analysis, the business unit is represented on the chart by a circle whose size (diameter or area) corresponds to the sales volume of the business. The axes may be divided into high, medium, or low categories, or "scores" of 0 to 100 may be assessed for each axis using some agreed-upon weighting scheme, such as the one just illustrated.

The final result of such an analysis, using the summary scores shown in Tables 4 and 5, is illustrated in Figure 2. This may be thought of as a classification of the *present* opportunity facing the business, using the *present* strategy of the business and its competitors, and the *present* character of the industry in which the business operates to make the assessment.

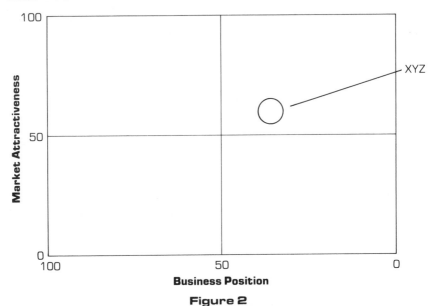

Figure 2

Plot of Rankings for Business Analyzed In Tables 4 & 5;
Area of Circle Indicates Sales

ASSESSING THE FUTURE OPPORTUNITY

The analysis of the current position of a business, just described, is relatively mechanical. Experienced analysts will differ somewhat in their assessments of individual factors but they are likely to be in substantial agreement about the present position of a business on the chart.

Far more difficult is the assessment of *future* opportunity. One frequently used approach is to make a single assessment of market attractiveness at some relatively close future date (such as a year from now) and to omit the current assessment. A variety of strategic options that might change "business position" are then explored against this background. While this approach saves time, it does not deal explicitly with changes in the market environment that alter its attractiveness over time.

A more rigorous approach is to do a thorough analysis of both present and future market environment and position. First, this should be carried out on the assumption that no major changes in strategy are made, and then repeated several times to explore new strategic options.

This is illustrated in Figure 3 for a market where attractiveness is forecast to decline. If no substantial strategic changes are made, the business may be expected to slide vertically downwards on the chart. Alternatively, the business may be moved into a commanding position in a decreasingly attractive market (strategy 1), or position may be allowed to slip as attractiveness declines (strategy 2). Implicit in this is a two-stage analytical process:

Stage 1: Exploring the Impact of a "No Change" Strategy

The analysis required at this step is an exact repeat of the current analysis except that assessments are made at some *future* time point, usually three or five years from now depending on the planning cycle.

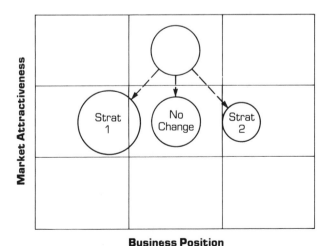

Business Position

Figure 3

Exploring Strategic Options

Such an analysis requires considerable skill. Forecasts have to be made of how the market will evolve competitively, financially, technologically, and environmentally. Unfortunately, theories of market evolution are only embryonic.

Product life cycle theory, as pointed out in Chapter 2, is the most well known theory of evolution, but it focuses on only a very small number of the variables required to assess market attractiveness. Its major focus is on sales and marketing mix variables. There is no explicit inclusion of segmentation changes, technological changes, external environmental changes, market share changes, financial performance changes, or cost changes due to experience, to name but a few. Furthermore the unit of analysis is usually a "product," not "business" or "market." Several other partial theories do exist,[2] but none are comprehensive enough to provide significant help at this step in the planning process.

Assessing the future is, therefore, largely a process of qualitative judgment. It involves answering questions such as:

- How will customer behavior change?
- How will segmentation be affected?
- How will competitors redefine their activities?
- How will competitors change their investment strategies?
- How will competitors' functional strategies change?
- How will product technology change?
- How will process technology change?
- What environmental changes will take place?
- What changes can be expected in the character of competition?
- How will costs change?
- How will financial performance be affected?

This is much more than "sales forecasting," encompassing a much more complex set of factors and relationships that influence future attractiveness.

Once such changes have been forecasted, the next task is to determine what impact they will have on the firm *if no significant change in strategy occurs*. Of crucial importance is understanding, as outlined in Chapter 2, how the "fit" between the firm's particular competence and the requirements of the marketplace may change as the market evolves. Even if this assessment is qualitative it provides some basis for making judgments about the future strength of a business' position in the light of forecasted changes.

---

[2]See Derek Abell, "Competitive Market Strategies: Some Generalizations and Hypotheses," Marketing Science Institute Report No. 75–107; See also William J. Abernathy and Kenneth Wayne, "Limits of the Learning Curve," *Harvard Business Review*, 50, No. 5 (September-October 1974), p. 109.

Stage 2: The Strategy Decision

The strategy decision requires that the process just described be repeated several times. However, the "no planned change" assumption is dropped in favor of planned changes in strategy to match the evolving marketplace. Each time the process is repeated, different assumptions are made about the objectives and investments to be made in the business. A final choice of strategy requires estimating the long-run costs and benefits of contemplated changes.

Again, this is a very difficult task. Cost estimates require at least an approximate idea of the actual functional strategies, budgets and fixed investments needed to pursue a particular option. An estimate of benefits requires an assessment of the expected financial and market performance which will result from a strategic change. *It is of paramount importance to consider the reaction of competitors to any strategic change.* This facet of the analysis is most often ignored with serious consequences for the final effectiveness of strategic market plans.

There are usually several major strategic investment options. These correspond closely to those described in Chapter 4. The main difference is that strategy choices are expressed in terms of changes in "business position," a composite of several different variables, rather than in terms of holding, gaining, or harvesting market share.

1. *Investing to hold* aims at maintaining the current position. It calls for sufficient investment to keep up with changes as the market evolves. Figure 4 shows this strategy in a market of declining attractiveness.

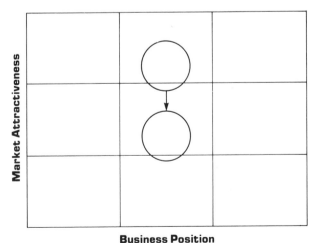

Business Position
Figure 4
Investing to Hold

223

2. *Investing to penetrate* (Figure 5) aims at improving business position. It requires sufficient investment to move the business to the left on the chart. Such a strategy is usually undertaken during the early development of a market or growth phase.

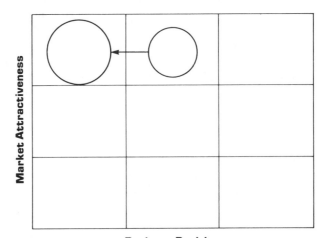

Business Position
Figure 5
Investing to Penetrate

3. *Investing to rebuild* (Figure 6) aims at restoring a position which has been lost. Such "revitalization" may take considerable investment if the market is entering maturity or declining.

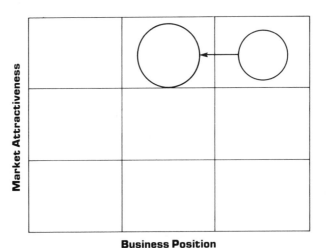

Business Position
Figure 6
Investing to Rebuild

4. *Selective investment* (Figure 7) aims at strengthening positions in in segments of the activity where the benefits of penetration or rebuilding appear to exceed the costs, and letting position weaken where costs exceed benefits.

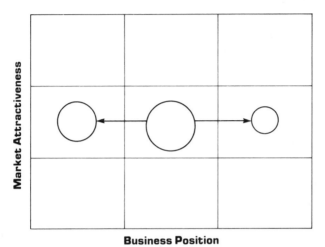

Business Position
Figure 7
Selective Investment

5. *Low investment* (Figure 8) aims at "harvesting" the business. Usually business position is exchanged for cash. This may be implemented over a fairly long time period, however. In the short

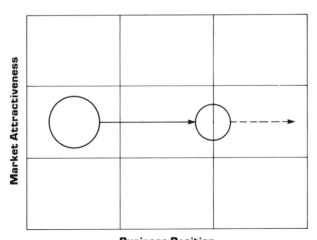

Business Position
Figure 8
Low Investment

run, selective investment may be made with a view to eventual sale of the business at the highest possible prices.

In practice, inexperienced planners tend to spend too much time on the assessment of *present* overall attractiveness, and too little time on the more difficult job of assessing future changes and strategic options for dealing with them. This is natural, perhaps, because the former is relatively easier and more "mechanistic"; the latter is more difficult and requires much more judgment.

DEFINING THE UNIT OF ANALYSIS

As noted earlier, these analytical methods may be applied at a variety of levels of aggregation provided that meaningful measures of the various factors can be made. Theoretically this could be an individual product, a product line, a market segment, a business unit, or even a division. In practice, a level of aggregation is usually chosen which is meaningful strategically, i.e., a level at which plans are drawn-up and implemented, and at which strategic decisions can be made relatively independently of strategic decisions in other organizational units. Thus it is more likely that an analysis would be made for the color-television business than television sets as a whole, and would encompass all color sets rather than focus on any particular size or model.

The choice of level at which to carry out market attractiveness-business position assessments rests with management. There are no easy prescriptions. Often the analysis may be repeated at several different levels. For example, corporate management may be interested in assessing the attractiveness of investing funds in a particular business unit and will ask the general manager of the business unit to provide such an analysis; the general manager may in turn ask his or her subordinate program managers to present an analysis of investment opportunity in each of several major product or market segments. Also, for planning purposes businesses are sometimes divided first on the basis of products, and then on the basis of user industries or geographic markets. In such cases the analytical procedures can be repeated across each of these dimensions.

SUMMARY

The analyses described in this chapter are based on separate assessments of market attractiveness and business position and the display of the results on a two-dimensional plot. The analysis of investment potential proceeds in three distinct stages. First, assessments of current market attractiveness and business position are made. Second, the analysis is repeated to portray the new position of a business as market conditions change with no corresponding change in strategy. Third, alternative strategic adaptions to a changed market environment are explored.

Market attractiveness-business position assessment focuses on the ROI potential of alternative strategic missions for a business. In this sense it complements portfolio analysis which is primarily concerned with the cash flow implications of strategy, and overall cash balances between various units in a division or company portfolio.

TEX-FIBER INDUSTRIES— PETROLOID PRODUCTS DIVISION (A)[1]

In late January 1975, Mr. J.T. (Jack) Simmons, General Manager of Tex-Fiber Industries—Petroloid Products Division (PPD), called a meeting of his key managers to solicit their views on what he perceived to be a worsening order and backlog situation.

Tex-Fiber's PPD had achieved record levels of sales and earnings in 1974 despite a severe economic recession and soaring raw materials costs. Fuelled by a large backlog of orders, the plant had operated at capacity for the first three quarters of the year. Management had then set two primary objectives: to raise prices to avoid a profit squeeze, and to obtain a product mix which yielded the maximum sales and earnings from the available resources.

By the fourth quarter of 1974, however, it seemed that the recession was going to have a direct and severe impact on the industry. Backlogs began to fall and new orders dried "to a trickle" (see Exhibit 1). By early 1975 plant utilization had dropped to 60 percent of capacity. Without rapid and decisive action, Mr. Simmons feared that profitability and liquidity for 1975 would be seriously threatened.

The Petroloid Products Division was somewhat unique among Tex-Fiber businesses in that it represented the company's only direct involvement in the petrochemicals industry. It was operated as a semiautonomous business unit (BU) within the Materials Group. All of Tex-Fiber's other divisions were involved in either synthetic fiber or textile related manufacturing activities. Tex-Fiber Industries ranked among the top 50 of *Fortune's* 500 largest industrial corporations.

The PPD was formed as an outgrowth of research and development conducted at Tex-Fiber laboratories in Philadelphia, Pennsylvania. During the 1940s scientists there were investigating the use of petroloids for textile fibers. When it was discovered that petroloids were likely to have many other still unexplored industrial applications, the Petroloid Products Division was created to carry on the manufacture and further development of these products. As it turned out, petroloids were never used in any quantity in the manufacture of synthetic fibers.

---

[1]This case was prepared by John Craig in collaboration with Derek F. Abell.

The PPD had proved to be a valuable addition to Tex-Fiber's portfolio of businesses. Following a period of initial losses, the department had reported 14 years of profit (see Exhibit 2). In the last ten years, it had generated a cumulative cash flow of over $84 million. Tex-Fiber Industries, however, levied a corporate assessment on each business unit in the form of an annual dividend. After these assessments, the PPD actually showed a very sizeable negative cumulative cash flow. In effect, part of the dividends returned to the corporate treasury were being reinvested to finance growth in PPD fixed assets and working capital.

Commenting on this pattern of growth via corporate investment, Mr. J.P. Means, Corporate Vice President-Finance, was on the record as having stated:

> For many years, at the operating level, we have tended to run our business in a one-dimensional financial environment. That one critical dimension was earnings. The name of the game was to make sales and consequently earnings grow as fast as we could and let the corporate treasury worry about financing the growth. During those years, our position as a triple-A rated company with a comparatively low level of debt allowed us to emphasize this sort of growth strategy.

> But with the inflation rate accelerating dramatically during the 1970s, investments in new plant and equipment have far exceeded capital cost recovery of older plants. Inventories and receivables have ballooned upward as sales have accelerated. With prices frozen, the return on sales hasn't brought in enough cash to support this inflated investment. Borrowings have increased and our capital structure has become more heavily weighted with debt. And now that the Federal Reserve Board has tightened up the money supply, funds have become hard to get and interest rates have skyrocketed. The days when the corporate treasury can provide a seemingly unending stream of cash to all of our businesses are over.

In this new cash constrained environment of the '70s, each division at Tex-Fiber Industries had been asked to pay particular attention to cash projections in their planning. PPD, historically a cash user after dividends, had been designated as a major net supplier of cash to the corporation over the 1976–80 period. Preliminary plans drawn up in late 1974 called, in fact, for a total of $84 million over and above dividend assessments, to be made available to the corporate treasury over the five-year period.[2] If achieved this would virtually eliminate the

---

[2] This amount might be increased or decreased depending on actual 1975 results. In the event of continued negative cash flow after dividends in 1975, the additional deficit would be added to the $84 million requirement. In the event of positive 1975 cash flow after dividends, this amount would be regarded as a "first installment" on the $84 million requirement.

cumulative deficit of the preceding ten years and put PPD on a break-even basis with respect to cash.

In calling the meeting of his key executives, Jack Simmons had asked them to bear in mind these longer run objectives, as well as make recommendations about how to react to the current downturn.

Simmons had emphasized that although each manager should be prepared to represent the views of his own department, he should also bear in mind the overall needs of the division.

THE PETROLOIDS BUSINESS

Petroloids were man-made substances based on the synthesis of organic hydrocarbons into a family of unique materials. The product lines were grouped into three major categories: oils; petro-rubbers; and foams, adhesives and sealants (FAS). Petro-oils were used as engine additives, lubricants, defoamers, water repellants, rust preventatives, hydraulic oils, damping oils, etc. In most applications, a relatively few large customers accounted for the bulk of sales. These customers generally used petro-oils in the production of their own end products.

Petro-rubbers were sold to molders for the manufacture of rigid and flexible rubber materials. Most molders were relatively small independent concerns who sold the finished product under contract to a wide variety of manufacturing industries. Because of the wide variety of potential applications for petro-rubbers, petroloid producers worked closely with end users as well as molders in developing new methods and uses.

Foams, adhesives, and sealants were sold both to industrial users and to consumer markets. Sealing materials could vary in consistency from liquid to stiff paste and were heat cured or vulcanized at atmospheric temperatures. Sealants could be applied by spraying, caulking, brushing, dipping, or pouring to form a permanent seal which was temperature and weather resistant.

Finished compounds exhibited many desirable qualities. For example, petro-rubber could easily be mistaken for natural rubber. It possessed the same elastic qualities as natural rubber but showed good resistance to heat, cold, chemicals and weathering properties usually associated only with inorganic compounds.

Nearly every basic manufacturing and processing industry used petroloid products in one form or another (Exhibit 3). Within the transportation sector the automotive industry served as a typical example of the range of petroloid applications. Petro-oil was used as the hydraulic medium in clutch and brake systems; as an additive for engine oils, coolants, and polishers; and as a lubricant for metallic and rubber parts. Petro-rubber was used for various seals, wire insulation, coolant hose, shock absorbers and external trim. Sealants found application as windshield sealants and gaskets for engine components.

The list of uses was equally impressive in other industries. Indeed if petroloids had limitations at all, it was in terms of product cost rather than product adaptability. Petroloids were synthesized in a complex and costly chemical process which rendered them more expensive than many substitute products. Applications were generally confined to those areas where petroloids had proven to be cost effective or where other products failed to stand up to exacting performance specifications.

History of the Industry

Although the synthesis of petroloids dated back to the nineteenth century, investigation of petroloids as a useful industrial product did not begin until the late 1940s.

In 1944 chemists at the American Adhesives Corporation began an investigation of the properties of synthetic polymer adhesives. They discovered that certain of these polymers possessed high tensile strength as well as adhesion and began work on textile fiber substitutes. In 1947 several variations had been developed and samples were sent to leading textile companies in the U.S., among them Tex-Fiber Industries.

The potential for these synthesized products in nonfiber applications was soon apparent. American Adhesives was still producing polymer in its laboratory with a slow, expensive process and was unable to satisfy demand. So, in 1952, the Standard Chemical Company was invited to join American in development of manufacturing facilities for meeting industry needs. American would supply the background in petroloid research, Standard, the experience in chemicals manufacturing. A joint venture, Standard American Corporation, was established in 1953 and soon afterwards the first commercial scale processing plant was constructed.

Basic research was being conducted at Tex-Fiber Industries at approximately the same time but followed a different tack from that taken by American. Top priority was given to the development of a novel and inexpensive method to synthesize petroloids. In 1950, Dr. P.Y. Ester succeeded in developing such a method. Known as the direct process, it was patented by Tex-Fiber and later licensed to Standard American and subsequent manufacturers. Initially, Tex-Fiber supplied products for various applications from its laboratory facilities. A separate petroloid plant was not built until 1956.

In turning their research efforts toward a broad base of specialty applications, the family of products was quickly expanded. Customized greases and rubbers were added to the oils already in use. Researchers discovered that petroloids were not only especially tough and weather resistant but had both water repellent and absorptive properties.

Standard American and Tex-Fiber Industries capitalized on their head start in petroloid research to dominate the rapidly developing industry. Until 1959, they remained the sole producers of petroloids with market shares of 76 percent and 24 percent, respectively. By 1962, however, they had been joined by ten other competitors in Europe, Japan, and the United States, virtually all of whom were large chemical companies. In the mid-1960s, a few additional companies entered the business, the last in 1965.

Commenting on the sudden rush of competitors into the petro-chemical business in the 1960s, a long-time industry observer remarked:

> I really can't attribute it to explosive growth. Petroloid sales volume has grown at a fairly steady rate of 14% over the last ten years. That's not bad, of course, but compared to the growth in demand for some specialty chemical compounds, it is modest. No, I'd have to attribute the new entries to speculation. In the late 1950s, each day seemed to bring news of a new petroloid product or property. There was talk of opening up a whole new world of chemistry which would replace many existing organic compounds.
>
> The business was and still is a highly capital and technical intensive industry. A new entrant needs sizeable financial and technical resources at its disposal. Only the larger chemical companies could provide both. The five-year head start enjoyed by Standard American and Tex-Fiber Industries served to deter some of them. But it compelled others to enter the business before they fell hopelessly behind. Spartan Chemicals began production in 1959 and several of the giant European chemical companies decided to take a crack at it, too. Among them were Le France Polymers, Crown Chemical Industries of Great Britain, and the Kruger Group and Hachst Chemie of Germany.
>
> The list of competitors was pretty well complete by 1962. It was clear by then that this would be a nice, profitable business but not the revolutionary one that some had hoped for. The big obstacle had been price. During the late 1950s and early '60s, petroloid products were ten times more expensive than many of their substitutes. But the gap has slowly been closing due to constant improvements in processing technology and increases in volume. Already the cost gap has closed from 10:1 to 3:1. In another twenty years we may see the petroloids industry enter a whole new era.

In addition to the number of competitors remaining constant over many years, market shares had also tended to stabilize. For example, in the United States, both Tex-Fiber Industries and Spartan Chemicals had gone through long periods with little or no change in market position (Exhibit 4).

The U.S. competitors had used different entry strategies for their initial penetrations. In the late 1950s, Tex-Fibers Industries positioned itself as a broad line producer like Standard American, serving as a second source for a variety of comparable products. It was not until the mid-1960s that Tex-Fiber Industries abandoned its follow-the-leader philosophy to become a leader in its own right in the FAS segment of the market.

Spartan Chemicals opted for a narrow product line to penetrate the market. Rather than attempt to take consumers and business away from established competitors, it developed the technology and became the dominant supplier in two new market areas, paint additives and dielectrics. Although other producers competed against Spartan Chemical in these segments, none were as successful. Similarly, Spartan Chemical was not a major factor outside this area of expertise.

Opinions differed on the importance of being first to develop and market new applications. Some believed that it was difficult to overtake a competitor once he had a lead in technology and market development. They argued that customers became habituated to the unique performance characteristics of the pioneer product and hence reluctant to change. Spartan Chemical was cited as an example of a company which had pioneered and maintained leadership in a particular market segment. Others argued that so long as the lead was not too great, superior product performance and marketing ability could compensate for a competitor's head start. Several Tex-Fiber Industries managers commented that although Standard American was frequently first into a market, the PPD was generally able to compete on an equal footing.

Alliance Chemical, the fourth and most recent competitor in the U.S. market, had also tried a broad line/second source penetration strategy. Alliance had no technological leadership in any market segment but competed aggressively on price and service. By taking advantage of its Ohio location, Alliance Chemical had gained a moderate share of the rubber and sealants business for the automotive industry.

The demand for petroloid products had grown steadily over the period from 1955 to 1974 (Exhibit 5). Meanwhile, the average price per pound had been declining despite the fact that many newer applications utilized more expensive product grades (Exhibit 6).

Recent changes in the world economy had caused reversals in these volume and price trends. By the last quarter of 1974 due to the widespread economic recession, the industrial production index had slipped 12.5 percent, automobile sales had fallen 27.2 percent and gross private investment had dropped 31.5 percent from 1973 levels. Given such major industrial contraction, the demand for petroloids was also expected to fall. However, by January 1975 exact assessments of the severity of the recession were difficult to make. A variety of factors, in particular the continued development of new petroloid applications, might, some executives believed, cushion sales. The appliance industry had actually increased its consumption of petroloids despite the declines in consumer purchases. Likewise, sales of sealants for renovation tended to rise when new building construction slowed.

While volume was falling, selling prices were rising for the first time since 1964. The cost of petrochemical feedstocks had doubled in two years and the tight money markets had forced competitors to generate funds internally. To protect margins, prices were raised in 1974 and were expected to rally further in the next five years.

Characteristics of the Industry

Since their inception, the development of new products and applications had been the primary source of new petroloid demand. In 1974, 50 percent of industry sales were products which had been introduced in the last five years. However, industry experts believed that major breakthroughs in technology would be less frequent in the future than in the past. Demand growth would stem more from applied research and the development of new applications for existing products than from the discovery of completely new grades and forms of materials.

Major producers competed with one another on a variety of dimensions. Among the most important were price, technical assistance, advertising and promotion, and product availability. Price was used as a competitive weapon primarily in those segments of the market where products and applications had become standardized. However, where products had been developed for highly specialized purposes and represented only a small fraction of a customer's total material cost, the market was often less price sensitive. Here customers were chiefly concerned with the physical properties of the product and operating performance.

Technical assistance was an important means of obtaining business. A sizeable percentage of total petroloid sales were accounted for by products developed to meet the unique needs of particular customers. Products for the aerospace industry were a primary example. Research engineers of petroloid producers were expected to work closely with customers to define performance requirements and to insure the development of acceptable products.

Advertising and promotional activities were important marketing tools in those segments which utilized distribution channels and/or which reached end users as opposed to OEMs. This was particularly true of foams, adhesives, and sealants which were sold both to industrial and consumer markets. A variety of packaged consumer products were sold to hardware, supermarkets, and "do-it-yourself" outlets by Tex-Fiber Industries as well as other competitors. Advertising increased awareness and stimulated interest among the general public while promotional activities improved the effectiveness of distribution networks. Since specialty petroloid products accounted for only a small percentage of a distributor's total sales, product promotion insured that specific products received adequate attention.

Product availability was a fourth dimension on which producers competed. With manufacturing cycles from 2–16 weeks in length and thousands of different products, no supplier could afford to keep all its items in stock. In periods of heavy demand, many products were often in short supply. Those competitors with adequate supplies and quick deliveries could readily attract new business.

As might be expected from the diversity of uses, the competitive environment in the industry varied from one market segment to another. The market was generally divided by type of product used, end user, and geographic location. Any segment might differ in terms of the number of competitors, intensity of competition, margin of profit, rate of growth, etc.

The earliest products and applications utilized oil-based materials. Many of these products had become near commodities with several competitors offering highly similar products. Although some oil applications were relatively new and showed high growth potential, many others provided lower margins and slower growth than other product grades. Price competition was common in this segment of the industry. Profit margins and growth rates were somewhat higher for some rubber products and significantly higher in FAS and those remaining rubber application segments which included larger proportions of new applications. A new application, once established, often yielded very substantial amounts of repeat business.

The largest differences in anticipated growth rates existed in the various industrial and end user markets. Among the fastest growing markets were certain construction sealants (29 percent), roofing materials (15 percent), consumer products (15 percent), health care applications (30 percent), and appliance applications (16 percent). The markets in aerospace, automotive, and mechanical goods were expected to slow to 5 percent, and a variety of oil additives and related products appeared to have reached maturity.

Market environments also differed from one geographic region to the next. The United States was the largest user of petroloid materials with 1974 sales of $1.19 billion. Four companies—Standard American, Tex-Fiber Industries, Spartan Chemicals, and Alliance—accounted for 99 percent of the U.S. sales. Prior to the recession, market growth had been expected to grow at an annual rate of 10 percent up to 1980.

Offshore demand was increasing more rapidly. Foreign markets which had accounted for 49 percent of worldwide sales in 1974, were expected to account for 52 percent in 1980.

Europe was the largest foreign market and was believed to lag the U.S. by two to three years in product and market development. Five foreign producers plus Standard American and Tex-Fiber Industries were competing for share in Europe. Each foreign producer maintained a stronghold in his home country while stiff competition existed in those nations with no local producers of their own. In general, materials prices tended to follow U.S. prices but at somewhat higher levels. Demand had been expected to grow at a faster rate than in the U.S.— about 12 percent annually.

The Japanese market had been expected to grow at the same rate as the U.S. market, approximately 10 percent. There were three Japanese producers, one of which enjoyed a commanding market share of 51 percent. Both Standard American and Tex-Fiber Industries had established joint ventures in Japan with market shares of 20 percent and 18 percent, respectively.

The smallest but fastest growing of the petroloids markets had been designated by PPD as the "Third World," although it included Canada, Latin America, South America, Australia, and Asia. Sales had been projected to grow 17 percent annually from 1975 to 1980. Additive and oil products accounted for more than 50 percent of the market but demand for rubbers and sealants was believed to be in a takeoff stage. There were no national producers in the Third World region. The European producers were active in Latin America, while the Japanese producers were mildly active in Far Eastern markets. Standard American held the dominant position with subsidiaries scattered throughout the Third World. Tex-Fiber Industries was a strong competitor in Canada but well behind Standard American in other locations.

Exhibit 7 summarizes the current sales, mix of products, and projected growth rates for the various geographic markets. Exhibit 8 provides the name and market share of competitors in each geographic region.

STANDARD AMERICAN CORPORATION

The undisputed leader in the industry was Standard American Corporation with total corporate 1974 sales of $1.08 billion and a worldwide petroloids market share of 35 percent. Standard American marketed a full line of products and had diversified into several related competitive fields. Petroloid product sales accounted for 75 percent of the business, non-petroloid sales for the remaining 25 percent.

The major manufacturing facilities and corporate headquarters were located in Houston, Texas. Several finishing plants[3] were located across the country. There was also a major manufacturing facility in the United Kingdom, two large finishing plants ($5–10 million in plant and equipment) in Belgium and Australia and several smaller finishing plants in Germany, Canada, Mexico, Brazil, and Japan. The company's spokesmen estimated that 80 percent of its aggregated investment in plant and equipment was in U.S. facilities. For 1975 it was reported that $100 million of investment in plant and equipment was planned. Seventy million dollars were to be spent on U.S. facilities, and $30 million on foreign operations. By early 1975 no reports had been received of any changes in these plans as a result of the recession.

Standard American marketed 2,500 products to over 30,000 customers throughout the world. No one customer accounted for more than 2 percent of total sales. The breakdown between industrial and consumer sales was approximately 80 percent–20 percent. Seventy percent of industrial sales and 20 percent of consumer sales were made through the company's 400 salesmen direct to customers, with the remainder being handled by distributors. The company operated ten regional offices in the U.S. and sixteen more in foreign countries.

Standard American was the technical leader and dominant force in the petro-oils segment of the business. These relatively mature products accounted for over 50 percent of all petroloid sales. The company was strong in the rubber and FAS segments, too, controlling 40 percent of the heat cured rubber business and 35 percent of the FAS business in the United States.

Standard American was the first company to investigate the industrial application of specialty petroloids and remained the unchal-

---

[3]Finishing plants received semi-finished goods from the central manufacturing facilities and performed the necessary final steps to complete the manufacturing process. The amount of value added at finishing locations varied widely depending on which manufacturing steps were performed centrally and which at the remote locations.

lenged leader in the development and improvement of products and processes. The company employed 675 people in research, development and technical service activities and spent a total of $324 million for R&D between 1970–1974. R&D expenditures amounted to 7.5 percent and 7.1 percent of sales in 1973 and 1974, respectively. By comparison Tex-Fiber Industries spent only $76 million on R&D during the same period. R&D expenditures for 1973 and 1974 had amounted respectively to 5.3 percent and 3.5 percent of sales.

Among the fruits of Standard American's product development activities were stannopetroloids, high grade specialty materials priced at $40 to $60 per pound. Standard American had developed and patented these products and was the sole supplier. Forty-eight million dollars of stannopetroloids were sold in 1975 with forecasts for $80 million by 1980.

The company also consistently outspent its competition in advertising and promotion, both in absolute and in percentage terms. Over $85 million had been spent in five years, more than three times the amount of its nearest competitor. Although Tex-Fiber had spent, as a percentage of sales, more than Standard American in 1973 (3.3 percent vs. 2.2 percent), this situation was reversed in 1974 (0.8 percent vs. 1.5 percent).

TEX-FIBER INDUSTRIES—
PETROLOID PRODUCTS DIVISION (PPD)

Tex-Fiber Industries—Petroloid Products Division was the second largest producer of petroloids worldwide. Although a pioneer in industrial petroloid research, Tex-Fiber Industries had never seriously threatened Standard American for industry leadership. One of PPD's managers who had been with the department since its beginning explained:

> Tex-Fiber Industries, as our names implies, is essentially a textile company. We didn't know much about the chemicals industry in the 1950s. Neither did American Adhesives for that matter, but they sought out Standard Chemical. It was Standard who supplied that joint venture with its marketing and manufacturing know-how.

> Tex-Fibers Industries, on the other hand, decided to develop talent from within rather than hire it from the outside. As a result, we started out as a collection of laboratory scientists who knew nothing about marketing— and recent college graduates who knew little about anything. For the first five years, we had all we could do to chase around after Standard American and try to copy what they did.

But by 1960s, we were more savvy. We recognized that we couldn't be all things to all people. Standard American already had a tremendous lead on oils so we focused on a segment that was just taking off—foams, adhesives, and sealants. By channeling our research and sales efforts into this segment we established ourselves as co-leaders with Standard American. Today, we actually enjoy a slight lead in this area.

It turned out to be a very fortunate decision. The sales growth and profit margins in FAS have exceeded those in other areas. As they have gained share in the total market, so have we. Our business philosophy continues to be one of selective penetration into the most attractive market segments.

In 1974, the PPD had record sales of $464 million and a worldwide market share of 20 percent. Twenty-three percent of 1974 revenues and 26 percent of profits were contributed by foreign sales. Exhibit 9 lists PPD's estimated sales and market share by product line and geographic market segment for 1974.

The department headquarters and main manufacturing facility were located in Philadelphia, Pennsylvania. In addition, through a joint venture arrangement, a small plant was operated in Osaka, Japan. A service center, consisting of a sales and technical service personnel and a small finishing department, had been opened in England in 1972. With these two exceptions, all petroloid products were shipped directly from the Pennsylvania plant.

The PPD organization was a somewhat complicated, quasi-matrix structure (see Exhibit 10). Currently, there were eight section managers reporting directly to the general manager. Three departments were organized by product: FAS, rubber, and oils. The rubber and oils departments were temporarily under the direction of one man. The staff functions of finance, planning and personnel each had their own section. There were also three departments organized by function: manufacturing, R&D, and the National Sales Organization. All product departments were profit centers; all functional departments were cost centers.

Sales and Marketing Activities

The PPD offered a full line of products with over 2,000 items. Approximately, 60 percent of sales were standard items sold directly from stock; the remaining 40 percent were items made to order. Products were marketed through a company sales force of 150 and an extensive distribution network consisting of 600 distributorships operating 870 locations and employing approximately 5,000 salesmen.

The National Sales Organization (NSO) accounted for two-thirds of the field sales force; the NSO served as the marketing arm for oils and for most of the FAS product line. While most of these salesmen sold a variety of items to a broad range of end user markets, approximately 30 salesmen functioned as industry specialists, concentrating on market segments which were considered especially attractive. Specialists were feasible where accounts were large and geographically concentrated.

The remaining 50 salesmen were divided equally between the Rubber Products Department and Consumer Products. Rubber Products salesmen devoted most of their time to 100 large accounts, predominately, automotive-related businesses in the mid-West. There were six automotive specialists located in Detroit. The specialists worked with OEM engineers to incorporate various products into new car designs and to authorize petroloid products for use in the auto supply aftermarket. The Consumer Products sales force reported to the FAS manager, and sold to large wholesalers and retail chains.

The typical salesman had a previous technical background, expertise in one or more market segments, a familiarity with all products, and an ability to cross sell items which fell outside his customary line. He was also responsible for the distribution channels in his territory and worked with individual distributorships to improve their effectiveness. In addition, he had to have the creativity and insight to discover new application possibilities. Each salesman had from 100 to 200 accounts in his territory, 50 of which might be active.

The distributorships provided broad, economical coverage of markets too small and fragmented to be served by a direct salesman. As a rule of thumb, accounts which purchased less than $50,000 per year were handled through the distribution network. Distributors were selected to reach the appropriate customer markets and included construction supply houses, auto supply houses, electrical and electronic distributors, chemical distributors, etc. The distribution network had been vastly expanded during the 1970s as a means of rapidly building sales volume. The number of distributorships had grown from 100 to 600 and their sales volume from 20 percent to 35 percent of domestic sales.

However, petroloids represented a small fraction of the items carried by most distributorships. To insure that company products received a disproportionate share of the distributors' attention, Tex-Fiber Industries used an incentive program in which distributors who met and exceeded their sales quotas were given all expenses paid trips to such spots as Spain, Hawaii, and Acapulco. These trips had become highly prestigious events among the distributors and had proved to be effective sales motivators. The PPD believed its incentive program to be unique in the chemical industry.

International sales were handled through a small direct sales force coupled with foreign distributors. The PPD had been a minor participant in the European market and was well behind Standard American in Japan and the Third World. Most managers agreed that without some minimum investment in service centers or finishing facilities to symbolize a commitment to foreign markets, Tex-Fiber Industries could not hope to be a significant factor internationally. The service center opened in England in 1972 had successfully raised local market share from 2 percent to 8 percent. Other service centers were being considered for France, Germany, and Mexico but no funds commitments had been made. The cost of maintaining a service center with local salesmen, a clerical staff, a technical service man, and a small finishing operation was approximately $200,000 per year. Investment costs associated with opening such a facility were estimated to be no more than $3 million. To date domestic opportunities had continued to receive funds priority over foreign investment.

Allocation of product to international was the responsibility of section managers responsible for each major line. But as one executive remarked:

> Section managers are not always responsive to international needs. In early 1974 when product was in short supply, the European organization had to come begging for goods—and often went away without any.

Manufacturing

The Central Manufacturing Section was responsible for producing materials for all three product lines. Plant and equipment at the Philadelphia facility represented a net investment of $170 million and covered an area of 35 acres. All final products were compounded from a few basic mainstreams of chemical intermediates. Production time varied from two to sixteen weeks depending on the product. Oils were among the simplest materials and required the shortest manufacturing times. Additional refining and additives were required to produce rubbers and FAS products. Approximately, 20 percent of the products could be manufactured with a continuous or semi-continuous process. The remaining 80 percent required further specialized and often lengthy manufacturing steps.

Due to the variety of products and manufacturing processes, capacity figures could vary sharply depending on the product mix. For planning purposes, Central Manufacturing assumed current rated capacity at approximately $420 million.

As general guidelines, Central Manufacturing had traditionally attempted to stock 10-20 percent of the grades, which accounted for 60 percent of sales volume, in finished goods inventory. Another 10-20 percent of the grades, representing 20 percent of sales volume, were held as work-in-progress, about 2-3 weeks from completion. The remaining 60-80 percent of the grades required 6-8 weeks to complete.

Research and Development

Research and development activities were conducted by a centralized R&D department and by technicians associated with each of the product sections. Research was aimed primarily at developing particular materials with particular properties. The R&D personnel in product sections focused primarily on defining the properties and chemical structure appropriate to new applications. Central R&D specialized more in developing the chemical processes necessary to produce the desired chemical structures. In early 1975, there were 25 research chemists and technicians assigned to Central R&D, 45 to FAS, 35 to rubber and 10 to oils.

Finance and Accounting

The Finance Department was responsible for credit and collections, cost accounting, budgeting, and systems analysis. The Manager of Finance also had overall responsibility for cash flow in the PPD. Credit terms in the industry were net 30 days with no discount for early payment. Due to the large number of small accounts, the department had a collection period which ranged from 55-60 days.

The Finance Department also administered the annual bonus scheme through which superior executive performance was rewarded. Bonuses were based on the achievement of a number of different objectives which were initially agreed upon when budgets were made up during the fall planning and budgeting cycle. Total corporate funds available for such bonuses were decided at the corporate level and then distributed to groups, divisions, and eventually departments. Within a division, bonuses were a function of the particular goals agreed to by a department manager and in turn by his subordinates. Departments were treated as profit centers and performance was measured primarily in terms of sales, market share, net income, and expense control. Cost centers were measured mainly on their ability to meet budget expense levels.

RECENT EVENTS

In 1974 the economy was moving from a period of rapid inflation into a period of steep recession. Fear of materials shortages had resulted in heavy buying and inventory surpluses. As the recession began to deepen the combination of falling demand and bloated inventories caused business activity in many sectors of the economy to plummet. Nonetheless, raw material costs continued to soar due to rising oil prices.

The recession hit the petroloids industry somewhat later than other sectors of the economy. At Tex-Fiber PPD, demand was heavy for the first three quarters of 1974. Benefiting from a large backlog of orders, the plant operated at peak capacity. At times it was necessary to improvise equipment or contract out work just to keep pace. Raw material inventories were allowed to balloon to insure against material shortages and the possibility of work stoppages. Raw materials costs had risen almost 70 percent since 1973.

The two primary objectives of management during this period had been to raise prices to protect margins and to optimize the product mix to maximize sales and earnings. Given that the last rise in the average selling price had occurred in 1958, the act of raising prices was a rather novel event. A variety of questions were encountered, many for the first time. Who should be the first in the industry to raise prices? Which items should be marked up and by how much? Which markets were most price sensitive? Should gross margin percentage or total contribution dollars be the main criterion? Mr. Bernie Grossinger, Department Manager for FAS, reflected on the problems he encountered:

> I remember how traumatic it was to change our way of thinking. Our first price increase was 2 percent. It was an extremely modest increase, but to us it represented a dramatic change in policy. We went around to all our customers explaining how our rising cost of materials had necessitated the price adjustment and trying to avoid an avalanche of negative reaction. They were facing the same problems and they understood our situation. Two months after that first difficult step we were raising prices 10-20 percent without a second thought.

> The psychological problems were easy enough to overcome. It was the business decisions that were really tough. We decided to assume the role of price leader in the FAS segment of the market. That created a dilemma. It would have been simple enough to raise prices 20 percent across the board. However, not all markets are equally price sensitive and not all

243

products have the same profit margins. Yet, if you raise prices 5 percent in one area, 10 percent in another, and 20 percent somewhere else, it becomes very confusing to your competitors.

Because of the pressure to keep margins up, we had a lot of decisions to make and we had to make them fast. In retrospect we may have made some poor ones.

Foam molding materials for the furniture industry were a prime example. Foam is molded to cast wood-like plastic parts for furniture. These products were among our highest margin items and represented a $12 million market in 1973, but the furniture industry was being hard hit by the recession and could ill afford additional costs.

In 1974 we raised prices on those molding products by 30 percent, Standard American did not, and we took a real beating. In the space of six months, our market share dropped from 75 percent to 50 percent and we lost $1,000,000–$1,500,000 of business. In October, 1974, when the furniture market caved in altogether, we put our prices back in line. Our market share has returned to 75 percent but the volume is now about a third of what it was a year ago. We should have played for contribution dollars rather than profit margin, but we were focusing so hard on gross margins that we didn't make the proper adjustment. Perhaps we should have dropped our prices back sooner, but we felt we had to make a stand.

As a result of price increases by all three product departments the average selling price per pound of finished material rose from $2.50 in 1973 to $3.00 in 1974. These increases reduced the profit squeeze but did not eliminate it entirely as gross margins dropped 7 percent. As a result of budget pruning, however, net income as a percentage of sales was slightly increased. Approximately 45 percent of this pretax net income was provided by FAS, 30 percent by rubbers, and the remainder by oils.

The second management objective, optimizing the product mix, had also required a change in thinking. Because of plant expansions in the late 1960s, the PPD had operated with excess capacity for several years. Sales orders were evaluated on an incremental cost basis and virtually any order which returned a positive contribution was accepted. However, as plant volume increased in the early 1970s and capacity became constrained, orders had to be evaluated not only in terms of contribution but also in terms of the amount of plant time, labor, and materials required. Consequently, sales efforts had to become far more selective.

In order to coordinate sales activities with manufacturing capabilities and financial objectives, the sales managers had, in 1974, begun development of a sales incentive program. The sales dollars for a product would be multiplied by the appropriate coefficient to arrive at an adjusted sales total. The adjusted total would then be used in evaluating and rewarding a salesman's performance. In this way, salesmen could be motivated to sell those items most profitable for the department under the current conditions. The strategic factors would be updated monthly to adjust for changes in plant volume, product mix, raw material cost, etc. However, development of the Strategic Factor Program was not completed until the fourth quarter of 1974.

The recession hit the industry with great suddenness. The forecasting models used at the PPD had predicted a sales downturn, but they failed to indicate just how acute the drop would be. One of the difficulties was estimating the impact for the huge number of different products and applications which existed. Just as management was becoming acclimated to the business environment which had existed in the first three quarters, the tables were dramatically turned. The long list of back orders disappeared, customers began drawing down the inventories which they had accumulated, and new orders were slumping badly. Oils were the hardest hit. As one executive put it, "we were swimming in the stuff."

In discussing the problems which he had encountered, Mr. Simmons stated:

> I only took over as general manager this past fall having worked in one of the company's textile divisions for the last seven years. I was surprised to see the plant running at full capacity because textiles were suffering from the recession. In textiles the drop in sales had come on us unexpectedly and we got caught with our pants down. But the PPD seemed to be just humming along. That's when I appeared on the scene.
>
> I hadn't met with the previous general manager to discuss the state of the business so it took me a couple of days to take stock of the situation. But I soon realized that the Petroloids Division was headed for the plunge. Our back orders were disappearing and nothing new was coming in. Nothing! Our costs and investments in working capital were way out of line and I knew we had to do some heavy cutting to meet our profit and cash flow commitments.

Original estimates for 1975 made in June of the previous year had anticipated sales of $550 million. This level of activity was expected to require plant and equipment additions of approximately $50 million and significant increases in working capital. By early 1975, however, it was realized that these original estimates would have to be sharply reduced and plant and equipment expenditures scaled down. Based on revised sales forecasts he had received from each product section Mr. Simmons asked Manager-Finance, Tom Eagle, to come up with a completely revised budget for 1975 (see Exhibit 11). After some discussion, the two agreed that, in spite of recent developments, the net income goal for the year should be set at $34 million. It was also agreed that fixed plant and equipment investment should be limited to the $15 million required for replacement and safety improvements. Tentative plans called for a reduction of working capital investment of approximately six million dollars compared to 1974 levels (see Exhibit 12).

In setting these goals Mr. Simmons remarked:

> I've already laid of 180 salaried and 150 hourly employees. That's a hell of a way to win friends and influence people. But I felt I had to set an example. I expect my department managers to be equally firm and to do the best they can under the circumstances.

Informal conversations with individual section managers prior to the scheduled meeting revealed, however, that attitudes about the impending cuts varied. Bernie Grosinger, Department Manager for FAS Products, commented:

> We have had to shift our emphasis from raising prices and bringing in high margin businesses to cutting costs and bringing in any business we can find. In FAS we are currently running a number of fire sales to liquidate the slower moving items in our inventories. We are also clamping down on expenses. I have asked our people to plan their traveling more carefully and to cut out first class air fares. We are also monitoring all expense statements closely.

> To keep our sales volume up, I've made it clear that all personnel in our department are expected to keep a sharp eye out for business. That includes our marketing staff, our research and technical service people, and myself. I am currently spending 30 percent of my time working on sales orders.

> With environmental changes occurring so rapidly in the last twelve months, it has been a real challenge to manage effectively. Our business is too fragmented to be able to carefully analyze all the decisions which have to be made, so we've attempted to sort out our priorities and to focus on the areas which matter most. Once we figure out what we want to do we have to communicate our objectives down through the organization and into the field. I hold department meetings every month and I try to smother the key objectives with attention. I also find it necessary to delegate less authority in order to keep tight control over operations.

> Price remains one of our key concerns. The cost of raw materials is still rising, creating a continuing squeeze on profit margins. We hope to pass these increases on to our customers, but Standard American has not always been quick to follow our pricing leads and with sales volume down, I am not certain we can afford to sacrifice share or volume.

Dr. Walner Hearter, Department Manager for Oils and Rubbers, noted several problems which the cost and investment cuts posed for his lines.

> I feel that a lean mentality is a healthy mentality for the business. But the cuts in R&D and promotion will severely limit our abilities to develop and promote profitable new applications for our rubber business. Tighter inventories will hurt our oil sales in several ways. When business is bad, delivery becomes a critical factor in soliciting orders, particularly for the oil products where competition is stiffest. As inventories are reduced, several grades can no longer be kept in stock. Sure, it is important to reduce our expenses and working capital, but we can't cover our fixed costs or turn a profit unless we fill the plant.

The proposed 1975 budget of the Sales Operation was down 15–16 percent from the previous year. Mr. Arnie Arthur, Manager for the Sales Operation, talked about the implications.

> The major adjustment we shall have to make is in the size of our sales force. We have already reduced our field sales force from 200 to 150. Fortunately, we accomplished the cutback largely by attrition. Some years ago, we took 15 of our top salesmen off commission, assigned several to each of our sales regions, and told them to prospect about and develop new business and new markets. We have now put them back on commission, filling several vacant spots. We feel that a salesman can cover his territory and still keep an eye open for new accounts and new applications.
>
> Our advertising and promotion budget will also be drastically reduced. In 1973 we had a budget equal to over 3 percent of sales. This year we have a budget of less than 1 percent of sales.[4] Our sales haven't suffered as much as one might expect, but these levels cannot be maintained for long. To a certain extent, we are able to benefit from the advertising of our competitors.
>
> Our sales incentive program seems to have come on-stream at the wrong time. I'm certain it will be useful in the future. Still, I wish there was a meaningful way to utilize it now.

The drop in sales was having a significant impact on the Finance Section. Mr. Tom Eagle, Manager of Finance, explained:

> When customers stop ordering they also stop paying. That means that receivables as well as inventories get out of line. We are concerned not

---

[4]These figures do not include distributor promotional programs.

only with when our customers can pay but if they can pay. We deal with many small companies and the incidence of bankruptcies among smaller businesses has increased dramatically. We are in the process of securing many of our more doubtful receivables. We also have several accounts which are solid, successful businesses but which have become illiquid in the recession. These are growing concerns which we would like to nurture. The problem is that they don't have the money to pay and we can't afford to extend our receivables further. We would like to help them out but I'm not sure how.

There is another dilemma which we have to resolve quickly. With large inventories on hand and salesmen far below their quotas, we've received considerable pressure from marketing people to ship more product to our customers. Many of these customers have large balances outstanding. It has been our policy not to make shipments unless the customer has paid his balance. If we ship to these people we may establish an undesirable precedent. We also strain customer relations by hounding for payment while shipping them more goods. On the other hand, if we ship out the goods we can recognize the sales and profits. Our salesmen's figures would be fattened up and our income statement much improved if we could be more assured of prompt collections.

Several department managers made comments that the budget cuts would further delay investments in foreign markets. "We are late already," said Mr. Arthur. "Standard American is in Mexico now, trying to influence the government to establish tariffs to protect the 'local' industry from foreign competition. We are at a significant competitive disadvantage by not having a local presence. But there is only so much money to go around and we have to balance our short- and long-term interests."

Exhibit 1

TEX-FIBER INDUSTRIES—PETROLOID PRODUCTS DIVISION [A]

Monthly Orders Annualized

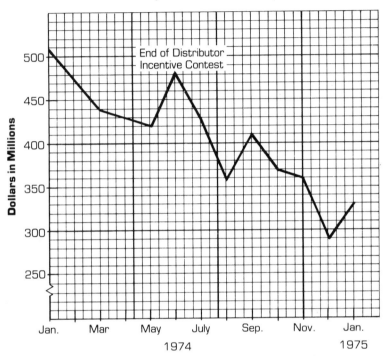

Source: Company records.

Exhibit 2

TEX-FIBER INDUSTRIES—PETROLOID PRODUCTS DIVISION [A]
PPD After-Tax Net Income, 1956–1974

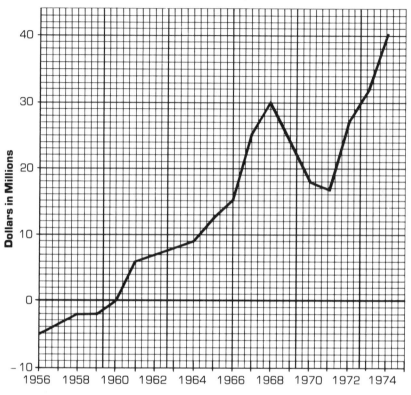

Source: Company records.

Exhibit 3

TEX-FIBER INDUSTRIES—PETROLOID PRODUCTS DIVISION [A]

Product Uses By Major U.S. Industrial Classification

PRODUCT TYPES \ INDUSTRIES	Consumer Products—General	Chemicals & Allied Prod.	Concrete, Cement, Bricks	Electrical, Electronic	Construction	Fabricated Products	Food, Related Industries	Mining	Non-Electrical Machinery	Paper Industries	Primary Metal Industries	Printing and Publishing	Rubber Products	Stone, Clay, Glass & Glass Prod.	Textile	Transportation, Communication	Miscellaneous Manufacturing	Paint	Aircraft & Missiles	Cosmetics & Polish	Photography Equipment & Supplies
Molded Materials (Foam)				X		X			X			X			X				X		
Additives (Oil)		X						X									X	X		X	X
Defoamers (Oil)		X					X								X		X				
Gaskets, Seals, Diaphragms (Rubber)		X	X	X	X	X	X			X						X	X		X		
Lubricants (Oil)		X	X	X			X				X						X		X		
Release Agents (Oils)		X		X		X	X	X	X	X	X		X				X				
Potting Compounds (Sealants)				X					X								X				
Release Coatings (Oil)								X	X	X	X		X				X				
Hydraulic Medium (Oil)								X								X		X			
Laminating Materials (Adhesives)				X					X				X	X		X	X		X		
Adhesive, Sealant, & Caulking Compound (Sealants)	X				X	X									X	X	X		X		X
Chemicals	X	X		X														X			
Molded-Extruded Parts (Rubber)							X									X			X		
Fabric Treatment (Oils)														X				X		X	

Source: Company data.

Exhibit 4

TEX-FIBER INDUSTRIES—PETROLOID PRODUCTS DIVISION [A]

Market Share Breakdown by Competitors for U.S. Market
1956–1974

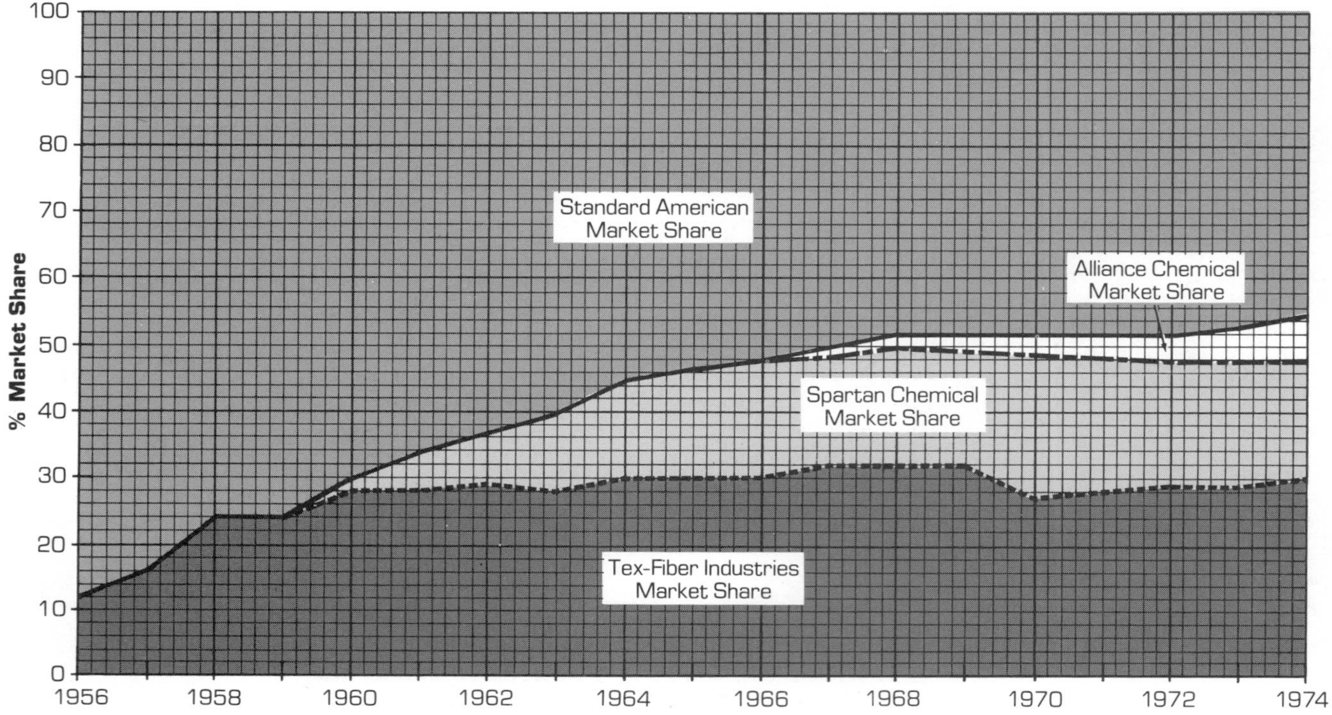

Standard American Market Share

Alliance Chemical Market Share

Spartan Chemical Market Share

Tex-Fiber Industries Market Share

% Market Share

Exhibit 5
TEX-FIBER INDUSTRIES—PETROLOID PRODUCTS DIVISION [A]
Petroloids Industry Worldwide Volume in Millions of Pounds
1956–1975

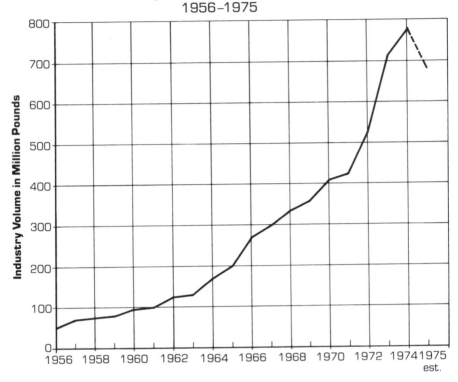

Exhibit 6
TEX-FIBER INDUSTRIES—PETROLOID PRODUCTS DIVISION [A]
Industry Average Selling Price Per Pound
1956–1975

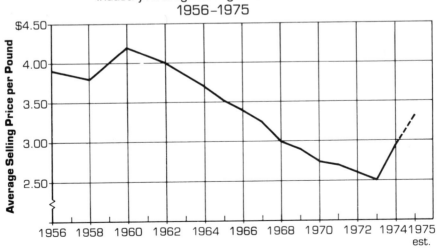

Exhibit 7
TEX-FIBER INDUSTRIES—PETROLOID PRODUCTS DIVISION [A]
Sales, Growth, and Product Mix for Geographic Markets

GEOGRAPHIC REGION	1974 SALES [BILLIONS OF $]	ORIGINAL· PROJECTED COMPOUND GROWTH RATE 1975–1980	% OF TOTAL SALES SOLD AS:		
			OILS	FOAM, ADHESIVES & SEALANTS	RUBBERS
United States	$1.19	10%	50%	29%	21%
Europe	0.62	12	39	32	29
Japan	0.33	10	63	21	16
Third World	0.18	17	66	21	13
Worldwide Totals	2.32	11*	50	28	22

Source: Company estimates.

*PPD executives had estimated compound growth rates by product category as: OILS, 8%; RUBBERS, 10%; FAS, 16%.

Exhibit 8
TEX-FIBER INDUSTRIES—PETROLOID PRODUCTS DIVISION [A]
Market Shares for Competitors by Geographic Region—1974*

PRODUCER	WORLDWIDE MARKET SHARE [$2.32B]	U.S. MARKET SHARE [$1.19B]	EUROPEAN MARKET SHARE [$0.62B]	JAPAN MARKET SHARE [$0.33B]	3rd WORLD MARKET SHARE [$0.18B]
Standard American	35%	45%	20%	20%*	50%
Tex-Fiber Industries	20	30	4	18 *	14
Spartan Chemical	9	17			5
Japan Petrochemical	8			51	9
Le France Polymer	7		23		9
Hachst Chemie	5		18		2
Kruger Group	5		16		9
Alliance Chemical	3	6			
Crown Chemical Industries	2		8		
Others	6	2	11	5	2

Source: Company estimates.

*Joint venture arrangements.

254

Exhibit 9

TEX-FIBER INDUSTRIES—PETROLOID PRODUCTS DIVISION [A]
PPD Sales and Market Share by Product Line and Geographic Region
1974

Key

Market Share
$ Millions Sales Volume

Product	United States	Europe	Japan	Third World	Total
Foam, Adhesives and Sealants [FAS]	45% / $154M	5% / $9M	18% / $12M	24% / $9M	28% / $184M
Rubbers	37% / $92M	4% / $8M	18% / $10M	22% / $5M	23% / $115M
Oils	18% / $110M	2% / $6M	18% / $38M	9% / $11M	14% / $165M
Total	30% / $356M	4% / $23M	18% / $60M	14% / $25M	20% / $464M

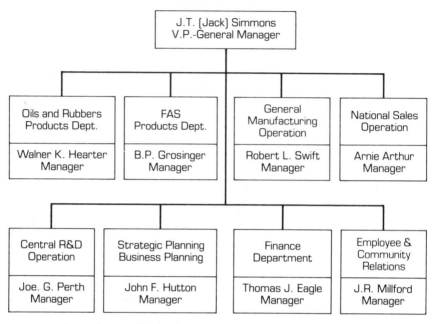

Exhibit 10

TEX-FIBER INDUSTRIES—PETROLOID PRODUCTS DIVISION [A]
Organization Chart

J.T. [Jack] Simmons
V.P.-General Manager

Oils and Rubbers Products Dept.	FAS Products Dept.	General Manufacturing Operation	National Sales Operation
Walner K. Hearter Manager	B.P. Grosinger Manager	Robert L. Swift Manager	Arnie Arthur Manager

Central R&D Operation	Strategic Planning Business Planning	Finance Department	Employee & Community Relations
Joe. G. Perth Manager	John F. Hutton Manager	Thomas J. Eagle Manager	J.R. Millford Manager

Source: Company files, 1975.

Exhibit 11

TEX-FIBER INDUSTRIES—PETROLOID PRODUCTS DIVISION [A]
Comparative Income Statements
(in $000,000)

	1974 ACTUAL	1975 ORIG. PLAN	1975 REVISED PLAN
Sales	464	550	400
FAS domestic	154	195	154
international	30	43	32
Rubbers domestic	92	110	84
international	23	30	20
Oils domestic	110	125	82
international	55	47	28
Cost of Goods Sold	204	258	188
Gross Margin	260	292	212
Total Dept. Exp.*	94	107	69
FAS	41	51	29
Rubbers	20	21	15
Oils	19	18	14
Sales Dept.	14	17	11
Other Overhead Exp.	92	105	83
Central R&D	1	1	1
Advertising	3	6	2
Other G&A Exp.	88	98	80
Income from Sales	74	80	60
Other Income	4	4	4
Total Income	78	84	64
Taxes	38	40	30
Net Inc. after Taxes	40	44	34
Depreciation	23	27	22
Dividends	20	24	18

*Generally about 70 percent of each department budget was allotted to R&D, application development, and/or marketing expenses. The division of these expenses depended on the department involved: the Rubbers Department spent most of its budget on applications R&D and market development; the FAS budget contained substantial allocations for distributor incentives and promotional programs as well as for R&D. The remaining 30 percent of each department budget covered general department overhead and administration.

Exhibit 12

TEX-FIBER INDUSTRIES—PETROLOID PRODUCTS DIVISION [A]
Comparative Balance Sheets
Financial Position at Dec. 31
[$000]

	1973	1974
ASSETS		
Current customer receivables	$44,992	$59,220
FIFO inventories	53,664	84,280
Plant and equipment first cost	286,220	326,404
depreciation reserves	(137,036)	(156,048)
Cost less accumulated		
depreciation	149,184	170,356
Investments in affiliates and		
associated companies	15,144	14,812
Cash and other assets	10,168	(20,692)
Total assets	$273,152	$307,976
LIABILITIES AND RESERVES		
Accounts payable	$(14,780)	$(18,776)
Other liabilities and reserves	(23,196)	(30,368)
Total liabilities and reserves	(37,976)	(49,144)
Net corporate investment	$235,175	$258,832

DISCUSSION QUESTIONS

TEX-FIBER INDUSTRIES [B]

1. What major pressures is Mr. Simmons faced with in early 1975?
2. What has PPD's historical performance been?
3. What are the essential characteristics of the petroloids markets?
4. How "attractive" is the business overall and by segments?
5. How would you describe competitor's approaches to this market?
6. What is Mr. Simmons now proposing? Would you, as a member of management, go along with his proposal?
7. What other alternatives does PPD have? In the long run? In the short run?
8. What would be the impact of following Simmon's proposal (or others) if 1975 sales are substantially different than forecast?

TEX-FIBER INDUSTRIES— PETROLOID PRODUCTS DIVISION (B)[1]

The sudden and severe business downturn which confronted Tex-Fiber's Petroloid Products Division in the fourth quarter of 1974 created a variety of challenges for its managers. But even as they set about trimming operations to ride out the current storm, plans were being made which would chart the future course of the business. Each June, a five-year business plan was submitted to corporate executives. The plan contained the key goals of the business and the specific policies which would be implemented to achieve them. It also enabled corporate management to coordinate long-term strategy among Tex-Fiber Industries' various operating divisions.

Mr. Jack Simmons, Vice President and General Manager of the PPD, had received from John F. Hutton, Manager of Strategic Planning, a wealth of historical data, general policies, and recommendations for future operations. Although he had been on the job only a few months, it was Mr. Simmons' responsibility to review these proposals with Mr. Hutton and to develop, with his assistance, a final five-year plan.

Early on, he had established the keynote of his administration by proclaiming that the primary mission of the Petroloid Products Division would be to strengthen its position as a strong number two in the industry. The PPD would maintain its leadership in foam, adhesives and sealants and capitalize on foreign market growth. Simmons' philosophy differed from that of previous general managers who had sought to supplant Standard American as industry leader. Mr. Simmons believed that such a goal was unattainable and felt that his approach was more realistic and more attuned to the changing objectives of the corporation.

In keeping with his philosophy, Mr. Simmons had established several specific goals for the division. He listed the following objectives for 1976–1980 period:

1. To maintain a minimum worldwide market share of 20 percent.
2. To increase sales in offshore markets to 30 percent of total PPD sales by 1980.
3. To maintain a 9 percent average return on sales after taxes.

---

[1]This case was prepared by John Craig in collaboration with Derek F. Abell.

4. To optimize net income, liquidity, and ROI through working capital and capacity investment management.

The last objective marked another departure from previous years when the primary goal had been to maximize earnings rather than to achieve an optimal balance among earnings, cash flow, and ROI. PPD, historically a cash user after dividends, had been designated as a major net supplier of cash to the corporation over the 1976–80 period. Preliminary plans drawn up in 1974 had called for $84 million, over and above dividend assessments, to be made available to the corporate treasury over the five-year period.[2] As Mr. Simmons commented:

> We have become much more sensitive to cash flow considerations. I'd guess that two years ago half the people in the division did not even know what cash flow was. But when it became a top priority for the corporation it became a top priority for us, too. We are all re-evaluating our operating policies in light of their effect on cash flow. Of course, the immediate actions we are taking are as much in response to the business decline as to the new emphasis on liquidity. But I'm certain there are many areas where cash flow considerations will have a significant and lasting impact on our way of doing business.

Mr. Simmons began a review of the materials supplied by Mr. Hutton. These included recommendations to conserve working capital, to adopt a new capacity investment strategy, and to fine tune the funds allocation procedure. These latter recommendations were of particular interest to Mr. Simmons for they would have a significant impact on the financial performance of the division.

WORKING CAPITAL CONSERVATION

The PPD monitored its levels of inventories and receivables in relation to sales volume. Historically, as Mr. Simmons learned, the division incorporated a margin of comfort into these levels to insure that no sales were lost due to overly strict credit terms or inventory shortages. But with the business downturn, inventories and receivables had climbed sharply.

---

[2]This amount might be increased or decreased depending on actual 1975 results. In the event of continued negative cash flow after dividends in 1975, the additional deficit would be added to the $84 million requirement. In the event of positive 1975 cash flow after dividends, this amount would be regarded as a "first installment" on the $84 million total requirement.

In preparing the five-year plan, Mr. Hutton estimated that by instituting tighter inventory controls and utilizing computer programs it would be possible to operate with significantly lower ratios of inventories and receivables. He calculated that by switching to a lean policy, working capital investment by 1980 would be $20 million less than it would be under the traditional "margin of comfort" policy.

CAPACITY INVESTMENT STRATEGY

As with inventories and receivables, the PPD had tended to program in a "margin of comfort" when determining capacity requirements. During the planning process, optimistic, pessimistic, and most likely sales forecasts were developed. Historically, plant and equipment had been added in more than sufficient amounts to accommodate the most likely demand forecasts. Lead times for investment varied considerably, from 12–18 months for equipment at the finishing end of the manufacturing process, to three years for new reactors and distillation columns. While the policy of investing in expectation of demand (or "front loaded investment") had enabled the division to capitalize on sudden spurts in demand, it occasionally had resulted in a premature commitment of funds. (See Exhibit 1 for capacity utilization.)

Given the new concern with cash flow, two alternatives were being considered—a back loaded investment strategy and a low investment strategy. The back loaded strategy would gear capacity requirements to the most likely sales forecast and would delay investment such that additional capacity came on-stream just as it was needed. In the low investment case, capacity would be maintained at its 1977 level[3] through 1980 with additional spending limited to environmental and safety measures.

Mr. Hutton had made several calculations on the three options (see Exhibit 2). He recommended that the PPD adopt the back loaded investment strategy. Under the most likely conditions, division net income would be maximized, ROI boosted sharply over current levels, and cash flow increased. The low investment case provided maximum cash flow. But income fell off sharply in the last years due to capacity shortages. And if sales approached optimistic forecast levels, the loss of revenue and market share would be severe. Under the optimistic forecast, losses would be incurred under the back loaded case as well.

---

[3]With an average lead time of two years, funds had already been committed for plant expansions coming on-stream in 1977.

However, by carefully monitoring actual and forecasted sales, the investment schedule could be accelerated, thus minimizing the negative effects.

FUNDS ALLOCATION PROCEDURE

The funds allocation proposal was especially interesting to Mr. Simmons. Mr. Hutton had developed a new approach to the allocation process. His objective was to strike an optimal balance between funding for high potential/fast growth products and low potential/slow growth ones. As Mr. Hutton explained:

> The most difficult allocations to make are the creative resource allocations. They include such items as research and product development, market development, and manufacturing process development. They are expensed in the period in which they are incurred, but they have a cumulative, positive impact on future sales and earnings. These allocation decisions occur continuously. They are difficult to quantify, highly discretionary, and present some tough trade-offs.

> To support a given level of sales, a certain amount of money is required for variable manufacturing and selling cost, inventories, and receivables. That leaves a pool of money which can be divided between nonvariable expenses and net income. Part of that pool must be drained off for what I call noncreative programs. These include staff functions like finance, planning, and personnel which make no direct contribution to sales. Then we must decide how much to channel into creative programs and how much to flow through to net income. The more we spend on R&D, advertising and promotion, and market development, the healthier our future business will be. But our current earnings and cash flow will suffer. It boils down to a classic trade-off: how to allocate a finite pool of resources to achieve the optimal balance between current and future income.

> The first step is to select a criterion on which funds allocations can be based. It has to be comprehensive enough to enable management to make sound decisions yet easy enough to calculate to make it usable on a daily basis.

> Sales dollars and contribution dollars are easy figures to calculate because they require no allocation of fixed costs. However, sales dollars give no indication of the profitability of a project, and contribution dollars tell only half the story. Contribution can be a useful consideration for certain short-term decisions, but in the long run, we are in business to generate net income, not contribution dollars.

> Clearly, net income is an important factor to consider. But it fails to reflect the productivity of the funds employed. So I have developed a measure which relates pretax operating income to the amount of creative resource dollars used.

Mr. Hutton had included for Mr. Simmons' inspection an exhibit listing the creative resources allocated to each of the Product Departments in 1973 and 1974, the pretax income generated by them, and their profitability per resource dollar spent. (See Exhibit 3.) Mr. Hutton contended that if high growth potential opportunities were to receive adequate funding, different investment and profit goals would have to be established for each of the product lines. A new product which required heavy spending to stimulate and expand demand could not be expected to be as profitable as one which was mature and well established in the market. Therefore, mature products would be funded at lower levels and expected to yield higher returns than high growth potential products.

In examining the funds allocations made over the last two years, Hutton believed that FAS had received too little funding and oils too much. He recommended the following targets for income per dollar of creative resources be established: FAS—$.70; rubbers—$1.75; and oils—$1.65.

DEVELOPING THE FIVE-YEAR BUSINESS PLAN

To aid him in his judgments, Mr. Simmons requested the PPD's balance sheets and income statements for the last five years (see Exhibits 4 and 5). He also wanted to compare the proposed strategy with the strategies which other competitors had pursued. At his request, comparative statistics between the Tex-Fiber PPD and Standard American were assembled (see Exhibit 6).

Mr. Simmons had collected several other pieces of information himself. He knew that Standard American had recently floated a debt issue for $240 million. The funds were earmarked primarily for a recapitalization of the company's financial structure. However, Standard American had also announced its intentions to spend $70 million in 1975 for plant and equipment in the United States and $30 million for foreign facilities. He was also aware that several years before Standard American had radically changed its organizational structure. Public statements by Standard American's chief executive described the organization as having a "matrix" form. As far as Mr. Simmons could tell, this included ten profit centers organized by component "businesses" and five additional profit centers organized by major geographic area.

In addition to the historical and competitive data available, Mr. Simmons wished to consider the comments of his department managers. The funds allocation proposal had generated the strongest reactions.

Mr. Bernie Grosinger, Department Manager for FAS Products, was concerned that his section would still not receive adequate resources over the next several years.

> FAS products are the fastest growing, highest margin products in the Division. But we have not received the support we need in R&D and market development to realize our full potential. Now we are on the verge of another major breakthrough in technology. If we don't receive sufficient resources we will be placed at a significant competitive disadvantage.

> And even if Hutton and Simmons decide to reallocate resources, there are practical problems to face. Some of those R&D professionals in the Oils Department have worked there for 20 years. They won't be nearly as effective doing FAS research. But do we lay them off and hire FAS specialists?

Dr. Walner Hearter, Manager of the Oils Product Department, was concerned that the well-being of his department might be threatened by the new allocation method.

> It is dangerous to speak in broad generalities about a business as diverse as petroloids. True, 40 percent of our oils products are commodities. But 60 percent are specialty items and many of these are as attractive as any in the FAS and rubbers line. Oil sales have suffered more than other lines because customers stockpiled more standard products back in 1974 than specialty items. Consequently, it has taken them longer to draw down their inventories and begin reordering.

> Now I'm afraid that oils will be tagged as the low margin, low growth segment of the business. If our allocations are trimmed any further we won't have the resources we need to push many attractive new applications and we will be the victims of a self-fulfilling prophecy.

> Strategically, oils have always been an important part of the PPD business. By maintaining a strong position in the oils segment, we keep Standard American honest. If we allow our position to slip, Standard American may be able to raise prices and margins in oils while cutting prices in FAS and rubbers. This could seriously jeopardize our leadership in FAS and undermine the profitability of our division.

Mr. Simmons sympathized with the views expressed by both managers. But resources were limited by the profit and cash flow goals for the division. As the new Vice President-General Manager, he was anxious to draw up a long-term plan which could accommodate corporate as well as divisional objectives.

Exhibit 1
TEX-FIBER INDUSTRIES—PETROLOID PRODUCTS DIVISION [B]

A] PERCENTAGE CAPACITY UTILIZATION 1965–1974

1965	105%	1970	88%
1966	103	1971	92
1967	99	1972	110
1968	101	1973	120
1969	99	1974	111

B] PERCENTAGE CAPACITY UTILIZATION BY MONTH—TYPICAL YEAR

J	86%	J	60%
F	88	A	75
M	108	S	109
A	108	O	110
M	110	N	110
J	123	D	113

Exhibit 2
TEX-FIBER INDUSTRIES—PETROLOID PRODUCTS DIVISION [B]
Analysis of Alternative Investment Policies
[in $000,000]

	FRONT LOADED CASE	BACK LOADED CASE	LOW INVESTMENT CASE
Plant expenditure required to expand capacity[1] (1976–1980)	$112	$ 92	$ 28
Impact on operations under most probable sales forecast: ($710 million in 1980)			
Market share loss through 1980	0%	0%	2%
Cumulative net income (1976–1980)	$236	$238	$231
Reconciliation of Δ net income to front loaded case:			
Depreciation savings		$ 13	$ 22
Additional manufacturing cost		$ (9)	$(32)
Pretax income		$ 4	$ (10)
After-tax income		$ 2	$ (5)
Impact on operations under optimistic sales forecast: ($845 million in 1980)			
Market share loss through 1980	2–3%	4–6%	8%
Net income loss (1976–1980)	$ 28	$ 52	$ 76
Impact on operations under pessimistic sales forecast: ($575 million in 1980)			
Market share loss through 1980	0	0	0
Net income loss (1976–1980)	0	0	0

Source: Tex-Fiber files, 1975.

[1]These amounts are net of expenditures required for replacement, and environmental and safety improvements. Such expenditures were estimated to continue at about $15 million per year throughout the period 1976–1980 regardless of which investment policy was chosen.

Exhibit 3

TEX-FIBER INDUSTRIES—PETROLOID PRODUCTS DIVISION [B]
Creative Resource Allocations and Income from Sales
[in $000,000]

PRODUCT LINE	CREATIVE RESOURCES SPENT		PRE-TAX OPERATING INCOME		INCOME PER DOLLAR OF CREATIVE RESOURCES	
	1973	1974	1973	1974	1973	1974
FAS	$45.0	$41.0	$24.9	$33.0	$.55	$.80
Rubbers	19.0	20.0	16.6	22.0	.87	1.10
Oils	18.1	19.0	12.8	18.9	.72	.99

Source: Company documents, 1975.

Exhibit 4

TEX-FIBER INDUSTRIES—PETROLOID PRODUCTS DIVISION [B]
PPD Income Statements, 1970–1974 [in $000,000]

	1970		1971		1972		1973		1974	
	$MM	%	$MM	%	$MM	%	$MM	%	$MM	%
Net Sales	201.8	100	223.1	100	287.6	100	374.0	100	464.0	100
Cost of Goods Sold	60.8	30.2	71.0	31.8	99.3	34.5	137.8	36.9	204.0	43.9
Contribution Margin	141.0	69.8	152.1	68.2	188.3	65.5	235.7	63.1	260.0	56.1
Creative Resources:										
FAS	N/A		13.9	6.2	17.6	6.1	45.0	12.0	41.0	8.8
Rubber	N/A		10.2	4.6	11.1	3.9	19.0	5.1	20.0	4.3
Oils	N/A		28.3	12.7	27.8	9.7	18.1	4.8	19.0	4.1
NSO	N/A		9.3	4.2	11.1	3.9	13.9	3.7	14.1	3.0
Other General and Administrative	110.9	54.9[1]	63.6	28.5	72.8	25.3	85.4	22.9	92.0	19.8
Income from Sales	29.9	14.9	26.8	12.1	47.9	16.7	54.8	14.6	73.9	15.9
Other Income	4.6	2.3	4.6	2.1	1.4	0.5	3.2	0.9	3.9	0.8
Taxable Income	34.5	17.2	31.4	14.1	49.3	17.2	58.0	15.5	77.8	16.8
Federal Income Tax	16.6	8.3	14.8	6.7	22.9	8.0	26.4	7.0	38.0	8.2
Net Income	17.9	8.9	16.6	7.5	26.6	9.2	31.6	8.4	40.0	8.6
Depreciation Expense	18.1	9.0	19.9	9.0	19.9	7.0	22.0	6.0	23.0	5.0
Pro Rata Dividends[2]	9.3	4.6	8.8	4.0	15.3	5.3	18.6	5.0	20.0	4.3
ROI		11.2		9.5		14.1		14.6		15.2

Source: Company files, 1975.

[1]Total of G&A plus section budgets.

[2]Dividend assessments were based on a complex formula involving sales, net income, and net corporate investment. Historically, however, dividends had averaged about 50 percent of net income after taxes.

Exhibit 5
TEX-FIBER INDUSTRIES—PETROLOID PRODUCTS DIVISION [B]
Financial Position at December 31
1970–1974 [in $000]

	1970	1971	1972	1973	1974
ASSETS					
Current Customer Receivables	$25,980	$28,924	$41,232	$44,992	$59,220
FIFO inventories	29,952	30,420	43,792	53,664	84,280
Plant & equipment—first cost	207,716	236,916	267,728	286,220	326,404
Depreciation reserves	(93,492)	(106,268)	(121,768)	(137,036)	(156,048)
Cost less accumulated depr.	114,224	130,648	145,960	149,184	170,356
Investments in affiliates and					
associated companies	0	5,472	11,336	15,144	14,812
Cash and other assets	304	3,560	2,984	10,168	(20,692)
Total assets	$170,460	$199,024	$245,304	$273,152	$307,976
LIABILITIES AND RESERVES					
Accounts payable	($ 5,648)	($ 3,356)	($15,532)	($14,780)	($18,776)
Other liabilities and reserves	(11,308)	(19,928)	(27,188)	(23,196)	(30,368)
Total liabilities and reserves	(16,956)	(23,284)	(42,720)	(37,976)	(49,144)
Net investment	$153,504	$175,400	$202,584	$235,176	$258,832

Source: Company files. 1975.

Exhibit 6
TEX-FIBER INDUSTRIES—PETROLOID PRODUCTS DIVISION [B]
Selected Comparative Statistics for Standard American
and the Tex-Fiber's PPD
(in $000,000)

		1970	1971	1972	1973	1974
DOMESTIC SALES	Standard American	308	320	376	448	536
	PPD	160	173	229	277	356
FOREIGN SALES	Standard American	124	140	190	260	280
	PPD	42	50	58	97	108
TOTAL SALES	Standard American	432	460	566	708	816
	PPD	202	223	287	374	464
RETURN ON SALES %	Standard American	10.0%	6.4%	10.0%	11.4%	11.0%
	PPD	8.9%	7.5%	9.2%	8.4%	8.6%
TOTAL MANUFAC-TURING AND OVERHEAD COST AS % OF SALES	Standard American	58%	60%	56%	54%	57%
	PPD	56%	58%	57%	60%	64%
R&D SPENDING AS % OF SALES	Standard American	9.8%	9.4%	8.3%	7.5%	7.1%
	PPD	8.0%	7.7%	6.3%	5.3%	3.5%
ADVERTISING AND PROMOTION AS % OF SALES	Standard American	2.7%	2.3%	2.2%	2.2%	1.5%
	PPD	1.6%	1.8%	2.7%	3.3%	0.8%

Source: Company files, 1975.

DISCUSSION QUESTIONS

1. What changes have been taking place at PPD over the last several years? What have been the implications of these changes for cash, NI, budget expenditures, in various categories?
2. What has Standard American been doing?
3. Evaluate Mr. Simmons' statement of goals for PPD in the light of these changes.
4. What forecasts of demand and market share should be made?
5. What is your reaction to the procedures used by Mr. Hutton to develop a long-range plan?
6. What broad alternatives does Mr. Simmons have in the future: a) in terms of financial strategy? b) in terms of product-market strategy? How are the two related?

The Use of Pooled Business Experience: The PIMS Project

The previous chapter, dealing with market attractiveness-business position assessment, noted three methodological problems:

1. The factors that impact on "attractiveness" or "position" have to be identified by the analyst.
2. The strength and direction of the relationship between a particular factor and attractiveness or position has to be assessed judgmentally.
3. Overall assessments of attractiveness or position depend on some implicit or explicit "weighting" of the different factors involved.

The so-called PIMS project[1] (for Profit Impact of Marketing Strategy) addresses these difficulties by using empirical evidence from a large number of businesses in a large number of situations. A computer model identifies the most important factors, shows how each factor is related to performance, and "weights" them according to their relative importance in the total equation.

---

[1]Schoeffler et al., "The Impact of Strategic Planning on Profit Performance," *Harvard Business Review*, March-April 1974.

To find better ways to explain and predict operating performance, the PIMS project was initiated in 1960 as an internal project at the General Electric Company (G.E.). After several years of intensive research and testing, a computer-based regression³ model was constructed that "explained" a substantial part of the variation in return-on-investment (ROI). The model used as input, data from a fairly large number of G.E. businesses in diverse markets and industries. (Such models are called "cross-sectional.") The model identified those factors that related most strongly to ROI and provided an indication of their relative role as explanatory variables.

Development of the model continued throughout the 1960s and early 1970s, first at G.E. and then later at the Harvard Business School and the Marketing Science Institute. At this stage the data base was enlarged to include many corporations in addition to G.E.. In 1975, the Strategic Planning Institute, a non-profit corporation governed by the member companies, was formed to manage the PIMS project. In 1977, membership included more than 150 companies operating more than 1,000 businesses, drawn mostly from the *Fortune 500* list. These companies contribute data on one or more of their businesses to the data pool and in return receive a variety of useful strategic planning information on each business submitted.

Among the most important questions which PIMS addresses are:

- What factors explain differences in typical levels of ROI and cash flow among various kinds of businesses?
- What rate of ROI and of cash flow is "normal" or "PAR" in a given type of business, under given market conditions, and using a given strategy?
- How will ROI and other measures of performance, in a specific business, be affected by a change in the strategy employed?
- What are promising directions to explore to improve the performance of a given business?

Answers to these questions are useful to management both in establishing overall objectives for a business and in identifying specific ways to reach them. Consequently PIMS contributes to several stages

---

²Additional background on the PIMS program is provided in Appendix A of the Tex-Fiber Industries (C) case (pp. 321–24).

³Regression is a statistical procedure for empirically determining how one variable may be affected by changes in one or more others.

of the strategic planning process outlined in Chapter 1. In addition, PIMS can be used to help forecast profits; to help make effective allocations of capital, manpower, and other scarce resources; to measure managerial performance (by comparing "expected" with "actual" profit results); and to appraise new business opportunities.

PIMS DEFINITION OF BUSINESSES AND MARKETS[4]

For purpose of PIMS analysis, a business is usually defined as an operating unit that:

- sells a distinct set of products or services
- to an identifiable group of customers
- in competition with a well-defined set of competitors.

Additionally the business must be defined broadly enough to avoid too many arbitrary allocations of joint costs.

The term "market" refers to a set of customers with similar requirements for products and/or services. However, a business may elect to serve only certain customers in the total market; thus when measuring market size and market share, PIMS uses the "served market" concept. A "served market" is usually smaller than the total market.

THE PIMS DATA BASE

Each participating company supplies more than 100 data items for each business, on five separate data forms. (These forms appear in the Tex-Fiber (C) case, pp. 291–320, following this chapter.)

- *Data Form 1:* asks for a description of the business, its products and/or services, its customers and the relationship of this particular business to other organizational components in the same company.
- *Data Form 2:* asks for operating results and balance sheet information.

---

[4]Appendix B of the Tex-Fiber Industries (C) case provides a fuller explanation of how to define businesses and markets in a particular PIMS application situation; see pages 325–27 in the case.

- *Data Form 3:* asks for data on leading competitors and the served market.
- *Data Form 4:* asks for a specification of the SIC[5] code or for certain other "industry" data.
- *Data Form 5:* asks for assumptions about future sales, selling prices, and raw materials costs.

Table 1 shows the composition of the data base in terms of industry, geography, and company size.

Table 1
COMPOSITION OF THE PIMS DATA BASE

INDUSTRY CLASSIFICATION	*% OF SAMPLE*	
Consumer product manufacturers	29	
Capital equipment manufacturers	19	
Raw materials producers	11	
Components manufacturers	23	
Industrial supplies manufacturers	14	
Service and distribution businesses	4	
	100%	
GEOGRAPHIC LOCATION		
U.S. based	85	
Foreign	15	
COMPANY SIZE [ANNUAL SALES]		
	OVER $100 MM	*UNDER $100 MM*
U.S.	55%	35%
Foreign	10	0
	65%	35%

Many first-time users of PIMS ask whether conclusions drawn from such a wide variety of businesses are really relevant for their particular business. Often, managers intuitively feel that their own situation is "unique" and "different." Sometimes they feel that more valid conclusions might be drawn from a subsample of the data more closely approximating their particular industry.

This line of reasoning overlooks the fundamental concept of the PIMS models, namely that certain strategic *characteristics* of the business and its market determine profitability. Each business is described in terms of 37 factors, such as growth rate, market share,

---

[5]SIC = Standard Industrial Classification. The SIC Code is used to classify firms and industries into standard groupings.

product quality, investment intensity, etc. It has been *empirically* determined that these factors provide more explanation of variation in performance than industry classification, geographic location, or size. Indeed, there are some "universal laws of the marketplace" and these laws apply equally well in a variety of industry sectors.

However, it does seem relevant to question whether the *same* 37 factors predict performance in equal measure in—say—a service industry, a manufacturing industry, and a distribution industry. "Sector" models are under development to ascertain if such differences are significant.

USING PIMS

There are two basically different ways that PIMS results can be used to facilitate strategic market planning:

1. By taking into account a series of general observations about the relationship of business performance with strategic and market variables. We shall report on this under the heading "Selected PIMS Findings."
2. By submitting data on a particular business to the PIMS models for detailed analysis of its performance relative to "PAR," and for assessing the implications of strategic changes. We shall report on this under the heading "Using PIMS on a Particular Business."

Each will be dealt with in turn.

SELECTED PIMS FINDINGS

Multivariate regression equations have been used to establish relationships between a variety of different factors and *two* separate measures of performance: ROI and cash flow. PIMS research indicates that these performance measures are largely determined by *general* factors: market growth rate, market share of the business, market share divided by the combined shares of the company's three largest competitors (a somewhat different measure of relative share than used for portfolio analysis in Chapter 4), the degree of vertical integration, working capital requirements per dollar of sales, plant and equipment requirements per dollar of sales, relative product quality, etc.

Cross tabulation analysis has been used to illustrate the most important relationships established by regression. The factors which have been tabulated may be grouped into five classes:

- attractiveness of market environment
  - —long run (4–10 years ahead) industry growth rate
  - —short run (up to 3 years ahead) industry growth rate
  - —stage in the product life cycle
- strength of competitive position
  - — market share
  - — relative market share
  - — relative product quality
  - — relative breadth of product line
- "effectiveness" of use of investment
  - — investment intensity (total investment/sales; also total investment/value added)
  - — fixed capital intensity (fixed capital/sales)
  - — vertical integration (value added/sales)
  - — percent capacity utilized
- discretionary budget allocations
  - — marketing expense/sales
  - — research and development expense/sales
  - — new product expense/sales
- current changes in market position
  - — change in market share

Tables showing these relationships appear below. The first group of tables shows the relationship between a variety of factors and ROI, and the second group shows the relationship to cash flow. (Specific definitions of each of the factors are given in the Tex-Fiber (E) case following this chapter, pages 369–71[6].) A word of caution is necessary in interpreting the tables. These tables show only the relationships between performance and one or two variables at a time, whereas actual performance would depend on all the other variables also. Therefore, these tabulated values must be interpreted as averages with "all other things being equal."

Statistically, the sample size of close to 1,000 businesses means that a fairly high "confidence level"[7] can be associated with the tabu-

---

[6]In a few cases reference should also be made to the input questionnaires contained in the Tex-Fiber (C) case, pp. 291–320.

[7]"Confidence level" is a statistical measure of the degree to which the results show a true relationship and are not due to chance. Generally speaking the larger the sample size, the higher the "confidence level" that the sample result approximates the true underlying relationships.

lated results. Differences of less than three percentage points between table entries in ROI, and less than one percentage point between table entries in cash flow/investment should be disregarded, however.

Determinants of ROI[a]

The major determinants of ROI are a) investment intensity, b) market share (or relative market share), c) market growth, d) life cycle stage, and e) marketing expense/sales ratio. Each has been tabulated alone or with another factor to determine its impact on ROI.

a) The Impact of Investment Intensity

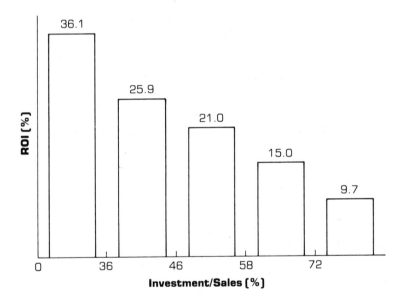

Figure 1

As Investment Intensity Rises ROI Declines

[a]ROI is measured throughout as: ROI = pre-tax income/average investment, where income is after deduction of corporate expenses, but prior to interest charges, and "investment" equals working capital plus fixed capital at book value. ROI is an average figure for the four years of reported data.

Table 2
LARGE INVESTMENT AND HIGH MARKETING INTENSITY EQUALS POOR ROI

	Marketing/Sales		
Investment/Value Added	LO 6% 11% HI		
LO	33*	29	25
89%	24	19	10
130%	11	9	9
HI			

*Read: The average return on investment for businesses with low investment/value added (less than 89 percent) and low marketing/sales (less than 6 percent) was 33 percent. Note that in all the tables in this chapter, "cut points" have been chosen so that each cell contains approximately equal numbers of observations (approximately 100 observations per cell).

Table 3
CAPACITY UTILIZATION IS VITAL WHEN FIXED CAPITAL INTENSITY IS HIGH

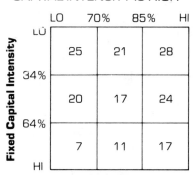

	Capacity Utilization		
Fixed Capital Intensity	LO 70% 85% HI		
LO	25	21	28
34%	20	17	24
64%	7	11	17
HI			

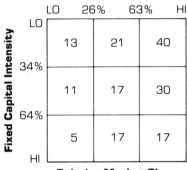

Table 4
HIGH CAPITAL INTENSITY & SMALL MARKET SHARE
EQUALS DISASTER

b) The Impact of Market Share[9]

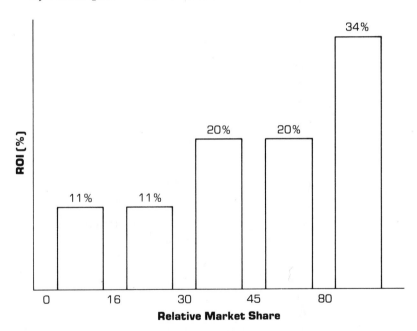

Figure 2
ROI is Closely Related to Relative Market Share

---

[9]Buzzell et al., ''Market Share: A Key to Profitability,'' *Harvard Business Review*, January-Feburary 1975.

Table 5
MARKET SHARE IS MOST PROFITABLE
IN VERTICALLY INTEGRATED INDUSTRIES

	LO	53%	68%	HI
LO				
	13	13	12	
26%				
	21	20	17	
63%				
	28	34	35	
HI				

Relative Market Share (y-axis)

Value Added/Sales

Table 6
HIGH R&D SPENDING DEPRESSES ROI
WHEN MARKET SHARE IS WEAK

	LO	1.3%	3.7%	HI
LO				
	17	12	4	
26%				
	14	20	10	
63%				
	27	30	30	
HI				

Relative Market Share (y-axis)

R&D/Sales

Table 7
CAPACITY UTILIZATION IS MOST IMPORTANT
FOR LOW SHARE BUSINESSES

	LO	70%	85%	HI
LO				
	9	11	17	
26%				
	17	18	22	
63%				
	33	31	34	
HI				

Relative Market Share (y-axis)

Capacity Utilization

280

Table 8

HEAVY MARKETING DEPRESSES ROI FOR LOW SHARE BUSINESSES

Relative Market Share	Marketing/Sales		
	LO	6%	11% HI
LO	20	13	7
26%	21	19	19
63%			
HI	34	31	34

Marketing/Sales

Table 9

MARKET SHARE AND QUALITY ARE PARTIAL SUBSTITUTES FOR EACH OTHER

Relative Market Share	Relative Product Quality		
	LO	6%	36% HI
LO	12	10	17
26%	17	17	26
63%			
HI	29	29	37

Relative Product Quality

c) The Impact of Market Growth Rate

Table 10

A RAPID RATE OF NEW PRODUCT INTRODUCTION IN FAST GROWING MARKETS DEPRESSES ROI

Long Run Market Growth Rate	New Products (% Sales)		
	LO	1%	12% HI
LO	21	18	18
6%	20	24	15
9%			
HI	24	25	15

New Products (% Sales)

Table 11
R&D IS MOST PROFITABLE IN MATURE, SLOW GROWTH MARKETS

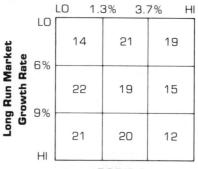

Long Run Market Growth Rate	LO 1.3%	3.7%	HI
LO	14	21	19
6%	22	19	15
9%	21	20	12
HI			

R&D/Sales

d) The Impact of Life Cycle Stage

Table 12
A NARROW PRODUCT LINE, IN EARLY OR MIDDLE STAGE OF THE LIFE CYCLE, IS LESS PROFITABLE THAN AT THE LATE STAGE

Stage in Life Cycle	Narrow		Wide
Early	11	16	27
Middle	13	18	29
Late	23	18	23

Relative Breadth of Product Line

e) The Impact of Marketing Expense/Sales

Table 13
HIGH R&D PLUS HIGH MARKETING DEPRESSES ROI

R&D Sales	LO 6%	11%	HI
LO	21	21	21
1.3%	22	23	19
3.7%	19	22	10
HI			

Marketing/Sales

Table 14
HIGH MARKETING EXPENDITURES DEPRESS ROI
ESPECIALLY WHEN QUALITY IS LOW

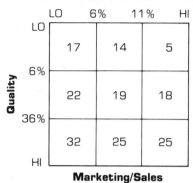

	LO	6%	11%	HI
LO	17	14	5	
6%	22	19	18	
36%	32	25	25	
HI				

Quality (vertical axis) — Marketing/Sales (horizontal axis)

Determinants of Cash Flow[10]

Among the major determinants of cash flow are relative market share and investment intensity. These two factors have been tabulated with other factors such as market growth, marketing/sales ratio, and rate of new product introductions, to determine their impact on cash flow.

a) The Impact of Relative Market Share on Cash Flow

Table 15
HIGH RELATIVE SHARE IMPROVES CASH FLOW;*
HIGH GROWTH DECREASES IT

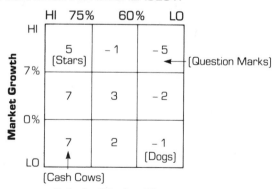

	HI 75%	60%	LO
HI	5 [Stars]	– 1	– 5 ← [Question Marks]
7%	7	3	– 2
0%	7	2	– 1 [Dogs]
LO	↑ [Cash Cows]		

Market Growth (vertical axis) — Relative Market Share (horizontal axis)

[10]Cash flow is measured throughout as: "cash flow" = cash flow/average investment, where cash flow on the right hand side of the equation is cash flow from operations minus changes due to fixed and working capital investment.

Table 15 generally corroborates the hypothesized relationship between share, growth, and cash that underpins portfolio display charts. It also provides a quantitative estimate of how these factors actually affect cash flow. Statistical analysis shows that only about 6 percent of the variability in cash flow among businesses in the sample can be explained by relative share and growth alone. This indicates that many other factors also influence cash flow. Some of these are shown in the tables that follow.

Table 16
HIGH SHARE AND LOW INVESTMENT INTENSITY PRODUCE CASH; LOW SHARE AND HIGH INVESTMENT INTENSITY RESULT IN A CASH DRAIN

	HI	62%	26%	LO
LO		14	6	1
80%		6	2	0
120%		1	-2	-5
HI				

Investment/Value Added (vertical axis)

Relative Market Share

Table 17
HIGH RELATIVE SHARE PRODUCES CASH—ESPECIALLY WHEN MARKETING INTENSITY IS LOW

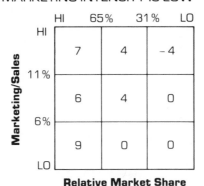

	HI	65%	31%	LO
HI		7	4	-4
11%		6	4	0
6%		9	0	0
LO				

Marketing/Sales (vertical axis)

Relative Market Share

b) The Impact of Investment Intensity on Cash Flow

Table 18

LOW OR MEDIUM GROWTH COUPLED WITH LOW INVESTMENT INTENSITY PRODUCES CASH; HIGH GROWTH COUPLED WITH HIGH INVESTMENT INTENSITY IS A CASH DRAIN

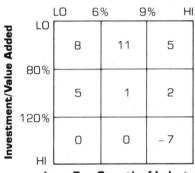

Long Run Growth of Industry

Table 19

HARVESTING SHARE WHEN INVESTMENT INTENSITY IS LOW PRODUCES CASH; BUILDING SHARE WHEN INVESTMENT INTENSITY IS HIGH IS A CASH DRAIN

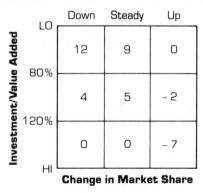

Change in Market Share

Table 20

INVESTMENT PLUS MARKETING INTENSITY RESULTS IN CASH DRAINS

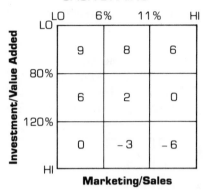

Marketing/Sales

Table 21

FEW NEW PRODUCT INTRODUCTIONS COUPLED WITH LOW INVESTMENT INTENSITY PRODUCES CASH

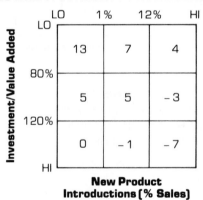

New Product Introductions (% Sales)

PIMS REPORTS FOR A PARTICULAR BUSINESS

While the foregoing tabulations provide a general indication of what to expect from following a particular strategy in a given market situation, more specific analyses for individual businesses are available to PIMS subscribers. Based upon the data supplied for each business a firm may receive four major kinds of reports. Examples and descriptions of each report are contained in the Tex-Fiber Industries (D) and (E) cases which follow this chapter. (See pp. 328–71.) Here, each will be outlined only.

"PAR" Reports indicate what ROI and cash flow are "normal" or "PAR" for a given kind of market environment, market position, degree of competitive differentiation, use of investment, budget allocation, company type, and historical pattern of strategic moves. It is based on the past performance of real businesses under comparable conditions.

In addition, the PAR Reports show how the PAR ROI and cash flow for a business compare with the average for *all* businesses in the PIMS sample (17 percent for pre-tax ROI and 2.7 percent for the ratio of cash flow to investment). PAR Reports also show what factors account for the variation of PAR from the overall average. If, for example, the PAR ROI for a business exceeds the average by 8 percent, then the PAR model will attribute a proportion of the 8 percentage points to each of the various factors, such as growth, investment intensity, or market share. (See Table 2 of the Tex-Fiber (D) case, pp. 331–32.)

PAR values are useful to management in assessing reasonable performance expectations for a particular business, and for setting a standard against which to control actual performance. Deviations of actual ROI from PAR can indicate that a business is particularly well or badly managed. PAR Reports are also useful for identifying critical success factors in any given situation. These are the factors that substantially contribute to the explanation of differences between PAR values and average ROI or cash flow for all businesses.

Strategy Sensitivity Reports predict what would happen (within the short and long term) if certain strategic changes were made. These reports are based on future values, supplied by the user, of industry sales, costs, and prices.

Strategy Sensitivity Reports show the effect of changes in market share, vertical integration, or capital intensity on performance measures such as ROI, net income, discounted net income, cash flow, and discounted cash flow. Management can, therefore, explore the implication of making fundamental changes in the strategy of a business, and the performance trade-offs that might be involved in the short and long run. For example, market share improvement typically depresses cash flow in the years it is undertaken, but may increase cash flow in the long run.

In reality, changes in these factors would also entail changes in other factors such as product quality, relative prices, capacity utilization, research and development/sales, and marketing expense/sales, etc. Market share improvement, for example, might require increases in marketing/sales and research and development/sales ratios. The model uses the PIMS data base to assess how the various factors typically relate to one another, and how a change in one affects changes in others.

Thus "consistency" between the various factors is determined by the historical experience of other real businesses making similar strategic moves. (See Table 8 in the Tex-Fiber (D) case, p. 341, as an example.)

Optimum Strategy Reports predict which *combination* of strategic moves results in the best ROI, discounted net income, or discounted cash flow. Individual reports are prepared to maximize each of these measures; each entails different strategic moves and results in suboptimal performance on the other performance measures. For instance, a strategy to maximize cash flow is likely to result in a sharp reduction in market share and lower long-run net income and ROI. (See, for example, Table 12 in the Tex-Fiber (D) case, p. 345.)

Limited Information Model (LIM) Report combines elements of both the PAR ROI and Strategy Sensitivity Reports, but in a less comprehensive way. It is designed for business planning situations in which it is difficult to collect all the data needed for a complete PIMS analysis. It uses 18 profit-influencing factors rather than 37; these explain more than 60 percent of the observed variation in ROI (as opposed to explanations of more than 80 percent when all the factors are used). (Examples of LIM Reports are in the Tex-Fiber (E) case, pp. 355–68).

Normally there is a progression in the utilization of the PIMS system. Companies usually begin by submitting data on only one or two businesses and define them at a rather aggregate level. A manufacturer of a range of portable typewriters, for example, might initially submit this as one single business. At a later stage, the numbers of businesses may be expanded and each *segment* of a business in which a differentiated strategy is possible might be explored. In the above example, the portable typewriter business might now be subdivided into geographic or product segments. Sophisticated users progress to developing strategies for "portfolios" of businesses, using a supplementary "model" (not described above) that takes overall cash constraints into account. In the process the hope is that using PIMS will become a routine part of the regular planning process.

In all phases PIMS is best used as an *aid* to management judgment, not as a substitute for management judgment. Strategy Sensitivity Reports, for example, are useful as "directional indicators"—to provide management with a sense of the trade-offs involved in undertaking various strategy alternatives. In other words, a liberal dose of business judgment should be applied in using PIMS print-outs to aid the preparation of actual plans and budgets. As Dr. Sidney Schoeffler, Executive Director of the Strategic Planning Institute and the originator of PIMS, says, "Don't ignore what the model says, but don't believe what the model says either."

SUMMARY

Using pooled business experience to aid planning—as PIMS does —addresses some of the difficulties associated with more judgmental methods for formulating business strategy. PIMS findings indicate that investment intensity, relative market share, industry growth rate, life cycle position, and marketing expense/sales ratios are among the most important factors affecting ROI and cash flow. Altogether 37 variables are used to "explain" variations in these performance measures for the nearly 1,000 businesses in the data base. The PIMS model requires as input more than 100 pieces of data concerning the business, its operating results, the market and competitive environment, and general industry characteristics; output is in the form of reports showing "normal" or "PAR" ROI, "PAR" cash flow, and the impact of strategic changes on various aspects of performance.

TEX-FIBER INDUSTRIES— PETROLOID PRODUCTS DIVISION [C][1]

In the course of drawing up five year business plans for the PPD division [see Tex-Fiber Industries—Petroloid Products Division (A) and (B)], Mr. John Hutton, PPD's Manager of Strategic Planning, had become intrigued with the PIMS model (see Appendix A) as a possible aid to strategic analysis and planning. He had since convinced Mr. Jack Simmons, his General Manager, that the division should explore the use of the PIMS model as an additional input to their thinking.

The PIMS model required as input more than 100 pieces of data concerning the business, its operating results, the market and competitive environment, and general industry characteristics. These data were to be provided in standard questionnaire format. Questionnaire forms had been made available to Mr. Hutton and with the help of other members of the management team he had already filled out most of the data required (see attached questionnaires). Two difficult questions still remained to be answered, however. First, Mr. Hutton had to decide at which stage petroloids were in their product life cycle (see Question #103). A related set of questions involved making future sales forecasts and price forecasts for the petroloids market (see Questions #501–504). Secondly, Mr. Hutton wanted to be certain that he had defined the "business" and its "served market" in the right way (see Questions #201, 301–302). He had, prior to completing these questions, carefully read relevant parts of the PIMS Data Manual (see Appendix B); he still wondered nevertheless, what the pros and cons of different definitions might be.

---

[1]This case was prepared by Joseph D'Cruz in collaboration with Derek F. Abell.

THE STRATEGIC PLANNING INSTITUTE

The PIMS Program

DATA FORM
1

DESCRIPTION OF THE BUSINESS: PRODUCTS AND SERVICES, CUSTOMERS, COMPANY RELATIONSHIPS

GENERAL INSTRUCTIONS: Please answer every question. If the best estimate of a quantity is zero, fill in "0", not a dash. If a question is not applicable, please check the box indicating this or write "N.A." prominently. Do not use these forms for businesses which are less than 3 years old. (For "start-up" businesses, obtain special forms from the PIMS office.)

IF YOU HAVE DIFFICULTY PROVIDING ANY OF THE INFORMATION REQUESTED IN THE FORM, please consult the PIMS Data Manual, or call the PIMS Office, Area 617, 492-3810

IDENTIFICATION OF BUSINESS

**IDENTIFYING NUMBER
FOR THIS BUSINESS
INTERNAL TO COMPANY**
(For New PIMS Businesses Only)

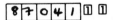

**PIMS IDENTIFYING
NUMBER**
(For Old PIMS Businesses: Use
Existing PIMS Number)

Line

100: SUITABILITY FOR RESEARCH

This business is real *(suitable for research)* — ☐ 0

is simulated *(not suitable for research)* — ☑ 1

has undergone dramatic short-term abnormalities *(possibly unsuited for research)* — ☐ 2

101: TYPE OF BUSINESS

This business is best described as . . . *(Check one of the following eight boxes)*

CONSUMER PRODUCTS MANUFACTURING:

. . . Durable Products — ☐ 1

. . . Non-Durable Products — ☐ 2

INDUSTRIAL/COMMERCIAL/PROFESSIONAL PRODUCTS MANUFACTURING:

. . . Capital Goods — ☐ 3

. . . Raw or Semi-Finished Materials — ☑ 4 CHECK

. . . Components for Incorporation into Finished Products — ☐ 5 ONE

. . . Supplies or Other Consumable Products — ☐ 6 ONLY

SERVICES — ☐ 7

RETAIL AND/OR WHOLESALE DISTRIBUTION — ☐ 8

PRODUCTS AND SERVICES

102: AGE OF PRODUCT CATEGORY OR TYPE

When were the *types* of products or services sold by this business first developed? (Please indicate date of development applicable to *current* basic technology.) *(Check one)*

Prior to 1930	1930–1949	1950–1954	1955–1959	1960–1964	1965–1969	1970–1974	1975–
☐ 0	☐ 1	☑ 2	☐ 3	☐ 4	☐ 5	☐ 6	☐ 7

103: "LIFE CYCLE" STAGE OF PRODUCT CATEGORY

How would you describe the stage of development of the product *category* or type sold by this business during the last three years? *(Check one)*

. . . Introductory Stage: Primary demand for product just starting to grow; products or services still unfamiliar to many potential users — ☐ 1

. . . Growth Stage: Demand growing at 10% or more annually in real terms; technology and/or competitive structure still changing — ☐ 2

. . . Maturity Stage: Products or services familiar to vast majority of prospective users; technology and competitive structure reasonably stable — ☐ 3

. . . Decline Stage: Products viewed as commodities; weaker competitors beginning to exit — ☐ 4

104: When did your company first enter this business? (Year of initial commercial sales.)

Prior to 1930	1930–1949	1950–1954	1955–1959	1960–1964	1965–1969	1970–1974	1975–
☐ 0	☐ 1	☐ 2	☑ 3	☐ 4	☐ 5	☐ 6	☐ 7

105: At the time your company first entered this business, was it . . . *(Check one)*

. . . One of the pioneers in first developing such products or services? □ 1

. . . An early follower of the pioneer(s) in a still growing, dynamic market? ☑ 2

. . . A later entrant into a more established market situation? □ 3

106–107: PATENTS AND TRADE SECRETS

Does this business benefit to a significant degree from patents, trade secrets, or other proprietary methods of production or operation?

106: PERTAINING TO PRODUCTS OR SERVICES?　NO ☑ 0　　YES □ 1

107: PERTAINING TO PROCESSES　NO □ 0　　YES ☑ 1

108: STANDARDIZATION OF PRODUCTS/SERVICES — Are the products or services of this business . . . *(Check one)*

. . . More or less standardized for all customers? ☑ 0

. . . Designed and/or produced to order for individual customers? □ 1

109: FREQUENCY OF PRODUCT CHANGES

Is it typical practice for the business and its major competitors to change all or part of the line of products/services offered. . . *(Check one)*

. . . Annually (for example, annual model changes) □ 1

. . . Seasonally? □ 2

. . . Periodically, but at intervals longer than one year? □ 3

. . . No regular, periodic pattern of change? ☑ 4

110: TECHNOLOGICAL CHANGE

Have there been *major* technological changes in the products offered by the business and/or its major competitors, or in methods of production, during the last 8 years? *(If in doubt about whether a change was "major", answer NO.)*

NO ☑ 0

YES □ 1

111: DEVELOPMENT TIME FOR NEW PRODUCTS/SERVICES

For your business and for its major competitors, what is the typical time lag between the beginning of development effort for a new product and market introduction? *(Check one)*

. . . Less than 1 year □ 1

. . . 1 – 2 years ☑ 2

. . . 2 – 5 years □ 3

. . . More than 5 years □ 4

. . . Not applicable; little or no new product development occurs in this business □ 5

END USERS AND IMMEDIATE CUSTOMERS

Lines 112 – 132 deal with (1) the *end users* of the products or services of this business, i.e., the persons or organizations that either consume your products or services OR incorporate them into other products; and (2) the *immediate customers* to whom you sell. Businesses and institutions that use your products or services are end users *unless* they re-sell products in *identical form.*

Line

112–116: DISTRIBUTION OF USE AMONG END USER GROUPS

Approximately what percentages (to the nearest 5%) of the output of the business are used by . . .

PER CENT

112: . . . Households, individual consumers   `0 0 5`

113: . . . Manufacturers (including use as components, materials, etc. in *their* end products)   `0 8 0`

114: . . . Institutional, commercial, professional customers (including farms)   `0 0 5`

115: . . . Government   `0 0 0`

116: . . . Contractors   `0 1 0`

NOTE: Please enter a percentage for every one of the above lines even if the percentage is zero.   TOTAL = 100%

117: NUMBER OF END USERS

During the most recent year for which you are entering data, within the served market, approximately how many end users were there for the products or services of this business *(Check one)*

19 or fewer	1	100,000 – 999,999		6
20 – 99	2	1,000,000 – 9,999,999		7
100 – 999	3	10,000,000 – 24,999,999		8
1,000 – 9,999	4	25,000,000 – or more		9
10,000 – 99,999	✓5			

118: NUMBER OF IMMEDIATE CUSTOMERS

During the most recent year for which you are entering data, approximately how many *immediate customers* were served by your business?

(NOTE: If this business sold directly and exclusively to end users, your answer to this question is simply a more detailed estimate than that given in Line 117, immediately preceding.) *(Check one)*

3 or fewer	1	50 – 99		5
4 – 9	2	100 – 999	✓6	
10 – 19	3	1,000 – 9,999		7
20 – 49	4	10,000 or more		8

119–121: CONCENTRATION OF PURCHASES – END USERS

119:   What proportion of the total number of *end users* account for 50% of total purchases of your products or services?

PER CENT

`3 0`

120: During the last 5 years, has this proportion (Check One)

... DECREASED? ☐ 1

... REMAINED STABLE? ☑ 2

... INCREASED? ☐ 3

121: Is the proportion reported in Line 119 ... *(Check one)*

... SMALLER than for leading competitors? ☐ 1

... ABOUT THE SAME AS leading competitors? ☑ 2

... LARGER than for leading competitors? ☐ 3

122–124: CONCENTRATION OF PURCHASES – IMMEDIATE CUSTOMERS

122: What proportion of the total number of *immediate customers* account for 50% of total sales?

PER CENT

| 1 | 5 |

123: During the last 5 years has this proportion (Check one)

... DECREASED? ☐ 1

... REMAINED SAME? ☑ 2

... INCREASED? ☐ 3

124: Compared to your major competitors, is the proportion reported in Line 122 ... *(Check one)*

... SMALLER than for leading competitors? ☐ 1

... ABOUT THE SAME AS leading competitors? ☑ 2

... LARGER than for leading competitors? ☐ 3

125–126: PURCHASE FREQUENCY – END USERS AND IMMEDIATE CUSTOMERS

How often do *end users* and *immediate customers* typically buy the products or services of your business? *(Check one in each column; focus on vendor selection or source decision rather than delivery schedule.)*

	125: END USERS	126: IMMEDIATE CUSTOMERS
Weekly or more frequently	☐ 1	☐ 1
Between once/week and once/month	☐ 2	☐ 2
Between once/month and once/6 months	☑ 3	☑ 3
Between once/6 months and once/year	☐ 4	☐ 4
Between once/year and once/5 years	☐ 5	☐ 5
Between once/5 years and once/10 years	☐ 6	☐ 6
Other	☐ 7	☐ 7

127–128: TYPICAL PURCHASE AMOUNT – END USERS AND IMMEDIATE CUSTOMERS

Is the typical *amount* of your products or services bought by an end user and an immediate customer in a single transaction . . . *(Check one in each column)*

	127: END USERS	128: IMMEDIATE CUSTOMERS
. . . Less than $1.00?	1	1
. . . From $1 up to $9.99?	2	2
. . . From $10 up to $99?	3	3
. . . From $100 up to $999?	4	4
. . . From $1,000 up to $9,999?	✓ 5	✓ 5
. . . From $10,000 up to $99,999?	6	6
. . . From $100,000 up to $999,999?	7	7
. . . From $1,000,000 up to $9,999,999?	8	8
. . . Over $10 Million?	9	9

NOTE: These amounts are in *actual* NOT disguised dollars. When customers buy on a contract basis covering a period of time, the total amount covered by such a contract should be regarded as a *single* transaction.

129–130: IMPORTANCE OF PRODUCTS/SERVICES TO END USERS AND IMMEDIATE CUSTOMERS

Indicate the proportion of the typical immediate customer's and typical end user's total annual purchases accounted for by purchases of the types of products and services sold by this business. *(Check one)*

	129: END USERS	130: IMMEDIATE CUSTOMERS
. . . Less than 0.25%	1	1
. . . Between 0.25% and 1.0%	✓ 2	✓ 2
. . . Between 1% and 5%	3	3
. . . Between 5% and 25%	4	4
. . . Over 25%	5	5

131: IMPORTANCE OF AUXILIARY SERVICES TO END USERS

Are installation, repair, customer education, or other product-related services provided to end users . . . *(Check one)*

. . . Of relatively little or no importance?

. . . Of some importance?

. . . Of great importance?

132: RELIANCE ON PROFESSIONAL ADVISERS

In making buying decisions, do end users rely on outside advisers – such as physicians, architects, or consulting engineers . . . *(Check one)*

. . . Never

. . . Occasionally

. . . Usually, always

☑ 0

☐ 1

☐ 2

133–136: DISTRIBUTION CHANNELS

Approximately what percentages of the sales of your businesses are made:

PER CENT

133...Direct to end users

134...To end users via company-owned retail or wholesale distribution facilities

135...To wholesalers

136...To retailers

0	6	0
0	0	0
0	3	8
0	0	2

TOTAL = 100%

NOTE: Please enter a percentage for every one of the above lines even if the percentage is zero.

137: GROSS MARGINS – DISTRIBUTION CHANNELS

What is the approximate total gross margin realized by wholesalers and/or retailers, expressed as a combined percentage of the selling price to end users? (Please estimate to the nearest 5 percentage points, e.g., 20%, 25%, etc. If all sales are made direct to users, answer zero.)

PER CENT

| 2 | 0 |

138–141: VERTICAL INTEGRATION

Compare the degree of vertical integration of <u>this business</u> relative to its leading competitors... Backward (toward raw materials)....Forward (toward customer).

DEGREE OF INTEGRATION

138: BACKWARD   139: FORWARD

. . . Less   ☐ 1   ☐ 1

. . . Same   ☑ 2   ☑ 2

. . . More   ☐ 3   ☐ 3

Compare the degree of integration of *your company* in this line of business with that of your leading competitors . . .

DEGREE OF INTEGRATION

140: BACKWARD   141: FORWARD

. . . Less   ☑ 1   ☐ 1

. . . Same   ☐ 2   ☑ 2

. . . More   ☐ 3   ☐ 3

COMPANY RELATIONSHIPS

Line Lines 142-148 apply to the most recent year for which you are entering data.

142—145: PURCHASES FROM AND SALES TO OTHER COMPONENTS OF THE COMPANY

142: Approximately what per cent of the total purchases of materials, supplies, etc. of this business were obtained from other components *of the same company?*

PER CENT

0	0	0

143: Estimate the average incremental profit on each additional dollar of sales to this business from other components of the same company. Express the estimate in before-tax dollars (e.g. $.10 = 10¢; $.00 = N/A)

$ | .0 | 0 |

144: Approximately what percent of the total sales of this business were made to other components of the same company?

PER CENT

0	0	2

145: Do the general managers of other organizational components that are significant suppliers or customers of this business report to the same immediate superior as the general manager of this business?

... Yes, for both "purchases from ..." and "sales to ..." □ 0

... No, for both "purchases from ..." and "sales to ..." □ 1

... Yes, for only "purchases from ..." □ 2

... Yes, for only "sales to ..." □ 3

... Not applicable ☑ 4

146: SHARED FACILITIES

To what extent did this business share its manufacturing or operating plant and equipment facilities and personnel with other components of the company? *(Check one)*

... Less than 10% of its plant and equipment ☑

... Between 10% and 80% of its plant and equipment □ 2

... 80% or more of its plant and equipment □ 3

147: COMMON MARKETS/DISTRIBUTION CHANNELS

Approximately what per cent of the sales of this business were to customers also served by other components of the same company? *(Check one)*

... Less than 25% ☑

... 25% – 49% □ 2

... 50% – 74% □ 3

... 75% or more □ 4

148: SHARED MARKETING PROGRAMS

To what extent were the products and services of this business handled by the same sales force and/or promoted through the same advertising and sales promotion programs, as those of other components of the company? *(Check one)*

... Less than 10% of its marketing expenditures

... Between 10% and 80% of its marketing expenditures   2

... 80% or more marketing of its expenditures   3

CAPACITY OR SUPPLY LIMITATIONS, PRICING RESTRICTIONS

Line

149—152: During the most recent data year were there any constraints on the ability of this business to increase its output by, say, 10%, on account of:

149: Scarcity of Materials?   NO 0   YES 1

150: Scarcity of fuels and energy?   NO 0   YES 1

151: Scarcity of Personnel?   NO 0   YES 1

152: Plant capacity limitations?   NO 0   YES 1

153: During 1972—73, did this business operate under governmental price controls?   NO 0   YES 1

154: If yes, to what extent do you estimate that controls affected profitability?

... Slightly (less than 0.1% on sales) or not at all   0

... Moderately   1

... Substantially (more than 1% on sales)   2

... Not applicable   3

SUPPLY CONDITIONS

Line

155: What per cent of *your* total external purchases are made from your three largest suppliers?   PER CENT 0 7 5

156: Express the sales of the three largest external suppliers to this business as a per cent of their total sales?   PER CENT 0 0 1

157: Does this business have good alternate sources of supply for the purchases referred to in Line 155?

... No   0

... Yes, but with difficulty   1

... Yes, with no difficulty   2

158: Are any of your three largest external suppliers integrated forward ... *(Check one)*

... No   0

... Yes but not into your served market   1

... Yes and into your served market   2

159: If your answer to Line 158 was "NO", is it economically feasable and likely that any would integrate forward?

NO ☑ 0
YES ☐ 1

ORGANIZATION

Line

160: Do other "Businesses" in your company offer products and services that compete directly with the products and services of this business?

NO ☑ 0   YES ☐ 1

161: What per cent of the employees of this business are unionized? Accuracy within 10% is adequate.

PER CENT
| 0 | 5 | 0 |

PRODUCTION PROCESS

Line

162–165: During the most recent data year what percentage of this business' sales was derived from products manufactured by each of the following methods? (Accuracy within 10% is adequate.)

PER CENT

162: Unit or small batch methods (production runs normally under 200);
| 0 | 0 | 0 |

PER CENT

163: Large batch or mass methods (e.g., assembly line);
| 0 | 0 | 0 |

PER CENT

164: Continuous process;
| 1 | 0 | 0 |

PER CENT

165: Non-manufacturing activities (e.g., service) (Businesses with no manufacturing should mark 100% in this box.);
| 0 | 0 | 0 |

NOTE: Please enter a percentage for every one of the above lines even if the percentage is zero.

TOTAL = 100%

End of Form 1

 THE STRATEGIC PLANNING INSTITUTE

CONFIDENTIAL

DATA FORM

2

OPERATING RESULTS
AND
BALANCE SHEET
INFORMATION

GENERAL INSTRUCTIONS: Please answer every question. If the best estimate of a quantity is zero, fill in "0", not a dash. If a question is not applicable, please check the box indicating this or write "N.A." prominently. Do not use these forms for businesses which are less than 3 years old. (For "start-up" businesses, obtain special forms from the PIMS office.)

IF YOU HAVE DIFFICULTY PROVIDING ANY OF THE INFORMATION REQUESTED IN THE FORM, please consult the PIMS Data Manual, or call the PIMS Office, Area 617, 492-3810

IDENTIFICATION
OF BUSINESS

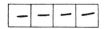

—	—	—	—

**IDENTIFYING NUMBER
FOR THIS BUSINESS
INTERNAL TO COMPANY**
(For new PIMS Businesses Only)

8	7	0	4	/

☑ 2 ☑ 5

**PIMS IDENTIFYING
NUMBER**
(For old PIMS Businesses
Use existing PIMS Number)

SALES AND EXPENSES

Please make certain that the disguise factor (designated by "D" on Form 2) *is the same* as that used for Line 301, "Size of Served Market". (Please note also that Line 301 should be scaled so that its largest value falls between $1,000 and $99,999.)

LINE	1971	1972	1973	1974	1975

201: NET SALES (TOTAL REVENUE) (D)

Revenue realized from goods shipped or services rendered net of (1) bad debts (2) returns (3) allowances. Include lease revenue and progress payments applicable to a given year. Exclude orders not covered by invoices.

201 | 223.1 | 287.6 | 374.0 | 464.0 | n.a.

202: LEASE REVENUES (D)

Revenue received from customers for use of equipment or facilities owned by this business. (Note: These revenues are also included above in Line 201.)

202 | 0 | 0 | 0 | 0 | n.a.

203: ORDER BACKLOG

Enter order backlog as a percentage of annual sales volume for each year (accuracy within 5% is adequate). (Enter "0" if not relevant.)

203 | 15 % | 15 % | 15 % | 5 % | n.a. %

204: PURCHASES (D)

Indicate the value of raw materials, energy, components, assemblies, supplies and/or services purchased or consumed. These may be obtained from other companies or from other businesses in your company. Exclude (1) capital expenditures and associated expenses (2) cost of modifying plant and/or equipment whether done in-house or contracted to others and (3) purchases for stockpile rather than use.

204 | 28.4 | 39.7 | 55.1 | 98.3 | n.a.

205: VALUE ADDED (D)

Value added = sales minus purchases (line 201 − 204).

205 | 194.7 | 247.9 | 318.9 | 365.7 | n.a.

206: MANUFACTURING & PHYSICAL DISTRIBUTION EXPENSES (D)

Indicate the cost of bringing inputs to this business to final form *plus* all logistical costs (e.g., warehousing, freight, insurance, breakage, etc.) (Depreciation expenses shown on Line 215 should not be included here.)

206 | 22.7 | 39.7 | 60.7 | 82.7 | n.a

207: PRODUCT OR SERVICE R&D EXPENSE (D)

Show all expenses incurred to secure innovations and/or advances in the products or services of this business. Include improvements in packaging as well as product design/features/functions. Exclude expenses for process improvement; these belong in Line 208.

207 | 10.3 | 10.8 | 11.9 | 9.7 | n.a.

208: PROCESS R&D EXPENSE (D)

Indicate all expenses for process improvements for the purpose of reducing the cost of manufacturing, processing, and/or physical handling of goods by this business.

208 | 6.9 | 7.2 | 7.9 | 6.5 | n.a.

209: GOVERNMENT—FUNDED R&D EXPENSE

Approximately what percentage of this business' total R&D expenditures (sum of line 207 and 208) were government-funded?

209 | 0 % | 0 % | 0 % | 0 % | n.a. %

210: SALES FORCE EXPENSES (D)

This includes (1) compensation and expenses incurred by salesmen, (2) commissions paid to brokers or agents, and (3) cost of sales force administration.

210 | 9.3 | 11.1 | 13.9 | 14.1 | n.a.

211: ADVERTISING & SALES PROMOTION EXPENSES (D)

Include all expenditures for (1) media advertising (2) catalogs (3) exhibits and displays (4) premiums (5) coupons (6) samples (7) *temporary* price reductions for promotional purposes whether to users, distributors or dealers.

211 | 4.0 | 7.7 | 12.3 | 3.7 | n.a.

212: ADVERTISING EXPENSES (D)

Isolate expenditures for *media* advertising within the total shown in Line 211.

212 | 2.5 | 4.0 | 7.0 | 3.0 | n.a.

213: OTHER MARKETING EXPENSES (D)

Include those marketing expenses not already reflected in Lines 210 or 211 (e.g., marketing and administration; market research; customer service).

213 | 31.2 | 30.8 | 50.0 | 60.1 | n.a.

214: TOTAL MARKETING EXPENSES (D)

The sum of Lines 210, 211 and 213.

214 | 44.5 | 49.6 | 76.2 | 77.9 | n.a.

215: DEPRECIATION EXPENSE (D)

Isolate, if possible, the annual depreciation charge on the major fixed assets of this business' manufacturing plant and equipment. (Depreciation expenses shown here should *not* be included in line 206.)

215 | 19.9 | 19.9 | 22.0 | 23.0 | n.a.

216: OTHER EXPENSES (D)

Indicate all other expenses or charges needed in order to compute net income but not called for in Lines 204 through 215. Include corporate assessments, if any. Exclude (1) charges for corporate debt (2) federal income taxes and (3) non-recurring costs. Your answer will be used as a "balancing" item.

216 | 63.6 | 72.8 | 85.4 | 92.0 | n.a.

217: NET INCOME (D)

Enter the operating profit of this business *prior* to deduction of (1) federal income taxes (2) corporate assessment for interest on corporate debt and (3) special non-recurring costs such as those linked to starting up a new facility. The conservative accounting principles reflected in your entries in Lines 201 or 202 apply to Line 217 as well.

CHECK: *Line 217 = (201) − (204+206+207+208+214+215+216).*

| 217 | 26.8 | 47.9 | 54.8 | 73.9 | n.a. |

BALANCE SHEET ITEMS

220: AVERAGE NET RECEIVABLES (D)

Show average receivables for the year net of allowances for bad debts.

| 220 | 28.9 | 41.2 | 45.0 | 59.2 | n.a. |

221: AVERAGE FINISHED GOODS INVENTORY (D)

Show average for the year, net of reserves for losses.

| 221 | 18.4 | 26.8 | 32.7 | 54.3 | n.a. |

222: AVERAGE INVENTORY OF RAW MATERIALS, COMPONENTS AND WORK IN-PROCESS (D)

Show average for the year, net of reserves for losses.

| 222 | 12.0 | 17.0 | 21.0 | 30.0 | n.a. |

223: GROSS BOOK VALUE OF PLANT AND EQUIPMENT (D)

Indicate the original value of buildings, real estate, manufacturing equipment, plus all transportation equipment owned. (Show average for each year)

| 223 | 236.9 | 267.7 | 286.2 | 326.4 | n.a. |

224: NET BOOK VALUE OF PLANT AND EQUIPMENT (D)

This is Line 223 net of accumulated depreciation to date. (Show average for each year.)

224 | 130.6 | 146.0 | 149.2 | 170.4 | n.a.

225: Express, as a percentage, your best estimate of current gross *replacement* cost of assets referred to in line 223 to the most recent gross *book* value in the last year listed on line 223.

225 | 180 %

226: CASH (D)

Show average for each year.

226 | 3.6 | 3.0 | 10.2 | -20.7 | n.a.

227: OTHER ASSETS (D)

Show average for each year.

227 | 5.5 | 11.3 | 15.1 | 14.8 | n.a.

228: AVERAGE INVESTMENT (D)

Indicate the average investment for each year identifiable as particular to this business. Include both fixed and working capital at book value. Exclude corporate investment not specific to this business (e.g., corporate aircraft). If a significant portion of total assets is leased, include the *capitalized* value of the annual lease obligation, i.e., estimate the book value of the assets as if they were owned.

228 | 175.4 | 202.6 | 235.2 | 258.8 | n.a.

229: SHORT TERM BORROWINGS (D)

Show average for each year.

229 | 19.9 | 27.2 | 23.2 | 30.4 | n.a.

230: OTHER CURRENT LIABILITIES (D)

(Such as accounts payable.) *Show average for each year.*

230 | 3.4 | 15.5 | 14.8 | 18.8 | n.a.

231: TOTAL ASSETS (D)

Enter the sum of Lines 228 and 229 and 230.

Check: Balance sheet figures should satisfy the equation: (226+227)+(220+221+222+224) = (228+229+230) = 231

231 | 199.0 | 245.3 | 273.2 | 308.0 | n.a.

OTHER DATA ON THE PRODUCTION PROCESS

235: STANDARD CAPACITY (D)

The sales value of the maximum output that this business can achieve with (1) facilities normally in operation and (2) current constraints (e.g., technology, work rules, labor practices, etc.). For most manufacturing businesses, this will consist of 2-shifts, 5-days per week. For process businesses, a 3-shift, 6-day period is typical.

235 | 240.0 | 260.0 | 310.0 | 420.0 | n.a.

236: CAPACITY UTILIZATION, PER CENT

The percentage of standard capacity utilized on average during the year.

236 | 92 % | 110 % | 120% | 111% | n.a. %

237: ACCOUNTING METHOD FOR INVENTORY VALUATION

237 | LIFO FIFO OTHER | | | | n.a.

238: SALES PER EMPLOYEE (*NOT DISGUISED*) *

Using *actual* data, divide annual sales volume plus lease revenues by the total number of persons (full-time equivalents) employed in the business. A precise figure is not required. Express in 1,000's of U.S. $'s.

238* | 42.0 | 46.0 | 49.0 | 54.0 | n.a. |

239: SALES PER SALESMAN (*NOT DISGUISED*) *

Again using *actual* data, divide annual sales volume plus lease revenues by the average number of (full-time equivalent) *salesmen* employed in the business. Express in 1,000's of U.S. $'s.

239* | 2479.0 | 2792.0 | 2899.0 | 2578.0 | n.a. |

* For Lines 238 and 239 enter the actual ratio, not a disguised ratio. Also, be sure to express in 1,000's of U.S. $'s.

End of Form 2

THE STRATEGIC PLANNING INSTITUTE

The
PIMS
Program

P
I
M
S

CONFIDENTIAL

DATA FORM

3

MARKET AND COMPETITION

GENERAL INSTRUCTIONS: Please answer every question. If the best estimate of a quantity is zero, fill in "0", not a dash. If a question is not applicable, please check the box indicating this or write "N.A." prominently. Do not use these forms for businesses which are less than 3 years old. (For "start-up" businesses, obtain special forms from the PIMS office.)
IF YOU HAVE DIFFICULTY PROVIDING ANY OF THE INFORMATION REQUESTED IN THE FORM, please consult the PIMS Data Manual, or call the PIMS Office, Area 617, 492-3810

IDENTIFICATION
OF BUSINESS

**IDENTIFYING NUMBER
FOR THIS BUSINESS
INTERNAL TO COMPANY**
(For New PIMS Businesses Only)

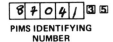

**PIMS IDENTIFYING
NUMBER**

(For Old PIMS Businesses:
Use Existing PIMS Number)

LINE	1971	1972	1973	1974	1975

SERVED MARKET

301: SIZE OF SERVED MARKET (D)

Indicate the total value of sales in the market actively served by this business. Your entry should (1) include price changes, (2) be comparable to your entry in Line 201 and (3) *reflect the same disguise factor as in Line 201.*

Please note that whenever the largest value entered for line 301 is less than $1,000 or more than $99,999.50 the computer will automatically rescale all Form 2 and 3 data designated "(D)". This automatic rescaling or moving of decimal points is necessitated by computer print-out constraints. In view of these constraints it is advisable to choose a disguise factor that limits the largest value on Line 301 to either four or five significant digits.

301 | 1150 | 1380 | 1790 | 2320.0 | n.a.

302: GEOGRAPHIC LOCATION OF SERVED MARKET

Was the served market for this business, as measured in Line 301, primarily located in . . . . *(Check one)*

Entire United States	☐ 1	Regional within U.S. and/or Canada ☐ 4	Regional within Europe * ☐ 7
All of Canada	☐ 2	United Kingdom * ☐ 5	Other * ☑ 8
U.S. and Canada	☐ 3	Common Market * ☐ 6	*world wide*

* If this box is checked, supplementary data forms will follow.

303: NUMBER OF COMPETITORS

Relative to the last year of data being entered, approximately how many competing businesses were there in the served market? Ignore competitors with less than 1% of the served market.

5 or fewer	6–10	11–20	21–50	51 or Higher
☐ 1	☑ 2	☐ 3	☐ 4	☐ 5

304: ENTRY OF COMPETITORS

During the past 5 years, have any major competitors entered the served market? ("Major" means competitors with at least 5% market share.)

NO ☑ 0   YES ☐ 1

305: EXIT OF COMPETITORS

During the past 5 years, have any major competitors dropped out of the served market? ("Major" means competitors with at least 5% market share.)

NO ☑ 0   YES ☐ 1

For each year, report the share of the *served* market accounted for by this business and by each of the three largest competing businesses. "Share of market" is defined as being the-sales of a business as a percentage of the served market (defined in Line 301).

306: THIS BUSINESS

306 | 19.3 % | 20.7 % | 20.9 % | 20 % | n.a %

307: COMPETITOR "A" (the largest competing business)

307 | 40 % | 41 % | 39.5 % | 35 % | n.a. %

308: COMPETITOR "B" (second largest competitor)

308 | 9 % | 9 % | 9 % | 9 % | n.a. %

309: COMPETITOR "C" (third largest competitor)

309 | 8 % | 8 % | 8 % | 8 % | n.a. %

310: THREE LARGEST COMPETITORS, COMBINED TOTAL
(*Not* including this business)

310 | 57 % | 58% | 56.5% | 52 % | n.a. %

311: YOUR MARKET SHARE RANK:

Relative to the latest year of data, what was the rank of this business in terms of market share within the served market?

311 | 2

312: INDEX OF PRICES (1973 = 100%)

For each year, estimate the percentage of selling prices charged by this business relative to the level in 1973. This percentage should reflect changes in prices of identical products, not changes in the product mix.

312 | 108 % | 104 % | 100% | 118 % | n.a.%

313: INDEX OF BASIC MATERIALS COSTS (1973 = 100%)

For each year, estimate the percentage of purchase prices for the most important category(ies) of materials (including fuel and energy, if important) used by this business, relative to the level in 1973.

313 | 90 % | 97 % | 100% | 170 % | n.a.%

314: INDEX OF AVERAGE HOURLY WAGE RATES (1973 = 100%)

For each year, estimate the average level of hourly wage rates paid by this business, relative to the level in 1973.

314 | 90 % | 95 % | 100% | 105 % | n.a %

COMPARISON WITH COMPETITORS

The questions in this section deal with the quality, price, cost of product and service offerings of this business relative to the major competitors referred to in Lines 307, 308 and 309 in the served market. The standard of comparison in each question is the *average* of leading competitors.

316–318: OVERALL RELATIVE PRODUCT QUALITY

For each year, estimate the percentage of your sales volume accounted for by products and services that *from the perspective of the customer* are assessed as "Superior", "Equivalent", and "Inferior" to those available from leading competitors. (Note: The sum of Lines 316-318 should total 100%)

316 *
SUPERIOR | 25 % | 25 % | 25 % | 25 % | n.a %

317 *
EQUIVALENT | 50 % | 50 % | 50 % | 50 % | n.a %

318 *
INFERIOR | 25 % | 25 % | 25 % | 25 % | n.a %

* The sum of lines 316–318 should total 100% in each column.

319: RELATIVE PRICES (Average for Leading Competitors = 100%)

For each year, estimate the average level of selling prices of your products and services, relative to the average price of leading competitors. (Example: If your prices averaged 5% above those of leading competitors, report 105%.)

319 | 100 % | 100 % | 100 % | 100% | n.a. % |

320: RELATIVE DIRECT COSTS PER UNIT (Average for Competitors = 100%)

For each year, estimate the average level of your direct costs per unit of products and services, relative to that of leading competitors. Include costs of materials, production, and distribution, but *exclude* marketing and administrative costs.

320 | 96.7 % | 101.7 % | 111.1 % | 112.3% | n.a. % |

321: RELATIVE HOURLY WAGE RATES (Average for Leading Competitors = 100%)

For each year, estimate the level of hourly wage rates paid by this business relative to the average level paid by leading competitors, regardless of their locations.

321 | 100 % | 100% | 100% | 100% | n.a. % |

322: RELATIVE SALARY LEVELS (Average of Leading Competitors = 100%)

For each year, estimate the average level of compensation paid to salaried workers by this business, relative to the average level paid by leading competitors, regardless of their locations.

322 | 100 % | 100 % | 100 % | 100% | 100% |

323–324: NEW PRODUCTS, PER CENT OF TOTAL SALES

For each year, estimate what percentage of the total sales was accounted for by products introduced during the 3 preceding years both for this business and for leading competitors.

(Example: for 1974, "New Products" should include those introduced in 1972, 1973, and 1974.)

323: THIS BUSINESS

| 323 | 20 % | 20 % | 20 % | 20 % | n.a. % |

324: LEADING COMPETITORS

| 324 | 20 % | 20 % | 20 % | 20 % | n.a. % |

325: BREADTH OF PRODUCT LINE

Relative to the product lines of leading competitors, estimate the breadth of the product line of this business.

... Less Broad   □ 1
... Same Breadth   ☑ 2
... Broader   □ 3

326–328: Estimate the breadth of this business's served market, relative to the average of its leading competitors.

	Less Than Competitors	Same As Competitors	More Than Competitors
326: ... Types of Customers	□ 1	☑	□ 3
327: ... Number of Customers	□ 1	☑	□ 3
328: ... Size of Customers	□ 1	☑	□ 3

329: SALES FORCE EXPENDITURES

Relative to leading competitors, did this business spend "About the Same" percentage of its sales on sales force effort? Or "Somewhat More" (or Less)? Or Much More" (or Less)?

NOTE: QUESTIONS 329-333 CALL FOR COMPARISONS OF RELATIVE LEVELS OF MARKETING EXPENDITURES, EXPRESSED AS PERCENTAGES OF SALES. IN THESE QUESTIONS "ABOUT THE SAME" is defined as within + 1 percentage point; "SOMEWHAT MORE OR LESS" means 1 to 3 percentage points more or less; "MUCH MORE OR LESS" means more than 3 points more or less.

329

1 = Much Less
2 = Somewhat Less
3 = About the Same
4 = Somewhat More
5 = Much More

n.a.

330: RELATIVE ADVERTISING EXPENDITURES

Relative to leading competitors, did this business spend "About the Same" percentage of its sales on media advertising Or "Somewhat More" (or Less)? Or "Much More" (or Less)?

330

1 = Much Less
2 = Somewhat Less
3 = About the Same
4 = Somewhat More
5 = Much More

331: RELATIVE SALES PROMOTION EXPENDITURES

Relative to leading competitors, did this business spend "About the Same" percentage of its sales on sales promotion efforts? Or "Somewhat More" (or Less)? Or "Much More" (or Less)?

331

1 = Much Less
2 = Somewhat Less
3 = About the Same
4 = Somewhat More
5 = Much More

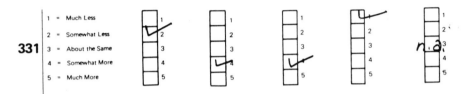

322: RELATIVE SALARY LEVELS (Average of Leading Competitors = 100%)

For each year, estimate the average level of compensation paid to salaried workers by this business, relative to the average level paid by leading competitors, regardless of their locations.

332

1 = Much Worse
2 = Somewhat Worse
3 = About the Same
4 = Somewhat Better
5 = Much Better

333: RELATIVE PRODUCT IMAGE/COMPANY REPUTATION

Were end users' perceptions of "product image" and/or company reputation (for quality, dependability, etc.) for this business "About the Same", "Somewhat Better" (or Worse) or "Much Better" (or Worse) than their perceptions of the image/reputation of leading competitors?

333

1 = Much Worse
2 = Somewhat Worse
3 = About the Same
4 = Somewhat Better
5 = Much Better

/3

End of Form 3

315

 THE STRATEGIC PLANNING INSTITUTE

 The PIMS Program

DATA FORM

4

INDUSTRY OR
LINE OF BUSINESS DATA

This Form *Requires* One Of The Following:

- Your SIC code, or

- Data for your industry

GENERAL INSTRUCTIONS: Please answer every question. If the best estimate of a quantity is zero, fill in "0", not a dash. If a question is not applicable, please check the box indicating this or write "N.A." prominently. Do not use these forms for businesses which are less than 3 years old. (For "start-up" businesses; obtain special forms from the PIMS office.)

IF YOU HAVE DIFFICULTY PROVIDING ANY OF THE INFORMATION REQUESTED IN THE FORM, please consult the PIMS Data Manual, or call the PIMS Office, Area 617, 492-3810

IDENTIFICATION
OF BUSINESS

**IDENTIFYING NUMBER
FOR THIS BUSINESS,
INTERNAL TO COMPANY**
(For New PIMS Businesses Only)

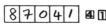

**PIMS IDENTIFYING
NUMBER**
(For Old PIMS Businesses:
Use Existing PIMS Number)

Respond *either* to

- Line 401, or to
- Lines 402 through 425

401: SIC CODE

Identify your Standard Industrial Classification group, using *at least* a 4-digit category (5 or 6 digits if possible or appropriate). Please enter zeros for the fifth and/or sixth digits if they are unknown or otherwise unavailable.

—	—	—	—	—

4 DIGIT GROUP   5TH 6TH DIGIT

OR

If you do not wish to identify your SIC category, please complete lines 402 – 425 below. Also, for any item on this form, if you feel that government-supplied statistics on the SIC code entered above are not appropriate for your served market, please enter your own estimates in the proper boxes. Any data so entered will be used in preference to government data for research and report purposes.

402–405: (USE MOST RECENT DATA AVAILABLE)

402: INDUSTRY CONCENTRATION RATIO

This is the percentage of industry shipments that is accounted for by the shipments of the four largest firms in that 4-digit SIC or a comparable industry grouping. If your industry spans several SIC groups, enter a weighted average, using dollar shipments as weights.

PER CENT
72%

403: INDUSTRY VALUE-ADDED PER EMPLOYEE

This is total dollars of value-added in your industry divided by total employment in your industry. For example, if industry value-added is 300 million dollars and industry employment is 15,000 then industry value-added per employee is $20,000.

NUMBER
45000

404: INDUSTRY EXPORTS

This is the value of *your* industry's exports from the geographic market defined in Line 301 to other countries as a per cent of the value of that industry's total shipments.

PER CENT
0 %

405: INDUSTRY IMPORTS

This is the value of imports from other countries into your market expressed as a percentage of "industry shipments, minus exports, plus imports." (If data is not available *enter your best estimate.*)

PER CENT
0 %

Note: Lines 404/5 — treat whole world as served market.

406—407: SIC GROWTH RATE AND INSTABILITY INDEX.

No entries are required for line 406-407. These values will be calculated from industry sales entered on lines 415-424. (The calculated values will be printed-out on the edit report for this business.)

408—414: (RESERVED FOR FUTURE USE)

415—425: INDUSTRY SALES

Supply the best data you have for Industry Sales and Lease Revenues for the last 10 years. Industry "Long-Run Growth Rate" and "Instability Index" will be calculated from this data. If you do not like the values calculated, you will have the opportunity to change them on the edit forms. *It is desirable but not necessary to fill out all 10 years.* The Growth Rate and Instability Index will be calculated from the years supplied. (Enter the first year of data on line 415 and the last year of data on line 424.)

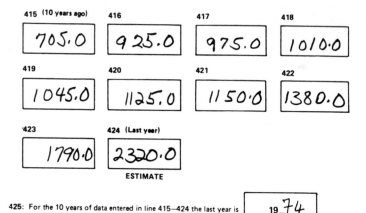

415 (10 years ago)	416	417	418
705.0	925.0	975.0	1010.0

419	420	421	422
1045.0	1125.0	1150.0	1380.0

423	424 (Last year)
1790.0	2320.0

ESTIMATE

425: For the 10 years of data entered in line 415—424 the last year is   19 74

THE STRATEGIC PLANNING INSTITUTE

The
PIMS
Program

CONFIDENTIAL

DATA FORM

5

ASSUMPTIONS OR FORECASTS OF SHORT—TERM AND LONGER TERM TRENDS IN MARKET SIZE, PRICES, AND COSTS

GENERAL INSTRUCTIONS: Please answer every question. If the best estimate of a quantity is zero, fill in "0", not a dash. If a question is not applicable, please check the box indicating this or write "N.A." prominently. Do not use these forms for businesses which are less than 3 years old. (For "start-up" businesses, obtain special forms from the PIMS office.)

IF YOU HAVE DIFFICULTY PROVIDING ANY OF THE INFORMATION REQUESTED IN THE FORM, please consult the PIMS Data Manual, or call the PIMS Office, Area 617, 492-3810

IDENTIFICATION
OF BUSINESS

**IDENTIFYING NUMBER
FOR THIS BUSINESS,
INTERNAL TO COMPANY**
(For New PIMS Businesses only)

| 8 | 7 | 0 | 4 | 1 | 5 | 1 |

**PIMS IDENTIFYING
NUMBER**
(For Old PIMS Businesses:
Use Existing PIMS Number)

MOST LIKELY ASSUMPTIONS (Actual results equally likely to be above or below these figures.)

	SHORT TERM (YEARS 0 – 3)	LONG TERM (YEARS 4 – 10)

Line

501–502: AVERAGE ANNUAL PER CENT CHANGE IN SIZE OF SERVED MARKET: This should be consistent with the definition of "served market" used in Line 301, Form 3. The estimate should be based on forecasts or assumptions of changes in market size *including price changes.*

501 (+ or –) % 502 (+ or –) %

503–504: AVERAGE ANNUAL PER CENT CHANGE IN SELLING PRICES OF PRODUCTS/SERVICES OF THIS BUSINESS: Corresponds to Line 312, Form 3.

503 (+ or –) % 504 (+ or –) %

505–506: AVERAGE ANNUAL PER CENT CHANGE IN COSTS OF BASIC MATERIALS USED BY THIS BUSINESS: Corresponds to Line 313, Form 3.

505 (+ or –) 0 8 % 506 (+ or –) 0 6 %

507–508: AVERAGE ANNUAL PER CENT CHANGE IN HOURLY WAGE RATES PAID BY THIS BUSINESS: Corresponds to Line 314, Form 3.

507 (+ or –) 0 8 % 508 (+ or –) 0 6 %

509: DISCOUNT RATE:

What internal interest rate should be used in computing the present value of streams of future income? 8% – 10% is often used. If your business does not discount future dollars, enter zero.

PER CENT 1 0

510: CAPITAL CHARGE RATE:

What capital charge rate should be applied to incremental investment in this business? (8 - 10% is commonly used.)

PER CENT 0

511: MAXIMUM MARKET SHARE:

What is the *maximum* market share that you believe this business could attain in 5 years through adopting a very aggressive growth strategy?

PER CENT 2 5

512: CAPACITY ADDITIONS:

What is the *minimum* economically efficient amount by which the *standard capacity* of this business could be increased, expressed as a percentage of the last year's standard capacity reported in Line 235, Form 2?

PER CENT 2

/5

End of Form 5

Appendix A

Extracts from a Speech Made by Dr. Sidney Schoeffler, Executive Secretary, the Strategic Planning Institute, to the SSP Conference at Indiana University in November 1975.

The "PIMS Program" of the Strategic Planning Institute is a large-scale, continuing empirical inquiry into the interrelationships among a group of factors representing the strategy, the competitive position, the business environment, and the operating results of businesses producing manufactured products or services. The program is organized around a data base reflecting the business-strategic experiences of about 600 individual businesses operated by 50-plus major corporations.

The PIMS Program is a *cross-sectional* study of business-strategic *experience*. It attempts to explain the experienced differences in operating results across the 600-plus businesses on the basis of differences in the strategic moves being made and differences in the competitive setting in which they were made.

HISTORY AND ORGANIZATION

The program originated as an internal planning study in the General Electric Company about 15 years ago. The G.E. study interpreted the experience of that company, in a considerable variety of products and service businesses, as if that company were a large laboratory for testing business strategy. Each of the various operating divisions was visualized as conducting a series of "experiments" designed to find out the consequences of business strategy in its particular market setting. The overall study interpreted these "experiments," with a view to detecting the underlying regularities—the "laws of nature" that operate in the marketplace—that govern which business action, in which business environment, produces what consequences.

In early 1972 the study was organized on a multi-company basis, under the umbrella of the Harvard Business School, and located initially at the Marketing Science Institute. The research team was drawn largely from General Electric, Harvard Business School, and the University of Massachusetts. Effective as of the beginning of 1975, the program was organized as the Strategic Planning Institute, an independent non-profit body.

321

DATA COVERAGE

At present, the data base includes 600-plus "businesses" for the five-year period from 1970 to 1974. The unit of observation, here called a "business," is a specific product line (or service line) that is reasonably homogeneous in terms of market served and technology employed.

Each "business" is documented by about 100 data items, supplied in standardized format by the company operating that business. The data items describe the *market* served by the business (in terms of growth, stability, etc.), the *competitive environment* (number and size of competitors, number and size of customers, etc.), the *position* of the business (market share, comparative product quality, comparative price, etc.). These data about market structure are supplemented by critical characteristics of the *strategy* of the business (changes in position, discretionary budget allocations, product quality, etc.), and finally, with information concerning the *operating results* obtained (profit, cash flow, and so on).

TESTS OF VALIDITY

We "believe" a particular observed pattern if it meets at least three tests:

— it is *statistically significant,* at the 95 percent level or better;

— it conforms to the best available *theory* of the case (which occasionally is constructed after the empirical observation);

— it *makes sense* to knowledgeable businessmen, who have direct experience with the phenomenon concerned.

The tests of statistical significance operate at both the micro-level (i.e., individual variables) and the macro-level (i.e., functions as a whole), with the latter being the more useful of the two. Since the key variables employed (to explain, say, ROI) are highly multicollinear, one should not attach much importance to individual coefficients of individual variables, and hence also not to the significance tests on such coefficients. The more useful test, though far more difficult to construct, is at the level of the function as a whole. The critical test is: does the "black box," taken as a whole, behave in the same way the "reality" does, as visible in the data base. Specifically, does the black box generate closely the same kinds of graphs and cross-tables, for example, as can be constructed from the original data. The key question is: how close is close?

BASIC FINDINGS

Taking our cross-sectional ROI-explaining equation as an example, we have so far identified 37 variables (each of them being significant in the micro sense at the 95 percent level or better, and theoretically sensible) that jointly explain about 80 percent of the variance of ROI. (See Exhibit 1 for a list of these factors.) These 37 variables operate in a highly inter-active way, being compounded into 58 separate cross-products or other combined terms. With over 500 degrees of freedom, plus good computer programs, even such a frighteningly complex equation becomes quite manageable. One of the main advantages of large-scale, cross sectional analysis is that it allows the delineation of very complex patterns.

One of the more interesting findings to date is that the 80 percent level of explanation appears to be a kind of *upper limit* for explaining ROI (or other measures of operating performance) with strategy/structure/environment kinds of data. Including the previous study at General Electric, so far there have been six separate attempts to estimate a cross-sectional ROI-explain-ing equation with that kind of data, covering the time period from the middle 1950s to the early 1970s, and also covering several different groups of businesses. In each case, the R^2 could be pushed to about 80 percent, but not beyond.

Equally interesting is that the same *key explanatory variables* appeared each time as being powerful and significant. There is some turnover in the relatively *minor* variables as we move from time period to time period, and from sample to sample, and also some changes in the precise values of the coefficients, but no major alterations in the pattern.

CONCLUDING OBSERVATIONS

The PIMS Program is uncovering a large number of impacts on profit and cash flow. In the aggregate, these impacts account for about 80 percent of the cross-sectional variance in ROI (or in other profit measures) across the whole base, excepting only a small number (about 5 percent) of extreme outliers.

It seems safe to conclude that micro-economic processes are indeed law-ful phenomena, obeying "laws of nature" that can be discovered in the way that is usual in many empirical sciences, and also applied in the usual way.

The laws of nature operating in the marketplace are not simple, or at least not yet. We can *simulate* simplicity by *fragmenting* the universe, particu-larly if we use simplicity of the resulting descriptive equation as the cri-terion of choosing a particular fragmentation scheme. But this approach loses many important insights, and is therefore not a good idea despite its many obvious operational advantages. Elegant simplicity will have to be won the hard way, by the formultion of new theory.

Exhibit 1

TEX-FIBER INDUSTRIES—PETROLOID PRODUCTS DIVISION (C)
Some Key Variables Explaining ROI

1. *Attractiveness of Business Environment*
   Market Growth, Long-Term
   Market Growth, Short-Term
   Percent Industry Exports
   Industry Concentration Ratio
   Customer Concentration Ratio
2. *Strength of Competitive Position*
   Market Share
   Relative Market Share (relative to 3 largest competitors)
   Relative Pay Scale (level of compensation relative to competition)
   Relative Product Quality
3. *Effectiveness of Use of Investment*
   Investment Intensity
   Value Added/Sales
   Sales/Employee
   Percent Capacity Utilized
4. *Discretionary Cost Allocations*
   Marketing Expense/Sales
   R & D Costs/Sales
   Rate of New Product Introductions
5. *Characteristics of the Owning Corporation*
   Company Size
   Company Diversity
6. *Current Changes in Position Variables*
   Change in Market Share
   Change in Vertical Integration
   Change in Relative Price
   Change in Product Quality
   Change in Capacity

Appendix B
Extracts from the PIMS Data Manual

GENERAL GUIDELINES
FOR DEFINING A "BUSINESS"

In defining business units to be submitted for PIMS analysis, four rules-of-thumb have evolved:

1. *60 Percent Rule on Joint Cost Allocation:* If 60 percent or more of the expenses of the proposed business unit represents arbitrary *allocations* of *joint costs* which are shared with other sister businesses, then the proposed definition of the business unit is not likely to be suitable for PIMS analysis. If possible, such joint-cost businesses should be combined.

2. *60 Percent Rule on Vertical Integration of Business Units:* if 60 percent or more of the "market" for a proposed business unit represents *shipments* to a *downstream subsidiary* of your own corporation, then it is best to integrate the downstream with the upstream business, and consider them as one business for PIMS analysis.

3. *Homogeneity of the Served Market:* Many businesses serve many markets, following diverse strategies, with diverse product lines flowing through several distribution channels. Should such businesses be further sub-divided for PIMS analysis? We have leaned toward answering "yes" if two out of three of the following statements are true:
   (a) each segment or channel contains markedly different *competitors*
   (b) each segment has markedly different market *growth* rates
   (c) you have markedly different *shares* in each segment
   and if the proposed sub-business unit also passes hurdles (1) and (2) above.

4. *Strategic Business Unit for Organizational Purposes:* In many instances, the issue of "what is a business" has been resolved by the organization framework within which strategies are analyzed in the individual firms. For obvious reasons, PIMS sponsors have tended to define businesses which conform easily to existing management units.

These guidelines are *not* to be taken as rigid tests, all of which a "business" must pass to warrant submission. There may be a number of ways around an apparent contradiction: for example, a complex unit may sell to different markets in the sense of guideline 3 and allocate costs arbitrarily to a degree which violates guideline 1, particularly if it feels obligated to integrate data for the manufacturing stages under guideline 2. Possible solutions are:

325

(a) divide the complex unit into three businesses, one joint manufacturing unit, and two marketing units serving the two distinct markets, taking the manufacturing unit's transfers to them as their cost of goods sold.

(b) divide the complex unit into two manufacturing and marketing units, allocating the manufacturing costs between them.

(c) submit the whole complex as one business unit.

(d) all of the above. It costs very little to conduct extra runs with PIMS software, which has led us in several instances to suggest that we analyze alternative configurations of the submitted businesses. However, the number of permutations can easily become excessive, so we have to limit the use of this expedient to only a few cases.

WHAT IS A SERVED MARKET?

The term "market" refers to a set of customers with similar requirements for products and/or services. A business may elect to serve only certain customers in the total market. For example, it may focus its entire marketing effort on:

- customers located in the same geographic area (e.g., the Eastern half of the U.S.: all of Canada; Canada and the United States; all homes within the broadcast range of a radio station)

- customers with annual purchases in excess of $1 million

- customers with one national purchasing office

- customers capable of servicing products without further support from their vendors.

- customers that emphasize high product quality rather than low price

- customers in search of a certain size product (e.g., TV sets with screen sizes under 12″)

- customers interested in products reflecting a given technology (e.g., *color* television sets; *nuclear* power plants; *hermetically sealed* motors; *flourescent* lamps)

- customers seeking to replace all or part of a product already owned.

A "served market" is usually smaller than the "total market."

Serving a market means that the business develops, manufactures, distributes, and/or services products appropriate to that segment of the total market. It addresses its sales efforts, direct or indirect, to particular customers or responds to "requests for bids."

Served markets can differ greatly even for products which appear identical. For example, kitchen appliances may be bought by a housewife or by general contractors for installation in an apartment complex or development. The size of a typical order, of course, varies dramatically between these two served markets. Large builders and contractors buy in carload (even trainload) lots with little variation in the features, functions, colors of models, etc.

It is important that you define the served market for each business carefully, since our analyses have shown that the *share* of its market achieved by a business is one of the most important single determinants of profitability. Generally speaking, the more *narrowly* the market is defined, the better. Of course, this means that it will often be necessary to make *estimates* of total market size based on appropriate allocations of published figures to specific regions, products, or types of customers.

DISCUSSION QUESTIONS

TEX-FIBER INDUSTRIES—[C]

1. What broad categories of questions are being asked by PIMS? Why these and not others?
2. How would you describe PPD in "PIMS" terms? What are some of its most important distinguishing characteristics?
3. Has Mr. Hutton defined the "business" and "served market" appropriately?
4. Given the data which has been provided, can you speculate about PPD's "PAR" performance in terms of ROI and cash flow?
5. What might be the financial impact for a business like this of increasing or decreasing market share?

TEX-FIBER INDUSTRIES— PETROLOID PRODUCTS DIVISION [D]¹

In early 1975, top management of Tex-Fiber Industries PPD were involved in the task of drawing up a five-year business plan for the division [see Tex-Fiber Industries—Petroloid Products Division (A) and (B)]. In addition to the data which had already been assembled, Mr. John F. Hutton, Manager of Strategic Planning, had convinced Jack Simmons, PPD's General Manager, that they should explore the use of the PIMS model as an analytical and planning tool. As a result, a wealth of input data [see Tex-Fiber Industries—Petroloid Products Division (C) and Appendix A of this case] had been supplied in standard question-naire format to the Strategic Planning Institute, a non-profit institution organized to serve PIMS member companies. Two weeks later, after some editing and revision of the initial input,² Mr. Hutton informed Mr. Simmons that output from the model was available, and that Mr. Good-man, an SPI representative, was ready to present these results to PPD management. A convenient date was quickly arranged for a PIMS pres-entation to be attended by Mr. Hutton, Mr. Simmons, and other key members of the PPD management team.

"PIMS" OUTPUT FOR PPD

Mr. Goodman started the meeting by explaining that runs of the PIMS model conducted so far had provided three different sets of out-put. The first two—the "PAR" Reports and the Cash Flow "PAR" Re-ports—were designed to analyze the performance of the business unit over the last three years and evaluate the contribution of a number of factors to return on investment and cash flow respectively. The third set of reports—the Strategy Sensitivity Reports—were designed to predict the outcome of various strategic moves for both the long and short run. Each set of reports was discussed in turn.

---

¹This case was prepared by Joseph D'Cruz in collaboration with Derek F. Abell.

²PIMS questionnaire input data was routinely subjected to a variety of tests for clerical accuracy and internal consistency. Input data for a particular business was compared to averages for all other businesses in the PIMS data base so that diagnostic checks could be performed on a variety of key ratios and interrelationships. In cases where input data fell outside certain limits established by reference to the whole data base, these values were "compressed" to prevent distortion of the final output.

THE "PAR" REPORTS

Mr. Goodman explained the concept of the "PAR" Reports in the following words:

The "PAR" Report addresses the question, "what profit rate is 'normal' for the combination of circumstances facing this business?" Our research covering over 600 businesses in approximately 100 medium and large corporations has demonstrated that the PIMS model can explain 80 percent of the variation in ROI by looking at 37 factors which describe the business unit and its competitive environment. ROI is defined for this purpose as Net Pre-Tax Income (*after* deduction of any corporate expenses included, but *prior* to interest charges) divided by average investment (i.e., working capital plus fixed capital at book value). The average ROI for all the businesses in the PIMS database was 16.7 percent for the years 1971 to 1974. The "PAR" Reports show how much higher or lower this business is expected to be from this average, given the external circumstances it is facing, and the strategy it has followed in the last four years. The "PAR" ROI is the return normally expected from an average management team with average luck. The net difference between the average ROI and the PIMS "PAR" ROI for this business is called the "Impact of strategic factors on "PAR" ROI." Each of the 37 factors used in the "PAR" model can influence this impact. Just as in real life, these factors are not independent of each other—rather, they interact in rather complex ways. Further, the contribution of each factor to the total impact is itself dependent upon the levels of other factors—a problem that statisticians call multicollinearity. It can therefore be deceptive to look at the impact of individual factors on "PAR" ROI, without taking these interrelationships into account. In the PIMS project, we have grouped factors which are related to each other into seven major categories. The contribution of each category to total impact is fairly stable and can be regarded as relatively independent; the impact of individual factors within a category must be interpreted with more care.

PPD management were then shown the "PAR" ROI reports for their business. The report showing the impact of each category on "PAR" ROI is shown in Table 1.

A lively discussion ensued about the meaning of the various terms in the report and their implications for PPD. Mr. Goodman suggested that they turn to the detailed findings of the "PAR" model (Table 2) and again cautioned them about interpreting the impact figures for each factor separately.

As discussion of the "PAR" Reports continued, questions were raised as to the precision and accuracy of the input data on which the reports were founded. Mr. Goodman addressed this problem as follows:

329

PRELIMINARY
FOR DISCUSSION ONLY
TABLE 1

"PAR" RETURN ON INVESTMENT (PRE-TAX) 1972-74

"PAR" RETURN ON INVESTMENT IS AN ESTIMATE OF THE PRE-TAX RETURN ON INVESTMENT (ROI) THAT IN 1972-74 WAS NORMAL FOR BUSINESSES FACING MARKET AND INDUSTRY CONDITIONS EQUIVALENT TO THOSE OF YOUR BUSINESS AND OCCUPYING A SIMILAR MARKET POSITION.

FOR BUSINESS NO. 87041, PRE-TAX

"PAR" ROI 26.3%

ACTUAL ROI 25.4

IMPACT ON "PAR" ROI OF THE FACTORS BY CATEGORY

"PAR" ROI EQUALS THE SUM OF THE TOTAL IMPACT AND THE AVERAGE ROI OF ALL BUSINESSES IN THE PIMS DATA BASE.

CATEGORY *	IMPACT ON "PAR" ROI (PRE-TAX) %
ATTRACTIVENESS OF BUSINESS ENVIRONMENT	3.1
STRENGTH OF YOUR COMPETITIVE POSITION	0.1
DIFFERENTIATION OF COMPETITIVE POSITION	1.2
EFFECTIVENESS OF USE OF INVESTMENT	13.4
DISCRETIONARY BUDGET ALLOCATION	-6.8
COMPANY FACTORS	-1.2
CHANGE/ACTION FACTORS	-0.2
TOTAL IMPACT	9.6
AVERAGE ROI, ALL PIMS BUSINESSES	16.7
"PAR" ROI, THIS BUSINESS	26.3%

* FACTORS MAKING UP THESE CATEGORIES ARE LISTED IN TABLE 2

TABLE 2   BUS. NO 87041
16-Dec-76

```
-----
  P
  I
  M
  S
-----
```

THE IMPACT ON "PAR" ROI OF EACH FACTOR
IN THE "PAR" PROFIT EQUATION (POINTS OF ROI)

F A C T O R S	BASE PERIOD VALUES FOR: ALL PIMS BUSINESSES	THIS BUSINESS	THIS TYPE OF BUSINESS	IMPACT OF FACTOR ON PAR ROI (%)
ATTRACTIVENESS OF				
BUSINESS ENVIRONMENT				3.1
INDUSTRY (SIC) GROWTH, LONG-RUN	8.0	21.3	8.2	3.2
MARKET GROWTH, SHORT-RUN	5.9	21.4	5.9	1.4
INDUSTRY EXPORTS (% TOTL SHPTS)	7.6	0.0	9.6	-1.1
SALES DIRECT TO END USER (%)	51.0	60.0	64.5	-0.4
STRENGTH OF YOUR				
COMPETITIVE POSITION				0.1
YOUR MARKET POSITION	22.5	20.5	24.2	-0.1
SHARE OF 4 LARGEST FIRMS (SIC)	51.6	72.0	52.1	0.6
INSTABILITY OF YOUR MKT SHARE	2.9	0.9	3.3	1.1
BUYER FRAGMENTATION INDEX	13.6	15.0	13.8	-1.5
DIFFERENTIATION OF				
COMPETITIVE POSITION				1.2
PRICE RELATIVE TO COMPETITION	2.7	3.0	2.7	-1.2
RELATIVE PAY SCALE	6.4	6.0	6.4	-0.4
PRODUCT QUALITY	23.2	0.0	24.7	1.1
NEW PRODUCT SALES (% TOT SALES)	12.1	20.0	12.1	0.6
MANUFACTURING COSTS/SALES	30.7	22.0	33.6	1.1
EFFECTIVENESS OF				
USE OF INVESTMENT				13.4
INVESTMENT INTENSITY	63.8	61.9	71.3	-12.1
FIXED CAPITAL INTENSITY	57.5	78.2	61.2	-0.5
RECEIVABLES/SALES	14.4	12.9	14.9	0.2
VERTICAL INTEGRATION	58.8	81.4	60.1	17.5
CAPACITY UTILIZATION	75.7	113.7	75.9	5.4
RAW & IN PROC. INVENT./PURCHASE	33.2	35.2	39.3	0.2
SALES/EMPLOYEES	47730.	50077.	42860.	2.7
DISCRETIONARY				
BUDGET ALLOCATION				-6.8
MKTG LESS SALES FORC EXP/SALES	4.1	14.6	3.0	-7.8
R&D EXPENSES/SALES	2.9	4.8	3.4	1.1

COLUMN 3, THE MEANS FOR THIS TYPE OF BUSINESS (INDUSTRIAL),
IS FOR REFERENCE ONLY AND NOT USED TO CALCULATE THE IMPACTS
EXCEPT WHEN USED TO REPLACE MISSING DATA (NOTED WITH AN *)

```
-----
 P
 I                                                    BUS. NO 87041
 M                                                    16-Dec-76
 S                      TABLE 2 (CONTINUED)
-----        THE IMPACT ON "PAR" ROI OF EACH FACTOR
             IN THE "PAR" PROFIT EQUATION (POINTS OF ROI)
```

| | BASE PERIOD VALUES FOR: | | | IMPACT OF FACTOR |
FACTORS	ALL PIMS BUSINESSES	THIS BUSINESS	THIS TYPE OF BUSINESS	ON PAR ROI (%)
COMPANY FACTORS				-1.2
CORPORATE PAYOUT (%)	62.0		63.2	-0.0
DEGREE OF CORP DIVERSIFICATION	2.1		2.3	-1.2
CORPORATE SIZE	1588.0		1431.0	0.0
GROWTH RATE OF CORPORATE SALES	10.1		10.3	0.0
CHANGE/ACTION FACTORS				-0.2
CHANGE IN YOUR MARKET SHARE	2.3	-3.4	3.1	-0.7
CHANGE IN PRODUCT QUALITY	3.2	0.0	3.3	-0.0
CHANGE IN PRICE INDEX	2.9	13.0	2.3	0.2
COMPETITIVE MARKET ACTIVITY	0.1	-6.5	0.1	-0.0
CHANGE IN CAPITAL INTENSITY	-3.3	-22.7	-4.3	-0.7
CHANGE IN VERTICAL INTEGR (%)	0.5	-9.2	0.3	0.6
POINT CHANGE ADV & PROM/SALES	-0.1	-1.9	-0.1	-0.7
CHANGE IN SALES FORC EXP/SALES	-0.3	-0.8	-0.3	-0.4
POINT CHANGE RETURN ON SALES	1.1	0.2	1.3	1.4

```
                         NOTES ON TABLE 2

   1. COMPONENTS OF "YOUR MARKET POSITION" IMPACT:
   YOUR MARKET SHARE               22.5       20.5       24.2
   YOUR MARKET SHARE/SHARE BIG3    54.3       37.0       58.8

   2. COMPONENTS OF "INVESTMENT INTENSITY" IMPACT:
   INVESTMENT/SALES                63.8       61.9       71.3
   INVESTMENT/(VALUE ADDED-.5NI)  120.0       82.5      125.3

   3. ONLY THE COMBINED NET EFFECT OF "INVESTMENT INTENSITY",
      "VERTICAL INTEGRATION" AND "SALES/EMPLOYEES" SHOULD BE
      GIVEN AN INTERPRETATION, NOT THE INDIVIDUAL IMPACTS:
          -12.14 + 17.48 +  2.68 =  8.03

   4. INTERPRETATION OF RELATIVE SCALES:
      "PRICE RELATIVE TO COMPETITION"      "RELATIVE PAY SCALE"
       IF "2" YOUR PRICE IS HIGHER     IF "4" YOUR PAY SCALE IS LOWER
          "4"               LOWER         "8"                 HIGHER


   COMPANY FACTORS ARE NOT SHOWN FOR REASONS OF DATA SECURITY
```

TABLE 3
SENSITIVITY OF "PAR" ROI (PRE-TAX) TO A CHANGE
IN A SINGLE FACTOR IN THE "PAR" PROFIT EQUATION

FACTOR	A TENTH OF A STANDARD DEVIATION	CHANGE IN "PAR" ROI IF THE FACTOR IS:	
		DECREASED BY COL 1	INCREASED BY COL 1
ATTRACTIVENESS OF BUSINESS ENVIRONMENT			
INDUSTRY(SIC) GROWTH,LONG-RUN	0.51	-0.11	0.11
MARKET GROWTH, SHORT-RUN	0.79	-0.08	0.08
INDUSTRY EXPORTS(% TOTL SHPTS)	0.89	-0.14	0.14
SALES DIRECT TO END USER (%)	4.30	0.22	-0.22
STRENGTH OF YOUR COMPETITIVE POSITION			
YOUR MARKET POSITION	1.68	-0.61	0.61
SHARE OF 4 LARGEST FIRMS (SIC)	2.48	-0.17	-0.01
INSTABILITY OF YOUR MKT SHARE	0.33	0.20	-0.20
BUYER FRAGMENTATION INDEX	0.91	-0.21	0.22
DIFFERENTIATION OF COMPFTITIVE POSITION			
PRICE RELATIVE TO COMPETITION	0.07	-0.37	0.37
RELATIVE PAY SCALE	0.14	0.15	-0.13
PRODUCT QUALITY	3.02	0.70	-0.70
NEW PRODUCT SALES(% TOT SALES)	1.45	-0.11	0.11
MANUFACTURING COSTS/SALES	1.44	-0.15	0.15
EFFECTIVENESS OF USE OF INVESTMENT			
INVESTMENT INTENSITY	3.21	2.40	-1.91
FIXED CAPITAL INTENSITY	4.00	-0.12	0.12
RECEIVABLES/SALES	0.78	0.11	-0.11
VERTICAL INTEGRATION	1.70	-1.46	1.46
CAPACITY UTILIZATION	1.59	-0.22	0.20
RAW & IN PROC.INVENT./PURCHASE	2.82	-0.12	0.12
SALES/EMPLOYEES	3089.00	-0.33	0.15
DISCRETIONARY BUDGET ALLOCATION			
MKTG LESS SALES FORC EXP/SALES	0.39	0.31	*******
R&D EXPENSES/SALES	0.27	0.27	-0.27

FIGURES IN COLUMNS 2 AND 3 INDICATE THE DIRECTION AND
NUMBER OF POINTS THAT "PAR" ROI MOVES WHEN THE FACTOR IS
CHANGED BY 0.1 OF A STANDARD DEVIATION.
   "COMPANY FACTORS" ARE NOT INCLUDED IN TABLE 4 BECAUSE A
BUSINESS CANNOT AFFECT THEM.

Table 3 of the "PAR" Report demonstrates what would happen to "PAR" ROI if an input factor is changed by a small amount. This is a way of looking at the sensitivity of the model to small data errors or changes in assumptions. These relationships are strictly true only for small changes (one tenth of a standard deviation).

As discussion returned to the details of Table 2, Mr. Thomas Eagle, Manager of the PPD's Finance Department, remarked that the actual ROI of the Division was 25.4 percent whereas the "PAR" ROI according to the PIMS model was 26.3 percent. Mr. Goodman responded:

We look upon this difference as a measure of the quality of operating management of the business. If the actual ROI is higher than "PAR," we feel that this is an indication that management has been making good operating decisions and using the resources of the business with above average skill. On the other hand, if the actual ROI has fallen below "PAR" it is likely that management has not taken proper advantage of the opportunities inherent in the strategic position of the business. However, the management quality factor is not the only variable that explains this difference. Occasionally a business may experience windfall profits or chance losses because of unusual circumstances or general economic conditions. Your people know this business better than I do, and it is up to you to decide whether or not this difference is an outcome of some special conditions facing this business. If so, you have to make a judgment as to whether or not these conditions are likely to continue into the future. But, for the difference from "PAR" to be sufficiently significant to be worthy of attention, it should be three points or better. This is *not* the case here; this business is essentially right on its strategic track.

THE CASH FLOW "PAR" REPORT

After some further discussion, the group turned to the Cash Flow "PAR" Reports on their business. Mr. Goodman described these reports as follows:

The PIMS Cash Flow "PAR" model is similar to the "PAR" ROI model, but addresses the question, "What cash flow can we reasonably expect from this business?" The cash flow/investment ratio used in our model is the average cash flow for this business from 1971 to 1974 divided by the average investment in the business during the period. The cash flow for the business is cash generated by after tax earnings plus depreciation, minus cash absorbed by increased working capital and increased gross investment in plant and equipment.[3] The average investment, as before, is the sum of working capital and the book value of fixed assets. The mean cash flow/investment ratio for all PIMS businesses is 2.0 percent. The ratio for the Tex-Fiber PPD business is 0.7 percent. In order to make a judgment as to whether this performance is good or bad, we would like to have an estimate of what ratio can be normally expected from an average management team with average luck, operating in a situation like this one, and making similar strategic moves. That is the "PAR" Cash Flow Ratio for this business, which is 0.3 percent according to our model. The PIMS Cash Flow "PAR" model is based on the 1972 to 1974 experience of the same 600 businesses used in the "PAR" model. It uses 19 cash flow influencing factors to explain 70 percent of the variance in the cash flow ratios of these businesses. These factors are summarized into six categories as shown in Table 4.

```
                              Table 4


-----                                            ( PRELIMINARY )
 SPI                CASH FLOW PAR REPORT           Bus. No. 87041
  I                                               17-DEC-76 15:32
  M                                                      Page  1
  S
-----                                            V-2B(761123)-03


            CASH FLOW / INVESTMENT   1972-1974

       ACTUAL   0.7%    PAR   0.3%    DEVIATION FROM PAR   0.4%



       IMPACT BY CATEGORY : CASH FLOW / INVESTMENT

       DECISION USE OF CASH                    -2.6
       CHANGE IN INVESTMENT/SALES               3.6
       FORCED USE OF CASH                      -7.0
       STRENGTH OF COMPETITIVE POSITION        -0.8
       DIFFERENTIATION FROM COMPETITORS        -0.5
       CAPITAL AND PRODUCTION STRUCTURE         5.6
       -----------------------------------   ------
            SUM OF IMPACTS                              -1.7
         +  AVERAGE  CASH FLOW / INVESTMENT              2.0
       -----------------------------------   ------   ------
            'PAR'  CASH FLOW / INVESTMENT               0.3%
```

---

[3]Cash flow as calculated by the PIMS model does *not* include deductions for corporate dividend assessments or repayments to the Corporation. These must be deducted separately from the figure shown to assess *net* PPD cash flow.

Mr. John Hutton asked Mr. Goodman if the factors of the Cash Flow "PAR" Model had the same multicollinear characteristics as the factors in the "PAR" ROI model. He answered as follows:

> To a large extent both models share this characteristic, though we have found that the cash flow factors are somewhat less collinear. Table 5 shows the impact of these cash flow factors, though again I should caution you against evaluating factors individually.

THE STRATEGY SENSITIVITY REPORTS

After looking at the PIMS analyses of the recent performance of Tex-Fiber Industries, the group turned their attention to the part of the model which attempted to project the business into the future. This required that certain assumptions about the "most likely environment" be fed into the model. Table 6 lists these assumptions.

Mr. Hutton explained that in making these judgments he had assumed that the real growth in the market for petroloids would be about 5 percent per year for the period 1975 to 1978, and then increase to about 9 percent per year from 1978 to 1984, once the industry had recovered from the recession. Since selling prices were expected to increase 5 percent per year and 3 percent per year respectively in these periods, the industry sales growth at current prices was assumed to be 10 percent per year in the 1975–1978 period and 12 percent per year in 1978–1984.

Further, he explained that the capacity utilization target had been set based on past experience as well as with an eye to cash flow. During the last few years the plant had often been run at over 100 percent of its rated capacity. It was decided to run the model with the assumption that capacity would be increased only when sales exceeded 113 percent of rated capacity. This was believed to correspond approximately to the "back loaded" investment policy currently under consideration by PPD manufacturing executives. The PIMS model usually assumed that targeted capacity was 95 percent; this assumption could be modified, however, if it was felt necessary.

The Strategy Sensitivity Report which Mr. Goodman showed first presented a scenario in which no changes were made in the firm's strategy. This report is shown in Table 7. He explained that for this report, the model forecasted trends in the market environment and in

Table 5

```
-----
 SPI                    CASH FLOW PAR REPORT                    ( PRELIMINARY )
  I                                                            Bus. No. 87041
  M                                                            17-DEC-76 15:32
  S                                                                Page  2
-----
```

		PIMS MEAN	THIS BUSINESS	IMPACT	--SENSITIVITY-CHANGES	
					CHANGE OF	IMPACT BY
	DECISION USE OF CASH			-2.6		
1	MARKET SHARE GROWTH RATE	3.2	-1.7	2.5	2.00	-1.02
2	MARKETING EXPENSE GROWTH RATE	10.3	25.3	-1.6	2.00	-0.22
3	NEW PRODUCT SALES (% TOT SALES)	13.1	20.0	-1.0	5.00	-0.96
4	R&D EXPENSE / SALES	2.4	4.8	-1.2	0.50	-0.34
5	MARKETING EXPENSE / SALES	10.3	18.1	-1.2	2.00	0.11
	CHANGE IN INVESTMENT/SALES			3.6		
6	POINT CHANGE INVESTMENT/SALES	-4.7	-7.3	3.6	2.00	-2.38
	FORCED USE OF CASH			-7.0		
7	REAL MARKET GROWTH, SHORT RUN	8.2	21.7	-7.3	2.00	-1.07
8	SELLING PRICE GROWTH RATE	6.4	6.5	-0.1	1.00	-0.75
9	INDUSTRY (SIC) GROWTH, LONG RUN	9.3	19.4	0.4	1.00	0.04
	STRENGTH OF COMPETITIVE POSITION			-0.8		
10	MARKET SHARE	23.3	20.5		5.00	1.23
	RELATIVE MARKET SHARE	60.6	37.0			
	DIFFERENTIATION FROM COMPETITORS			-0.5		
11	PRICE RELATIVE TO COMPETITION	1.030	1.000	0.0	0.01	-0.01
12	RELATIVE PRODUCT QUALITY	23.5	0.0	-0.1	5.00	0.15
13	PRICE DIFF FROM COMPETITORS	0.040	0.000	-0.5	0.01	0.13
	CAPITAL AND PRODUCTION STRUCTURE			5.6		
14	INVESTMENT / SALES	58.3	61.9	-2.3	5.00	-1.04
15	VERTICAL INTEGRATION	59.8	82.5	5.8	2.00	0.62
16	VALUE ADDED PER EMPLOYEE	29.3	40.3	0.5	5.00	0.11
17	CAPACITY UTILIZATION	80.6	113.7U	1.7	5.00	0.00
18	REPLACEMENT VALUE / GBV OF P&E	185.4	180.0	-0.1	10.00	0.11
19	EMPLOYEES UNIONIZED (%)	51.3	50.0	0.1	5.00	-0.08

FOOTNOTES

(U) CAPACITY UTILIZATION   COMPRESSED TO UPPER LIMIT OF   110.0

```
                                  Table 6


  ---                                                         BUS.  NO.  87041
   P                      STRATEGY SENSITIVITY REPORT            16-Dec-76
   I                      VERSION 002C(611010)-5                  (19:39)
   M                             SUMMARY                          PAGE   1
   S                             -------
  ---
                         "MOST LIKELY" ENVIRONMENT
                           KEY ASSUMPTIONS
                         -----------------


                                        1975-78      1978-84
                                        -------      -------
        INDUSTRY SALES GROWTH RATE       10.0%        12.0%
        ANNUAL CHANGE IN SELLING PRICE    5.0%         3.0%
        ANNUAL CHANGE IN WAGE RATES       8.0%
        ANNUAL CHANGE IN MATERIAL COST    8.0%
        ANNUAL CHANGE IN PLANT COST       8.0%         6.0%
                                        -------------------
        TIME DISCOUNT RATE                    10.0%
        CAPITAL CHARGE RATE                    0.0%
        TAX RATE                              50.0%
        DIVIDEND PAYOUT RATE                   0.0%

        "QUANTUM" OF ADDITIONAL CAPACITY       2.0%
        TARGETED CAPACITY UTILIZATION        113.0%
        ANNUAL DEPRECIATION RATE              12.0%

                                    ACTUAL      ASSUMED
                                   HISTORICAL    FUTURE
                   DEVIATIONS FROM:  ------      ------
                          PAR ROI    -1.3         -1.3
                        DELTA ROI    -3.0          0.0
```

the cost structure of the firm, based on its recent performance. It then
used these forecasts to predict the performance that could be expected
of the firm in the future. The model assumed that deviations from PAR
would be the same as the average for the last three years.

Mr. Goodman continued by explaining that the model could also be
used to investigate the likely impact of various changes in strategy.
Such factors as market share, degree of vertical integration, and investment intensity could be varied and the probable outcomes of such
moves studied. The "no planned change" scenario was used as the
base line for comparison. One set of output which was of particular
interest to the PPD group concerned the outcome expected if the business allowed its market share to change. A decline in market share was
accompanied in the model by decreasing expenditures in marketing and

338

Table 7

```
 ---                                          BUS. NO. 87041
  P               STRATEGY SENSITIVITY REPORT    16-Dec-76
  I                VERSION 002C(611010)-5         (19:39)
  M                      DETAILS                  PAGE   3
  S                      -------
 ---
            STRATEGY MOVE:      NO PLANNED CHANGE
```

	RECENT POSITION[1] (1972-74)	DURING STRATEGY IMPLEMENTATION (1977)	NEW STEADY-STATE POSITION (1979)	NEW LONG-TERM POSITION (1984)
NET SALES (CURRENT$)	476.4	643.0	803.3	1415.7
NET INCOME	74.7	101.4	128.1	225.1
AVERAGE INVESTMENT	294.8	345.3	472.6	862.4
NET CASH FLOW	9.3	33.8	0.4	34.6
RETURN ON INVESTMENT	25.4%	29.4%	27.1%	26.1%
RETURN ON SALES	15.7%	15.8%	15.9%	15.9%

FACTORS

COMPETITIVE POSITION:				
MARKET SHARE	20.5	20.8	21.1	21.1
RELATIVE MARKET SHARE	37.0	37.7	38.3	38.3
RELATIVE PRICE INDEX	3.0	3.1	3.0	3.0
PRODUCT QUALITY	0.0	-12.5	-3.0	-3.0

USE OF INVESTMENT:				
INVESTMENT/VALUE ADDED	82.5	73.0	78.6	81.3
INVESTMENT/SALES	61.9	53.7	58.8	60.9
FIXED CAPITAL INTENSITY	78.2	68.7	71.2	74.1
NET BOOK/GROSS BOOK VALUE	52.9	49.6	54.0	54.7
VALUE ADDED/SALES	81.4	79.9	81.4	81.4
WORKING CAPITAL/SALES	20.5	19.6	20.4	20.4
CAPACITY UTILIZATION	113.7	112.8	111.5	113.0
SALES/EMPLOYEES	50077.	50671.	53431.	61648.

BUDGET ALLOCATIONS:				
MARKETING EXPENSES/SALES	18.1	17.8	18.1	18.1
R+D EXPENSES/SALES	4.8	4.0	4.8	4.8

PERFORMANCE MEASURES:

DISCOUNTED NET INCOME 10YR	816.2
DISCOUNTED CASH FLOW 10YR	99.7
AVERAGE NET INCOME 3YR	92.5
DISCOUNTED CASH FLOW YIELD RATE 10YR	15.1%
AVERAGE RETURN ON INVESTMENT 5YR	27.9%

[1]"Recent position" is not a simple average of the last three years. Net sales ($476.4), for example, are calculated by multiplying industry sales in 1974 ($2.32 billion) by average market share (20.5 +). Other factors are calculated to be consistent with the net sales calculation.

R&D between 1975 and 1977, and a subsequent return to average levels for 1972–1974 in order to prevent share from slipping further. The forecasts of the outcome of a small decrease in market share are shown in Table 8.

There was considerable discussion about the implications of this table. Mr. Goodman explained:

> These strategy sensitivity reports should be read in conjunction with the report on what is likely to happen if no changes are planned. For example, look at the investment/value added ratio. In Table 8, the model shows the ratio dropping from 82.5 in 1972–1974 to 71.5 in 1977. This looks like a considerable drop. However, if you look at the "no planned change" report in Table 7, you will see a drop to 73.0 in 1977. In other words, the model is telling us that a business in your strategic position is likely to experience a drop in its investment/value added ratio if it makes no changes in its current strategy, i.e., if only such time-related factors as inflation and depreciation are assumed to be operating. The position in Table 8 is only a shade lower than the position in Table 7—in other words, if you plan for a slight decrease in market share, your investment/value added ratio is likely to be slightly lower than if you try to maintain your market position. All the other factors in this report should be evaluated similarly.

The group then went on to consider the report which analyzed a strategy move consisting of a small increase in PPD's market share. This is shown in Table 9.

In response to questions about larger increases or decreases in market share, Mr. Goodman presented the summary data shown in Table 10.

Mr. Goodman then called the group's attention to the optimization section of the Strategy Sensitivity Report. He described this section as follows:

> We can ask the model what type of strategy is most likely to optimize a particular performance measure. For example, you may be interested in seeing how to obtain the highest possible ten-year discounted net income. We can run the model to estimate the type of strategy which is most likely to produce this outcome. This is shown in Table 11. Again, this report should be read in conjunction with the forecast of the most likely position with no change in strategy (Table 7).

Since the PPD group were highly interested in the capacity of their business to generate cash, they asked Mr. Goodman to show them the report on strategy to optimize discounted cash flow. This is shown in Table 12.

Table 8

```
---
P
I
M
S
---
```

STRATEGY SENSITIVITY REPORT
VERSION 002C (611010)-5
DETAILS

STRATEGY MOVE: SMALL DECREASE IN MARKET SHARE

	RECENT POSITION (1972-74)	DURING STRATEGY IMPLEMENTATION (1977)	NEW STEADY-STATE POSITION (1979)	NEW LONG-TERM POSITION (1984)
NET SALES (CURRENT$)	476.4	595.4	688.8	1213.9
NET INCOME	74.7	121.1	114.6	185.3
AVERAGE INVESTMENT	294.8	307.5	373.5	753.1
NET CASH FLOW	9.3	56.3	24.3	16.7
RETURN ON INVESTMENT	25.4%	39.4%	30.7%	24.6%
RETURN ON SALES	15.7%	20.3%	16.6%	15.3%

FACTORS

COMPETITIVE POSITION:				
MARKET SHARE	20.5	19.3	18.1	18.1
RELATIVE MARKET SHARE	37.0	34.2	31.7	31.7
RELATIVE PRICE INDEX	3.0	3.1	3.0	3.0
PRODUCT QUALITY	0.0	-14.4	-4.7	-4.7
USE OF INVESTMENT:				
INVESTMENT/VALUE ADDED	82.5	71.5	72.7	82.5
INVESTMENT/SALES	61.9	51.6	54.2	62.0
FIXED CAPITAL INTENSITY	78.2	69.5	68.8	75.2
NET BOOK/GROSS BOOK VALUE	52.9	47.4	48.2	54.4
VALUE ADDED/SALES	81.4	80.4	81.4	81.4
WORKING CAPITAL/SALES	20.5	18.7	21.1	21.1
CAPACITY UTILIZATION	113.7	111.5	112.3	110.9
SALES/EMPLOYEES	50077.	49520.	51470.	61821.
BUDGET ALLOCATIONS:				
MARKETING EXPENSES/SALES	18.1	16.9	18.2	18.2
R+D EXPENSES/SALES	4.8	3.5	4.7	4.7

PERFORMANCE MEASURES:

DISCOUNTED NET INCOME 10YR	775.2
DISCOUNTED CASH FLOW 10YR	155.4
AVERAGE NET INCOME 3YR	105.6
AVERAGE RETURN ON INVESTMENT 5YR	33.8%
DISCOUNTED CASH FLOW YIELD RATE 10YR	16.6%

Table 9

STRATEGY SENSITIVITY REPORT
VERSION 002C(611010)-5
DETAILS

STRATEGY MOVE: SMALL INCREASE IN MARKET SHARE

	RECENT POSITION (1972-74)	DURING STRATEGY IMPLEMENTATION (1977)	NEW STEADY-STATE POSITION (1979)	NEW LONG-TERM POSITION (1984)
NET SALES (CURRENT$)	476.4	692.3	931.3	1641.3
NET INCOME	74.7	78.8	143.0	259.0
AVERAGE INVESTMENT	294.8	394.1	569.8	1003.8
NET CASH FLOW	9.3	6.3	-16.3	42.7
RETURN ON INVESTMENT	25.4%	20.0%	25.1%	25.8%
RETURN ON SALES	15.7%	11.4%	15.4%	15.8%

FACTORS

COMPETITIVE POSITION:				
MARKET SHARE	20.5	22.4	24.5	24.5
RELATIVE MARKET SHARE	37.0	41.4	46.4	46.4
RELATIVE PRICE INDEX	3.0	3.2	3.0	3.0
PRODUCT QUALITY	0.0	-10.3	-1.1	-1.1

USE OF INVESTMENT:				
INVESTMENT/VALUE ADDED	82.5	75.9	81.4	81.6
INVESTMENT/SALES	61.9	56.9	61.2	61.2
FIXED CAPITAL INTENSITY	78.2	69.6	72.1	74.9
NET BOOK/GROSS BOOK VALUE	52.9	52.4	57.7	55.5
VALUE ADDED/SALES	81.4	79.5	81.4	81.4
WORKING CAPITAL/SALES	20.5	20.5	19.6	19.6
CAPACITY UTILIZATION	113.7	111.7	112.2	112.6
SALES/EMPLOYEES	50077.	52120.	54478.	62234.

BUDGET ALLOCATIONS:				
MARKETING EXPENSES/SALES	18.1	18.6	17.9	17.9
R+D EXPENSES/SALES	4.8	4.6	4.9	4.9

PERFORMANCE MEASURES:

DISCOUNTED NET INCOME 10YR	846.9
DISCOUNTED CASH FLOW 10YR	22.3
AVERAGE NET INCOME 3YR	77.4
DISCOUNTED CASH FLOW YIELD RATE 10YR	13.6%
AVERAGE RETURN ON INVESTMENT 5YR	22.8%

Table 10

M A R K E T   S H A R E

SUMMARY RESULTS OF:	DECREASE		NO PLANNED	INCREASE	
	MAJOR	SMALL	CHANGE	SMALL	MAJOR
	-----	-----	------	-----	-----
MARKET SHARE 1979	15.	18.	21.	24.	28.
NET SALES BILLED 1979	572.	689.	803.	931.	1075.
NET INCOME 1979	96.	115.	128.	143.	158.
AVERAGE INVESTMENT 1979	282.	373.	473.	570.	683.
ROI 1977 (%)	48.	39.	29.	20.	10.
ROI 1979 (%)	34.	31.	27.	25.	23.
ROI 1984 (%)	25.	25.	26.	26.	26.
DISCOUNTD NET INCOME 10YR	705.	775.	816.	847.	863.
DISCOUNTED CASH FLOW 10YR	213.	155.	100.	22.	-73.
AVERAGE NET INCOME 3YR	108.	106.	92.	77.	56.
DISC CSH FL YLD RATE 10YR (%)	18.	17.	15.	14.	12.
AVERAGE ROI 5YR (%)	39.	34.	28.	23.	18.

Table 11

STRATEGY SENSITIVITY REPORT
VERSION 002C(6 11010)-5
DETAILS

STRATEGY: TO OPTIMIZE
DISCOUNTED NET INCOME 10YR

	RECENT POSITION (1972-74)	DURING STRATEGY IMPLEMENTATION (1977)	NEW STEADY-STATE POSITION (1979)	NEW LONG-TERM POSITION (1984)
NET SALES (CURRENT$)	476.4	735.1	1050.0	1850.4
NET INCOME	74.7	37.2	222.6	410.6
AVERAGE INVESTMENT	294.8	471.1	782.9	1300.7
NET CASH FLOW	9.3	-40.1	-44.6	101.7
RETURN ON INVESTMENT	25.4%	7.9%	28.4%	31.6%
RETURN ON SALES	15.7%	5.1%	21.2%	22.2%

FACTORS

COMPETITIVE POSITION:				
MARKET SHARE	20.5	23.8	27.6	27.6
RELATIVE MARKET SHARE	37.0	44.7	54.6	54.6
RELATIVE PRICE INDEX	3.0	3.1	3.0	3.0
PRODUCT QUALITY	0.0	-5.7	0.7	0.7

USE OF INVESTMENT:				
INVESTMENT/VALUE ADDED	82.5	77.1	88.3	83.7
INVESTMENT/SALES	61.9	64.1	74.6	70.3
FIXED CAPITAL INTENSITY	78.2	73.6	83.6	86.2
NET BOOK/GROSS BOOK VALUE	52.9	55.7	63.4	56.5
VALUE ADDED/SALES	81.4	85.3	94.5	94.5
WORKING CAPITAL/SALES	20.5	23.1	21.6	21.6
CAPACITY UTILIZATION	113.7	113.0	113.0	113.0
SALES/EMPLOYEES	50077.	49321.	47725.	53766.

BUDGET ALLOCATIONS:				
MARKETING EXPENSES/SALES	18.1	20.1	17.8	17.8
R+D EXPENSES/SALES	4.8	5.3	5.8	5.8

PERFORMANCE MEASURES:

DISCOUNTED NET INCOME 10YR	1125.2
DISCOUNTED CASH FLOW 10YR	-30.6
AVERAGE NET INCOME 3YR	49.7
DISCOUNTED CASH FLOW YIELD RATE 10YR	14.2%
AVERAGE RETURN ON INVESTMENT 5YR	19.0%

Table 12

BUS. NO. 87041
16-Dec-76
(19:39)
PAGE 13

```
---
 P
 I
 M
 S
---
```

STRATEGY SENSITIVITY REPORT
VERSION 002C(611010)-5
DETAILS

STRATEGY: TO OPTIMIZE
DISCOUNTED CASH FLOW 10YR

	RECENT POSITION (1972-74)	DURING STRATEGY IMPLEMENTATION (1977)	NEW STEADY-STATE POSITION (1979)	NEW LONG-TERM POSITION (1984)
NET SALES (CURRENT$)	476.4	537.9	562.2	990.8
NET INCOME	74.7	111.3	97.3	185.4
AVERAGE INVESTMENT	294.8	235.2	213.7	535.3
NET CASH FLOW	9.3	75.5	59.4	28.4
RETURN ON INVESTMENT	25.4%	47.3%	45.5%	34.6%
RETURN ON SALES	15.7%	20.7%	17.3%	18.7%

F A C T O R S

COMPETITIVE POSITION:				
MARKET SHARE	20.5	17.4	14.8	14.8
RELATIVE MARKET SHARE	37.0	30.2	24.8	24.8
RELATIVE PRICE INDEX	3.0	3.1	3.0	3.0
PRODUCT QUALITY	0.0	-16.0	-6.7	-6.7
USE OF INVESTMENT:				
INVESTMENT/VALUE ADDED	82.5	58.9	48.4	69.3
INVESTMENT/SALES	61.9	43.7	38.0	54.0
FIXED CAPITAL INTENSITY	78.2	62.5	56.4	66.4
NET BOOK/GROSS BOOK VALUE	52.9	39.9	34.3	53.2
VALUE ADDED/SALES	81.4	82.8	86.0	86.0
WORKING CAPITAL/SALES	20.5	18.8	18.7	18.7
CAPACITY UTILIZATION	113.7	113.0	113.0	113.0
SALES/EMPLOYEES	50077.	43289.	40470.	52808.
BUDGET ALLOCATIONS:				
MARKETING EXPENSES/SALES	18.1	16.6	18.4	18.4
R+D EXPENSES/SALES	4.8	3.2	4.9	4.9

P E F F O R M A N C E   M E A S U R E S :

DISCOUNTED NET INCOME 10YR	721.9
DISCOUNTED CASH FLOW 10YR	273.0
AVERAGE NET INCOME 3YR	99.1
DISCOUNTED CASH FLOW YIELD RATE 10YR	20.0%
AVERAGE RETURN ON INVESTMENT 5YR	41.5%

FURTHER DISCUSSION

After considerable further debate, Mr. Simmons proposed that the meeting be adjourned to allow he and his managers to study in more detail the implications of what they had seen. Mr. Goodman departed to catch his plane for a planned meeting with another client over 1,000 miles away. As the management group broke-up, Mr. Jack Simmons commented as follows to John Hutton, his Strategic Planning Manager:

> All this is very interesting, John. The next job is to figure out how to put it to use. Firstly, how well does the PIMS model succeed in analyzing and describing the strategic position of our business? What, if anything, have we learned from this exercise that we did not already know. Next, how can those Strategic Sensitivity Reports help us in deciding what strategy we should pursue for PPD. My current problem is that I soon have to present our five year plans to corporate headquarters. What I need from you is a set of recommendations for our future strategy and some concrete ideas about what performance you think PPD can achieve.

Appendix A

Edit Report Obtained by Running the Tex-Fiber [A] [B] and [C] Data on the "PIMS" Model.

```
                                                        EDIT (1970-1974)
---                                                     V-OY(761124)-03
SPI                                                     DATA FORM 1
 I
 M
 S
---

100 RESEARCH SUITABILITY                  1   SIMULATED BUSINESS
101 TYPE OF BUSINESS                      4   MANUFACTURING RAW OR SEMI-FINISHED MATERIALS

102 AGE OF PRODUCT CATEGORY              2   1950 - 1954
103 STAGE OF PRODUCT LIFE CYCLE          3   MATURITY STAGE
104 YEAR OF YOUR INITIAL SALE            3   1955 - 1959
105 ORDER OF MARKET ENTRY                2   EARLY FOLLOWER

106 PROPRIETARY PRODUCTS                 0   NO
107 PROPRIETARY PROCESSES                1   YES

108 STANDARDZATION OF PRODUCTS/SERVICES  0   MORE OR LESS STANDARD
109 FREQUENCY OF PRODUCT CHANGES         4   NO REGULAR PATTERN
110 TECHNOLOGICAL CHANGE                 0   NO
111 DEVELOPMENT TIME FOR NEW PRODUCTS    2   1 - 2 YEARS

112 USED BY INDIVIDUAL END USER          5  **
113 USED BY MANUFACTURERS END USER      80  **
114 USED BY INSTITUTIONAL END USER       5  **
115 USED BY GOVERNMENT END USER          0  **
116 USED BY CONTRACTORS END USER        10  **

117 NUMBER OF END USERS                  5   10,000 - 99,999
118 NUMBER OF IMMEDIATE CUSTOMERS        6   100 - 999

119 %CONCENTRATN OF PURCHASERS-END USER 30  **
120 CHANGE IN PURCHASER CONCEN END USER  2   NO CHANGE
121 RELATIVE PIRCHASERS CONCEN END USER  2   ABOUT THE SAME AS LEADING COMPETITORS

122 %CONCN OF PURCH-IMMEDIATE CUSTOMERS 15  **
123 CHANGE IN PURCH CONCEN IMMED CUSTS   2   NO CHANGE
124 RELATIVE PURCH CONCN IMMEDIAT CUSTS  2   ABOUT THE SAME AS LEADING COMPETITORS

125 PURCHASE FREQUENCY - END USER        3   BETWEEN ONCE/MONTH AND ONCE/6 MONTHS
126 PURCH FREQUENCY-IMMEDIATE CUSTOMERS  3   BETWEEN ONCE/MONTH AND ONCE/6 MONTHS

127 TYPICAL PURCHASE AMOUNT - END USER   5   $1,000 TO $9,999
128 TYPICAL PURCH AMT - IMMED CUSTOMERS  5   $1,000 TO $9,999

129 IMPORTANCE OF PRODUCT - END USER     2   BETWEEN 0.25% AND 1.0%
130 IMPORTANCE OF PRODUCT - IMMED CUSTS  2   BETWEEN 0.25% AND 1.0%

131 IMPORTANCE OF AUX SERVICES-END USER  1   SOME IMPORTANCE
132 RELIANCE ON PROFESSIONAL ADVISORS    0   NEVER

133 % SOLD TO END USER                  60  **
134 % SOLD TO DISTRIBUTION FACILITY      0  **
135 % SOLD TO WHOLESALERS               38  **
136 % SOLD TO RETAILERS                  0  **

137 % GROSS MARGINS-DISTRIBUTORS        20  **
```

EDIT (1970-1974)
V-OY(761124)-03
DATA FORM 1

```
---
SPI
I
M
S
---
```

138 REL VERT INTEGRATN BUSINES-BACKWDS	2	SAME
139 REL VERT INTEGRATN BUSINES-FORWRDS	2	SAME
140 REL VERT INTEGRATN COMPANY-BACKWRDS	1	LESS
141 REL VERT INTEGRATN COMPANY-FORWARDS	2	SAME
142 % PURCHASED FROM COMPANY COMPONENTS	0.0	
143 % PROFIT MARGIN - INTERNL SUPPLIERS	0.0	
144 % SALES TO COMPANY COMPONENTS	2	%
145 INTERNAL CUSTOMERS - SAME MANAGER	4	NOT APPLICABLE
146 SHARE FACILITIES WITH OTHERS	1	LESS THAN 10% OF ITS PLANT AND EQUIPMENT
147 COMMON MARKET OR DISTRIB CHANNELS	1	LESS THAN 25%
148 SHARED MARKETING PROGRAMS	1	LESS THAN 10% OF ITS MARKETING EXPENDITURES
149 PRODUCTION LIMITATON-LACK MATERIALS	0	NO
150 PRODUCTION LIMITATON-LACK ENERGY	0	NO
151 PRODUCTION LIMITATON-LACK PERSONNEL	0	NO
152 PRODUCTION LIMITATON-LACK PLANT	1	YES
153 GOVERNMENT PRICE CONTROLS	0	NO
154 GOVERNMENT CONTROLS AFFECT PROFITS	3	NOT APPLICABLE
155 %PURCHASES FROM 3 LARGEST SUPPLIERS	75	%
156 %SALES TO BUSINESS, BIG-3 SUPPLIERS	1	%
157 ALTERNATE SUPPLY SOURCES	2	YES, WITH NO DIFFICULTY
158 SUPPLIERS INTEGRATED FORWARD	1	YES, IN OTHER MARKET
159 SUPPLIERS MIGHT INTEGRATE FORWARD	0	NO
160 COMPETITION FROM WITHIN COMPANY	0	NO
161 % OF EMPLOYEES UNIONIZED	50	%
162 % PRODUCED IN SMALL BATCHES	0	%
163 % PRODUCED ON ASSEMBLY LINE	0	%
164 % PRODUCED BY CONTINUOUS PROCESS	100	%
165 % PRODUCED - NOT MANUFACTURED	0	%

EDIT (1970-1974)
V-OY(761124)-03
DATA FORM 2

OTHER PRODUCTION DATA

	------1970------	------1971------	------1972------	------1973------	------1974------
225 % REPLACEMENT / GROSS BOOK VALUE	180 %				
235 STANDARD CAPACITY		240.00	260.00	310.00	420.00
236 % CAPACITY UTILIZATION		92.00	110.00	120.00	111.00
237 ACCOUNTG METHOD-INVENTORY VALUATION		2.00	2.00	2.00	2.00
203 % ORDER BACKLOG		15.00	15.00	15.00	5.00
238 SALES PER EMPLOYEE ($1000)		42.00	46.00	49.00	54.00
239 SALES PER SALESMAN ($1000)		2479.00	2792.00	2899.00	2578.00
% RETURN ON INVESTMENT		15.28	23.64	23.30	28.55
% RETURN ON SALES		12.01	16.66	14.65	15.93

EDIT (1970-1974)
V-DY(761124)-03
DATA FORM 2

BUSINESS 87041
16-DEC-76
PAGE 3

SPI
I
M
S

INCOME STATEMENT DATA

	1970 AMOUNT	1970 %SALES	1971 AMOUNT	1971 %SALES	1972 AMOUNT	1972 %SALES	1973 AMOUNT	1973 %SALES	1974 AMOUNT	1974 %SALES
201 NET SALES (+ LEASE REVENUES)			223.10	100.0	287.60	100.0	374.00	100.0	464.00	100.0
202 LEASE REVENUES			0.00	0.0	0.00	0.0	0.00	0.0	0.00	0.0
204 PURCHASES			28.40	12.7	39.70	13.8	55.10	14.7	98.30	21.2
205 VALUE ADDED			194.70	87.3	247.90	86.2	318.90	85.3	365.70	78.8
206 MFG & PHYSICAL DISTRIBUTION EXPENSE			22.70	10.2	39.70	13.8	60.70	16.2	82.70	17.8
207 PRODUCTS & SERVICES R&D EXPENSES			10.30	4.6	10.80	3.8	11.90	3.2	9.50	2.1
208 PROCESS R&D EXPENSES			6.90	3.1	7.20	2.5	7.90	2.1	6.50	1.4
210 SALES FORCE EXPENSES			9.30	4.2	11.10	3.9	13.90	3.7	14.10	3.0
211 ADVERTISING & SALES PROMO EXPENSE			4.00	1.8	7.70	2.7	12.30	3.3	3.70	0.8
212 MEDIA ADVERTISING EXPENSES			2.50	1.1	4.00	1.4	7.00	1.9	3.00	0.6
213 OTHER MARKETING EXPENSES			31.20	14.0	30.80	10.7	50.00	13.4	60.10	13.0
214 TOTAL MARKETING EXPENSES			44.50	19.9	49.60	17.2	76.20	20.4	77.90	16.8
215 DEPRECIATION EXPENSE			19.90	8.9	19.90	6.9	22.00	5.9	23.00	5.0
216 OTHER EXPENSES			63.60	28.5	72.80	25.3	85.40	22.8	92.00	19.8
217 NET INCOME			26.80	12.0	47.90	16.7	54.80	14.7	73.90	15.9

IMPLICIT BALANCE SHEET

	1970 AMOUNT	1970 %ASSTS	1971 AMOUNT	1971 %ASSTS	1972 AMOUNT	1972 %ASSTS	1973 AMOUNT	1973 %ASSTS	1974 AMOUNT	1974 %ASSTS
ASSETS										
226 CASH			3.60	1.8	3.00	1.2	10.20	3.7	-20.70	-6.7
220 AVERAGE NET RECEIVABLES			28.90	14.5	41.20	16.8	45.00	16.5	59.20	19.6
221 AVERAGE FINISHED GOODS INVENTORY			18.40	9.2	26.80	10.9	32.70	12.0	54.30	17.6
222 AVERAGE RAW MATERIALS+WIP INVENTORY			12.00	6.0	17.00	6.9	21.00	7.7	30.00	9.7
TOTAL CURRENT ASSETS			62.90	31.6	88.00	35.9	108.90	39.9	122.80	39.9
223 GROSS BOOK VALUE - P & E			236.90	119.0	267.70	109.1	286.20	104.8	326.40	106.0
LESS ACC. DEPRECIATION			106.30	53.4	121.70	49.6	137.00	50.1	156.00	50.6
224 NET BOOK VALUE - P & E			130.60	65.6	146.00	59.5	149.20	54.6	170.40	55.3
227 OTHER ASSETS			5.50	2.8	11.30	4.6	15.10	5.5	14.80	4.8
231 TOTAL ASSETS			199.00	100.0	245.30	100.0	273.20	100.0	308.00	100.0
LIABILITIES										
229 SHORT TERM BORROWINGS			19.90	10.0	27.20	11.1	23.20	8.5	30.40	9.9
230 OTHER CURRENT LIABILITIES			3.40	1.7	15.50	6.3	14.80	5.4	18.80	6.1
228 AVERAGE INVESTMENT - BOOK VALUE			175.40	88.1	202.60	82.6	235.20	86.1	258.80	84.0
231 TOTAL ASSETS			199.00	100.0	245.30	100.0	273.20	100.0	308.00	100.0

EDIT (1970=1974)
V=OY(76112A)=03
DATA FORM 3

SPI
I
M
S

	1970	1971	1972	1973	1974
301 SIZE OF SERVED MARKET		1150.00	1380.00	1790.00	2320.00
302 GEOGRAPHIC LOCATON OF SERVED MARKET	8 OTHER				
303 NUMBER OF COMPETITORS	2 6 - 10				
304 MAJOR COMPETITOR ENTER MARKET	0 NO				
305 MAJOR COMPETITOR EXIT MARKET	0 NO				
311 MARKET SHARE RANK	2				
306 % MARKET SHARE - THIS BUSINESS		19.30	20.70	20.90	20.00
307 % MARKET SHARE - LARGEST COMPETITOR		40.00	41.00	39.50	35.00
308 % MARKET SHARE=2ND LARGE COMPETITOR		9.00	9.00	9.00	9.00
309 % MARKET SHARE=3RD LARGE COMPETITOR		8.00	8.00	8.00	8.00
310 % MARKET SHARE=TOP 3 COMPETITORS		57.00	58.00	56.50	52.00
312 % INDEX OF PRICES (1973=100%)		108.00	104.00	100.00	118.00
313 % INDEX BASIC MATERIAL COST(73=100%		93.00	97.00	100.00	170.00
314 % INDEX AVG HOURLY WAGES(1973=100%)		90.00	95.00	100.00	105.00
316 % PRODUCT QUALITY - SUPERIOR		25.00	25.00	25.00	25.00
317 % PRODUCT QUALITY - EQUIVALENT		50.00	50.00	50.00	50.00
318 % PRODUCT QUALITY - INFERIOR		25.00	25.00	25.00	25.00
319 % RELATIVE PRICES VS COMPETITORS		100.00	100.00	100.00	100.00
320 % RELATIVE DIRECT COSTS PER UNIT		96.70	101.70	111.10	112.30
321 % RELATIVE HOURLY WAGE RATES		100.00	100.00	100.00	100.00
322 % RELATIVE SALARY LEVELS		100.00	100.00	100.00	100.00
323 % NEW PRODUCTS - THIS BUSINESS		20.00	20.00	20.00	20.00
324 % NEW PRODUCTS - COMPETITORS		20.00	20.00	20.00	20.00
325 RELATIVE PRODUCT BREADTH	2 SAME AS COMPETITORS				
326 RELATIVE TYPES OF CUSTOMERS SERVED	2 SAME AS COMPETITORS				
327 RELATIVE NUMBER OF CUSTOMERS	2 SAME AS COMPETITORS				
328 RELATIVE SIZE OF CUSTOMERS	2 SAME AS COMPETITORS				
329 RELATIVE SALES FORCE EXPENDITURES		3.00	3.00	3.00	3.00
330 RELATIVE ADVERTISING EXPENDITURES		2.00	4.00	4.00	1.00
331 RELATIVE SALES PROMO EXPENDITURES		2.00	4.00	4.00	1.00
332 RELATIVE QUALITY CUSTOMER SERVICES		3.00	3.00	3.00	3.00
333 REL PRODUCT IMAGE/COMPANY REPUTATON		3.00	3.00	3.00	3.00

EDIT (1970-1974)
V-OY(761124)-03
DATA FORM 4

```
---
SPT
I
M
S
---
```

401 SIC CODE   9607

402 % INDUSTRY CONCENTRATION RATIO   72   %
403 % INDUSTRY VALUE-ADDED / EMPLOYEE   45000
404 % INDUSTRY EXPORTS   0   %
405 % INDUSTRY IMPORTS   0   %

406 INDUSTRY GROWTH RATE   19.4
407 INDUSTRY INDEX OF INSTABILITY   0.1

415 - 424 INDUSTRY SALES - 10 YEARS   705.00   925.00   975.00   1010.00   1045.00
                                        1125.00   1150.00   1380.00   1790.00   2320.00

EDIT (1970-1974)
V-OY(761124)-03
DATA FORM 5

```
---
SPI
I
M
S
---
```

	SHORT TERM 1976 - 1978	LONG TERM 1979 - 1983
501 % FUTURE MARKET GROWTH - SHORT TERM	10.0	
502 % FUTURE MARKET GROWTH - LONG TERM		12.0
503 % FUTURE SELLING PRICE - SHORT TERM	5.0	
504 % FUTURE SELLING PRICE - LONG TERM		3.0
505 % FUTURE MATERIALS COST - SHORT TERM	8.0	
506 % FUTURE MATERIALS COST - LONG TERM		6.0
507 % FUTURE HOURLY WAGE - SHORT TERM	8.0	
508 % FUTURE HOURLY WAGE - LONG TERM		6.0

509 % INTERNAL DISCOUNT RATE   10   %
510 % INCREMENTAL CAPITAL CHARGE RATE   0   %
511 % MAXIMUM MARKET SHARE IN 5 YEARS   25   %
512 % MINIMUM CAPACITY ADDITIONS   2   %

TEX-FIBER INDUSTRIES—[D]

1. Read carefully through the case and try to understand *each* exhibit and its implications.
2. What has been learned from the PIMS analysis which we did not know already from analysis of the (A) and (B) cases?
3. How may the output be used to aid in drawing up plans for PPD?
4. What sort of a job did Mr. Goodman do in presenting PIMS to PPD management?
5. What additional PIMS analysis might be useful to PPD management?

TEX-FIBER INDUSTRIES—
PETROLOID PRODUCTS
DIVISION (E)[1]

Following Mr. Goodman's initial presentation of the PIMS output to PPD management, there was a general feeling that additional insights might be gained if each segment of the business could be analyzed separately. Cognizant of the fact that it might be difficult to assemble by segment all the data required by the normal PIMS data forms, Mr. Goodman proposed that the Limited Information model (LIM) might be employed. The LIM model contained only 18 variables (see Appendix A) in comparison to the 37 variables used in the full PIMS model. Yet it could "explain" more than 60 percent of the variations in ROI.

The decision was made to conduct PIMS runs for segments defined first by product (i.e., oils, rubbers, FAS), and second by geographic market (i.e., U.S., Europe, Japan, 3rd World). The results of these runs are shown in the following exhibits.

---

[1]This case was prepared by Derek F. Abell in collaboration with Robert D. Buzzell.

Exhibit 1
OILS

```
-----
 P                                              RUS. NO.    1
 I
 M                                                         PAGE  1
 S
-----
```

LIMITED INFORMATION MODEL

ESTIMATE OF NORMAL ROI
BY CATEGORY OF IMPACT

F A C T O R S	PIMS MEAN	THIS BUSINESS	IMPACT OF FACTOR ON ESTIMATE OF ROI(%)
1 MARKET SHARE (%)	23.6	14.0	
2 RELATIVE MARKET SHARE (%)	61.7	18.0	
			−3.3
3 RELATIVE PRODUCT QUALITY	25.9	0.0	−2.9
4 RELATIVE PRICE	103.5	100.0	−0.0
5 PERCENT EMPLOYEES UNIONIZED	48.3	50.0	−0.1
6 %NEW PRODUCT SALES / SALES	11.9	15.0	−0.4
7 R&D EXPENSE / SALES (%)	2.4	1.8	0.3
8 MARKETING EXPENSE / SALES (%)	10.8	10.9	−0.4

COMPETITIVE POSITION & ACTION IMPACT   −6.8

	PIMS MEAN	THIS BUSINESS	IMPACT OF ROI(%)
9 INVESTMENT / SALES (%)	56.1	61.9	
10 INVESTMENT/VALUE ADDED (%)	96.7	100.0	
			−3.7
11 FIXED CAPITAL INTENSITY (%)	52.3	78.2	−1.2
12 VERTICAL INTEGRATION (%)	58.8	62.0	0.4
13 VALUE ADDED/EMPLOYEE ($1000)	30.0	31.0	0.2
14 CAPACITY UTILIZATION (%)	79.6	110.0C	7.3

CAPITAL & PRODUCTION STRUCTURE IMPACT   3.0

	PIMS MEAN	THIS BUSINESS	IMPACT OF ROI(%)
15 REAL MARKET GROWTH RATE	8.2	8.0	0.2
16 SHARE OF 4 LARGEST FIRMS (%)	56.5	90.0	1.3
17 % OF CUSTOMERS = 50% SALES	12.2	5.0	0.3
18 PURCHASE AMOUNT−IMMED. CUSTS	5.2	6.0	−1.2

MARKET ENVIRONMENT IMPACT   0.6

TOTAL IMPACT   −3.3
AVERAGE ROI, ALL PIMS BUSINESSES   22.1*

ESTIMATED ROI, THIS BUSINESS   18.8

C ... EXTREME VALUE COMPRESSED TO THIS LIMIT

* .... Average ROI differs from that in Tex-Fiber (D) because the LIM
       model is based on a more recent data base.

Exhibit 2
OILS

```
-----
 P
 I                                              BUS. NO     1
 M
 S                                              PAGE   3
-----
```

STRATEGIC MOVES

ASSUME: INDUSTRY SALES GROWTH OF   8.0% PER YEAR FOR   5 YEARS
THIS CURRENT DOLLAR GROWTH REFLECTS
REAL MARKET GROWTH RATE OF   8.0%
SELLING PRICE GROWTH RATE OF   0.0%

	PRESENT	FUTURE
INDUSTRY SALES:	1178.6	1731.7

STRATEGIES CHANGING MARKET SHARE (%)

	PRESENT	1979 DOWN 20%	1979 HOLD	1979 BUILD 20%
MARKET SHARE (%)	14.0	11.2	14.0	16.8
RELATIVE MARKET SHARE (%)	18.0	13.9	18.0	22.3
RELATIVE PRODUCT QUALITY	0.0	-1.7	0.0	1.7
CAPACITY UTILIZATION (%)	110.0	95.0	95.0	95.0
INVESTMENT/VALUE ADDED (%)	100.0	115.8	115.8	115.8
INVESTMENT / SALES (%)	61.9	71.7	71.7	71.7
FIXED CAPITAL INTENSITY (%)	78.2	87.5	87.5	87.5
VALUE ADDED/EMPLOYEE ($1000)	31.0	32.2	32.2	32.2
: SALES	165.0	194.0	242.4	290.9
: NET INCOME	19.2	17.3	23.3	29.8
: INVESTMENT	102.1	139.0	173.8	208.5
: ROI	18.8	12.5	13.4	14.3
: CASH FLOW		1.3	-2.7	-6.4
PAYOFF : INCREMENTAL ROI (DOWN TO BUILD)*			17.9	

*Read as the incremental return on incremental investment required to move from a "down 20%" strategy to a "build 20%" strategy. In this case it is $\dfrac{29.8-17.3}{298.5-139.0} = \dfrac{12.5}{69.5} = 17.9\%$

Exhibit 3
RUBBERS

```
-----
 P
 I
 M
 S
-----
```

LIMITED INFORMATION MODEL

ESTIMATE OF NORMAL ROI
BY CATEGORY OF IMPACT

FACTORS	PIMS MEAN	THIS BUSINESS	IMPACT OF FACTOR ON ESTIMATE OF ROI(%)
1 MARKET SHARE (%)	23.6	23.0	
2 RELATIVE MARKET SHARE (%)	61.7	30.0	
			-1.0
3 RELATIVE PRODUCT QUALITY	25.9	0.0	-2.8
4 RELATIVE PRICE	103.5	100.0	-0.3
5 PERCENT EMPLOYEES UNIONIZED	48.3	50.0	-0.1
6 %NEW PRODUCT SALES / SALES	11.9	20.0	-1.1
7 R&D EXPENSE / SALES (%)	2.4	6.1	-2.6
8 MARKETING EXPENSE / SALES (%)	10.8	17.4	-4.4

COMPETITIVE POSITION & ACTION IMPACT			-12.1
9 INVESTMENT / SALES (%)	56.1	61.9	
10 INVESTMENT/VALUE ADDED (%)	96.7	77.0	
			-1.1
11 FIXED CAPITAL INTENSITY (%)	52.3	78.2	-1.2
12 VERTICAL INTEGRATION (%)	58.8	80.0	1.8
13 VALUE ADDED/EMPLOYEE ($1000)	30.0	40.0	2.2
14 CAPACITY UTILIZATION (%)	79.6	110.0C	5.9

CAPITAL & PRODUCTION STRUCTURE IMPACT			7.7
15 REAL MARKET GROWTH RATE	8.2	10.0	0.3
16 SHARE OF 4 LARGEST FIRMS (%)	56.5	100.0C	1.7
17 % OF CUSTOMERS = 50% SALES	12.2	15.0	-0.1
18 PURCHASE AMOUNT-IMMED. CUSTS	5.2	5.0	0.3

MARKET ENVIRONMENT IMPACT			2.3

```
                       TOTAL IMPACT    -2.2
       AVERAGE ROI, ALL PIMS BUSINESSES   22.1
                                        ------
          ESTIMATED ROI, THIS BUSINESS    19.9
```

C ... EXTREME VALUE COMPRESSED TO THIS LIMIT

Exhibit 4
RUBBERS

```
-----
P
I                                                        BUS. NO    2
M
S                                                        PAGE   3
-----
```

STRATEGIC MOVES

ASSUME: INDUSTRY SALES GROWTH OF 1C.0% PER YEAR FOR 5 YEARS
         THIS CURRENT DOLLAR GROWTH REFLECTS
            REAL MARKET GROWTH RATE OF   8.0%
            SELLING PRICE GROWTH RATE OF   2.0%

	PRESENT	FUTURE
INDUSTRY SALES:	5C0.0	805.3

STRATEGIES CHANGING MARKET SHARE (%)

	PRESENT	DOWN 20%	1979 HOLD	BUILD 20%
MARKET SHARE (%)	23.0	18.4	23.0	27.6
RELATIVE MARKET SHARE (%)	30.0	22.6	30.0	38.3
RELATIVE PRODUCT QUALITY	0.0	-2.9	0.0	2.9
CAPACITY UTILIZATION (%)	110.0	95.0	95.0	95.0
INVESTMENT/VALUE ADDED (%)	77.0	89.2	89.2	89.2
INVESTMENT / SALES (%)	61.9	71.7	71.7	71.7
FIXED CAPITAL INTENSITY (%)	78.2	85.4	85.4	85.4
VALUE ADDED/EMPLOYEE ($100J)	40.0	40.9	40.9	40.9
: SALES	115.0	148.2	185.2	222.3
: NET INCOME	14.2	13.1	18.5	24.5
: INVESTMENT	71.2	106.2	132.7	159.3
: ROI	19.9	12.4	13.9	15.4
: CASH FLOW		-0.4	-3.1	-5.4
PAYOFF : INCREMENTAL ROI (DOWN TO BUILD)			21.4	

Exhibit 5
FAS

LIMITED INFORMATION MODEL

ESTIMATE OF NORMAL ROI
BY CATEGORY OF IMPACT

F A C T O R S	PIMS MEAN	THIS BUSINESS	IMPACT OF FACTOR ON ESTIMATE OF ROI(%)
1 MARKET SHARE (%)	23.6	28.0	
2 RELATIVE MARKET SHARE (%)	61.7	39.0	
			0.7
3 RELATIVE PRODUCT QUALITY	25.9	10.0	-1.6
4 RELATIVE PRICE	103.5	100.0	-0.3
5 PERCENT EMPLOYEES UNIONIZED	48.3	50.0	-0.1
6 %NEW PRODUCT SALES / SALES	11.9	25.0	-1.8
7 R&D EXPENSE / SALES (%)	2.4	4.9	-1.8
8 MARKETING EXPENSE / SALES (%)	10.8	21.7	-7.1

COMPETITIVE POSITION & ACTION IMPACT   -12.0

9 INVESTMENT / SALES (%)	56.1	61.9	
10 INVESTMENT/VALUE ADDED (%)	96.7	72.0	
			-0.4
11 FIXED CAPITAL INTENSITY (%)	52.3	78.2	-1.2
12 VERTICAL INTEGRATION (%)	58.8	86.0	1.9
13 VALUE ADDED/EMPLOYEE ($1000)	30.0	43.0	2.9
14 CAPACITY UTILIZATION (%)	79.6	110.0C	4.7

CAPITAL & PRODUCTION STRUCTURE IMPACT   7.9

15 REAL MARKET GROWTH RATE	8.2	16.0	0.8
16 SHARE OF 4 LARGEST FIRMS (%)	56.5	100.0C	1.7
17 % OF CUSTOMERS = 50% SALES	12.2	30.0	-1.5
18 PURCHASE AMOUNT—IMMED. CUSTS	5.2	5.0	0.3

MARKET ENVIRONMENT IMPACT   1.2

TOTAL IMPACT   -2.8
AVERAGE ROI, ALL PIMS BUSINESSES   22.1

ESTIMATED ROI, THIS BUSINESS   19.3

C ... EXTREME VALUE COMPRESSED TO THIS LIMIT

Exhibit 6
FAS

```
                        STRATEGIC MOVES

     ASSUME:  INDUSTRY SALES GROWTH OF  16.0% PER YEAR FOR  5 YEARS
              THIS CURRENT DOLLAR GROWTH REFLECTS
                        REAL MARKET GROWTH RATE OF      11.0%
                        SELLING PRICE GROWTH RATE OF     5.0%

                          PRESENT              FUTURE
              INDUSTRY SALES:   657.1          1380.2


                 STRATEGIES CHANGING MARKET SHARE (%)
                                         1979
                              PRESENT    DOWN 20%   HOLD   BUILD 20%
MARKET SHARE (%)                28.0       22.4     28.0     33.6
RELATIVE MARKET SHARE (%)       39.0       28.9     39.0     50.7
RELATIVE PRODUCT QUALITY        10.0        6.5     10.0     13.5
CAPACITY UTILIZATION (%)       110.0       95.0     95.0     95.0
INVESTMENT/VALUE ADDED (%)      72.0       83.4     83.4     83.4
INVESTMENT / SALES (%)          61.9       71.7     71.7     71.7
FIXED CAPITAL INTENSITY (%)     78.2       84.9     84.9     84.9
VALUE ADDED/EMPLOYEE ($1000)    43.0       43.9     43.9     43.9
             : SALES           184.0      309.2    386.5    463.8
             : NET INCOME       21.9       26.9     38.7     52.0
             : INVESTMENT      113.9      221.6    277.0    332.4
             : ROI              19.3       12.1     14.0     15.6
             : CASH FLOW                   -8.1    -13.3    -17.7
     PAYOFF  : INCREMENTAL ROI (DOWN TO BUILD)      22.6
```

Exhibit 7
U.S.

```
-----
 P                                              BUS. NO    4
 I
 M                                              PAGE   1
 S
-----
```

LIMITED INFORMATION MODEL

ESTIMATE OF NORMAL ROI
BY CATEGORY OF IMPACT

F A C T O R S	PIMS MEAN	THIS BUSINESS	IMPACT OF FACTOR ON ESTIMATE OF ROI(%)
1 MARKET SHARE (%)	23.6	30.0	
2 RELATIVE MARKET SHARE (%)	61.7	44.0	
			1.3
3 RELATIVE PRODUCT QUALITY	25.9	0.0	-2.8
4 RELATIVE PRICE	103.5	100.0	-0.3
5 PERCENT EMPLOYEES UNIONIZED	48.3	50.0	-0.1
6 %NEW PRODUCT SALES / SALES	11.9	20.0	-1.1
7 R&D EXPENSE / SALES (%)	2.4	4.8	-1.7
8 MARKETING EXPENSE / SALES (%)	10.8	19.9	-5.9

COMPETITIVE POSITION & ACTION IMPACT   -10.6

9 INVESTMENT / SALES (%)	56.1	61.9	
10 INVESTMENT/VALUE ADDED (%)	96.7	76.0	
			-1.1
11 FIXED CAPITAL INTENSITY (%)	52.3	78.2	-1.2
12 VERTICAL INTEGRATION (%)	58.8	81.0	1.9
13 VALUE ADDED/EMPLOYEE ($1000)˙	30.0	40.0	2.2
14 CAPACITY UTILIZATION (%)	79.6	110.0C	5.9

CAPITAL & PRODUCTION STRUCTURE IMPACT   7.8

15 REAL MARKET GROWTH RATE	8.2	10.0	0.3
16 SHARE OF 4 LARGEST FIRMS (%)	56.5	98.0	1.6
17 % OF CUSTOMERS = 50% SALES	12.2	15.0	-0.1
18 PURCHASE AMOUNT-IMMED. CUSTS	5.2	5.0	0.3

MARKET ENVIRONMENT IMPACT   2.2

```
                            TOTAL IMPACT         -0.6
          AVERAGE ROI, ALL PIMS BUSINESSES       22.1
                                                ------
             ESTIMATED ROI, THIS BUSINESS        21.5
```

C ... EXTREME VALUE COMPRESSED TO THIS LIMIT

Exhibit 8

U.S.

```
-----
  P                                              BUS. NO    4
  I
  M                                              PAGE    3
  S
-----
```

STRATEGIC MOVES

ASSUME: INDUSTRY SALES GROWTH OF 10.0% PER YEAR FOR 5 YEARS
          THIS CURRENT DOLLAR GROWTH REFLECTS
                REAL MARKET GROWTH RATE OF   7.0%
                SELLING PRICE GROWTH RATE OF   3.0%

                         PRESENT   FUTURE
        INDUSTRY SALES: 1190.0   1916.5

                STRATEGIES CHANGING MARKET SHARE (%)
                                              1979

	PRESENT	DOWN 20%	HOLD	BUILD 20%
MARKET SHARE (%)	30.0	24.0	30.0	36.0
RELATIVE MARKET SHARE (%)	44.0	32.4	44.0	57.7
RELATIVE PRODUCT QUALITY	0.0	-3.7	0.0	3.7
CAPACITY UTILIZATION (%)	110.0	95.0	95.0	95.0
INVESTMENT/VALUE ADDED (%)	76.0	88.0	88.0	88.0
INVESTMENT / SALES (%)	61.9	71.7	71.7	71.7
FIXED CAPITAL INTENSITY (%)	78.2	85.3	85.3	85.3
VALUE ADDED/EMPLOYEE ($1000)	40.0	40.9	40.9	40.9
: SALES	357.0	460.0	575.0	689.9
: NET INCOME	47.6	43.2	61.8	82.8
: INVESTMENT	221.0	329.7	412.1	494.5
: ROI	21.5	13.1	15.0	16.7
: CASH FLOW		-0.2	-7.3	-13.3
PAYOFF : INCREMENTAL ROI (DOWN TO BUILD)			24.0	

Exhibit 9
EUROPE

```
-----
  P
  I
  M
  S
-----
```
                                                        BUS. NO   5

                                                        PAGE   1

                    LIMITED INFORMATION MODEL

                      ESTIMATE OF NORMAL ROI
                      BY CATEGORY OF IMPACT

                                                    IMPACT OF
                                                    FACTOR ON
                                    PIMS   THIS   ESTIMATE
        F A C T O R S   MEAN   BUSINESS OF ROI(%)
        ------------------   -----   -------- ---------

 1 MARKET SHARE (%)   23.6   4.0
 2 RELATIVE MARKET SHARE (%)   61.7   5.0C
                                                       -7.4
 3 RELATIVE PRODUCT QUALITY   25.9   0.0   -2.6
 4 RELATIVE PRICE   103.5   100.0   0.0
 5 PERCENT EMPLOYEES UNIONIZED   48.3   50.0   -0.1
 6 %NEW PRODUCT SALES / SALES   11.9   20.0   -1.1
 7 R&D EXPENSE / SALES (%)   2.4   4.8   -1.7
 8 MARKETING EXPENSE / SALES (%)   10.8   10.0   0.1

            COMPETITIVE POSITION & ACTION IMPACT   -12.8

 9 INVESTMENT / SALES (%)   56.1   61.9
10 INVESTMENT/VALUE ADDED (%)   96.7   76.0
                                                       -0.9
11 FIXED CAPITAL INTENSITY (%)   52.3   78.2   -1.2
12 VERTICAL INTEGRATION (%)   58.8   81.0   1.8
13 VALUE ADDED/EMPLOYEE ($1000)   30.0   40.0   2.2
14 CAPACITY UTILIZATION (%)   79.6   110.0C   5.4

            CAPITAL & PRODUCTION STRUCTURE IMPACT   7.3

15 REAL MARKET GROWTH RATE   8.2   12.0   0.5
16 SHARE OF 4 LARGEST FIRMS (%)   56.5   65.0   0.4
17 % OF CUSTOMERS = 50% SALES   12.2   20.0   -0.4
18 PURCHASE AMOUNT-IMMED. CUSTS   5.2   5.0   0.3

                      MARKET ENVIRONMENT IMPACT   0.8

                          TOTAL IMPACT   -4.8
        AVERAGE ROI, ALL PIMS BUSINESSES   22.1

            ESTIMATED ROI, THIS BUSINESS   17.3

        C ... EXTREME VALUE COMPRESSED TO THIS LIMIT

Exhibit 10
EUROPE

STRATEGIC MOVES

ASSUME: INDUSTRY SALES GROWTH OF 12.0% PER YEAR FOR 5 YEARS
THIS CURRENT DOLLAR GROWTH REFLECTS
REAL MARKET GROWTH RATE OF   9.0%
SELLING PRICE GROWTH RATE OF   3.0%

	PRESENT	FUTURE
INDUSTRY SALES:	620.0	1092.7

STRATEGIES CHANGING MARKET SHARE (%)

	PRESENT	1979		
		DOWN 20%	HOLD	BUILD 20%
MARKET SHARE (%)	4.0	3.2	4.0	4.8
RELATIVE MARKET SHARE (%)	5.0	0.8	1.0	1.2
RELATIVE PRODUCT QUALITY	0.0	-0.5	0.0	0.5
CAPACITY UTILIZATION (%)	110.0	95.0	95.0	95.0
INVESTMENT/VALUE ADDED (%)	76.0	88.0	88.0	88.0
INVESTMENT / SALES (%)	61.9	71.7	71.7	71.7
FIXED CAPITAL INTENSITY (%)	78.2	85.3	85.3	85.3
VALUE ADDED/EMPLOYEE ($1000)	40.0	40.9	40.9	40.9
: SALES	24.8	35.0	43.7	52.4
: NET INCOME	2.7	3.0	3.8	4.7
: INVESTMENT	15.4	25.1	31.3	37.6
: ROI	17.3	11.8	12.1	12.4
: CASH FLOW		-0.5	-1.3	-2.1
PAYOFF : INCREMENTAL ROI (DOWN TO BUILD)			13.5	

Exhibit 11
JAPAN

```
-----
P                                          BUS. NO    6
I
M                                          PAGE   1
S
-----
```

LIMITED INFORMATION MODEL

ESTIMATE OF NORMAL ROI
BY CATEGORY OF IMPACT

			IMPACT OF FACTOR ON
F A C T O R S	PIMS MEAN	THIS BUSINESS	ESTIMATE OF ROI(%)
1 MARKET SHARE (%)	23.6	18.0	
2 RELATIVE MARKET SHARE (%)	61.7	24.0	
			-2.5
3 RELATIVE PRODUCT QUALITY	25.9	0.0	-2.8
4 RELATIVE PRICE	103.5	100.0	0.0
5 PERCENT EMPLOYEES UNIONIZED	48.3	50.0	-0.1
6 %NEW PRODUCT SALES / SALES	11.9	20.0	-1.1
7 R&D EXPENSE / SALES (%)	2.4	4.8	-1.7
8 MARKETING EXPENSE / SALES (%)	10.8	10.0	0.1

COMPETITIVE POSITION & ACTION IMPACT   -8.0

9 INVESTMENT / SALES (%)	56.1	61.9	
10 INVESTMENT/VALUE ADDED (%)	96.7	76.0	
			-0.9
11 FIXED CAPITAL INTENSITY (%)	52.3	78.2	-1.2
12 VERTICAL INTEGRATION (%)	58.8	81.0	1.9
13 VALUE ADDED/EMPLOYEE ($1000)	30.0	40.0	2.2
14 CAPACITY UTILIZATION (%)	79.6	110.0C	6.7

CAPITAL & PRODUCTION STRUCTURE IMPACT   8.8

15 REAL MARKET GROWTH RATE	8.2	10.0	0.3
16 SHARE OF 4 LARGEST FIRMS (%)	56.5	94.0	1.5
17 % OF CUSTOMERS = 50% SALES	12.2	10.0	0.0
18 PURCHASE AMOUNT-IMMED. CUSTS	5.2	5.0	0.3

MARKET ENVIRONMENT IMPACT   2.1

TOTAL IMPACT   2.9
AVERAGE ROI, ALL PIMS BUSINESSES   22.1

ESTIMATED ROI, THIS BUSINESS   25.0

C ... EXTREME VALUE COMPRESSED TO THIS LIMIT

Exhibit 12
JAPAN

P
I
M
S

BUS. NO 6

PAGE 3

STRATEGIC MOVES

ASSUME: INDUSTRY SALES GROWTH OF 10.0% PER YEAR FOR 5 YEARS
THIS CURRENT DOLLAR GROWTH REFLECTS
REAL MARKET GROWTH RATE OF 7.0%
SELLING PRICE GROWTH RATE OF 3.0%

	PRESENT	FUTURE
INDUSTRY SALES:	330.0	531.5

STRATEGIES CHANGING MARKET SHARE (%)

	PRESENT	1979 DOWN 20%	1979 HOLD	1979 BUILD 20%
MARKET SHARE (%)	18.0	14.4	18.0	21.6
RELATIVE MARKET SHARE (%)	24.0	18.4	24.0	30.1
RELATIVE PRODUCT QUALITY	0.0	-2.2	0.0	2.2
CAPACITY UTILIZATION (%)	110.0	95.0	95.0	95.0
INVESTMENT/VALUE ADDED (%)	76.0	88.0	88.0	88.0
INVESTMENT / SALES (%)	61.9	71.7	71.7	71.7
FIXED CAPITAL INTENSITY (%)	78.2	85.3	85.3	85.3
VALUE ADDED/EMPLOYEE ($1000)	40.0	40.9	40.9	40.9
: SALES	59.4	76.5	95.7	114.8
: NET INCOME	9.2	9.5	12.8	16.3
: INVESTMENT	36.8	54.9	68.6	82.3
: ROI	25.0	17.3	18.6	19.9
: CASH FLOW		1.1	0.0	-0.9
PAYOFF : INCREMENTAL ROI (DOWN TO BUILD)			25.0	

Exhibit 13
THIRD WORLD

```
-----
 P
 I                                               BUS. NO     7
 M
 S                                                 PAGE    1
-----


                    LIMITED INFORMATION MODEL
                    --------------------------
                       ESTIMATE OF NORMAL ROI
                       BY CATEGORY OF IMPACT


                                                 IMPACT OF
                                                 FACTOR ON
                                   PIMS    THIS   ESTIMATE
          F A C T O R S           MEAN  BUSINESS OF ROI(%)
          -------------------     ----- -------- ---------

 1 MARKET SHARE (%)               23.6    14.0
 2 RELATIVE MARKET SHARE (%)      61.7    21.0
                                                   -3.6
 3 RELATIVE PRODUCT QUALITY       25.9     0.0     -2.5
 4 RELATIVE PRICE                103.5   100.0      0.0
 5 PERCENT EMPLOYEES UNIONIZED    48.3    50.0     -0.1
 6 %NEW PRODUCT SALES / SALES     11.9    20.0     -1.1
 7 R&D EXPENSE / SALES (%)         2.4     4.8     -1.7
 8 MARKETING EXPENSE / SALES (%)  10.8    10.0      0.1
                                                  ------
            COMPETITIVE POSITION & ACTION IMPACT   -8.9

 9 INVESTMENT / SALES (%)         56.1    61.9
10 INVESTMENT/VALUE ADDED (%)     96.7    76.0
                                                   -0.9
11 FIXED CAPITAL INTENSITY (%)    52.3    78.2     -1.2
12 VERTICAL INTEGRATION (%)       58.8    81.0      1.6
13 VALUE ADDED/EMPLOYEE ($1000)   30.0    40.0      2.2
14 CAPACITY UTILIZATION (%)       79.6   110.0C     6.7
                                                  ------
            CAPITAL & PRODUCTION STRUCTURE IMPACT   8.4

15 REAL MARKET GROWTH RATE         8.2    17.0      1.0
16 SHARE OF 4 LARGEST FIRMS (%)   56.5    82.0      1.0
17 % OF CUSTOMERS = 50% SALES     12.2    10.0      0.0
18 PURCHASE AMOUNT-IMMED. CUSTS    5.2     5.0      0.3
                                                  ------
                  MARKET ENVIRONMENT IMPACT         2.3



                          TOTAL IMPACT              1.9
          AVERAGE ROI, ALL PIMS BUSINESSES         22.1
                                                  ------
              ESTIMATED ROI, THIS BUSINESS         24.0


        C ... EXTREME VALUE COMPRESSED TO THIS LIMIT
```

STRATEGIC MOVES

ASSUME: INDUSTRY SALES GROWTH OF   17.0% PER YEAR FOR   5 YEARS
          THIS CURRENT DOLLAR GROWTH REFLECTS
             REAL MARKET GROWTH RATE OF   14.0%
             SELLING PRICE GROWTH RATE OF   3.0%

	PRESENT	FUTURE
INDUSTRY SALES:	180.0	394.6

STRATEGIES CHANGING MARKET SHARE (%)

	PRESENT	1979 DOWN 20%	HOLD	BUILD 20%
MARKET SHARE (%)	14.0	11.2	14.0	16.8
RELATIVE MARKET SHARE (%)	21.0	16.3	21.0	26.0
RELATIVE PRODUCT QUALITY	0.0	-1.7	0.0	1.7
CAPACITY UTILIZATION (%)	110.0	95.0	95.0	95.0
INVESTMENT/VALUE ADDED (%)	76.0	88.0	88.0	88.0
INVESTMENT / SALES (%)	61.9	71.7	71.7	71.7
FIXED CAPITAL INTENSITY (%)	78.2	85.3	85.3	85.3
VALUE ADDED/EMPLOYEE ($1000)	40.0	40.9	40.9	40.9
: SALES	25.2	44.2	55.2	66.3
: NET INCOME	3.7	5.3	7.0	8.9
: INVESTMENT	15.6	31.7	39.6	47.5
: ROI	24.0	16.7	17.7	18.7
: CASH FLOW		-0.6	-1.3	-1.9
PAYOFF : INCREMENTAL ROI (DOWN TO BUILD)			22.8	

Appendix A

Definitions of the Input Data Items

1. PERCENT MARKET SHARE—The share of the served market for this business, expressed as a percentage.
2. PERCENT RELATIVE MARKET SHARE—The market share of this business relative to the combined market shares of its three leading competitors, expressed as a percentage. For example, if this business has 30 percent of the market and its three largest competitors have 20 percent, 10 percent, and 10 percent:

$$\text{Rel. Market Share} = \frac{30\%}{20\% + 10\% + 10\%} = 75\%$$

3. RELATIVE PRODUCT QUALITY—The percentage of sales volume from products and service that, from the perspective of the customer, are judged as superior to those available from leading competitors, minus the percentage judged as inferior. For example, if 60 percent of the sales volume of this business is from products that are thought of as superior and 20 percent is from those thought of as inferior:

$$\text{Rel. Product Quality} = 60\% - 20\% = 40\%$$

Note that the mean of Relative Product Quality is 22.1 percent, indicating that the typical PIMS business has a higher product quality than its competitors.
4. RELATIVE PRICE—The average level of selling prices of the products and services of this business, relative to the average level of its leading competitors. The average price of the competitors is 100 percent; if the average prices of the business are 5 percent higher, its price relative to competition is 105 percent.
5. PERCENT EMPLOYEES UNIONIZED—The percentage of total employees of this business who are unionized.
6. PERCENT NEW PRODUCT SALES/SALES—Percentage of sales accounted for by new products. New products are those products introduced during the three preceding years.
7. PERCENT R&D EXPENSES/SALES—Product or Service R&D expenses plus Process R&D expenses expressed as a percentage of sales. Product or Service R&D expenses include all expenses in-

curred to secure innovations and advances in the products or services of this business.

8. PERCENT MARKETING EXPENSES/SALES—The sum of sales force, advertising, promotion, and other marketing expenses expressed as a percentage of sales. Do not include costs of physical distribution.

9. PERCENT INVESTMENT/SALES—Investment as a percentage of sales. Investment can be measured in any of the following ways:

   - net book value of plant and equipment plus working capital
   - equity plus long-term debt
   - total assets employed minus current liabilities attributable to the business

10. PERCENT INVESTMENT/VALUE ADDED—Investment expressed as a percentage of value added. Value added is adjusted for profits to minimize that portion of the relationship with ROI which is caused by under- or over-stated earnings.

$$\frac{\text{Investment}}{\text{Value Added} - .5\,(\text{Net Income} - \text{PIMS mean ROI} \times \text{Investment})}$$

11. PERCENT FIXED CAPITAL INTENSITY—The gross book value of plant and equipment, expressed as a percentage of sales.

12. PERCENT VERTICAL INTEGRATION—Value added as a percentage of sales. Both value added and sales are adjusted for profits to minimize that portion of the relationship with ROI which is caused by under- or over-stated earnings.

$$\frac{\text{Value Added} - .5\,(\text{Net Income} - \text{PIMS mean ROI} \times \text{Investment})}{\text{Net Sales} - .5\,(\text{Net Income} - \text{PIMS mean ROI} \times \text{Investment})}$$

13. VALUE ADDED/EMPLOYEE ($1000)—Value added (adjusted for profits), expressed as thousands of dollars per employee.

$$.001 \times \frac{\text{Value Added} - .5\,(\text{Net Income} - \text{PIMS mean ROI} \times \text{Investment})}{\text{Total Number of Employees}}$$

14. PERCENT CAPACITY UTILIZATION—The average percentage of standard capacity utilized during the year. Standard capacity is the sales value of the maximum output this business can sustain with (a) facilities normally in operation and (b) current constraints

(e.g., technology, work rules, labor practices, etc.). For most manufacturing businesses, this will consist of 2 shifts, 5 days per week. For process businesses, a 3-shift, 6-day work week is typical.

15. REAL MARKET GROWTH RATE—The historical annual real (unit) growth rate of the market which this business serves, expressed as a percentage.

16. PERCENT SHARE OF 4 LARGEST FIRMS—The combined market shares of the four leading firms in the industry, expressed as a percentage.

17. PERCENT OF CUSTOMERS = 50% SALES—The best estimate of the percentage of immediate customers accounting for 50 percent of the sales of this business.

18. PURCHASE AMOUNT-IMMED. CUSTS.—The typical amount of products or services bought by an immediate customer in a single transaction. This factor is coded as follows:

    1 – between 0 and $1
    2 – between $1 and $10
    3 – between $10 and $100
    4 – between $100 and $1,000
    5 – between $1,000 and $10,000
    6 – between $10,000 and $100,000
    7 – between $100,000 and $1 million
    8 – between $1 million and $10 million
    9 – over $10 million

DISCUSSION QUESTIONS

TEX-FIBER INDUSTRIES—[E]

1. What do the "PAR" ROI reports show?
2. What do the "Strategic Moves" reports show?
3. What are the pros and cons of the LIM model?
4. What are the pros and cons of doing analysis at this level?

The
Formal Methods
Compared

Many would-be users of portfolio analysis, the market attractiveness-business position display, and PIMS are uncertain as to how they differ, whether they are substitute or complementary approaches, and when and how they may be used. This chapter, therefore, compares each methodology on a variety of dimensions including: (1) the dependent and independent variables utilized and the theoretical relationships on which each is based; (2) their role in the planning process; (3) the ability to assess past, present, and future competitive dynamics; (4) ways in which strategic *changes* can be explored; and (5) the organizational unit of analysis to which each can be applied. Each of these will be addressed in turn.

VARIABLES UTILIZED AND
THEIR THEORETICAL RELATIONSHIPS

Portfolio Analysis

The relative market share-market growth display rests on two major sets of assumed relationships:

1. Cash from operations is a function of cost/unit which in turn is a function of scale and experience, which finally is a function of relative market share.

2. Cash-need for investment in plant, equipment, and working capital is a function of industry growth rate.

Points 1 and 2 lead to the conclusion that:

3. Total cash flow is a function of relative market share and industry growth.

Plotting products (or "businesses") on a two-dimensional matrix where the axes are relative market share and growth can be used to classify products approximately as cash "cows," "stars," "question marks," or "dogs" according to cash-flow potential. However, *actual* cash flow can deviate from cash flow predicted by such a classification for a variety of reasons, as explained in Chapter 4.

1. Strategic changes are underway to increase or decrease market share. These may have short-run positive or negative effects on cash flow.
2. The supposed relationship between relative market share and cash flow may be weak.
3. The supposed relationship between industry growth rate and cash flow may be weak.

It is also important to note that while the two major relationships upon which the market share-market growth concept is based are intuitively appealing and seem to correspond closely to general experience; there is still only limited published *empirical* demonstration of their validity. This is not to say that the relationships are not true, but most of the empirical data are in the hands of management consultants who, understandably, have difficulty publishing client data. Table 15 in Chapter 6 is one of the few pieces of evidence available concerning the relationship between growth, share and cash flow. This shows that the hypothesized relationship certainly exists but that the amount of explanation provided by these two factors is relatively low.

Market Attractiveness-Business Position Analysis

This analysis is fundamentally different from portfolio analysis in three major respects. First, there is significantly less emphasis on relative costs (due to experience, or scale, or relative market share) and considerably more emphasis on other non-cost elements that distinguish one business from another. Second, there is considerably more emphasis on elements other than growth rate to assess the attractiveness of one market as opposed to another. Third, the dependent variable is usually presumed to be return on investment (ROI), not cash flow. High market attractiveness coupled with a strong business position could presumably result in high ROI but not necessarily high positive cash flow. Such might be the case, as pointed out in Chapter 5, in a high growth industry.

The inclusion of additional variables may lead to better predictions of performance than are possible with the simpler portfolio display. In particular, where performance is associated with other market elements than simply market growth, e.g., capital intensity or patent protection, these elements can be included. Further, the inclusion of other *company* variables such as relative technical capability, product quality, and marketing effectiveness, allows the prediction of performance where *effectiveness* as opposed to efficiency (due to scale or experience) is a key marketing requirement.

In spite of the inclusion of many more variables, only two dimensions, market attractiveness and business position, are usually included in a final display. Sometimes efforts are made to create these composite measures using some kind of weighting scheme. This is, of course, an arbitrary judgmental procedure. Appropriate weights may vary from market to market and business to business. Where the market is clearly segmented between, say, a price-oriented and performance-oriented segment, weights may be applied that reflect the business' strength in one dimension or another, i.e., each segment analyzed separately.

PIMS

The PIMS program employs considerably more variables than either of the previous methods. Taken together, PIMS' 37 factors account for over 80 percent of the observed variation in profitability across the 1,000 businesses in the data base.

This much longer list of explanatory variables includes industry growth rate and relative market share (although defined slightly differently), many of the additional variables suggested in the market attractiveness-business position approach, as well as other variables. The inclusion of these variables leads to specific predictions of ROI and cash flow, in contrast to the more general classifications which result from the two other techniques. All three of the major reasons, just cited, that might lead to disparity between actual and predicted cash flow in the market share-market growth display (i.e., strategic change, weak relative share-cash flow relationship, or weak industry growth-cash flow relationship), are dealt with explicitly in the PIMS model by the inclusion of other variables.

However, the employment of such a large variety of explanatory factors inevitably leads to statistical problems. In many cases, since the variables themselves are related to one another, the impact of *individual* factors on performance cannot be clearly isolated.[1] This would be the case, for instance, in trying to separate the impact of long- and short-run growth rate. Therefore, PIMS researchers have grouped variables into relatively independent clusters (industry/market environment, market position, extent of competitive differentiation, etc.). Within a cluster, the effects of individual variables are very hard to isolate from one another, but the effects of the clusters are more easily isolated.

In addition to the employment of many more *independent* variables, PIMS also differs from the other approaches in its selection of *dependent* variables. PIMS is actually based on two separate models, one used for predicting ROI, and the other for predicting cash flow, i.e.,

Model 1: ROI is a function of 37 factors.

Model 2: Cash flow is a function of 19 factors.

Some of the factors in the cash flow model are also in the ROI model; some are only used to predict cash flow.

PIMS is an *empirical* model. The 37 factors have been isolated through multiple-regression technques using real data from a large variety of businesses. Not only does PIMS include more variables and group them in more than two dimensions, it also replaces the somewhat arbitrary weighting scheme used to assess "company position" and "attractiveness," with an empirically derived weighting scheme. Furthermore, differences between actual and predicted cash flow or profit based on the PIMS model are made explicit in the form of "PAR" Reports. As the word implies, a "PAR" value of cash flow or profit is that value which might be predicted given the characteristics of that particular business and market. Since most, if not all, of the major strategic variables that might be expected to affect performance are included in the model, differences between PAR and actual performance can be at-

---

[1]The reason is a phenomenon that econometricians call multicollinearity. Other concerns have been levelled at the data base. First, that the period over which most of the data was collected, i.e., the early 1970s, was highly inflationary, and therefore not representative of less inflationary conditions. Second, that procedures for "cleaning" the input data by omitting "outliers," i.e., data that lie outside a predetermined range, bias the results and artificially improve the model's explanatory power. PIMS advocates maintain that while all these criticisms have statistical merit, no *better* way currently exists to deal with the complexities involved.

tributed mainly to non-strategic variables (such as operating management). This is in sharp contrast to the market share-market growth display and the market attractiveness-business position display, in which performance is not explicitly predicted.

It is important for users of the three methods to recognize that the data inputs differ substantially in terms of their measurability. Portfolio analysis and PIMS use measures that are mostly quantifiable. They are ambiguous only to the extent that the business and market can be defined ambiguously. As a result, it is difficult for planners located in a business unit to "fudge" the analysis and misrepresent the true investment opportunity to corporate management: this is *not* the case with the market attractiveness-business position display. Numerous qualitative judgments have to be made. It is possible, either through plain misjudgment or deliberate misrepresentation, to classify almost any unit so as to make it look like a strong candidate for further investment funds. It is up to corporate-level management, therefore, to fully understand the basis on which a display has been constructed. It should accept no display simply at its face value.

Apart from measurability, the difficulty of assembling the data required by the three approaches is very different. Whereas a simple display of relative share and growth can be easily and quickly constructed, a thorough analysis of market attractiveness and business position, or the preparation of PIMS input data for a business, is very demanding and time consuming.

ROLE IN THE PLANNING PROCESS

The three analytical approaches have different roles in the planning process.

Portfolio Analysis

The fundamental concept of a portfolio chart is that it allows the *simultaneous* comparison of many different products or businesses, however they are defined. It emphasizes the inherent balance between growth and cash.

Particularly in a cash-constrained environment, where outside debt or equity financing is limited, it provides graphic illustration of the fact that cash needed for one component of the portfolio must come from another. Thus portfolio analysis focuses attention on the dynamics of cash flow *among* businesses and forces the user to consider the reality of business interdependence in a resource allocation sense.

"Good," "balanced" portfolios can quickly be distinguished from "bad," "unbalanced" ones.

Portfolio analysis is of primary help in defining the "mission" for a particular business. It helps upper-level management to evaluate the cash consequences of strategic options proposed by managers responsible for lower-level business units. It also provides a visual display of a company's overall competitive stance in a number of related businesses vis-à-vis competitors. For lower-level management, portfolio analysis provides a framework for evaluating the current strategic role of a business vis-à-vis its competitors, and for considering future changes in strategy. Such changes cannot be evaluated directly, however. The costs and benefits have to be analyzed "off the chart" and a new display plotted showing future positions resulting from strategic changes.

Market Attractiveness-Business Position Analysis

The market attractiveness-business position display also allows simultaneous comparison of several businesses, but it does not indicate the internal cash relationships between one business and another. Rather, businesses usually are compared in terms of their expected ROI performance. This provides different and additionally useful information to strategic planners, since both cash flow and ROI potential are important ingredients to any designation of the unit's role in a portfolio.

Like portfolio analysis, this analytical approach is primarily used to define the mission of a business. But the display of market attractiveness and business position can be used to assess the *relative* attractiveness of different business investments, a feature portfolio analysis does not provide. Also, the underlying analyses needed to construct such a chart often help to identify critical requirements for success in that business.

Market attractiveness-business position analysis has one great advantage over other methods if it is done rigorously. In the second stage of analysis where *future* industry attractiveness and company position are considered, management must make explicit its assumptions about how the market will evolve. This includes changes in such factors as technology, segmentation, competitive structure, customer needs, distribution, etc. Thus the approach *forces* future oriented strategic thinking.

PIMS

Since it focuses on one business at a time, PIMS has typically been less concerned with portfolio relationships among businesses and more concerned with the strategy of each business unit. PIMS is useful at several stages in the planning process. First, it can be used to assess performance expectations of each business in terms of cash ·flow and ROI. This is of help to both upper- and lower-level management in defining a reasonable mission for each business. Second, the PAR Reports identify critical success factors. Third, strategy changes in terms of several key strategic factors can be explored quantitatively. Fourth, an approximate idea of the changes required in some key functional measures (such as marketing/sales and research and development/sales) is provided.

Although the list of capabilities sounds impressive, users often make the point that PIMS is more helpful in defining major strategic improvements that need to be made than in defining the specific actions needed to be taken to reach a new strategic position. The three variables that can be manipulated strategically—relative share, investment intensity, and vertical integration—are all relatively "high-level" variables, which cannot be controlled directly by management. For instance, to *achieve* greater market share, functional programs must be devised including marketing activities and budgets, research and development programs and budgets, decisions with respect to new plant expansion and process improvements, sales and service plans, etc. Although the experience of other businesses making such moves is incorporated in PIMS reports, judgment is still needed in deciding how functional strategies relate to, say, market share changes in a specific situation. In many cases, where more programs are being proposed than can be accepted, options have to be ranked on the expected contribution of each activity. PIMS provides no direct assistance in this task.

PIMS also takes no explicit account of future market evolution except in terms of sales, prices, and costs. Unlike market attractiveness-business position analysis, it cannot be used directly to explore the changing fit between company skills and the changing market environment in which the business competes. Table 1 summarizes these comparisons.

ASSESSING COMPETITIVE DYNAMICS

Portfolio Analysis

The portfolio display can be used to overlay the position of competitive products or businesses on company displays. Each competitive product may be plotted *separately* and represented by a circle whose position denotes its market share and industry growth rate, and whose size represents its sales volume.

Table 1

USEFULNESS OF THE THREE APPROACHES AT VARIOUS STAGES OF THE PLANNING PROCESS

	PORTFOLIO ANALYSIS	MARKET ATTRACTIVENESS/ BUSINESS POSITION ANALYSIS	PIMS
Step 1 Defining the business	Not applicable, although the "unit of analysis" must be defined before any of the methods can be used		
Step 2 a) Determining the current performance of the business in the portfolio	In terms of cash flow	In terms of ROI	In terms of cash flow and ROI
b) Determining the future mission	Useful for checking cash balance	Useful for assessing opportunity in terms of ROI	Useful for exploring goal trade-offs quantitatively
Step 3 Formulating functional plans	Not applicable	Judgmental only	Empirical association between mission and functional budgets
Step 4 Setting budgets	Not applicable	Not applicable	Empirical association between mission and functional budgets

This information can be used in three different ways. First, it provides a graphic representation of the relative size and strength of each major competitor in a market, making relationships much more apparent than they would be in a table of numbers. Determination of the relative strength or weakness of a competitive position sometimes may be made on visual evidence alone. Second, *changes* in competitive position may be plotted and competitive dynamics explored. Third, and perhaps most important, a plot of a competitor's *total* portfolio often provides considerable insight into where each competitor is relatively weak or strong and which businesses are slated for growth and which for harvesting. Competitive offenses may then be launched against positions of relative weakness and not against positions of strength. Sometimes companies may even deliberately launch an offensive in a unit of only limited potential in order to prevent a competitor using a strong cash position in such a segment to finance growth elsewhere.

Market Attractiveness-Business Position Analysis

Individual competitors can also be evaluated and plotted in a two-dimensional display using the market attractiveness-business position approach. However, comparisons are not in terms of an overall competitive portfolio, but in terms of individual products or businesses. Such an evaluation may be used to "second guess" competitors' plans to invest, hold, or liquidate position. It has to be borne in mind, however, that inputs about competitors are much more subjective than they are for portfolio analysis.

PIMS

The PIMS model cannot provide competitive insight about individual competitors. Competitive comparisons are made on several dimensions, such as relative market share, relative product quality, relative prices, relative marketing effort, etc. But, each comparison is made in terms of the value for the individual business versus the average for the three "leading" competitors. It is not possible to assess either the impact of individual competitor's moves over time, or the overall balance in terms of strong and weak positions in a competitor's portfolio.

This does not mean that competitive response is completely ignored in assessing strategic moves using the Strategy Sensitivity Reports. Instead, some "average" response based on the experience of other businesses in the data base making similar moves is implied by the costs and benefits predicted. Competitive response is thus automatically assumed in the model, but in a general way. It is, of course, theoretically possible to do a PIMS analysis of a competitor by entering data about its business instead of yours. Usually such data is very difficult to assemble, however.

EXPLORING STRATEGIC CHANGES

Portfolio Analysis

Movements of individual products or businesses on the portfolio chart are often highly indicative of actual or impending performance. The normal "success" sequence described in Chapter 4 is one in which share is captured during the growth phase of the market and then held in order to generate cash during maturity. There are many "disaster" sequences. The most common is never to achieve sufficiently high share during the growth phase so that in maturity costs are uncompetitive and cash flow is low. Another is to let a "star" dwindle in share as growth slows so that in maturity a "dog" rather than a "cash cow" results.

These patterns do indicate some generally desirable and undesirable strategic choices. But though suggestive, they by no means provide guidance on all the strategic options that occur. For example, when should a "cash cow" be slowly harvested for cash? When should a "dog" be divested? Which "question marks" should be selected for investment and which should be de-emphasized? Questions of this type can only be assessed as a result of a thorough analysis of customers, competitors, environmental trends, market characteristics, and internal company strengths as described in Chapter 2. The chart should not and cannot be used alone to assess the costs and benefits of strategic moves.

Nevertheless, in its simplicity portfolio analysis is very easy to use and discuss. It does provide a quick and easy organizing framework within which broad alternatives can at least be considered.

Market Attractiveness-Business Position Analysis

The market attractiveness-business position chart is simply a convenient display device for a thorough strategic analysis of a business and its market. Admittedly, the first stage of the analysis only serves to assess the present opportunity; however, the second stage, which takes into account future market changes and a variety of strategic moves to anticipate and respond to such changes, produces conclusions as to the relative desirability of different alternatives. These conclusions usually are not quantified empirically, but depend on management judgments and assessments of the weights to apply to various factors.

Thus this approach goes beyond portfolio analysis in its ability to aid management in assessment of future strategic changes. Necessarily it is far more time consuming, far more demanding in its data requirements, and much harder to use unambiguously as a framework for discussions between managers at different levels.

PIMS

Of the three methodologies, only PIMS quantitatively predicts the financial outcome of strategic changes. It allows the manager to explore the approximate impact of a variety of strategic moves in terms of cash flow, ROI, net income, and a variety of other derived measures. The manager using PIMS relies on the experience of many other businesses in a wide range of situations, making similar strategic moves from similar starting points.

But PIMS does not provide the user with a way to analyze the impact of *future changes in the market* (except sales, prices, and costs) on business strategy. The strategic changes that can be explored are limited to "realigning" current strategy. PIMS is most useful in assessing the viability of *today's strategy in today's market* and in suggesting ways to improve it. In this respect it falls short of market-attractiveness-business position analysis, which does provide the user with at least a qualitative way to consider future market changes and their impact on a firm's stragegy.

THE "UNITS OF ANALYSIS"

Portfolio Analysis

To be worthwhile, portfolio analysis should be carried out using "units of analysis" for which relative market share bears some relationship to costs. Otherwise the display becomes meaningless.

This means that a "circle" drawn on a portfolio chart ideally should represent an organizational unit that has its own dedicated manufacturing, sales, and research and development. If this is not the case and these or other resources are shared with other units, costs are hard to distinguish and the market share/cost relationship become less predictable.

In spite of these problems, however, portfolio displays are often drawn for individual products or market segments that share resources. One major reason is that share of a segment is easier to measure unambiguously than share of a total business; and so is market growth. A further reason is that some strategic *changes* are actionable at the individual program level and not at the overall business level. The user should, however, recognize the trade-offs that are implicitly being made. Measurability and the need to make actionable recommendations suggest defining the units of analysis narrowly; correspondence between relative market share and costs argues for defining the unit of analysis more broadly. If a narrow definition is used, it is often better to estimate actual costs and to view relative share skeptically as a relative cost surrogate.

Portfolio analysis may be carried out both for individual products and for market segments. Electro Industries might, for example, decide to (1) plot watches and calculators as circles on a portfolio chart and (2) repeat the analysis for watches and calculators combined, but with separate circles for branded- and private-label merchandise.

Because there are no assumed relationships between relative share and costs, assessments of attractiveness and position can be made equally well at several levels of aggregation as long as meaningful measures of the various factors can be made. Thus such analyses might be used by corporate management to assess competing business opportunities or by business-level management to assess competing program opportunities. In practice, as pointed out in Chapter 5, a level of aggregation is usually chosen that is meaningful strategically, i.e., a level at which plans are drawn up and implemented, and at which strategic decisions can be made relatively independently of strategic decisions for other units.

As with portfolio analysis, this methodology can be applied equally well to programs defined by products or market segments and may be repeated for both. For example, a business manager first may look at major product lines as contenders for scarce resources, and then at user industries or geographic market segments.

PIMS

Guidelines have been established by PIMS for deciding on an appropriate level and definition at which to conduct PIMS analysis (see Appendix B in the Tex-Fiber (C) case). These guidelines usually point to the "business unit" as a more appropriate level of analysis than individual program units such as products or market segments. However, it is suggested that in certain circumstances, it may be desirable to split an organizational unit into several parts for analytical purposes.

Users of PIMS should be aware of the trade-offs usually involved in choosing a particular level of analysis. Because the variables in PIMS have to be quantified, there is no opportunity to judgmentally combine perspectives from several different levels as there is in making assessments of market attractiveness or business position. PIMS is like portfolio analysis in this respect. If the "business unit" is chosen as the level of analysis, measures of market share and market growth rate may suffer from ambiguity since several distinct programs of activity are being combined. If, however, a lower level of aggregation such as an individual product or market segment is chosen, there is considerable difficulty in disentangling joint costs.[2] The relationship between market

---

[2]Joint costs are costs which result when two or more products share a common resource (e.g., a manufacturing facility) and the costs cannot be clearly allocated to one product or another.

share and profitability at the product or market segment level may just not be as pronounced as it is at the business level—the level at which the PIMS model has been constructed and "fitted" to empirical data.

These trade-offs are inevitable. Since choice usually involves a compromise, it is often wise to carry out PIMS analyses using several different definitions of the business. Indeed, this is true of all the analytical methods.

SUMMARY

The aids to strategic planning described in this chapter are used today in many enterprises. In spite of some of the conceptual difficulties pointed out, all these methodologies—properly applied—can be valuable to management seeking to bring order to the highly complex task of planning in a complex multiproduct, multimarket business environment. To use each properly requires understanding the underlying logic of each, which aspects of strategy they try to address, and the scope and limitation of each in the total planning process. As one consultant commented on portfolio analysis:

> The portfolio charts we use are simply partial aids to understanding highly complex relationships. We constantly caution executives to recognize that strategy formulation itself takes one into competitive, market-oriented, economic analyses which go far beyond these simple two-dimensional displays.

It seems to the authors that this perspective is a healthy one. The analytical approaches are *aids* to strategic planning and in no sense total strategic planning systems. In particular, none of the methods deal with the question of how to define the business, nor explicitly with the bridges between definition and other elements of strategy. This subject is taken up in the next chapter.

EXERCISE

The Tex-Fiber Industries Case Series (A through E) provides a variety of opportunities for applying each of the methodologies contrasted in this chapter, as well as for other more traditional qualitative analyses.

Using whatever methods, concepts, and analyses appear relevant, prepare a strategic market plan for the PPD division based upon all the cases in the series. The plan should include (but not necessarily be limited to):

1. A general statement of the strategy you propose.
2. The goals you believe should be targeted.
3. Pro forma profit and loss statements for the years 1975–1980.
4. The implications of your proposal for market share, net income and cash flow.
5. The relative emphasis on the various market segments in which PPD is active.
6. How you plan to implement your proposal.
7. Any other implications of your proposals, e.g., organizational changes, bonus schemes, and compensation schemes.
8. How the long-range plan and the short-range decision that must be taken for dealing with the recession in 1975, relate?
9. Comments about how portfolio analysis, the industry attractiveness-business position display, and/or PIMS have been used to aid in the development of the plan.

Creative and Managerial Aspects of Planning

PART

III

Defining the Business[1] and Making the Bridge to Other Strategic Decisions

8

While the answer to the question "What business are we in?" (i.e., defining the business) can be considered the starting point of strategic planning, we have deferred considering it until now for three reasons. First, you by now have a better appreciation of the significance of the problem, having wrestled with a variety of real-life cases in which firms confronted such issues. Second, there is a "chicken and egg" relationship between business definition and other elements of strategy. We have to define the business before we can make other decisions, yet these decisions often implicitly redefine the business. Such is the case with a decision to invest in product or market development, for example. Third, some aspects of definition require a creative skill in addition to the analytical skills and methodological skills discussed in earlier chapters.

What do we really mean by "defining the business"? In the case of Docutel Corporation, it took the form of deciding whether to expand internationally or into new customer areas such as gasoline dispensing and supermarket POS systems; whether to add "systems" capability to compete more effectively with NCR and Burroughs; and whether to offer regular human-operated bank terminals as well as automatic units. Decisions to change in any of these dimensions would have altered the scope of Docutel's business. Also, Docutel had to consider how to

---

[1]The subject matter of this chapter is dealt with in much greater detail in the forthcoming book by Derek F. Abell, *Defining the Business: The Starting Point of Strategic Planning,* to be published by Prentice-Hall in 1980.

segment the market it served, and to what extent its offerings should reflect differences among such segments. Should the major segmentation be by bank type? Geography? Product line within the bank system? Some other relevant dimension? Should different approaches be used for each chosen segment, or should differences be ignored and the offering standardized?

Differentiation, as pointed out in Chapter 2, is a double-edged sword; by tailoring the offering to more precisely meet the needs of each segment, a firm also seeks to differentiate itself from its competitors. The word "differentiation" is, unfortunately, often used so loosely that it is unclear whether differentiation exists across segments, among competitors, or both. We have already pointed out that as markets develop it is common to see product differentiation among competing suppliers diminish due to imitation, while product differentiation across segments increases as customer needs are satisfied more precisely. For instance in the soft-drink industry—many consumers perceive little difference between Coke and Pepsi, yet there are substantial differences between the diet and regular varieties offered by both brands.

Speer Industries provides us with another example of a firm wrestling with its business definition. Should the Brite Division have redefined itself by adding a low-cost chromotograph? To what extent should this offering differ from the high-priced line? Should the Reliance Division develop new specialty products in contrast to the relatively low-technology products aimed at satisfying standard customer functions today? How should the SPD Division define its scope, given so many apparent options to choose from? (Look back, for example, at Exhibit 7 in the Speer (A) case, p. 40.) And, of course, should all four divisions be integrated in some way and defined as a "Scientific Products" business? If so, what scope should it have and how and to what extent should the various activities be differentiated from one another and from the activities of competitors?

In other cases, the Electro Industries and the Tex-Fiber Industries series, for example, the question of definition was less explicit. Nevertheless, both companies had to deal with this question in their planning. Should Electro offer a full line of consumer electronic products? Should Tex-Fiber segment its markets and differentiate its approach by geographic region and end-use industry as well as by major product lines?

Business definition is the first step in strategic market planning for two major reasons. First, business definition is a creative decision in its own right that can fundamentally affect the health of the business. Docutel, for example, lost market share rapidly once major computer manufacturers redefined the business as a "systems" purchase. To remain viable, Docutel was under pressure either to redefine its activities by extension to new non-bank applications (supermarkets, gasoline stations, etc.), or to find a creative way to segment the bank business to insulate itself from competition. It appears from this case example that some definitions of a business are strategically superior to others, either because they better satisfy customers' requirements, and/or because they lead to competitively lower costs, and/or because they fit the distinctive competence of the company particularly well, and/or because they insulate the business from competition.

Second, in spite of the "chicken and egg" relationship between business definition and other strategic decisions, a definition of the business and its segmentation logically precedes all other strategic decisions. An assessment of the relative viability ("attractiveness") of a particular definition is an input to decisions with respect to *mission*, i.e., to invest in, maintain, or withdraw from a business, as we have seen in earlier chapters. But definition also influences *organizational strategy* (and, therefore, indirectly the choice of a unit of analysis for planning purposes), and *functional strategy*. Specific functional plans for actually satisfying customer needs can only be formulated once business scope, segmentation, and differentiation have been explicitly considered. We say "considered" as opposed to "decided" to explicitly recognize that business definition influences, and is influenced by, other strategic decisions.

This chapter first takes up the question of how to conceptualize business definition. This is then extended to ways to conceptualize market boundaries and hence to measure market share. Guidelines are then offered on how to actually reach decisions about business scope, segmentation, and differentiation—and the major factors that have to be considered in the process.

From this foundation, we shall consider how bridges have to be made between (1) business definition and mission, (2) business definition and organizational strategy (even though organzational strategy is *not* a major theme of this book, it will be considered here because of its relationship to the strategic definition of the business), and (3) business definition and functional strategies.

CONCEPTUALIZING BUSINESS DEFINITION

A business may be defined in one of two ways: either in terms of its served market, or in terms of the products or services of which it is comprised. Served market is a definition from the demand side, whereas products or services constitute a supply-side definition. Thus we may describe Docutel as a company serving the bank customers' needs for automated cash dispensing and withdrawal (its served market) or as a company manufacturing automatic cash dispensing and withdrawal machines (its product line).

Descriptions of product and served market together encompass three dimensions:

1. The *customer group* dimension, or *WHO* is being served. Several alternative classification schemes may be possible, based on such familiar dimensions as geography, user industry, demography, buying behavior, etc. In the case of Docutel, *banks in the United States* are the primary customer group.
2. The *customer function* dimension, or *WHAT NEED* is being satisfied. Sometimes products are multifunctional in that they serve clusters of related needs; in other cases, the business serves multiple customer functions but with separate products. Docutel serves the *cash dispensing and withdrawal* function.
3. The *technological* dimension, or *HOW* customer functions are being satisfied. Often several different possibilities (technologies) exist for satisfying the same function. Docutel, for example, defines its business in terms of *automatic* teller machines. (Human-operated teller terminals are an alternative "technology" for performing the same functions, but were not part of Docutel's original definition.)

Usually it is necessary to define a business in terms of its "product-market" strategy rather than in terms of either products or served markets alone. First, descriptions of products typically are in terms of technology and function performed; descriptions of served markets are typically in terms of customer groups and functions served. Thus neither description alone usually provides a complete *three-dimensional* definition in terms of customer groups, customer functions, and technologies. The three dimensions are important for determining *scope, segmentation,* and *differentiation.*

Scope defines the *extent* to which a business participates in one or more customer groups, one or more customer functions, and one or more technologies. Initially Docutel focused on one major customer group (banks), a narrow range of functions (cash dispensing and deposit), and one technology (automatic tellers). This definition was in sharp contrast to the definitions of its much larger competitors.

Segmentation and differentiation define *how* a business participates along *each* of the three dimensions, even though we usually think of it in terms of customer groups only: One customer group may, of course, differ from another in its needs (e.g., banks versus supermarkets or savings banks versus commercial banks); but also one customer function may require different marketing approaches than another (e.g., cash dispensers versus computer CPUs and software); and products based on one technology may differ in their marketing requirements from products based on an alternate technology (e.g., automatic versus human tellers). A company may or may not decide to recognize such potential segmentation on each dimension and to differentiate its offering accordingly. Creativity enters in deciding, from among the many ways to segment either customer groups, customer functions, or technologies, which ways provide distinctly improved customer satisfaction, the chance to bring distinctive competence to bear, and insulation from imitation by competitors.

In addition to being defined by customer groups, customer functions, and technologies, which may be regarded as "horizontal" dimensions, a business may also be defined "vertically." Is the business integrated backward into the manufacture of components or raw material supplies—as some automobile companies are with respect to glass manufacture? Conversely, is the business integrated forward into "downstream" activities? This may mean owning and operating a channel of distribution—as major gasoline producers operate filling stations, or fabricating, say, a raw material into finished products—as aluminum manufacturers produce beverage cans and household foil.

Let us now look at the implications of individual business definition for overall market definition.

DEFINING MARKET BOUNDARIES
AND MEASURING MARKET SHARE

The product-market definitions of a business used by competitors can be similar or different from ours—as, for example, Docutel's definition of the business as an "automatic bank teller" business differs from Burroughs' definition as an "Electronic Funds Transfer System" business. When similar definitions are used, market-share measurement is straight-forward; when they are different, several interpretations are possible. In the former case, the "total" market has the same boundary definition as the product-market of each competitor. Market share is then measured simply by the proportion of sales that each competitor has in this market. In the case of different definitions, the "total" market has no clear meaning since competitors differ in their product and served market definitions. If market shares of each individual competitor are measured in terms of their *own* product definition and served market, they will probably not add up to 100 percent.

In the market for laboratory ovens, for example, two major types of competitors coexist. The first type is an oven-maker, selling ovens (both electric and microwave) to institutional and consumer markets as well as to laboratories. The second type is a specialist in the manufacture and distribution of laboratory apparatus. This type sells a wide line of laboratory equipment including ovens, incubators, baths, pumps, measuring instruments, and laboratory hardware. The first type of competitor defines its business broadly by customer group and technology, and narrowly by customer function (ovens); the second type of competitor defines its business narrowly by customer group (laboratories only) but broadly by customer function.

We shall now consider in more detail the measurement of market share when competitors define their activities similarly, and when they define them differently.

Competitors Similarly Defined

Although there is no ambiguity about the meaning of market share and total market when competitors are similarly defined, there is still a question as to the appropriate *level* at which share should be measured —for the business as a whole or for each separate program within the business. For example, General Foods might measure its overall share of the coffee business or it might measure its share of instant coffee, or decaffeinated coffee, or coffee sold in the New England region. The measure chosen depends on the *purpose* for which the measure is used.

There are two major ways in which market share measures can be used: (1) as a yardstick of market performance, and (2) as an indicator of relative cost position or relative market power. When it is used as a measure of performance, share should be measured *for each individual program* of activity. General Foods might, for example, measure its performance in instant coffee, decaffeinated coffee, or in different geographic regions. It might even choose to measure performance in subsegments of these markets. When market share is used as an indicator of relative costs or market power, a broader measure is usually needed. The total market in which share is measured should be broad enough to allow differences between competitors in resource scale or experience to be accounted for. If, for example, a single manufacturing plant supplies a product nationwide, market share measures at the regional level are unlikely to indicate much about relative manufacturing costs. Only nationwide share measures can do that. Likewise, if a "pooled" sales force is used to sell many different products in a product line, individual product-market shares are unlikely to accurately indicate relative selling costs. A measure of the share of *total* sales volume is important to do this. The key is to define market boundaries so that major cost components are encompassed in the definition.

Competitors Differently Defined

The number of ways in which competitors may define a business differently is infinite. It helps, however, to try to visualize, in a three-dimensional display, how each separate competitor defines its own business. Figure 1 shows, using only a limited number of competitors as an example, how this might look. Figure 1a shows a situation in which only one major technological solution is feasible; Figure 1b shows a situation in which several technological solutions are feasible (e.g., frozen versus refrigerated packaged foods versus fresh foods).

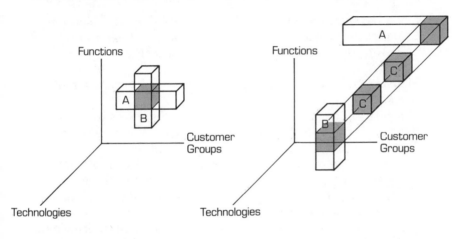

**1a—One Feasible
Technological Solution**   **1b—Several Feasible
Technological Solutions**

Figure 1
Contrasting Competitive Definitions

In Figure 1a, Competitor A is broadly defined in terms of customer groups served but focused in terms of customer functions and technologies; Competitor B is broadly defined in terms of customer functions served but focused in terms of customer groups and technology. This corresponds quite closely to the two classes of competitors described earlier in the laboratory oven example. In Figure 1b, Competitor A is broadly defined by customer group and narrowly by function; Competitor B is defined broadly by function but narrowly by customer groups, while Competitor C is narrowly defined by both customer and function but offers products based on several substitute technologies.

In these situations, "market share" can take on a variety of meanings depending on which "market" definition is used. There are three major possibilities:

1. as a percentage of *all* sales in the various product lines/served markets of the different competitors,
2. as a percentage of the sales for which all competitors compete (the shaded areas in Figure 1), or
3. as a percentage of a *particular* competitor's product/served market definition only.

Using the same dichotomy as before between market share as a measure of performance and market share as an indicator of cost or market power, we may draw the following conclusions:

- Measure (a) is probably meaningless and inappropriate for either purpose.
- Measure (b) should be used as a measure of performance only. In the case of ovens described above, the share of laboratory ovens should be looked at solely as a performance measure.
- Measure (c) cannot be used directly to assess *relative* cost position since each competitor's share is measured in a different served market. Competitors' shares will therefore not add up to 100 percent. In the laboratory oven example, the costs of laboratory ovens for firms specializing in ovens must be assessed from data on their total oven sales; the costs of laboratory ovens for firms specializing in laboratory apparatus must be assessed from data on their total laboratory apparatus sales.

CHOOSING A DEFINITION
OF THE BUSINESS

Unfortunately, it is relatively rare to find managements consciously and explicitly setting guidelines for defining a business. Businesses are often defined by accident rather than design—by new product activity in one, two, or all three dimensions. Each product (or market) extension is looked at primarily on its own merits and not on the basis of its overall strategic impact. Thus actions shape the definition rather than the definition shaping actions.

To make matters worse, the business literature offers little beyond general exhortations to be defined in one dimension or another. Theodore Levitt[2] has suggested that companies should avoid "marketing myopia." This implies presumably that they should define themselves broadly in terms of the *function* being performed as opposed to a particular technology ("we are in the transportation business not the railroad business"; "the energy business not the oil business"; etc.). Mack Hanan[3] has suggested alternatively that *customers* should be the basis for business definition and that growth should occur by asking the question "What other needs of the customers we know so well can we serve profitably?" Still others have argued that skill in a particular technology should provide the basis for growth and new product development. None of these prescriptions tells management which factors should be considered in any *particular* situation. Nor are any guidelines provided as to either scope or degree of segmentation (and differentiation) along dimensions other than the one highlighted by each advocate. The problem is to decide: (a) what scope is desirable along each axis, and (b) how the market should be segmented and to what extent differentiation should be pursued.

Scope

In addition to a critical evaluation of each new product addition, deletion, or market extension in its own right, four questions have to be considered at an overall strategic level:

1. What *potential customer benefits* result from broad or narrow definition along any of the three dimensions? In terms of functions, customers may favor buying a complete "system," as in the case of automatic teller machines; in terms of customer groups, there may be benefits to selling to more than one group, as in the case of branded products having "international" identity such as Coke; in terms of technologies, customers may favor a source offering several alternative technological solutions, as in the case of building-insulation supply.

2. Are there any *potential cost efficiencies* from broad definition along any of the three dimensions? This might occur as a result of

---

[2]Theodore Levitt, "Marketing Myopia," *Harvard Business Review*, September–October 1975.
[3]Mack Hanan, "Reorganize Your Company Around Its Market," *Harvard Business Review*, November–December 1974.

either scale or shared experience. Quite often, a broad definition in terms of customer groups served may lead to manufacturing efficiencies; a broad definition in terms of customer functions served may lead to distribution and marketing efficiencies (as a result of carrying a broad product line). In all likelihood, the oven manufacturers described earlier have lower manufacturing costs, while laboratory apparatus manufacturers have lower sales, distribution, and service costs.

3. How different are the marketing, manufacturing, research and development, service, and distribution *requirements* along each of the three dimensions? If, for example, the manufacturing task to produce an ATM and a human-operated teller are very different, it might argue against being in both "technologies." If the marketing task in selling automatic dispensing devices to supermarkets and gas stations is very different from that required in banks, this might argue against selling to these other customer groups. If the research and development requirements for building a whole bank EFTS system are very different than that for ATMs alone, this might argue against a broad functional definition.

4. Does the *company* have the skill to span a definition of activity that seems to make sense from other viewpoints? Docutel, for example, may believe that ATMs are becoming part of an EFTS system purchase and that there are some cost advantages to selling a broad line of equipment to banks, but simply not have the expertise to design, manufacture, or sell EFTS systems.

Segmentation and Differentiation

Knowing how to segment a market and knowing when and to what extent to differentiate the offering to each segment is often the most creative part of strategy formulation. Segmentation (and its counterpart, differentiation) usually has a cost and a benefit. Costs are incurred because segmentation implies *customization* of the offering to meet customer needs more precisely; benefits result because customers are likely to be attracted to the manufacturer who comes closest to satisfying their needs.

As pointed out in Chapter 2, an *efficient* strategy usually results when a company defines its activity broadly on one or more dimensions and pursues an *undifferentiated* product strategy across segments along each of these dimensions. It is generally relying on low-cost position to achieve competitive market advantage (possibly through low prices). The company relies on *standardizing* marketing, manufacturing, distribution, research and development, services, etc. The advantages of such an approach are the potential scale economies and/or experience effects asssociated with higher volumes of standardized products. The emphasis is on process improvement as opposed to product performance improvement. Ford Motor Company's approach to automobile marketing in the early 1920s typifies this approach ("you can have any color you want as long as it's black").

If, by contrast, a company either defines itself narrowly along each of the three dimensions (a so-called "concentrated" strategy) or *differentiates* its offering to each major segment, it is usually seeking to be particularly *effective* in meeting the needs of customers. The advantages of such an approach are in the potential benefits of specialization. While there are often non-price benefits such as superior product quality, technical assistance, or channel services, in some cases price may be the particular benefit sought. Such might be the case when a manufacturer, by virtue of being a dominant factor in a specialized niche, achieves a superior cost position as a result of its specialized experience.

Making the trade-off between an undifferentiated, broad, efficiency-based strategy and a differentiated or focused effectiveness strategy requires consideration of similar factors to those used to define scope. This time the questions appear in a slightly different guise, however.

1. What is the nature of *customer buying behavior*—in particular, how much do customers value low price in relation to non-price benefits?
2. Are *cost economies* available through standardization, or alternatively through achieving a dominant position in a specialized niche? Conversely, what are the *cost penalties* of specialization?
3. What impact will segmentation and differentiation have on the relative similarity or difference in marketing, manufacturing, research and development, service, and distribution requirements?
4. Does the *company* have the skill to span the differentiated requirements of a segmented market?

Often only qualitative answers can be given to these questions. Nevertheless, the questions must be asked, and repeated as segmentation/differentiation possibilities on each of the three dimensions are considered.

You may well conclude from the foregoing that segmentation is not so much a creative task as a judgmental one. But that is because the foregoing is concerned with the *extent* of segmentation/differentiation and not with *how* the market should be segmented in the first place. Creativity is particularly important in addressing this latter question.

Let us consider some examples:

- The Norton Company, a manufacturer of abrasives of many different types, recognized significant differences in the needs of large customers buying large orders. These customers needed substantial inventory backup, fast delivery, and other specialized distribution services. By segmenting their market in terms of customer size and order size instead of by type of grinding wheel sold, they were able to make considerable gains in market share to that particular segment.
- "Plug compatible" computer peripheral-manufacturers correctly identified the fact that a segment of IBM's customer base did not need all the extra services that IBM supplied; this segment included experienced purchasers who were prepared to buy individual peripheral components as opposed to computer systems if prices were lowered sufficiently. In the late 1960s, they began to make considerable inroads into IBM's previously impregnable market position.

These two examples illustrate the creative (and complex) nature of segmentation. There are usually many *different* ways to subdivide and categorize customer groups, customer functions, or technologies. Banks, for example, may be described as large or small, metro or rural, innovative or conservative, commercial or S&L's. These are all different ways to subdivide on the customer group dimension. The function performed by a supplier for a bank may be divided into terminal functions (e.g., cash dispensing) and computer-software functions. Alternatively, they may be subdivided in terms of whether the supplier provides a full-service backup or a partial-service backup. These are different ways to subdivide on the customer function dimension. Finally, technologies may be subdivided as human-operated or automatic, electromechanical or electronic, and optical-card reading or magnetic-card reading.

Creative segmentation involves the identification of a fruitful way to subdivide on one or more of these dimensions, as Norton did in abrasives, and as plug compatible computer manufacturers did for computer peripherals. In the former case, segmentation was in terms of customer groups (large customers having special needs related to large-volume purchasing). In the second case, segmentation was in terms of specific customer functions (initially, tape drives) purchased by specific customer groups (those with substantial buying experience—initially, the Federal Government).

Let us review what we have said about business definition so far, before moving ahead and discussing how it relates to other strategic decisions:

First, we have stated that each business can be defined along three axes—customer groups served, customer functions served, and technologies used to serve those functions.

Second, we have stated that two measures, scope and segmentation/differentiation, are necessary to describe the way a business is defined.

Third, we have stated that a business may or may not choose to recognize differences in the requirements of satisfying different customers and different functions, and of satisfying them with different technologies. Usually, the *physical* product will differ in the case of different functions and technologies, but there is still a question as to how much to standardize marketing and service arrangements.

Fourth, we have stated that competitors often choose dissimilar definitions of the business and do not compete from the same perspective. This makes it difficult to define market boundaries and to measure share.

Fifth, we have stated that choice of business definition should be made *explicity* with due consideration for customer satisfaction, costs, differences/similarities in resource requirements, company skills, and competitive position.

Sixth, we have stated that there is a creative aspect to segmentation, and that the *basis* on which the market is segmented is as important as the extent to which segment differences are recognized by differentiated approaches.

Now we are in a position to go on and examine how such definitional decisions relate to other strategic decisions—in particular, the mission of the business, organizational choices, and functional strategy choices.

RELATING BUSINESS DEFINITION AND MISSION

Business definition and mission are interrelated in two ways. First, mission choices can affect business definition. A decision to invest (or disinvest) in a particular segment of activity will expand (or contract) the scope of the business in that particular direction. For example, a shift in emphasis by Tex-Fiber Industries toward FAS and away from oils would ultimately alter the scope of the business. FAS products perform certain functions that oils do not perform; also, the customers served differ. A decision to drop out of Europe in favor of the Third World would also directly alter scope in terms of customer groups served.

Second, business definition can affect the choice of mission. When, as a result of market evolution, a particular business definition becomes less attractive over time (as happened to Docutel), serious consideration should be given to redesignating the mission of the business—for example, from "star" to "cash cow" or from "question mark" slated for heavy investment to "question mark" slated for liquidation. In many cases, of course, the definition can be changed to protect the long-term viability of the business, or new ways can be found to creatively segment the market. Even if this is possible, the mission of the business may need to be reconsidered. Conversely, the emergence of a new attractive opportunity to change scope (as Golden Wonder confronted in the U.K. potato chip industry described in Chapter 2) may call for an increase in investment funds directed toward a particular business.

RELATING BUSINESS DEFINITION AND ORGANIZATIONAL STRATEGY[4]

In modern diversified corporations, the lines that delineate one business from another are redrawn frequently. Two separate but related divisions may be consolidated; one large division may be split into two; a new business may have its early development as a spin-off from an existing business; or an acquisition may be integrated into an existing division. More fundamental regroupings may take place—for example, a corporation previously organized around geographic markets may be reorganized into world-wide product divisions, or vice versa.

Organizational redesign is necessary because businesses are being redefined strategically in a never-ending process. For example, new applications are found for one division's technology among customers previously served only by another division; or decisions are reached to market the products of two separate divisions as complete "systems." In such cases, organization design should reflect market strategy. As market conditions evolve and as businesses are redefined strategically to take advantage of new opportunities, organizational structure must change also.

But the organizational structure may frequently lag behind the proper strategic definition, or occasionally lead it. This happens be-

---

[4]A thorough treatment of this subject can be found in E. Raymond Corey and Steven H. Star, *Organizational Strategy: A Marketing Approach* (Boston: Division of Research, Harvard Business School, 1970), Chapters 1–5.

cause strategic redefinition is a continuous process, but reorganization occurs only occasionally at isolated points in time. Thus, a division or product department may contain several relatively autonomous "businesses" that have not yet been given distinct organizational recognition. This often happens when the businesses are not large enough yet to support the administrative and overhead burden associated with complete organizational independence. Or, two divisions may continue to operate independently even though their activities are closely related. Or, organizational separation may occur in advance of the strategic evolution of a fully fledged independent business with the objective of stimulating such development.

The recognition that organizational lines may *not* correspond at a particular time period with lines drawn on the basis of strategic considerations is of vital concern to strategic market planners. Often, hard choices have to be made between carrying out strategic analyses, such as portfolio or PIMS analyses, using business definitions corresponding to established organizational entities (making internal data relatively easy to obtain) or using definitions that are superior strategically, but have no organizational counterpart.

Just as product-market scope has its analog in the organizational definition of a business unit, product-market segmentation has its analog in the organization's program units. And just as the organizational definition of a business may not correspond exactly with the strategic definition of product-market scope at a particular time period, program unit definition may lag behind strategic segmentation schemes. On the other hand, creative market segmentation is often implemented through a creative redesign of the organization's program structure in *anticipation* of the emergence of important new segments.

Sometimes, businesses are subdivided into programs in more than one way. In the 1970s, for example, IBM had both product and market managers. Product managers had responsibility for major product lines (such as the IBM 360, 370, etc.); market managers had responsibility for each of the major customer groups (such as hospitals, banks, educational institutions, etc.) to which the products were sold. This is called a *bilateral* program structure. Organizations that divide into program units along only one dimension (e.g., product lines only) are said to have *unilateral* program structures.

Recognition that program units may not correspond at a particular time period with strategic segmentation *also* presents an analytical problem for planners. It is analogous to the lack of correspondence between organizational lines and strategic definition at the level of the overall business. Choices may have to be made as to whether organizational units or units defined in terms of market segmentation schemes are to be used for purposes of analysis. Often, when the choice is not clear, we recommend doing both.

It is worth reiterating that there is a "chicken and egg" relationship between strategic business definition, organizational design, and the choice of appropriate units for planning. Often, management cannot plan effectively because organizational "program" units do not exist for which planning can be conducted. This was the case at Tex-Fiber Industries' PPD division. It was virtually impossible to develop strategic market plans or to allocate resources selectively to either geographic areas or end-user industries because these segments of the overall business had no organizational counterpart. PPD's major competitor, Standard American, reputedly operated with a much more elaborate program structure.

In such cases, some preliminary planning may be needed to identify relevant segmentation schemes. This is a necessary prelude to reorganization. Subsequently, planning becomes the responsibility of program management for the newly defined organizational units. This process is a continuing one. Planning results in business redefinition and innovative segmentation; reorganization then redefines the business and program units around which planning itself is organized.

RELATING BUSINESS DEFINITION TO FUNCTIONAL STRATEGIES[5]

Functional strategy decisions (i.e., marketing mix[6] decisions, and decisions about policies and programs for manufacturing, distribution, R&D,[7] procurement, etc.) derive from the definition of the business. For this purpose, we may think of a definition described, as before, in terms of

1. scope, and
2. the basis for segmentation and extent of differentiation. Each of these will be dealt with in turn.

---

[5]See John M. Hobbs and Donald F. Heany, "Coupling Strategy to Operating Plans," *Harvard Business Review*, May–June 1977.

[6]The term "marketing mix" was coined by Professor Neil Borden in the 1950s. It refers to "the apportionment of effort, the combination, the designing, and the integration of the elements of marketing into a program or 'mix' which on the basis of an appraisal of market forces will best achieve the objectives of an enterprise at a given time." The most important elements of the "mix" are product policy, channel policy, advertising and promotion policy, and prices.

[7]See Gluck, Foster, and Forbes, "Cure for Strategic Malnutrition," *Harvard Business Review*, November–December 1976.

Relationship Between Scope and Functional Strategy

Choices of scope have, or should have, their primary impact on product development activities. In many companies that do not explicitly consider overall scope as an important determinant of customer satisfaction or costs, the converse is probably true: product development activities ultimately determine scope. Ideally, consideration of the four factors suggested earlier should alert management to the pros and cons of being broadly or narrowly defined on each of the three axes— and should be a central consideration in the selection of new products, decisions to expand into new markets, and product abandonment. Thus, scope affects R&D, sales, and distribution strategy. Indirectly, it impacts on manufacturing because decisions to broaden or narrow scope will alter the mix of products flowing through the plant.

Relationship Between Segmentation/ Differentiation and Functional Strategies

At this point, we must take care to remember the distinction between differentiation of the offering *across segments* and segmentation leading to differentiation of the offering from competitive offerings, i.e., *across competitors*. Docutel, for example, treats small rural S&Ls differently from large, metropolitan commercial banks. The former purchase fewer units, have less sophisticated systems requirements, and generally demand less uptime. But Docutel also differentiates itself from its competitors by offering higher levels of uptime and service in *all* applications. In this sense, it is appealing to a class of customers who value, and are prepared to pay for, reliability. Both forms of differentiation influence functional strategies.

Segmentation/Differentiation Across Segments When a company differentiates its offering across customer groups, customer functions, or technologies, fragmentation of functional activities can result. Marketing programs have to be tailored to each segment. R&D programs are aimed at developing special products to suit special functional or technological needs; and manufacturing is likely to be customized. Conversely, when an undifferentiated approach across segments is chosen, marketing, R&D, and manufacturing can become more standardized.

Segmentation/Differentiation Across Competitors When a company differentiates itself from its competitors, functional activities may or may not be fragmented. They will, however, reflect the "theme" that distinguishes the company from its rivals. "Theme" is often difficult to quantify and measure but may nevertheless unify marketing, manufacturing, and R&D, etc., around the satisfaction of a particular set of customer needs. In the television industry, for example, Zenith has traditionally emphasized product reliability; Silvertone (Sears' brand) has relied on superior service, credit facilities, and Sears' store image; others have emphasized portability, color tone, or the set as a piece of furniture.[8] In the photography field, Kodak has traditionally emphasized "ease of use" while Polaroid has emphasized "instant" photography.

Whatever the theme, there are implications for all functional strategies. Let us take Zenith, for example. Reliability implies superior product quality, advertising and promotion designed to reinforce the consumer's perception of reliability, channel and service policies that back up the claim, manufacturing policies that emphasize tight quality-control, and R&D policies designed to improve product reliability as opposed to, say, color tone or aesthetic values.

Functional strategies, therefore, are influenced, or should be influenced, by several aspects of business definition. Where companies fail to *think* strategically, the reverse is often true. Functional strategy decisions, often reached without regard for broader strategic considerations, implicitly determine scope, differentiation across segments, and differentiation from competitors. This is putting the cart before the horse.

SUMMARY

Business definition may be considered as the starting point of strategic planning, yet in practice other strategic decisions may have to be at least considered before any final decisions are made. There is thus, we believe, a "chicken and egg" quality to definitional choices as they relate to other strategic questions.

Businesses may be defined in terms of their scope and segmentation/ differentiation along the three axes of customer groups, customer functions, and technologies. Since an almost infinite variety of possibilities exist for defining a business, in many markets competitors define their activities differently. This makes it difficult to define market boundaries and to measure market share unambiguously.

Business definition requires that four major factors be considered *in addition* to individual assessments of the desirability of entering new

---

[8]See Nelson W. Foote, "Market Segmentation as a Competitive Strategy." Presented to the Consumer Market Segmentation Conference, American Marketing Association, Chicago, February 24, 1967.

product markets. They are (1) customer behavior with respect to scope and segmentation, (2) cost behavior and potential cost efficiencies, (3) similarities/differences in "resource" requirements, and (4) company skills.

Choices of business definition relate to choices of business mission, organizational choice, and functional strategy choices. Successful planning requires that the "bridges" between these various strategic decisions are clearly understood and explicitly considered.

SANDS, TAYLOR & WOOD[1]

Sands, Taylor & Wood and its subsidiary companies sold a line of over 1,000 items to the food industry. In July 1976, following three substantial acquisitions over the preceding eight years, Frank Sands, the President, found himself pondering some very fundamental questions about the future of the business. As he put it:

Who Are We?

What Do We Do?

What Business Are We In?

How Do We Conceive of Ourselves?

How Should We Conceive of Ourselves Five Years from Now?

In particular, he believed that with the acquisitions behind him, he needed some clear criteria for introducing new products and evaluating their performance prospects on a long range basis. Many options for new development seemed open. The challenge was to shape the choices in a way which would fully exploit the potential for growth which he believed the acquisitions provided.

As a first step towards the resolution of these issues, two committees were appointed "to take a closer look at Sands, Taylor & Wood's current and future product offerings." These were:

1. A new Products Development Committee (see Exhibit 1).
2. A Product Elimination Committee.

COMPANY BACKGROUND

Sands, Taylor & Wood was founded in 1790 by Henry Wood who commissioned imported flour on Boston's Long Wharf under the name of Henry Wood & Son. Wood acted as a distributor for the flour to bakers and other distributors. In 1800, Henry Wood hired a salesman named John L. Sands—great-great-grandfather to the present president—who

---

[1]This case was prepared by Ashis Gupta in collaboration with Derek F. Abell.

was eventually to acquire an interest in the firm. Importing at first from England, the company turned increasingly to United States sources as the domestic milling industry developed. Practically all the domestic centers grew up around metropolitan areas, providing easy access to transportation. Among these, the Buffalo, New York, and Minneapolis regions quickly emerged as major centers for the flour trade. The former dominated the navigation system of the Great Lakes while the latter stood at the edge of the world's largest wheat growing areas. With the development of new milling processes and a proliferation of suppliers, product consistency and quality were difficult to maintain. Thus, in 1896 the company decided to distribute its own brand of flour—King Arthur Flour—endeavoring to market a consistently high quality product.

Through the decades, the company had remained in the hands of the Sands family. When Frank Sands II (Harvard Business School, class of 1963) joined the company as a salesman in 1963, flour continued to make up the bulk of Sands, Taylor & Wood's business. Sugar and shortening also contributed a small percentage of sales. Soon, Frank Sands began widening the company's line through the introduction of items such as canned sliced apples, raisins, nuts, and pie fillings for sale to the bakery and institutional trade. "It was an extremely fragmented business," said Frank Sands. "Anybody sold anything they could to distinguish himself." As in flour, Sands, Taylor & Wood acted only as a distributor. By 1968, when Frank Sands II became president, the company was distributing out of its Cambridge, Massachusetts, warehouse a considerable line of edible baking supplies.

One of the first things Frank Sands recalled having recognized was the enormous difficulty in increasing market share, given the highly competitive nature of the business. Relationships between salesmen and customers took years to develop, and, once established, were highly resistant to any disturbance. "Our salesmen have to fight to sell one or two items, simply to establish their credibility. It may be years, if at all, before any sizable business results," said Frank. However, in 1969 a chance to grow faster presented itself in the form of an opportunity to acquire a competitor. This competitor was roughly equal in sales volume, distributed a similar product line, and offered the potential to double Sands, Taylor & Wood's existing share of the market.

ACQUISITIONS

In February 1969, Sands, Taylor & Wood acquired the assets of Allied Bakers, another bakery supply house similar to Sands, Taylor & Wood. The purchase required the company to borrow a sum of $200,000.

While this gave Sands, Taylor & Wood the expected larger market share, it caused a formidable expansion of their total line. Accounting for subtle differences within each specific line (as a result of the industry having to meet small, but *ad hoc* requests of customers), the newly enlarged company found itself carrying a total of almost 1,000 items of different sizes and specifications. For instance, the new company carried fourteen different varieties of lemon filling alone. One specific result of the reorganization which ensued was the transference of the "family flour,"[2] business over to the corporate framework of Allied Bakers and the consolidation of the remaining distributorship under Sands, Taylor & Wood. The new "family flour" entity assumed the name of King Arthur Flour Company.

As a distributor, one of the hard facts Frank Sands learned early in his apprenticeship was the excessive vulnerability of the distributor's high volume accounts. While personal relationships played no insignificant part in these "connections," the very size of these larger accounts tempted manufacturers to try to by-pass the distributor by offering the customer large savings through "direct" sales and the elimination of the distributor's margin. Frank Sands saw a clear need to develop some kind of production capability to protect Sands, Taylor & Wood from encroachments by manufacturers prepared to sell "direct." All too often, the company had lost sizable chunks of business to manufacturers after the company had painstakingly developed the market.

In view of such problems, Frank Sands proved particularly receptive when an executive of the Joseph Middleby Company, a century-old bakery and ice cream ingredient manufacturing and supply house in Boston, confided in him early in 1973 that the owner was attempting to sell the flagging Middleby Company. Frank Sands succeeded in purchasing the Middleby company in September 1973 for a sum less than the company's asset value. What made the acquisition even more attractive was the $400,000 Middleby tax loss which Sands, Taylor & Wood was able to carry forward. Once a very successful organization, the Middleby Company had been faced with a rapid downturn in the sixties. Sales stood at $1 million at the time of its acquisition. One of the problems to which Frank Sands addressed himself was the elimination of "deadwood" in and around the newly acquired factory. A sales force of eleven was reduced to three within one year. Not only did this acquisition fill a need for production capability, it appeared to provide Sands, Taylor & Wood a faster path to growth than would otherwise be available to

---

[2]*Family flour* is the trade name given to all-purpose flour which the housewife purchases in supermarkets for cooking, baking and other uses. It is usually packaged in sizes ranging from 2 pounds to 25 pounds. The baker generally requires specialized types of flour to meet his specific needs for bread, cakes, cookies, etc., and buys in 100-pound bags.

them. Frank Sands himself viewed the acquisition as a major turning point. He stated:

> Having manufacturing was the breakthrough. It opened up lots of new opportunities. When we were just a distributor, somebody else conceived the products. We didn't have the chance to be creative or to innovate. All we could do was to work out better ways to distribute the products. The distributor is very vulnerable. He gets hacked around. Just as he gets set up to meet a market need the market changes or disappears and he can't do anything about it.

The last of three acquisitions to date was made by Frank Sands in early 1976. This was at a time when further changes needed to be made at the Middleby Company. There were too many problems associated with trying to operate out of the very old premises at South Boston.[3] Frank Sands had been looking for a new place to move for some time when he heard that the H. A. Johnson Company was up for sale. This company, a competitor of the Middleby Company, was founded in 1877 by H. A. Johnson who was at one time a partner of Joseph Middleby. In 1972 the company had been purchased by Aerojet, a California aerospace firm, who relied on a West Coast-based team of engineers to run the food company. The business plummeted downhill. By August 1975, Aerojet was searching for a buyer for the Johnson Company. Aerojet's negotiation with a group of local investors fell through in December 1975.

H. A. Johnson Company had a modern running plant. They had essentially the same customers as the Middleby Company. And they had virtually the same line of products being offered by Sands, Taylor & Wood and the Middleby Company. Finding it an attractive buy, Frank Sands persisted in making his interest known to Aerojet. When the original negotiations fell through in December 1975, Frank Sands stepped in. In February 1975, the H. A. Johnson Company was acquired, and its operations consolidated with those of the Middleby Company as a wholly-owned subsidiary renamed the Johnson-Middleby Company. The price of over $1,500,000 entailed payment through a half-million-dollar note and the rest in cash. Although the H. A. Johnson Company had recorded 1974 sales of over $14 million, the price paid was for the company's assets as valued by Aerojet. Since the 1974 sales figures reflected the skyrocketing cost of sugar, the major raw material used in production, both Aerojet and Frank Sands agreed to limit the figure's relevance to

---

[3]The Middleby Company was located in a factory building known as the Daylight Company, built in 1907. The building received its name from its considerable glass windows which allowed daylight over the working areas.

the value of the H. A. Johnson Company. Reflecting on this acquisition, one executive observed:

> The mouse swallowed the cat! Now we have to make some hard-nosed decisions about where to go with it.

The corporate picture, following the acquisition of the H. A. Johnson Company, is presented in Exhibit 2. Exhibit 3 presents the organizational structure in the latter half of 1976, and Exhibit 4 excerpts the performance of the three companies from the 1975–76 income statement.

OPERATIONS: SANDS, TAYLOR & WOOD

Sands, Taylor & Wood distributed products manufactured by a wide variety of sources, as well as some of those of the Johnson-Middleby Company. In effect, the company carried every edible item a baker used. Ninety-eight percent of the merchandise was distributed in the packing under which it had left the original manufacturer. Estimated sales for fiscal 1976 were slightly in excess of $12 million.

Sales were broken down approximately as follows:

Flour and mixes	40%
Sweeteners (including sugar)	10
Shortening	15
Fillings, toppings and flavorings	5
Fruits and nuts	9
Milk products	4
Other miscellaneous	17
	100%

Joe Hennessey, a widely respected professional in the trade and childhood friend of House Speaker Tip O'Neill, controlled a sales force consisting of ten "outside" and three "inside" salespersons. In fiscal 1975–76, this team was responsible for sales totalling $11,650,000. With a single exception, all the "outside" salesmen operated on a straight commission basis—calculated at 10% of the gross profit on the items sold. The three "inside" salespersons were salaried employees who monitored customer orders, received telephone orders, and phoned certain specific customers (e.g., Mister Donut, Hayes-Bickford) who preferred to place their orders exclusively over the telephone. These three salespersons wrote orders averaging $100,000 each month. These orders involved no commission.

Sands, Taylor & Wood was generally considered to be the largest bakery distributor in New England. The region was clearly divided among nine salespeople (see Exhibit 5) with no territorial overlaps. However, there was a tenth salesman, a salaried individual, who handled special accounts throughout New England. Well-known local retail and wholesale bakers like Eagerman's Bakery, supermarket bakeries like DiAngelo and Fernandes Supermarkets, restaurants like Anthony's Pier 4, Jimmy's Harborside, Durgin Park, and the Colonnade, and business and educational institutions like Servomation, Harvard and Northeastern University were among the company's more prominent customers.

Every salesman structured his sales around flour, shortening, and sugar. "Without these," said Joe Hennessey, "you won't be able to sell anything." By and large, salesmen tried to reach a compromise with respect to these items which were subject to fierce competition. Flour sales were especially sensitive in this respect. Prices per cwt. varied by nickels and dimes from day to day, and salesmen carried no price lists. They operated from day to day with a minimum price beyond which they were not permitted to sell. Sugar, too, was sold on a day-to-day basis, with sugar coming into the warehouse one day, being sold the next. Salesmen carried price lists for one week at a time. "All we can do with these higher-volume items," said Joe Hennessey, "is keep our ears to the ground and find some kind of tradeoff between low margins on sugar and flour and the more profitable items in our line." He indicated that spreads on flour prices, in particular, had become much tighter since the Russian wheat deal.

The company's gross margin on items manufactured by Johnson-Middleby ranged up to 40 percent. Margins on other resale items averaged 15 percent. To motivate higher sales on the low-profit items, the company was seriously contemplating a move to a more sophisticated compensation plan with finer graduations.

Joe Hennessey identified a wide range of competitors for his products. In flour, the company was competing with other distributors as well as the big mills like Pillsbury, PV, Gold Medal, and IMCO. Likewise, in shortening, there were large corporations like Hunt-Wesson, Durkee, and P&G selling both through distributors and direct. With respect to other items, Sands, Taylor & Wood had to face challenges from corporate giants such as Kraft and Donut Corporation of America as well as many smaller distributor/jobber operations. Longstanding business relationships and a very personalized service enabled Sands, Taylor & Wood's salesmen to maintain what was considered a fairly steady volume of sales. Some executives, however, viewed the future with concern. One vice president stated:

> Every time a baker dies, we lose a customer for good. Sometimes we wonder whether the traditional baking industry will disappear altogether! Overall consumption of bread is actually decreasing; supermarkets are taking over the function of the retail baker; and the food service industry is taking over everything as people eat more and more outside the home.

OPERATIONS:
KING ARTHUR FLOUR COMPANY

Following the company reorganization when Allied Bakers was acquired in February 1969, the King Arthur Flour Company handled only the "family flour" business of the group. Sales for the 1975-76 fiscal year amounted to nearly $2 million, this revenue being generated by flour sold in bags of various sizes from two to twenty-five pounds through supermarkets and retail food stores. Bert Porter, Vice President of Sales for the company, did not anticipate any appreciable growth during fiscal 1977.

Bert Porter had been with the company for some thirty years. He believed that the national family flour market was declining at the rate of five percent each year. He was quick to point out, however, that sales of King Arthur Flour had increased almost 100 percent in the last ten years. He attributed this success not only to the carefully differentiated nature of the product, but also to a sustained promotional activity on the part of the company.

The King Arthur family flour was aimed principally at the home breadmaker. In a market where there was no United States Department of Agriculture standards for family flour, the company consistently marketed a product containing significantly higher protein. Bert Porter believed that, at this level of protein content, King Arthur Flour showed a discernible difference in volume and texture (obtained by hand kneading) compared to other family flours in the supermarket which normally carried a protein content 20 to 25 percent lower. The unbleached quality of the flour had been for decades a strong selling point in favor of the King Arthur brand. This was not only because "protein" and "gluten"[4] were difficult words to merchandise, but also because the discriminating food buff preferred his flour unbleached. Although bleaching destroyed the natural color of flour, Bert Porter readily conceded that "unbleached" did not constitute a major difference between flours. The same protein strength was possible in bleached as well as unbleached flours. Besides, all family flour was "enriched" by order of the U.S. Government to contain niacin, thiamine, riboflavin, and iron. While some might look upon enrichment as artificial additives, Bert Porter maintained that they helped ensure that U.S. wheat flour was the most nutritious in the world.

The King Arthur Flour Company was the only division of the group which advertised directly to the general public. The advertising budget for fiscal 1976 was $175,000, a figure which included traveling expenses

---

[4] "Gluten" is the name for the sticky vegetable protein found in all wheat flours. It is gluten which gives the dough its elasticity and unique ability to rise. The better the wheat, some experts say, the higher the gluten level.

incurred by Bert Porter in the course of giving actual baking demonstrations on television. He was responsible for one show each week, either on television or radio, over nearly a six-month period each year. Following these demonstrations, listeners and viewers normally called in for brochures describing the baking procedures (see Exhibit 6). A three-hour Sunday afternoon radio show on Boston's station WEEI, in 1974, brought forth nearly 6,000 requests for brochures. Lately, the requests ranged in the hundreds. Bert Porter ascribed this drop in interest to the state of the economy which drove increasing numbers of housewives to work. Even though she could save substantially (not including the "value" of her time), a working housewife was more likely to buy bread off supermarket shelves than bake at home.

Frank Sands and other executives recalled highlights of earlier promotional pitches involving the flour. For instance, in the 1800s, the company pioneered transit advertising on Boston streetcars. And in 1927 the company hired an intrepid "knight," a student from Bates College, who averaged twenty-four miles a day on a Kentucky thoroughbred visiting the towns and villages of Massachusetts. He participated in parades, town celebrations, and garnered along the way a constant throng of astonished children and fascinated onlookers. This flair for promotion surfaced again a year later. Walter Sands, Frank Sands' father, outfitted a truck with a large pipe organ and woodcarving of a mounted knight. He played through the streets until stopped by police for not having a license. But the Mayor of New York City supplied Walter Sands with a license as an itinerant musician and the sale went on.

With the exception of southern Connecticut, the King Arthur Flour Company was distributed throughout New England. Sales in the New England region were handled exclusively by a single broker, the George William Bentley Company of Waltham, Massachusetts. Beginning in 1971 and 1976, respectively, the company also sold through brokers in Albany and Syracuse, New York. Brokers' commission was a normal five percent. They sold through their direct salesmen who wrote orders from the brokers' offices and retail salesmen who visited outlets at regular intervals, constantly looking for greater shelf space. Higher costs prevented these salesmen from calling upon the small independent grocer who thus had to depend entirely on "jobbers"[5] if they responded at all to the King Arthur Flour advertising. Grocery chains bypassed jobbers and enjoyed gross margins of at least twenty percent.

The company's major competitors were Pillsbury and Gold Medal, both of whom sold through their own salesmen. Based on records avail-

---

[5]The "jobber" is the institution which actually handles the flour and sells to grocery stores. The broker handles no flour. The jobber is invoiced by King Arthur Flour Company and sells for whatever price his own overheads allow. His margin is usually five percent of the invoiced value.

able at the King Arthur Flour Company, sales and market shares for the Boston area are presented in Exhibit 7 and 8. Neither Pillsbury nor Gold Medal stressed "unbleached" flour in their advertising. In 1975, however, Heckers, a New York distributor, announced it would enter the New England market with an unbleached brand. But Heckers abruptly dropped its advertising campaign for New England in 1976, after it appeared that it had made virtually no impact on this market. Frank Sands, the company president, voiced the belief that the company enjoyed a dominant market share in the twenty-five-pound-bag sales of family flour in New England. He considered King Arthur sales greater in this size and category than the combined sales of Pillsbury and Gold Medal. Frank Sands also believed that his company sold more ten-pound bags of family flour in New England than any other competitor.

OPERATIONS: JOHNSON-MIDDLEBY COMPANY

Johnson-Middleby sold a combination of seven broad product categories to three separate segments of the food market. These were sold under their own prestigious labels, as well as some private labels. Table 1 states the current position:

Table 1

PRODUCT CATEGORIES	BAKERIES	SUPPLIED TO: SODA FOUNTAIN ICE CREAM & YOGURT MANUFACTURERS	INSTITUTIONAL FOOD SERVICE COMPANIES
1. Fondant[6] and icing preparations	X		
2. Crunch	X	X	
3. Sundae toppings, fountain syrups		X	X
4. Pastry and fruit fillings	X		X
5. Yogurt, ice cream, fruits, and flavors		X	
6. Relishes			X
7. Resale items	X		

[6]Fondant is the trade name for a high quality form of icing sugar.

Under an agreement signed in 1971 between the H. A. Johnson Company and Hall-Smith, a New England institutional food service company, the former agreed not to solicit business from Hall-Smith's competitors. The agreement, renewable each year, now permits Johnson-Middleby to sell to other food service companies *only* private labels, not such prestigious brands as the company's own "Murray" and "Bestovall" names.

Johnson-Middleby sales were controlled by Harold Porter, another industry veteran, who was with the H. A. Johnson Company at the time it was acquired by Sands, Taylor & Wood. Items from this manufacturing arm of the company were sold through a sales team of three industry sales managers and six salesmen operating independently of the Sands, Taylor & Wood sales force. In fiscal 1976 sales totaled approximately $9,500,000,[7] broken down approximately as follows:

Fondant and icing preparations	23%
Crunch products	5
Sundae toppings and fountain syrups	13
Pastry and food fillings	19
Yogurt, ice cream, fruits, and flavors	15
Relishes	1
Resale items	24
	100%

Sales for the 1977 fiscal year were projected at $10,600,000. Sales to January 1977 were keeping close to the projected figures. The summer months traditionally recorded higher than average sales of Johnson-Middleby's products. Real growth, however, was anticipated in supplies to the yogurt industry. Between September 1976 and January 1977, sales to yogurt manufacturers exceeded $500,000 and Harold Porter expected sales of yogurt preparations to reach $1 million for the fiscal year.

The current sales analyses available to the Johnson-Middleby Company were a carryover from the old H. A. Johnson Company. These were somewhat more sophisticated than reports available at either Sands, Taylor & Wood or the King Arthur Flour Company. Not only was there a unit report of every item sold each month, there was also a monthly customer analysis of products sold and corresponding dollar amounts. The latter analysis suggested the following broad categories of customers for Johnson-Middleby products:

CUSTOMER	% OF TOTAL SALES
Retailers	35
Distributors (including Sands, Taylor & Wood)	30
Manufacturers	35

---

[7]This figure differs substantially from the corresponding figure in Exhibit 3 because the Sands, Taylor & Wood income statement has accounted for Johnson-Middleby figures only for eight months from February 1976, the date when Sands, Taylor & Wood acquired the company. Furthermore, $80 to $100 thousand monthly sales of Sands, Taylor & Wood were from distributing Johnson-Middleby products.

These customers numbered approximately 2,500 in all, and were additionally classified by Harold Porter as follows:

CUSTOMER DESCRIPTION	% OF TOTAL SALES
Bakery and confectionary	60
Dairy and ice cream	15
Food service (soda fountain)	25

The company estimated that about 300 of its customers accounted for 80% of the business, the balance being shared by the remaining 2,200.

The six field salesmen were responsible for clearly defined territories which sometimes overlapped with those of the three industry sales managers as well as those of the Sands, Taylor & Wood sales force. This was particularly the case in terms of the following specific markets:

1. Soda fountain and syrups
2. Ice cream and yogurt
3. Bakery products

In addition to these commissioned salespeople, some of whom earned as much as $60,000 annually, the company also sold directly to six brokers located in Detroit, Buffalo, Philadelphia, Western Massachusetts, Atlanta, and Washington, D.C. Generally speaking, brokers received a commission of five percent on sales totaling nearly $1 million.

One of the problems facing the commissioned salespeople was that they were reluctant to sell the low-profit items in their line. They were afraid this would adversely affect their total compensation. This apprehension was seen by Sands, Taylor & Wood executives as a direct outcome of the compensation plan under which the sales force operated. On the assumption that a 16% rate of gross profit represented the average "break-even" over its total product line, the company paid its sales force as follows:

1. 10% of gross profit on items with a gross profit margin lower than 16%.
2. A sliding percentage of gross profit ranging from 10% to 18% on items with a margin of 16% or above.

Typically, the company's line of syrups and toppings possessed the highest margins, while fondant and resale items possessed the lowest. Across the board, Frank Sands believed that average gross margins exceeded those available in Sands, Taylor & Wood's distributing operations.

Frank Sands was sufficiently realistic to agree that his entire sales force, including that of Johnson-Middleby, was not extending itself sufficiently. Their average age was nearly sixty, they were well paid and satisfied. Under the circumstances, he believed there was little incentive to devote extra energy to the development of extra sales. The incremental commission rewards were simply not attractive enough. As with the sales capability, Frank Sands also believed that manufacturing capacity utilization left much to be desired. Although Johnson-Middleby operated on a single shift (except occasionally for the production of "fondant"), Frank Sands regretted that even the entire capacity of a single shift was not being fully utilized. "We have a long way to go here," he said, "especially in the area of lowering labor intensive operations, installing sophisticated machinery, and generally streamlining the manufacturing arm."

The Johnson-Middleby Company had to contend with a long list of competitors in each of its major product categories. In the bakery goods area, Harold Porter conceded that Globe Manufacturing, a New York producer, was clearly the industry leader in pie fillings. Their high quality and wide product line made it necessary even for Sands, Taylor & Wood to carry some Globe products. Harold Porter pointed out, however, that Johnson-Middleby's quality had improved considerably over the last two years. New machines made it possible for Johnson-Middleby to cook the fruits in the very cans in which they were to be shipped. This gave the fruits a superior shape and appearance. "Today we are definitely selling on quality alone," he said. While Globe Manufacturing as well as another major competitor, Orchard Foods, possessed this unique manufacturing capability, Orchard prices were considerably lower than those of Globe and Johnson-Middleby, which were on a par. Sands, Taylor & Wood's executives pointed out, however, that Orchard's quality was far from consistent. Time and again, Johnson-Middleby salesmen found it possible to demonstrate the superiority of their products through an accepted trade practice whereby they "cut" cans—their own as well as those of a competitor's products. When respective cans, particularly those of fruit fillings, were opened, there appeared tangible proof of Johnson-Middleby's product superiority.

The executives also maintained that Johnson-Middleby was clearly the leader in price and quality in the "syrups and toppings" category. Apart from Orchard Foods, the major competitors were J. Hungerford-Smith, and Richardson Corporation, as well as many "bathtub" operators.[8] "Our competitors have to be fought in terms of dollars as well," said Harold Porter. "Lately we have been doing business for

---

[8]These were small manufacturers who were content to supply one or more large customers. They tended to be family businesses with relatively low overheads and inconsistent quality.

price differences of a nickel per case." To meet this growing threat, the company decided in 1977 to introduce a line of low-priced items. Johnson-Middleby executives believed, as a rough "ballpark" estimate, that they enjoyed 50% of the New England Market for the superior line of these products.

Supplies to ice cream and dairy manufacturers represented a strong growth area. The major competitors here were Crown Preserving and Alpha Aromatics. Johnson-Middleby held a major share of the H. P. Hood business and a lesser share of Columbo. A major competitor for supplies of vanilla was McCormick Tea and Spices. "We belong to the Retail Ice Cream Association," said Harold Porter. "We sell some portion of the flavoring requirements to every one of its list of members."

As institutional suppliers, Johnson-Middleby executives saw their major strength in their wide product line. Exclusive supplies to Hall-Smith currently totaled $600,000 annually. The executives believed that Hall-Smith had clear potential of a $1 million volume in the immediate future. Another major strength for Johnson-Middleby lay in its extensive network of "candy, paper and tobacco" distributors. These sold to retail ice cream and "dairy freeze" outlets. At the end of 1976, they totaled nearly 100 located throughout the Northeast.

ALTERNATIVE COURSES OF ACTION CONSIDERED

Frank Sands clearly recognized the need to streamline the company's overall product line. One of the committee tasks he had assigned related specifically to product elimination. With Sands, Taylor & Wood's 1977 corporate gross profit budgeted at $1,625,000, and with the company's distributive capacity estimated at 1,000 pallets,[9] the company considered it necessary for its products to show at least a $135/pallet/ month gross profit. There were many "overlapping" items in inventory, as well as those which appeared to move very slowly or not at all. In this respect, the stock status report for mid-January 1977 pointed to such items as Bakerfond, a type of icing sugar (389 cases valued at $5,700 in stock; average monthly sales $475); Sweetex, a cake shortening (203 cases valued at $3,500 in stock; average monthly sales $760); and Betrikake, another cake shortening (274 cases valued at $4,800 in stock; average monthly sales $225) as typical examples.

It was, of course, agreed that any attempt at product elimination had to acknowledge the contending claims of customers who often had

---

[9]Each pallet represented 40 × 50-pound bags or 20 × 100-pound bags.

singular product preferences which had somehow to be met. It was brought to Frank Sand's notice that, in the past, members of the sales force had been known to approach the Research and Development section with informal customer requests for new or special items. In the same spirit of informality, Research and Development had always honored such requests. This peculiarity of the business encouraged the proliferation of product lines. As an alternative to product elimination, Frank Sands also proposed the possibility of promotional programs aimed at pushing dormant items.

Sands, Taylor & Wood executives were also encouraged to search for fresh growth opportunities. The particular areas which the New Product Committee initially planned to investigate were:

a. The possibility of marketing a chocolate syrup under the King Arthur label. This would compete with Hershey's 16-ounce package on the supermarket shelves. However, present packaging capabilities would not allow such an attempt on economical terms.

b. Manufacturing for private labels such as those of major supermarket chains, etc. A syndicated market information report provided Sands, Taylor & Wood with reliable information on supermarket sales within specific geographical areas. These reports indicated a substantial market share for private labels in many product categories other than those currently packed by Johnson-Middleby.

c. Substituting Johnson-Middleby "mixes" for items currently purchased from other sources and distributed by Sands, Taylor & Wood. These mixes were used primarily as muffin and pancake ingredients. "I have no doubt there's a lot of money in specialty mixes," said Frank Sands, "but somehow we seem to be missing the boat." For instance, one reason why Sands, Taylor & Wood distributed mixes manufactured by Donut Corporation of America was a clear preference shown by some customers for this product. Donut Corporation of America products were well advertised in food and bakery trade magazines. "How can we push our own formulations instead of those of the Donut Corporation?" asked Frank Sands. Discussion on this subject seemed to indicate that the only way to initiate a breakthrough with a new or substitute product lay in demonstrating to the baker the superior qualities of, say, a mix formulated by Johnson-Middleby. It was recognized that this might involve presenting in-shop demonstrations and even "seminars" on how to make donuts and muffins. A baker, it was argued, was not one to make changes unless he was clearly dissatisfied with the product he was currently buying.

d. Yogurt particularly represented an area which the company found promising and attractive. The Johnson-Middleby division was a major supplier of yogurt fruit flavorings to H. P. Hood, a company with which it had collaborated long and patiently in the development of frozen yogurt, better known as "Frogurt." "We're servicing the hell out of Hood's," said Sal Pascuito, Director of Research and Development. "We're doing just about everything they want. The question is, can we work as closely with other companies without straining our resources? If we tackle six yogurt manufacturers, are we not likely to multiply sixfold the problems we are currently encountering with Hood?" Notwithstanding these perceived difficulties, Frank Sands agreed to hire a dairy technologist to study the possibilities of expanding into the yogurt/frogurt[10] industry. When submitted, the young dairy expert's report identified no less than fifteen yogurt flavoring prospects scattered in Illinois, Wisconsin, North Carolina, Pennsylvania, New York and New Jersey. Three of these prospects were identified as especially "hot." One, estimated at buying 1½ trailers (i.e., 60,000 pounds) of flavoring each week, was apparently interested in a long-term deal with a major supplier on a cost plus 6% basis. Another yogurt manufacturer, currently buying from Borden, was interested in switching to "natural" flavors. Although no specific F.D.A. (Food and Drug Administration) guidelines defining "natural" had yet been issued, it was believed that Johnson-Middleby might have an edge in this specific expertise. The reason for this optimism lay in the vast experience gathered by the company in formulating a wide range of flavors for H. P. Hood as well as Columbo.

e. Regional expansion of family flour as well as other product lines to new geographical areas. This might include Connecticut, additional parts of upstate New York, or even the Midwest.

Although the exact costs and benefits associated with each of these options were not known, it was believed that some would require less investment than others. Increased manufacture of private labels, for example, would require little direct investment. Nor would expansion of Johnson-Middleby output in either existing or similar product lines that might be sold by Sands, Taylor & Wood. On the other hand, introduction of a new branded product under the King Arthur label might require considerable investments in advertising and promotion. Likewise, expansion to new geographic areas was reckoned, from experience, to involve at least a three-year payback. Within reason, however, Frank Sands believed that capital could be found to undertake such steps if that seemed desirable.

---

[10]Frogurt is a frozen yogurt.

CONCLUSION

Frank Sands was particularly interested in the Harvard Business School developing a case study out of the current situation in his company. Even though he was unable to put his finger on any problem of major proportions, he hoped that the study might help present him with a much needed sense of direction. He conceded that while he was understandably enthusiastic over his recent acquisitions, he was perfectly aware that each of the individual businesses were fairly solid and mature, with little or no possibilities of dramatic growth. "Of course they're profitable, each one of them," he declared. "But while we seem poised on the threshold of circumstances which might offer us great momentum, each of my businesses appear to be characterized by a deep inertia which threatens to defeat this momentum."

Frank Sands wanted to make his present operations bigger, more aggressive, and he hoped his senior executives fully appreciated the rationale behind his acquisitions. He wanted to capitalize upon the numerous opportunities that he believed were available to his current organization, but recognizing a limit to his various assets including people, facilities, capital and his own time, he wanted to commit those assets to the opportunities with the greatest potential for maximum return. In particular, he wondered whether there were other options than the ones he was specifically considering, for example, integration forward into bakery outlets, fast-food activities, or maybe ice cream chains. Another suggestion was further acquisition. One possibility which he knew existed was the major New England producer of branded frozen dough products, with distribution in supermarkets and institutional markets.

Although he confessed to a perception that the parent distributor company, Sands, Taylor & Wood, had somehow been overshadowed in terms of possibilities by the Johnson-Middleby Company, he wondered whether the $135 plus/pallet/month gross profit was sufficient as a financial criterion for judging and justifying the introduction of new products. "I hope we can take the best advantage of these evolving circumstances," said Frank Sands. Adding, with a smile, "What I'd most like to do is spend my days in New Hampshire, somewhere near my old college, Dartmouth, and let this thing run as efficiently as it can."

Exhibit 1
SANDS, TAYLOR & WOOD
CHARTER OF NEW PRODUCT DEVELOPMENT COMMITTEE

H.a.JOHNSON A DIVISION OF AEROSENCE CORPORATION

SINCE 1877

TO: DISTRIBUTION   DATE: 8 June 1976

FROM:

SUBJECT: Product Development Committee

DISTRIBUTION: F. Sands, D. Crandall, J. Hennessy, T. Callahan,
                H. Porter, S. Pasciuto, R. Renna

The purpose of the Product Development Committee is to insure
that the Johnson-Middleby Research and Development resources
are applied to projects which have the best chances of maximizing the profitability of the Company.

It is the responsibility of the Chairman to coordinate the
total Company effort in this area and to keep the President
informed as to the progress, success, and failures of the
various projects.

It is the primary responsibility of J. Hennessy, H. Porter,
and P. Higgins to identify market requirements, estimate
volume, price/cost relationships, assess competition and any
other factors which may affect the sales/marketing viewpoint.
The assignment of this responsibility is not intended to
preclude recommendations or suggestions from any other employee of the Company; but should be used as a vehicle to
funnel ideas through the channels which have the resources
to fully explore their potential.

It is the primary responsibility of S. Pasciuto and R. Renna
to analyze competitive products when available, develop formulations, investigate alternative ingredients, evaluate end
use and advise on the overall technical feasibility of all
ideas discussed in the Committee.

It is the primary responsibility of T. Callahan to identify
manufacturing methods and capabilities, storage and handling
problems or advantages, investigation of equipment purchases
and labor requirements, advise on raw material problems and
the overall impact on Production.

Exhibit 1 [cont.]

TO: DISTRIBUTION   8 June 1976
Product Development Committee

It is the primary responsibility of D. Crandall to explore
financial implications with regard to inventory, capital
investment requirements, and the overall financial impact.

The assignment of priorities will be a Committee decision.
I suggest that the following guidelines be used in assigning
priorities.

    1.   Existing products for current customers.

    2.   New products specifically requested by current
        customers.

    3.   New product ideas based on profit x volume x
        probability of attainment.

This letter was written as an attempt to organize the Committee
into a functioning body with responsibilities defined as I see
them at present. I would appreciate comments or suggestions
to improve the efficiency of the Committee.

Exhibit 2
SANDS, TAYLOR & WOOD COMPANY

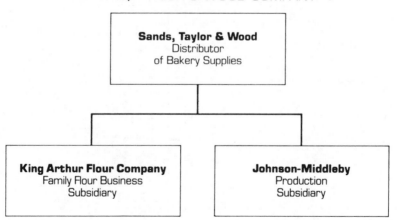

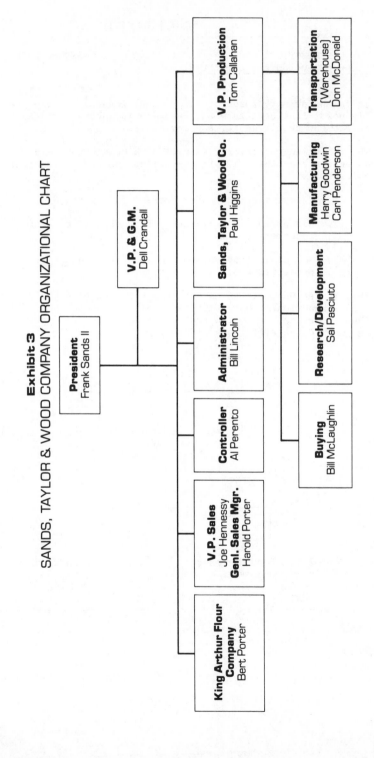

Exhibit 3
SANDS, TAYLOR & WOOD COMPANY ORGANIZATIONAL CHART

President
Frank Sands II

V.P. & G.M.
Dell Crandall

King Arthur Flour Company
Bert Porter

V.P. Sales
Joe Hennessy
Genl. Sales Mgr.
Harold Porter

Controller
Al Perento

Administrator
Bill Lincoln

Sands, Taylor & Wood Co.
Paul Higgins

V.P. Production
Tom Callahan

Buying
Bill McLaughlin

Research/Development
Sal Pasciuto

Manufacturing
Harry Goodwin
Carl Penderson

Transportation
[Warehouse]
Don McDonald

Exhibit 4

SANDS, TAYLOR & WOOD COMPANY

Financial Peformance for Fiscal Year Ending September 30, 1976

	APPROXIMATE SALES	APPROXIMATE NET INCOME, PRE-TAXES	APPROXIMATE ASSETS EMPLOYED
King Arthur Flour	$ 2,000,000	$ 62,000	$ 222,000
Johnson-Middleby (Feb.–Sept. 1976 only)	8,000,000	340,000	4,000,000
Sands, Taylor & Wood (excluding Johnson-Middleby sales)	12,000,000	40,000	3,133,000
	$22,000,000	$442,000	$7,455,000

Source: Company's annual reports.

Exhibit 5

SANDS, TAYLOR & WOOD COMPANY

Salesmen's Territories

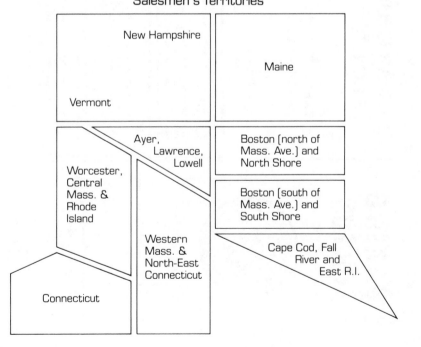

Exhibit 6
SANDS, TAYLOR & WOOD COMPANY
King Arthur Flour Brochure

"More Bread Recipes, As Easy As Ever."

King Arthur Flour Company
155 North Beacon Street, Brighton, Mass. 02135

KING ARTHUR FLOUR

"BREAD BAKING MADE EASY"

Remember the aroma in Grandmother's kitchen when she made her own bread. It brings back some wonderful memories, doesn't it?

But Grandmother's bread-baking was a major task, requiring almost 10 hours from start to finish. Now, however, by using this new easy method, only 4 hours are needed. Start your bread after breakfast, eat it for lunch.

And you can use the same flour Grandmother used, NEVER BLEACHED KING ARTHUR FLOUR, higher in protein for better bread, yet unexcelled for cakes and pastries, milled only from hard spring wheat, and white as nature intended it to be, without any bleaching.

In a day when food additives are so much the subject of doubt and misgivings, isn't it reassuring to know that KING ARTHUR FLOUR is still pure and unbleached? For your health's sake, use it always.

"AMERICA'S OLDEST FLOUR COMPANY"
—SINCE 1790—

BAKING FOR FUN

8 new and easy-to-prepare recipes, plus tips for better baking.

"AMERICA'S OLDEST FLOUR COMPANY"

Unbleached flour since 1790

King Arthur Flour Co.
155 North Beacon Street
Brighton, Mass. 02135

428

Exhibit 7

SANDS, TAYLOR AND WOOD COMPANY

Comparison of Flour Sales

[Boston Area Only]

	YEAR	BLEACHED BALE 24 × 2 LB.	BLEACHED BALE 10 × 5 LB.	UNBLEACHED BALE 10 × 5 LB.
King Arthur	1973–74	7,279	All unbleached	
	1974–75	5,281	All unbleached	
	1975–76	5,368	All unbleached	
Gold Medal	1973–74	28,846	119,298	1,914
	1974–75	24,199	129,708	1,170
	1975–76	24,071	148,749	1,591
Pillsbury	1973–74	32,329	95,450	11,040
	1974–75	35,578	90,425	13,396
	1975–76	33,162	134,959	13,030
Robin Hood	1973–74	—	—	—
	1974–75	14	—	—
	1975–76	140	—	—
Private Label	1973–74	—	—	—
	1974–75	—	—	—
	1975–76	—	—	—

Exhibit 7 [cont.]

	TOTAL BALES 10 × 5 LB. *	BALE 5 × 10 LB.	BALE 2 × 25 LB.	TOTAL ALL SIZES
King Arthur	64,786	22,107	27,218	121,390
	56,015	20,286	25,068	106,650
	66,080	22,958	24,546	118,952
Gold Medal	121,212	26,654	22,699	199,411
	130,878	25,918	17,999	198,994
	150,340	22,444	15,550	212,405
Pillsbury	106,490	20,313	10,325	169,457
	103,821	24,180	6,988	170,567
	147,989	18,964	11,047	211,162
Robin Hood	4,207	890	3,978	9,075
	6,440	577	5,455	12,486
	5,518	595	2,887	9,140
Private Label	—	—	—	93,077
	—	—	—	97,621
	—	—	—	129,723

Source: Company records.

*Total of bleached and unbleached bales, 10 × 5 lb., listed in last two columns of upper portion of this exhibit.

Exhibit 8
SANDS, TAYLOR & WOOD COMPANY
Flour Sales
Total Market & Shares of Market
[Boston Area Only]

TOTAL MARKET			
	1973–1974	592,411 bales	
	1974–1975	586,309 bales	
	1975–1976	682,417 bales	

	1973–74	1974–75	1975–76
King Arthur	20.5%	18.2%	17.5%
Gold Medal	33.6	34.0	31.1
Pillsbury	28.6	29.1	30.9
Robin Hood	1.6	2.1	1.3
Private Label	15.7	16.6	19.0
Heckers	—	—	0.2

Source: Company records.

DISCUSSION QUESTIONS

SANDS, TAYLOR & WOOD COMPANY

1. Who are they (Sands, Taylor & Wood Company)?
   What should they do?
   What business are they in?
   How should they conceive of themselves?
   How should they conceive of themselves five years from now?
2. What strategic actions should Mr. Sands now take?
3. What administrative processes should he set in motion?
4. If you think he is short of information, what specifically should he collect? Where? How? At what cost?

Making Planning Work: The Human Side of Planning

PROBLEMS IN MAKING PLANNING WORK

Advocates of planning in large organizations usually start out optimistically. Armed with new conceptual tools, such as the ones described in this book, they look forward to bringing order to an important process which has been too haphazard in the past. But far too often their optimism is unfounded; serious problems—of which the following are examples—arise:

- Planning becomes a mindless ritual—the "rites of fall"—rather than an opportunity for sound strategic thinking.
- Higher-level (for example corporate) staff people become embroiled in "we-they" battles with lower levels of the organization.
- Information that exists in other parts of the organization is withheld or begrudgingly surrendered to those who need it for planning.
- Other information presented in plans—such as sales estimates—is "slanted" to justify a particular position rather than provide a sound basis to compare alternatives.
- Future strategies often are unimaginative projections of present strategies.
- Attractive new strategies are proposed but are rejected, and seemingly inferior ones are selected instead.
- The results of the planning process are ignored when actual decisions of long-range consequence, such as acquisitions, are made.

THE UNDERLYING CAUSES
OF THE PROBLEMS

The underlying causes of these problems are seldom technical deficiencies with the planning process or the analytical approaches. Instead they are human and administrative problems. Planning requires that people work together on complex issues with a large number of alternatives, great uncertainties, and consequences far into the future. The stakes are enormous for themselves and their organizational unit. When these are added up it seems that the human and organizational deck is stacked against planning. More specifically:

- Planning is fundamentally a resource allocation process; managers perceive that their power base and career prospects are enhanced by receiving a large share of resources. Therefore their inputs to the planning process are geared to achieve these ends. They become advocates for their position rather than seekers of the corporate good.
- Short-range issues with near-term financial consequences are of far greater importance to most managers than the longer-range issues addressed by strategic planning. Thus managers are unaccustomed to thinking about the more distant future and find it difficult and unrewarding to do so.
- The above two reasons stem, by and large, from a common source: the organization's explicit and implicit reward-punishment system. Managers observe that those who are in key positions in faster-growing, larger organizational units are better paid, have better careers, and have more prestige than those in their smaller, slower-growing counterparts. Furthermore, they know that short-range measures (for example, this year's sales and earnings) receive far greater weight in evaluating their performance than longer-run measures. It is not surprising, therefore, to see them put emphasis where the personal rewards seem to be the greatest.
- Most resource and program managers' jobs are performed at a hectic pace, with constant interruptions, short, verbal encounters, and great varieties of subject matter and issues, primarily having to do with current, *ad hoc,* specific issues. Such jobs tend to attract managers who *prefer* doing business this way.[1] But planning requires longer periods of deeper, uninterrupted thought having to do with more general, long-range complex issues. Thus many managers are ill-equipped and ill-disposed to plan.

---

[1] Henry Mintzberg, "The Manager's Job: Folklore and Fact," *Harvard Business Review,* 53, no. 4 (July–August 1975), pp. 49–61.

- Many key people are misinformed about planning. A surprisingly large number of those who are expected to plan simply don't understand how to. They don't understand planning, what is expected of them in the planning process, the purpose of the information they are to provide, the importance of their contribution, or the planning tools (such as portfolio analysis) they are to use. Even worse, most organizations have planning sophisticates in planning departments who are often misinformed about their role. They think they are to *do* planning rather than to *facilitate* planning by general managers, resource managers, and program managers. When their clients are similarly misinformed, which is too often the case, planning ends up being abdicated to those too unfamiliar with their businesses to do an adequate job.
- The necessary knowledge to make planning work is unevenly distributed in the organization. This makes it possible for lower-level people with intimate knowledge of individual businesses, products, and markets to present information selectively, or in a manner that favors a preferred strategy. Central staff types, responsible for evaluating and integrating plans, are poorly equipped to challenge them. For their part, higher-ups, in their ignorance of markets, can assign roles to lower units that are strategically unsound. Moreover, upper-level types think their lower-level counterparts "don't know how to plan" whereas lower-level (e.g. division personnel), in turn, view the high-level (e.g. corporate) people as "in the ivory tower," "too theoretical," or "don't know our business." This results in suspicion and disdain on the part of each side for the other, a source of the "we-they" behavior described earlier.
- Managers often hide their actual activities or results from higher-level management by arbitrary allocations within the accounting system. When information required for planning can potentially expose some of this activity and reduce a manager's flexibility, requests for the information will be resisted.
- Politics, informal alliances, and friendships among key managers may cause less-than-optimal planning decisions for the organization as a whole.
- Good communication and dialogue necessary for successful planning are made difficult by the large number of people who must interact. They have widely varying backgrounds and are often physically and organizationally remote from one another. The problem is compounded by the need to summarize complex ideas succinctly, such as in portfolio charts or in terse written statements. The analysis and plans for a substantial business may be only allotted a few pages in planning documents.

As can be seen, these causes of planning problems have as their source the nature of human beings—especially their concern about their own well-being, the nature of modern-day corporations—especially their reward-punishment systems, and the nature of planning—especially its complexity, large stakes, and long-range outlook. There is relatively little that those involved in planning can do to change the causes, but there is a great deal that can be done to work within or around them. Doing so starts with the fundamental realization that the techniques described in earlier chapters are insufficient, by themselves, to ensure that planning works. The ability to successfully address these human and organizational problems is an added ingredient required for success.

Here are a dozen ways to help ensure success:

1. *Get the support of senior management.*
   The support of senior management is an absolute must, because planning is ultimately designed for *them* to set strategy and allocate resources. Their support may start with words, but must ultimately be reflected in their deeds. Senior management behavior sends important signals to the rest of the organization about what is expected; if it doesn't take planning seriously then the rest of the management won't either. Senior management must be actively involved in planning, and see that decisions subsequent to the plan are consistent with it (or made along with a clearly communicated modification of the plan).

2. *Educate those who will be involved in planning.*
   It is important for those involved in planning to have an overview of the planning process, understand the key analytical approaches to be used, and understand what is required at each major step of the process. A common understanding of the corporation's "model" for planning is essential for proper communication and to ensure that each person's contribution properly fits in.

   Often, education is required before strategic thinking can really take place. We suggest that such education be conveyed in a seminar of several days duration. In it, every effort should be made to support concepts with concrete examples; in fact discussion of cases such as those in this book and ones drawn from company files would be ideal. Presentations should make clear the benefits of planning to those involved. Ample time should be allowed for questions. Answers should be forthright; the difficulties of planning should not be papered over.

A good example of the need for face-to-face education occurred in a major accounting firm.[2] The partner in charge of planning had developed a time-sharing computer model which could be used for planning by the managing partners at each of the branch offices. It was hardly used until he made a personal tour to each office to introduce and explain it. Great enthusiasm followed; some of the managers became so fascinated that they stayed late at night exploring alternatives and analyzing consequences. On the other hand, a large insurance company developed an elaborate and comprehensive planning system which was only partially successful. Its limited success was due in large measure to inadequate attention to the need for education. Instead, there was over-reliance on a thick, abstract planning manual developed by the planning department, which few managers read and most didn't understand.

3. *Ensure that all general managers, resource managers, and program managers are actively involved in planning.*

   All types of management—general management, resource management, and program management—must be active in planning; after all, the future of each part of the operation is being planned in conjunction with planning the whole. All viewpoints will be required in shaping the overall plan. Of course, they can delegate a great deal to staff subordinates but they must be involved and ultimately responsible for the results.

4. *Make heavy, but appropriate, use of staff analyses.*

   The quality of planning will depend in large measure on how effectively staff can be used to conduct analyses, gather data, explore the implications of alternatives, prepare position papers, etc. While some of the staff might be called "planners," managers should remember that planners don't plan; *they help managers do so.*

   For example, this distinction is not understood in a large, diversified corporation, noted as a sophisticated developer and user of the latest planning techniques. Unfortunately, the sophisticated techniques are used outside of the main management stream by planners with relatively little interaction with managers. The resultant "plans" have little impact on actual corporate decisions; they are not managers' plans but planners' plans. In fact, the head of planning and the chief-executive officer are locked in continual battle over the appropriate future course of the organization. It is

---

[2]John S. Hammond, "Do's and Don'ts of Computer Models for Planning" *Harvard Business Review*, 52, no. 2, (March–April 1974), pp. 110–123.

not hard to guess who wins. Thus planners and other staff people may put in the majority of the hours, but they should be just decision *facilitators;*[3,4] the managers to whom they report are the decision *makers.*

5. *Keep planning simple, and add complexity when the organization is ready for it.*

   To be effective, planning must be simple and easy to understand. However, what is simple for one organization may be complex for another; clearly an organization that is planning for the first time must use a simpler system and simpler techniques than would be suitable for an organization experienced with planning. This suggests an evolutionary approach, for instance introducing only a few new concepts (such as experience curves and portfolio analysis) each year. What John Little[5] said about computer models applies equally to planning systems.

> The manager carries responsibility for outcomes. ... We should not be surprised if he prefers simple analysis that he can grasp, even though it may have a qualitative structure, broad assumptions, and only a little relevant data, to a complex model whose assumptions may be partially hidden or couched in jargon, and whose parameters may be the result of obscure statistical manipulations ...

> The best approach is to lead the potential users through a sequence of models of increasing scope and complexity. ... Often the user, having learned a simple model, will start to ask for just the additional considerations found in the advanced models.

Introduction of new techniques should use as their starting point the attitude and knowledge of the managers about current techniques. While this seems obvious, too often new approaches to planning are introduced as if nothing had come before; when this occurs confusion and resistance can result.

While standardization of procedures and techniques is desirable for consistency and ease of communication, it is important not to be doctrinaire. For instance, techniques should be matched to

---

[3]John S. Hammond, "The Roles of the Manager and Management Scientist in Successful Implementation," *Sloan Management Review*, 15, no. 2 (Winter 1974), pp. 1–24.

[4]John W. Drake, *The Administration of Transportation Modeling Projects* (Lexington, Mass.: D. C. Heath, 1973).

[5]John D. C. Little, "Models and Managers: The Concept of a Decision Calculus," *Management Science*, 16, no. 8 (April 1970), p. B-466.

decisions, i.e., experience curves for analysis of strategies of individual products and portfolio analysis for decisions among products. The "bottom line" of planning is to come up with good plans based on sound strategic thinking; the techniques are just means to this end.

6. *Be concerned about data inputs.*
   A recurring difficulty in planning is the availability of appropriate data, especially about markets and market share. When it is unavailable, ingenuity is required to collect it or to estimate it. Important judgments must be made when the information is "available" but in the wrong form. For instance, market share data from an industry association may assume a market definition different from the organization's market definition. This forces the difficult decision of whether to collect or estimate data according to the proper definition—often at considerable cost and reduced accuracy—or to plan, using the industry data. Other problems arise when data is potentially biased, often because its source is trying to prove a point. Then the issue becomes how to obtain an independent verification or to remove the bias from the data. Sometimes the bias arises because the data is intended for a purpose other than planning. For example, insurance companies are required to keep books according to special accounting rules for regulatory agencies monitoring company solvency. These public data are among the most easily available in the industry, and the most accurate, yet rarely give a true picture of the current performance and competitive position of the companies. It must be considerably adjusted if used for planning.

7. *Make creation of a good plan the objective, rather than simply planning.*
   The distinction between planning and creating a good plan is subtle yet important for creating the right attitude in the minds of those doing planning. If people feel they will be rewarded for planning they will put in their time but a good plan won't necessarily result. On the other hand, if a good plan is expected then chances of it resulting are greatly increased. The distinction is akin to that between working and accomplishing the job, or between traveling and arriving.

8. *Make the reward-punishment system work for planning.*
   Planning works best when the organization's reward-punishment system rewards planning, rewards longer-term performance, and is consonant with the behavior required to implement the plan. For instance, if regional exploration managers of an oil company are rewarded for the percentage of successful wells drilled, they

will resist a plan which calls for drilling a high percentage of wildcat wells. Thus, to the extent possible, those responsible for implementing plans and planning should adjust the reward-punishment system to reward action consistent with the realization of the plan, or adjust the plan to fit the reward-punishment system.

9. *Tailor the planning approach to the characteristics of key people.*
The characteristics of those involved in planning (i.e., "typical" managers of various types and upper-level management) must be taken into account in designing planning procedures and selecting approaches. Approaches that result in good strategic plans from one manager won't necessarily get the same results for another. For instance, the former chief executive of one company was a reader who liked substantial written support for all decisions. His planning system generated notebooks of information for his review prior to entering the final stages of planning. His successor was not a reader; he preferred terse oral summaries. When faced with the first planning cycle in his new administration he balked at all the material. As a result, planning was nearly scrapped and was revived only when the system was revised to meet his needs. Unless there is specific information to the contrary, the system should be designed assuming that the managers like verbal communication, short encounters, and prefer "live action" to deep thought. Ways of accomplishing this include: initiating the planning process at some sort of "retreat" away from daily interruptions, verbal discussions to "prime" the thinking process, and conducting as much dialogue as possible verbally (with subsequent documentation) rather than by memoranda. Once the planning process is well underway as many decisions as possible should be made in a number of short encounters, to fit the managers' natural style, rather than a few long meetings.

10. *Have a specific schedule for planning.*
As mentioned earlier, planning is something that few managers enjoy; they will postpone it in favor of fighting short-term "fires" if given a chance. To avoid this, a strict schedule, enforced from the top, is essential. The old management adage "scheduled activities drive out unscheduled activities" works well in planning.

11. *Allow sufficient time for planning.*
The schedule should allow sufficient time in two ways: enough hours and enough elapsed time. The hours are necessary because planning is time consuming; the elapsed time is necessary for data to be collected, staff work to be done, and, more importantly, for subconscious reasoning to take place. Participants do a great deal of the best thinking about planning by "mulling things over"

between planning sessions. This subconscious process is especially valuable during the alternative-generation phase. It works best when it has time and stimulation, such as a series of four two-hour meetings, each a few days apart, rather than a single eight-hour session.

12. *Tie planning to year-round decision making.*

Annually, most large corporations create or update a long-range plan. Quite naturally, attention focused on planning is at its highest during this time of the year; it must remain high during the rest of the year if the benefits of planning are to be achieved. As mentioned previously, all major long-range decisions including capital budgeting, financing, new product introduction, acquisitions, and divestitures should be related to the plan. Special long-range studies of products, markets, etc., should continue throughout the year. Competitive, environmental, economic, and other sorts of analysis should be ongoing. Major changes in environmental or competitive conditions should cause the plan to be updated.

SUMMARY

Mastery of the techniques, described in earlier chapters, dealing with the economic side of planning, is not sufficient, by itself, to ensure good results. Success requires consideration of human and administrative issues because humans conduct planning in an organizational setting—not in isolation.

Many problems result; the following are some of the underlying causes. Most corporate reward-punishment systems reward short-run performance more than long-run, so managers spend relatively little time thinking about long-run issues. They use the planning system to enhance the share of the corporate resources that their organizational unit receives. Their jobs are so hectic that they have become attuned to dealing with current *ad hoc* issues in brief verbal encounters; the long periods of deep reflection required to plan effectively are foreign to them. Planning is often misunderstood. Organizational politics further complicate complex technical issues. Communication among far-flung organizational units with widely differing orientations is difficult.

Most of these causes are unavoidable, and the challenge is to succeed in spite of them. We have listed a dozen suggestions for doing so:

1. Get the support of senior management.
2. Educate those who will be involved in planning.
3. Ensure that all general managers, resource managers, and program managers are actively involved in planning.

4. Make heavy, but appropriate, use of staff analysis.
5. Keep planning simple, and add complexity when the organization is ready for it.
6. Be concerned about data inputs.
7. Make the objective creation of a good plan, rather than simply planning.
8. Make the reward-punishment system work for planning.
9. Tailor the planning approach to the characteristics of key people.
10. Have a specific schedule for planning.
11. Allow sufficient time for planning.
12. Tie planning to year-round decision making.

BUTLER & HAMMER, INC.[1]

Walter Schmidt, planning specialist and PIMS representative[2] for Butler & Hammer, Inc., and his boss, Carl Philips, vice president for corporate planning were about to conclude their meeting on a study requested by Ralph Barnes, the corporate president. The results suggested some significant changes in the strategy of the company's Power Drive Division which were likely to arouse strong feelings. Consequently, the two men were discussing a "game plan" for introducing the results into the organization. In conducting the study Mr. Schmidt had been heavily influenced by various PIMS analyses. He was one of eight in the corporate planning group; Mr. Philips reported directly to Mr. Barnes. (See Exhibit 1 for an organizational chart.)

Butler & Hammer, Inc. (B & H), with sales of $3.1 billion, was a diversified manufacturer, primarily of industrial products. It was organized into four product groups, each of which had a group vice president to whom reported from four to ten product line divisions. The publicly-held company was among the top hundred in the *Fortune 500* and had plants in twenty-two U.S. and twelve foreign locations.

B & H was considered to be a well-managed "blue chip" but not a great innovator. Rather, it had compiled a solid record through "bread and butter" conservative management practices. Most of its management had risen through the ranks with a preponderance having engineering and manufacturing backgrounds.

The Power Drive Division, the subject of the study, was located about 1,000 miles from the corporate headquarters, just over two hours by frequent commercial jet service. Management concern about this mature business was growing because it had been slowly losing profitability and share during the past five years of its 45-year life.

The division manufactured and sold power drives to about twenty heavy equipment manufacturers. Annual sales which were $85,000,000, had been growing at 6.5 percent in recent years compared to an estimated industry growth rate of 8 percent. With an 18 percent share of the

---

[1]This case was prepared by John S. Hammond and Donald F. Heany.

[2]A PIMS representative is the person in a PIMS member organization responsible for handling the organization's relationship with the PIMS project.

market it was second to a more vertically integrated, efficient competitor that had about one-third of the market. The division's prices were competitive with quality just below average. It did little R & D and employed a small sales force.

The company's participation in the PIMS program had been through the impetus of Messrs. Schmidt and Philips. Walter Schmidt had read an article about PIMS in the *Harvard Business Review* at about the same time his boss was attending an American Management Association (AMA) conference on corporate planning at which he had heard Dr. Sidney Schoeffler, of the Strategic Planning Institute, describe the PIMS program. The two decided that PIMS membership would be very helpful to their planning activities. Thereafter, Mr. Philips proposed to Mr. Barnes that the company join PIMS. The president's reply was, "Well, Carl, I'll defer to you on this one. If you think it's worthwhile, you have my blessings to go ahead and spend some of your budget on it."

PIMS had been warmly received when it was introduced to the rest of management in a two-hour presentation by Messrs. Schmidt and Philips at the next quarterly Division Manager's meeting. However, after getting data on ten businesses initially, Mr. Schmidt had encountered significant difficulties in getting another year's data on the ten businesses at the close of the corporation's fiscal year. With the exception of data on five businesses in the International Group, his attempts to get data on additional businesses had met with a cold response.

Furthermore, he had been recently involved in a battle with a quantitatively oriented subordinate of one of the group vice presidents over an appropriations request. Mr. Schmidt's conclusions, based on PIMS, had not supported the major plant expansion which the Belt Division had requested. The issue was still unresolved but the odds were somewhat greater than 50-50 that the group vice president would prevail.

PERSONNEL INVOLVED

Ralph Barnes, 57, had been president and chief executive officer for five years capping a long career at B & H, which was interrupted only by service as an officer in World War II. He had held engineering, marketing, and manufacturing posts, rising at the early age of 37 to a general management position.

An easy-going Westerner, he was a master at managing by persuasion and consensus, relying heavily on the counsel of his four group vice presidents and his financial vice president in reaching important decisions. He enjoyed their solid support and vice versa.

Mr. Barnes initiated relatively little. Instead he responded to problems and to proposals brought to his attention from below. Although he liked numerical support of any proposal, Mr. Barnes had no financial training. His formal management education was confined to three industrial engineering courses as an undergraduate and a few short courses by the American Management Association.

While tolerant of others' viewpoints and willing to listen to their arguments, Mr. Barnes usually had his own ideas about how to deal with business problems which were brought to his attention. His long experience in the industry and what his staff termed a "masterful intuition," had been the basis on which he could, with some confidence, reach sound business decisions. However, recent raw material shortages and surpluses, energy shortages, rapid inflation, environmental controls, minority hiring, and recession had perplexed him. Furthermore, these unusual and rapidly changing conditions had caused increasing disagreement about difficult situations among his trusted advisors.

Carl Philips, 48, was a respected middle-level manager whose experience at the divisional level included a unit manager's position as well as a long list of staff positions. He had compiled a solid record of per-formance on every assignment and had been promoted steadily. His ambition, which he had mentioned to Mr. Schmidt, was to become a division manager before Mr. Barnes retired five years hence. Therefore, he had welcomed his appointment to corporate planning as a place to gain visibility and to learn how the corporate executive office functioned.

Under Mr. Philips, the Planning Department had grown from two people to eight at a time when many other staff operations had steady or constricting budgets. This expansion had been in spite of the occasional strong protest of the Vice President for Finance who expressed concern about growing overhead in periods of flat earnings. Mr. Barnes tended to seek Mr. Philip's advice on about half of the important decisions involving the corporation's resource allocation and frequently requested studies of difficult situations. While many were longer-term studies, often the requests were for several-day efforts. A corporate planning system, introduced by Mr. Philips soon after assuming his position, was just beginning to succeed after a shaky start.

Mr. Philips had a reputation for being a down-to-earth realist who knew well the absorption rate of top management for new ideas. He seemed particularly to prize the credibility which he and his planners had built with senior management. His life-long career at B & H gave him a thorough knowledge of the company and direct acquaintance with most general managers from the division level up.

It was Mr. Barnes who, two and a half years earlier, had asked Mr. Philips to come to corporate headquarters to assume the newly created post of Director of Corporate Planning and then, two years later, promoted him to Vice President, Corporate Planning. (Some years earlier Mr. Philips had been staff to Mr. Barnes at the division level.) The two paragraphs in this year's annual report were the first in which the planning function had been described in any depth. They had been written by Mr. Philips for his superior.

Walter Schmidt, 36, had both engineering and M.B.A. degrees. Of his ten years with B & H, five were in the divisions as a market analyst and five were in the corporate staff.

Intrigued with analytic approaches, Mr. Schmidt felt that PIMS analyses gave him great insights into the businesses which he was asked to analyze. He also got considerable intellectual reward from his involvement with PIMS and he especially enjoyed attending PIMS conferences.

Robert McCloud, 38, manager of the Power Drive Division, had held a variety of manufacturing positions in several divisions, prior to assuming his current position a year earlier. As manufacturing manager for the Power Drive Division for the previous seven years he had been the architect of the division's production strategy. He had integrated backward, somewhat, including into specialized castings and the custom blending of some gear oils and greases.

Based on his results-oriented style, he had been promoted to division manager when his group vice president became disenchanted with the division's performance. The organizational changes and overhead cuts he had introduced and the elimination of marginal products from the line had improved earnings but not to the level of several years earlier. He was proudest of the record of more output from the same work force and the slightly increased market share of the last year. However, within the past month he had confided in Mr. Philips that he was concerned that time was running out on his two-year mandate to turn around the division. He had been frustrated at how much time it had taken him to get a handle on the business and understand all of its problems; a year after taking over he felt he was still learning about it. While he was very strong in manufacturing, he had little experience in marketing, finance, and other functions. Because of his relatively recent promotion he was known to less than half of B & H's general management.

THE STUDY

Mr. Philips' charge from Mr. Barnes (which in turn was conveyed to Mr. Schmidt) was to "take a look at the Power Drive Division and see what you can suggest about improving its strategy. I think we need a fresh view from outside and young McCloud could use some help." Mr. Schmidt first familiarized himself with the division by reading some of its marketing literature and by rereading its contributions to the past two years' corporate plans. This revealed plans to trim the product line, increase efficiency by acquiring several million dollars worth of computer-controlled manufacturing equipment, and backward integrate somewhat. He next decided to use PIMS to get an assessment of how the division's performance compared with PAR and to identify promising areas for strategy improvement. To do so, however, required information from the division so he sought Mr. Philips' advice on how to proceed. Mr. Philips suggested that the two meet with Mr. McCloud at the division's headquarters. After checking with Mr. Rubin, the group vice president of the Industrial Systems Group (who seemed concerned about the study), the meeting was arranged.

At the meeting Mr. Philips introduced Mr. Schmidt and explained the purpose of the study. Then Mr. Schmidt reviewed the PIMS concepts and explained how PIMS could be used to assess the division's strategy and look for areas of improvement. Mr. McCloud seemed interested but skeptical. Mr. Schmidt then explained the need for data and suggested he obtain it directly from the division's comptroller. Mr. McCloud asked to see the list of desired information and then said that he would get the data and provide it to Mr. Schmidt in about ten days. The meeting adjourned after an hour's discussion.

The information from Mr. McCloud arrived about a week late so that it was nearly a month after the meeting when the PIMS runs were available. Mr. Schmidt analyzed them carefully; they indicated that PAR ROI should be 32 percent compared with the division's 25 percent figure. It suggested, among other things:

1. A major increase in market share would be desirable.
2. No increase in backward integration should be made.
3. Investment intensity should remain at current levels.

DEALING WITH THE RESULTS OF THE POWER DRIVE STUDY

It was the usual practice at the end of a study for Mr. Schmidt to review the results with Mr. Philips and then present them to the appropriate constituencies. Before making the presentation, Mr. Philips usually would give his subordinate elaborate counsel regarding the politics of the situation. One of his favorite reminders was, "We didn't get where we are overnight or by taking big chances." Another was, "It doesn't pay to have enemies in the divisions."

Occasionally Mr. Philips felt he had to temper Mr. Schmidt's enthusiasm for quantitative analysis. Usually Philips allowed Schmidt to make his own presentations, being content only to introduce Schmidt and participate in the subsequent discussion of the presentation.

In this particular case the men realized they had a difficult problem. They decided to meet the next day on a "game plan" for what to do with the results. Mr. Philips closed with, "Now, Walter, I realize what a fine job you've done on this analysis. But don't forget that Sam Rubin (the group vice president of the Industrial Systems Group) has had a lot to do with shaping the current strategy of the Power Drive Division. And he was the one who picked Bob McCloud as the division manager. His O.R. (Operations Research) man is likely to come down on us like a ton of bricks, just as he did on that appropriations request in the Belt Division. I think we're walking on eggs here.

"I don't think I can hold off Ralph Barnes for more than a couple of weeks. He called yesterday and asked how we were coming on this study. I suspect that while we are going to have to take a position soon, it will be several months before definitive action, if any, will be taken. We need a *specific* plan on how to proceed. How are you going to handle this one?"

DISCUSSION QUESTIONS

BUTLER & HAMMER, INC.

1. What do you think of the way Mr. Schmidt has handled the study so far?
2. What characteristics of the organization are relevant in deciding how Messrs. Schmidt and Philips should proceed?
3. What characteristics of the people involved are relevant?
4. What characteristics of the decision problem which the study addresses are relevant?
5. What are the most serious potential obstacles to Mr. Schmidt in getting his recommendations accepted and implemented?
6. How should the two men proceed?

Exhibit 1
BUTLER & HAMMER, INC.
Partial Organization Chart

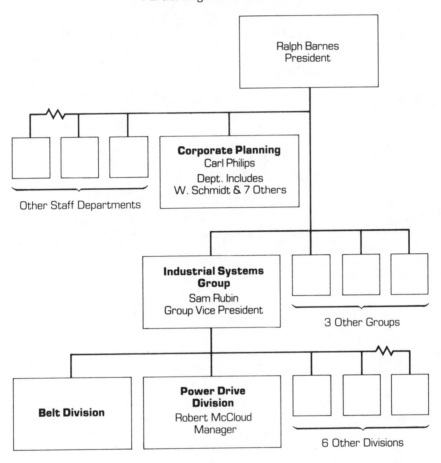

Preparing a Strategic Market Plan

By now you should have a good understanding of the kinds of problems that strategic marketing planning entails, as well as a firm grasp of the kinds of approaches and concepts that should be employed. What remains is to describe how these ideas can be incorporated into the preparation of actual plans.

The actual planning format is important only so far as it ensures that deep strategic thinking occurs. It provides—in effect—a checklist of important issues to be addressed. However, simply going through the format as a blind ritual will not assure that strategic planning is occurring. Companies that believe they have a good planning system simply because they have a well-organized and highly detailed set of instructions with fancy forms and all the trimmings do so at their own peril.

In this chapter we want to describe how the planning process should work and how plans should be drawn up to encourage, not discourage, the process of strategic thinking. While sound procedures can never substitute for strategic thinking, they can reinforce it.

THE PLANNING PROCESS

In Chapter 1 we described a three-cycle planning process. In cycle 1, planning involves a determination of the pros and cons of broad strategic *alternatives*. These alternatives relate primarily to the definition of the business and its future mission. In cycle 2, the definition of the business and its mission are "given" and the emphasis shifts to the formulation of functional strategies required to accomplish the chosen strategy. In cycle 3, the emphasis shifts from long-range strategy to the one-year plan detailing programs of activity and budgets.

When a three-cycle planning process is implemented in a diversified company, a second process of *vertical interaction between levels of the organization* must occur as an integral part of the decision-making flow. Corporate, business, and program (or functional) managers have to reach agreement on various aspects of the plan as it passes through the various steps in the planning process. Table 1 shows how the flow through the three cycles of decisions combines with the flow through three levels of management.[1] [In this particular diagram, the levels have been designated as corporate, business, and program (or functional department). In some companies, the levels might be designated by other terms such as "groups," "divisions" (or "departments"), and "products" (or "markets"), respectively.]

As can be seen, each cycle of the planning process involves all three levels of management. In the first cycle, tentative agreements are made between corporate, business, and program managers about definitional alternatives and missions. These broad strategic choices are made with an eye to corporate requirements as well as an eye to the realities of the various markets in which the business competes. The decisions that are reached provide a framework for more detailed planning in the next cycle. In the second cycle, business and program managers work with functional managers (e.g., managers of manufacturing, R&D, sales, etc.) to develop tentative plans about the functional programs to be undertaken. In so doing, the strategic issues debated in the first cycle achieve additional definition. Finally, in the third cycle, specific resource allocations are made as functional plans are solidified and converted into budgeting terms.

In the remainder of this chapter we shall wear the hat of a manager of a business unit and consider how he/she should prepare plans for presentation to corporate management at each cycle. However, nearly all that will be said could equally apply to a program manager preparing plans for presentation to his/her next level, namely, the management of a business unit. The key point to bear in mind is that both the purpose and output of planning are quite different in each cycle;

---

[1]This graphic representation of the planning process is based on a similar representation proposed by Peter Lorange and Richard F. Vancil. See Lorange and Vancil, *Strategic Planning Systems* (Englewood Cliffs, N.J.: Prentice-Hall, Inc., 1977), Chapter 1, p. 26.

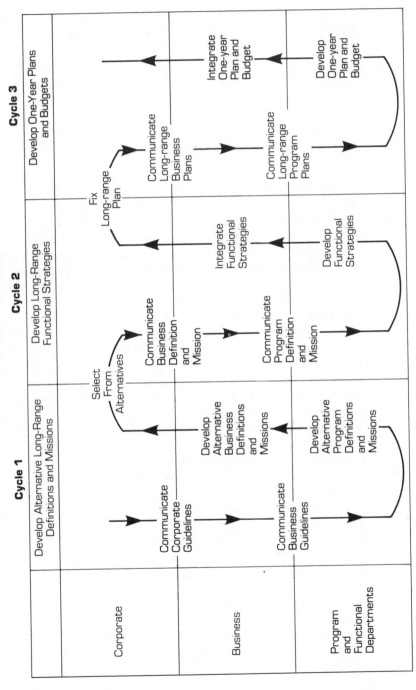

the format and content of first-, second-, and third-cycle plans should reflect these differences. In many companies this is not done. Either only one plan is prepared (in which case the company usually gets "locked in" too early to a single alternative) or the first-cycle plan is simply modified in subsequent cycles as planning progresses.

PREPARING FIRST-CYCLE PLANS

The emphasis in preparing first-cycle plans is on long-range *alternatives* and on understanding the pros and cons of alternative definitions of the activity and alternative missions. The process starts with corporate management providing broad guidelines to business management who in turn provide guidelines for program management. These guidelines may include assumptions about the overall economic climate, about the presumed scope of the activity, as well as some guidelines as to what management is seeking in terms of cash flow, net income, return on investment, or other measures of performance. It is important that these requirements be viewed only as highly tentative. Final decisions as to the appropriate mission for a business (or program) and its role in the corporate (or business) portfolio should depend just as much on analysis of the market opportunity as they do on corporate requirements. Tex-Fiber Industries, for example, may be criticized for its overly strong "top-down" orientation. Corporate management apparently designated the Petroloid Products Division (PPD) as a future cash cow without detailed analysis of the market. Had they analyzed the market, they would have realized that funds would be withdrawn from PPD just at the point in time when PPD's major competitor was increasing its investment in that business.

Functional strategies and their financial implications have to be considered, but only at a level of detail sufficient to support the analyses of business definition and mission. As in each cycle, "the numbers have to be pushed"—understanding the financial implications of alternatives is essential—but the projections need only be approximate at this stage.

Although many variations in specific format are possible, a cycle-1 plan should include the general headings shown in Table 2. A plan of this type should be drawn up for each business unit within the corporation (or with slight modification for each program unit within a business).

Table 2

TYPICAL CYCLE-1 PLAN FOR A BUSINESS UNIT

A. *Management Summary* (by business manager/planner)
    1. Key assumptions, alternatives, recommendations
B. *Corporate Guidelines* (from corporate manager/planner)
    2. Corporate economic guidelines
       — overall
       — in this sector
    3. Presumed business scope
    4. Tentative statement of corporate requirements (five years)
       — overall (growth, earnings per share, net income, ROI)
       — for this business (sales, market share, net income, ROI, cash flow)
C. *Business and Market Analyses* (by business manager/planner)
    5. Customer analysis and segmentation
    6. Competitor analysis
    7. Analysis of market characteristics
    8. Major trends/changes
    9. Company self-assessment
    10. Cost analysis
D. *Strategic Alternatives* (by business manager/planner)
    11. Alternative definitions of business activity
       — pros/cons
       — impact on mission
       — functional strategy implications
       — approximate financial implications
    12. Alternative missions for the business
       — current portfolio role
       — impact of no planned change
       — analysis of alternative "moves" and functional strategy implications
E. *Recommendations* (by business manager/planner)
    13. Definition
    14. Mission
    15. Congruence with corporate requirements
    16. Contingency analysis—"what if" the market doesn't evolve as expected?
    17. Implementation

PREPARING SECOND-CYCLE PLANS

The outcome of negotiations in the first cycle is a tentative decision on the future definition of the business and the mission which will be pursued. At the lower level, programs get defined and *their* missions are tentatively decided.

These decisions set the scene for the second planning cycle. At this stage, business and program managers start to work closely with functional managers, i.e., managers of manufacturing, sales, research and development, service, physical distribution, etc. Whereas in the first planning cycle functional strategies were only considered in enough detail to allow decisions to be made about the strategic questions of definition and mission, in this cycle detailed functional strategies to accomplish these directions are worked out. In practice, many companies fail in their planning because functional strategies are developed in the absence of any clear overall strategic definition and mission.[2]

The detailed development of functional strategies consistent with the various programs of activity requires more detailed elaboration of financial implications than occurred in the first cycle. Each functional program which is proposed will be roughly costed out and the total impact on expenses, net income, and cash flow will be considered. Still, however, the resultant budgets, pro forma income statements, and balance sheets are only approximate.

With the same caveat that many variations in format are possible, a cycle-2 plan should include the general headings shown in Table 3.

Table 3
TYPICAL CYCLE-2 PLAN FOR A BUSINESS

A. *Management Summary* (by business manager/planner)
    1. Key assumptions, recommendations
B. *Corporate Inputs* (in negotiation with corporate manager/planner)
    2. Business definition
    3. Business mission
C. *Market Analyses* (repeated from cycle-1 plan but highlighting aspects relevant to functional strategy formulation—by business manager/planner)
    4. Customer analysis and segmentation
    5. Competitor analysis
    6. Analysis of market characteristics
    7. Major trends/changes
    8. Company self-assessment
    9. Cost analysis
D. *Long-Range Business Plan* (by business and program managers/planners)
    10. Overall summary
    11. Program A
    12. Program B, etc.
E. *Long-Range Resource/Functional Plans and Tentative Budgets* (by functional managers)
    13. Manufacturing
    14. Sales
    15. Research and development
    16. Service
    17. Physical distribution

---

[2]See Gluck, Foster, and Forbes, "Cure for Strategic Malnutrition," *Harvard Business Review*, November–December 1976.

Note how this cycle-2 plan differs from the cycle-1 plan presented previously. First, there is much less attention to broad strategic alternatives. Decisions about these alternatives have already been tentatively made in negotiations between business and corporate management. Here the focus shifts to detailed functional planning. Both program managers and functional managers are involved in such planning and each draws up a part of the plan from his/her own perspective. Each program manager draws up functional plans for his/her particular program; these are then integrated into an overall plan for the business (section D in Table 3). Also, functional managers draw up complete functional plans for their particular activity (section E in Table 3).

PREPARING THIRD-CYCLE PLANS

In the final cycle, attention shifts to the preparation of the one-year plan for the upcoming fiscal year. As a result, the major concern is with *specific* program and functional plans, budgets, and implementation.

Between the second and third cycles, business management will have reviewed cycle-2 program and functional plans, and corporate management will have reviewed cycle-2 business plans. The long-term strategic plan, including definition, missions, functional strategies, and approximate budget implications, will have been agreed. This agreement forms the context within which the one-year plan gets formulated.

In this third cycle, *sales forecasting* becomes extremely important as an input. Specific forecasts for various segments of activity have to be made and their implications for resource commitments agreed to. This will include manufacturing commitments, sales-force commitments, research and development commitments, etc. As this is done, pro forma income statements, balance sheets, and cash flow statements are prepared. These provide the basis for final budget decisions for the forthcoming year. At this point they are highly specific and detailed.

A typical format for the one-year plan is shown in Table 4.

RELATIVE IMPORTANCE OF THE THREE CYCLES

The relative importance of the three cycles varies considerably depending on the particular business situation at hand. In some businesses, little debate is necessary each year about long-term strategic alternatives or long-term functional plans. This is usually true in mature, relatively stable businesses where careful planning has taken place in

Table 4
TYPICAL CYCLE-3 PLAN FOR A BUSINESS

A. *Management Summary* (by business manager/planner)
    1. Key assumptions, recommendations
B. *Corporate Inputs* (from corporate manager/planner—approved cycle-2 plans)
    2. Long-range business plan (outline form)
    3. Long-range resource plans (outline form)
C. *One-Year Business and Program Plans and Budgets* (by business and program managers/planners)
    4. Overall business
    5. Program A
    6. Program B, etc.
D. *One-Year Resource/Functional Plans and Budgets* (by functional managers)
    7. Manufacturing
    8. Sales
    9. Research and development
    10. Service
    11. Physical distribution
E. *Contingency Plans* (by business manager/planner)
    12. Major assumptions on which plan is based
    13. Sensitivity of results to assumptions
    14. Contingency plans
F. *Implementation* (by business manager/planner)
    15. People responsibilities
    16. Timetable

---

the past, and management is clear about the long-term strategic directions that are being followed. Attention, instead, is directed at shorter-term annual planning and budgeting in line with established longer-term objectives. The long-term plan is simply "tuned up" to reflect changes that have occurred since the last complete planning cycle.

In other businesses, either those that are in earlier developmental stages or those where little planning has taken place in the past, major attention must be given to the first- and second-planning cycles. This may go on annually for a number of years as major strategic moves are made in response to market evolution or as management begins to articulate and implement a clear long-term strategy.

WHAT HAPPENED
TO THE MARKETING PLAN?

The process which has been described above has been called "strategic market planning." Many companies call it "business planning" or simply "strategic planning." How does the preparation of such plans relate to the so-called "marketing plan"? In such a system as the one just described the answer is that there probably will be no separate "marketing plan." Marketing management (product managers, market managers, sales managers, etc.) plays a key role in the preparation of a strategic market plan, and this plan subsumes the major elements of the marketing plan. In particular, the strategic market plan includes: a) plans for individual "programs" within a business and b) the way *marketing* resources will be used to accomplish the plan.

Many companies—especially functionally organized ones—still have a "marketing plan," although it is often little more than a "sales plan." However, in multiproduct, multimarket, diversified companies that are organized into businesses and programs, it is increasingly common to find strategic market planning (or "business planning") replacing marketing planning. When a marketing plan is prepared in these situations, it is usually for defined programs of activity within the business and provides an elaboration of the marketing task that has to be accomplished as part of such a program.

USING A STRATEGIC MARKET PLAN

In some companies months are spent in the planning process yet, once it is completed, plans are filed away in managers' desks and are never referred to until the next planning cycle. In too many companies, the plan is not communicated beyond a few key managers; actions are not initiated to build strength in the long term; one-year planning goes on independently of longer-range strategic planning (as at Tex-Fiber); capital budgets are approved as a completely separate activity organized by the controller's office; new product development, acquisitions, and diversification have a life of their own; and plans are seldom used as control devices. This attitude toward planning and plans is unfortunate since the plan is intended to be a *working* document with many uses. Among the most important are:

1. To communicate a sense of direction to all parts of the organization;
2. To identify near-term actions needed to prepare the company for the long run;
3. To help assess the long-term impact of shorter-range plans;
4. To provide a basis for short-range, one-year planning;
5. To provide a basis for capital budgeting and financial strategy;
6. To provide guidelines for new product development, diversification, acquisition, and divestiture;
7. To provide a control device against which to compare actual progress.

---

[3]John M. Hobbs and Donald F. Heany, "Coupling Strategy to Operating Plans," *Harvard Business Review*, May–June 1977.

Unless the plan is *used* for these purposes, much of the effort that goes into planning will have been wasted.

A CONCLUDING NOTE

This book has been about techniques to facilitate perhaps the most important organizational decision-making process: the determination of a strategy for a business and for its subunits and the allocation of its resources to businesses and among the subunits. To arrive at these decisions, properly, requires time-consuming, complex interaction of many human beings who must consider large amounts of information. The techniques we have described provide ways of conceptualizing the process and structuring the information to facilitate better decision making.

Many people lose sight of the fact that planning is a study of the future, designed to assist the making of *current* decisions. It is *not* a vehicle for making future decisions; in fact, its role is less often narrowing options than keeping them open.

Planning requires prodigious amounts of time, energy, and thought, as does any complex problem-solving process. It is a job for corporate management, business management, functional management, and program management, supported and stimulated by very substantial amounts of good staff work. It is a job, not for planners, but for managers supported by planners. Making planning work effectively in an organization takes practice and refinement; it is not unusual for at least three years to elapse before planning functions smoothly, so patience is the watchword.

In practice, planning provides the framework for a dialectic—a great debate. The debate is among the organization's constituencies, each with a combination of conflicting and consonant interests and each out to get a goodly share of the corporate resources.[3] The state of the art of planning will advance to the degree that new techniques and procedures can be devised that shed more light than heat on this process. The techniques described in this book are major steps in that direction.

---

[3] Joseph L. Bower, *Managing the Corporate Resource Allocation Process* (Boston: Division of Research, Harvard Business School, 1970).

SPEER INDUSTRIES (B)[1]

On April 1, 1975, the Special Task Force appointed by the president of Speer Industries, Inc., to study Speer's approach to the Scientific Instrumentation market, met for the first time. At that meeting it was agreed that the work of the Task Force should proceed in two parallel directions:

1. A report should be compiled on the "scientific instrumentation" industry. This task was assigned to Mr. Guy Converse, a member of the Task Force and part-time assistant to the president, Mr. Paul Berger.
2. Each of Speer's four divisions involved with scientific instrumentation should draw up a "strategic plan." These plans were scheduled for presentation to the Task Force at the next meeting. The responsibility for drawing up individual plans was assigned to the general manager of each division involved. However, in each case, two "shepherds" were appointed from among the Task Force members to guide the planning activity and to ensure some measure of uniformity in the final result.

In settling on these two next steps, the minutes of the April 1st meeting documented five reasons which the Task Force believed justified such an effort:

1. It would provide a qualitative statement of directions already underway or contemplated.
2. It would allow the Task Force to see the cash flow and net income implications of each of these separate planned activities.
3. The individual plans themselves would be improved simply from the process of formalizing them.
4. Eventually some ranking of the relative desirability of some of the new directions planned might be possible in terms of:
   a. their relative profitability, cash requirements, fit with the company, etc.,

---

[1]This case was prepared by Derek F. Abell.

    b. their contribution toward a strategy for Speer's scientific instrumentation activities, as a whole, and

    c. their potential for allowing integration/sharing of manufacturing, R&D, or sales activities at some time in the future.

5. A statement of Speer's current and planned activities in this market might be compared with an overall analysis of the whole scientific instrumentation area to ascertain whether Speer was generally devoting itself to growth and profitable areas. This might suggest overall new directions, acquisitions, markets to be considered for entry, etc., etc.

The remainder of this case contains the first of the two items called for by the Task Force, a description of the scientific instrumentation industry compiled under the direction of Mr. Guy Converse (see following Appendix).

Appendix A

Speer Industries, Inc. [B]

To: Task Force on Scientific Products
From: Guy Converse
Subject: The Scientific Instrumentation Industry

    According to United States government statistics,[2] 1975 shipments of instrumentation of all types amounted to $12.01 billion. 1976 shipments were estimated to be $13.18 billion, an increase of 11 percent. Table 1 shows an overall breakdown of these shipments by SIC code.

    SAMA[3] classifies "scientific" instrumentation in a somewhat different manner than the United States government. The association operates six major "sections" within which virtually all of Speer's products fall.

analytical instruments	optical
laboratory apparatus	process measurement and control
measurement and test equipment	scientific laboratory furniture and equipment

---

[2]United States Industrial Outlook, 1976.
[3]SAMA is an abbreviation for the Scientific Apparatus Makers Association. SAMA has more than 200 member firms.

Table 1

Shipments of Instrumentation
[$000,000]

	1976	1975
INSTRUMENTS FOR MEASUREMENT, ANALYSIS & CONTROL		
3811 Engineering and science	$ 1,680	$ 1,480
Aerospace, nautical, navigational (50%)		
Laboratory apparatus and furniture (43%)		
Other (7%)		
3822 Automatic environmental controls	870	720
3821 Measuring and controlling instruments	2,780	2,400
Process control (46%)		
Fluid metering and counting devices (30%)		
Other measuring and controlling instruments (24%)		
3821 Electricity measurement	2,380	2,180
Test (70%)		
Other (30%)		
3832 Optical instruments and lenses[4]	870	785
MEDICAL AND DENTAL INSTRUMENTS AND SUPPLIES	4,900	4,400
Total (all instruments)	13,180	12,010

[4]Includes gas chromatographs, spectrophotometers, electron microscopes and other related instrumentation.

Some idea of the breadth and scope of equipment implied by even these broad categories can be gained by reference to Exhibit 1. This exhibit contains a partial list of "analytical instruments and related supplies and equipment" used by a leading technical journal[5] in describing brand preference for individual items of equipment.

The markets for analytical instruments are equally diverse. Prior to the second world war scientific instruments were primarily used for research purposes in scientific laboratories. By contrast, in the present day, analytical instruments are used in industrial plants, in clinical laboratories, in educational institutions, in the field, and in other situations both inside and outside the laboratory. As a result, the analytical instrument market has grown from virtually nothing to an estimated $600 million in 1974.

The growth has been accompanied by a change in the nature of the market. Fifty years ago, consumable supplies, e.g., reagent chemicals and supplies, constituted the major part of the market. In 1974 consumables constituted only 25–35 percent of the total market, the rest being accounted for by instruments. The reasons behind the growth and the change are described below. Their likely future impact is also assessed:

[5]Research/Development Magazine.

1. Economic expansion: Between 1944 and 1974 the gross national product had quintupled in dollar terms. Growth in the future can be expected to be slower as the philosophy of conservation becomes dominant.

2. New technology: New technology has made practicable a whole range of new measurements and analyses. Also as industrial production techniques become more sophisticated, need for instrumentation increases. Adaptation of solid state technology can be expected to have a positive impact in the future.

3. Cost reduction: New technology and increased demand have led to significant cost reductions in instruments, thus enlarging the market. This process is expected to continue in the future despite inflationary pressure.

4. Increasing labor costs: The increase in personnel costs provides a financial incentive for replacing manual processes by instrumentation. This trend, combined with cost reduction in instrumentation, will lead to ever increasing use of instrumentation in the future.

5. Federal funding: In the post-Sputnik era, federal funding for all branches of science and technology were sharply increased. This both created a demand for analytical instruments and fostered the development of much of the sophisticated instruments available today. Federal funding is still increasing but its relative importance is declining. This trend is likely to continue in the future. However, some areas such as energy, environment and health are receiving a substantial increase in funding. The direction of funding is changing from basic research to development and this may reduce the range of technical breakthroughs in comparison to previous years.

6. Computerization: Introduction of computers with their vast data processing capacity made automation possible in a number of areas like industrial process control or clinical testing. This, in turn, created a demand for instruments to generate the data needed by the computer. A. W. Fisher recently forecast that new instruments will be based on advances in electronics and data processing rather than in the sciences.

7. Federal regulation: Regulations in the area of environment (air and water pollution, employee health and safety), product quality and other areas have increased the demand for instruments. The impact of federal regulation can be expected to be higher in the future.

8. Energy cost: The high cost of energy has encouraged the use of instruments to conserve energy. Energy cost can be expected to rise in the future, thus aiding the growth of instrumentation.

All these factors point to a continued expansion of the market for analytical instruments. Exhibit 2 summarizes the growth of the market by use between 1967 and 1974, and projects the market in 1982. It shows a slower growth between 1974–82 (8.4% p.a.) than in 1967–1974 (10.1% p.a.). The process control, production and quality control, and hospital and biomedical segments will grow at an above average rate.

Exhibit 3 presents the same data by product class. Above average growth during 1974–1982 is expected in electro-analytical instruments, special purpose instruments and instrument data systems.

MARKET ANALYSIS

Industry. At approximately 60 percent of the domestic market, industry is the largest purchaser of analytical instruments. This dominance is expected to remain unchanged between 1974 and 1982.

However, the use of instruments is expected to change significantly —process control and quality control are expected to grow faster than research and development.

It is estimated that two-thirds of the process control expenditures are related to new plant and equipment. So this market depends heavily on capital investment. The increase in investment tax credit to 10 percent and a general upturn in the economy are expected to boost capital spending. Planned expenditures show a steady increase through 1978. Several industries which are major users of process control equipment are expected to show a much higher rate of increase. These include iron and steel, petroleum, chemicals, and paper.

Four factors are likely to foster increased use of process control equipment—government regulation (product safety, environmental), increased cost and scarcity of energy, increasing sophistication of industrial processes requiring sophisticated control instrumentation, and the development of advanced computerized control systems. It is expected that the federal government will spend $10 billion in energy research and development between 1974 and 1979. This is expected to be supplemented by a large investment by industry. The bulk of the government funds will be spent in nuclear technology but substantial investments will be made in energy conservation (14 percent) and coal technology (19 percent) both of which will use analytical instruments. One study estimates that there will possibly be twenty synthetic natural gas plants by 1990 which will mean a $50–60 million market for process instrumentation and control. Turning next to computer-based control systems it is estimated that by 1982 there will be 30,000 such systems in the United States (1972—3,000).

Market growth will also come from application of process control instrumentation to new industries. New users include food and beverage, pulp and paper, iron and steel, nonferrous metals, and building materials.

One area of product opportunity seems to be in improved measuring instruments. A survey by a trade magazine found that inability to obtain reliable measures of process variables is a major limitation in the growth of automatic control systems. The demand for such instruments is expected to grow 20 percent per year between 1974 and 1982.

The production and quality control instrument market is less dependent on capital expenditure and hence is more stable. The recent emphasis on product quality has encouraged the use of analytical instruments in this area. The pharmaceutical industry has been strongly affected by the range of tests required by the FDA and by the increase in the number of products. The food and beverage and cosmetic industries have been similarly affected. Growth markets in this area include mining as well as several industries mentioned in the process control section.

Industrial research and development is expected to hold steady during 1974 and 1975 but to show a steady increase in coming years. The new emphasis on conservation and the acceptance of a lower rate of economic growth will continue to restrict growth in this area. Petroleum and chemicals industries are the largest purchasers of analytical instruments for research and development purposes.

Hospital and Biomedical. The hospital and biomedical market is divided amongst three types of laboratories—independent clinical laboratories (6,000–7,000 establishments), hospital laboratories (6,000–7,000 establishments), and small laboratories for individual physicians or groups of physicians (40,000–50,000 establishments).

This market has grown faster than others during 1967–74 and is expected to enjoy the highest growth rate (9.4 percent) in 1974–82. The factors fueling growth are: more comprehensive health care (Medicare, Medicaid, health maintenance organizations), increases in personnel costs (a unionization effort is currently underway in the health care field), increased government research funding, and advances in health care technology requiring more comprehensive tests.

The bulk of the market growth is likely to come from the growing size and number of clinical laboratories. They are in the best position to increase automation and cut costs on a high volume of routine tests.

Universities and Other Nonprofit Laboratories. The universities and nonprofit laboratories constitute a mature market. Most sales are likely to be for replacement and modernization.

The university/college market has been severely restricted by the reduced growth in enrollment. Enrollment in chemistry courses has actually declined. University budgets have been cut and their purchasing power eroded by inflation. So there is no prospect for a general increase in budgets in this market. However, the National Science Board has defined six areas of future scientific importance (population, world food supply, energy, materials, climate, and the environment) and these may offer growth opportunities.

Government. The direct government purchase is the smallest segment (9 percent in 1974). However, government funds a substantial portion of industry and university research and development. These funds, together with government regulatory activity, give it a substantial influence on the other segments.

The growth of research and development is expected to continue at the 4 percent p.a. rate achieved in 1969–75. Between 1969 and 1975 research and development funds were shifted from space research (1969—24 percent of total, 1975—13 percent) to health (1969—7 percent, 1975—10 percent), energy (1969—2 percent, 1975—5 percent) and environment (1969—2 percent, 1975—5 percent).

In the environment area, government will impact demand for analytical instruments both directly through research funds and indirectly through legislation and promulgation of standards.

COMPETITION

The scientific instrument industry is composed of a preponderance of small firms specializing in one or more types of instruments. In addition, there are a number of larger firms which devote part or all of their facilities to instrumentation. Currently it is estimated that there are about 600 companies active in various aspects of the scientific instrument manufacturing industry. Because many firms are small and have difficulty in obtaining the financial and management resources for growth, mergers and acquisitions are quite prevalent.

Requirements for instrument servicing must be met by successful firms in the field. Generally, larger well-established organizations benefit in this respect and have a strong comparative advantage over small competitors with poor service organizations.

Four well-established companies—Beckman Industries, Hewlett Packard, Perkin Elmer, and Varian Associates—account for more than 50 percent of analytical instrument sales by domestic firms. Each have field sales and service forces numbering 100–200 persons. In virtually every market segment in which one of these firms competes, they hold one of the top three or four market positions.

Beckman Instruments is one of the strongest firms in the instrumentation field, especially in the medical and pollution area. Principal development efforts appear to be in clinical medicine, pollution control, production and quality control, and biomedical research. Beckman produces mini computers and has been active in the laboratory data systems market. In the clinical laboratory market Beckman has tried to emphasize supplies as well as instruments.

Hewlett Packard, a major producer of test and measurement instruments, is active in the manufacture of gaseous analyzers, desk-top and hand-held calculators, gas and liquid chromotographs with mini-computer capabilities, computer interfaces, strip chart recorders, and spectrophotometers. The firm is widely known in the industrial community and has a strong reputation in data systems and automation.

Perkin Elmer is a leading producer of analytical instruments, and a leading factor in precision optics and electro-optical systems for the government. The company is believed to offer one of the most complete lines of analytical instruments in the world. Foreign sales account for more than 30 percent of total volume. The company has been active in the laboratory computer systems market and has built its own computer processors to analyze instrumentation output. Users of Perkin Elmer's instruments include clinical, educational, and industrial purchasers, with the petroleum and chemical fields accounting for a large market share. The company's growth has been both internal and by means of acquisition.

Varian Associates is a leading producer of microwave and special purpose tubes for voice and data communications, navigation, radar, and various industrial control systems. The company also offers a broad line of analytical instruments for use in chemical research, life sciences and diagnostic medicine. Varian has become a large factor in the instrument field by means of acquisitions plus extensive research and development.

The company has placed a great deal of emphasis on the market for mini-computer systems for laboratory analytical use. It offers a wide variety of data systems for practically every analytical device it markets. Varian has shipped a substantial proportion of the total number of physical science turnkey systems to date. In 1971 a new instrument division was formed which pulled together a variety of instrument and related equipment activities.

Additional Firms. Fisher Scientific is a large manufacturer and distributor of analytical instruments, laboratory equipment, and reagent chemicals. The product line includes emission spectrometers, atomic absorption and laser Raman spectrophotometers. In addition, Fisher distributes a wide variety of apparatus and instrument products manufactured by other firms. In the 60's, Fisher made a major move in the clinical laboratory market and sales increased from $11 million in 1966 to $66 million in 1974 (34 percent of total Fisher sales).

Digital Equipment Corporation is the leading manufacturer of mini-computers, which are being used increasingly with analytical instruments. Mini-computer demand continues to grow very rapidly. A minor portion of the mini-computer market is supplied by IBM and Honeywell but sales are only a small factor in overall corporate revenues. The marketing, technical and financial strengths of these firms could eventually pose a threat to well-established firms in the analytical instrument field if they choose to compete in instrumentation systems.

Exhibit 1

SPEER INDUSTRIES, INC. [B]

PRODUCT CATEGORIES

Activation analysis systems
Analytical balances
Analyzers, C–H–N
Analyzers, carbon dioxide
Analyzers, chemical (automated wet)
Analyzers, oxygen
Analyzers, particle size
Analyzers, polarographic
Analyzers, (DTA, TGA), thermal
Blenders
Calculators, desk top
Calculators, hand held
Calorimeters
Centrifuges
Chemicals, radioactive labeled
Chemicals and reagents
Chromatographs, gas
Chromatographs, liquid
Chromatographs, thin layer
Compressed gases
Digital computers
Electron spin resonance equipment
Electrophoresis equipment
Fume hoods
Hot plates

Interfaces (computer to scientific instruments)
Ion microprobes
Laboratory furnaces and ovens
Laboratory furniture
Laboratory glassware
Microscopes, optical
Microscopes, scanning electron
Microscopes, transmission electron
Nuclear magnetic resonance equipment
Optical rotary dispersion equipment
pH meters
Plastic labware
Recorders (strip-chart)
Recorders (x-y plotting)
Refractometers
Specific ion electrodes
Spectrometers, electron (ESCA)
Spectrometers, mass
Spectrometers, raman
Spectrometers, x-ray
Spectrophotometers, atomic absorption
Spectrophotometers, atomic fluorescence
Spectrophotometers, ultraviolet
Spectrophotometers, visible
X-ray fluorescence equipment

Exhibit 2
SPEER INDUSTRIES, INC. [B]
Analytical Instruments
Market Trends

	1967		1974		1982		ANNUAL GROWTH RATE 1967–74	1974–82
	$*	%	$	%	$	%	%	%
MARKET SEGMENT								
Industrial	160	61	300	59	575	59	9.4	8.5
Process control	35	13	80	16	175	18	12.5	10.3
Product and quality control	50	19	100	20	210	22	10.4	9.7
R&D	75	29	120	23	190	19	6.9	5.9
Hospitals and biomedical	45	17	110	22	225	23	13.6	9.4
Universities and nonprofit	30	12	55	11	95	10	9.0	7.1
Government agency	25	10	45	9	80	8	8.8	7.5
TOTAL	260	100	510	100	975	100	10.1	8.4
Overseas markets	60		150		325		14.0	10.1
	320		660		1300		10.9	8.8

Source: Adapted from Frost and Sullivan, *Analytical Instruments Markets,* Report #272, June 1974. They define analytical instruments as "devices for determining chemical composition or molecular structure."

*Dollar amounts are in millions.

Exhibit 3
SPEER INDUSTRIES, INC. [B]
Analytical Instruments
Product Trends

	1967		1974		1982		ANNUAL GROWTH RATE 1967–74	1974–82
	$*	%	$	%	$	%		
PRODUCT CLASSIFICATION								
Electro magnetic radiation	119	37	197	30	335	26	7.5	6.9
Thermal techniques	6	2	14	2	35	3	12.9	12.1
Surface techniques	6	2	13	2	24	2	11.7	8.0
Magnetic field effects	37	12	66	10	98	8	8.6	5.1
Electro-analytical	12	4	31	5	75	6	14.5	11.7
Physical-chemical	48	15	80	12	145	11	7.6	7.7
Special purpose instruments	55	17	124	19	240	18	12.3	8.6
Instrument data systems	37	12	140	21	348	27	20.9	12.1
TOTAL	320	100	660	100	1300	100	10.9	8.8

Note: These totals include overseas markets.

*Dollar amounts are in millions.

468

SPEER INDUSTRIES, INC. [C]⁴

On April 1, 1975, the Special Task Force appointed by the president of Speer Industries to study Speer's approach to the scientific instrumentation market, decided on two major directions for its further activities. The first of these involved the completion of a report on the scientific instrumentation industry [see Speer Industries, Inc. (B)]. In addition, the Task Force requested each General Manager to submit a written "strategic plan" for his division prior to the next meeting. Two "shepherds" were chosen from among the Task Force members to oversee the preparation of each plan and to ensure some uniformity in the final results.

The "shepherds" were appointed as follows:

Division and General Manager	Shepherds
Reliance Instrumentation Company (Mr. John Wayne)	Alan Fayerweather, Guy Converse
Brite Instrument Company (Mr. Alvin Brite)	Alan Fayerweather, Otto Poensgen
Intron, Inc. (Mr. Robert McNaulty)	Alan Fayerweather, Otto Poensgen
SPD, Inc. (Mr. Otto Poensgen)	Alan Fayerweather, Otto Poensgen⁵

As a first step in this process, the three shepherds met with Mr. James Young, executive vice president and chairman of the Task Force, on April 10, 1975. Two conclusions were reached at that meeting. First, a format was drawn up for the eventual presentation of each plan in summary budget form (see Exhibit 1). Secondly, it was agreed that each General Manager should be encouraged to submit plans containing whatever major alternatives he believed worthy of consideration. Each alternative was to be supported by a budgeted profit and loss and cash flow projection. It was believed that alternatives needed to be presented

---

⁴This case was prepared by Derek F. Abell.

⁵Mr. Poensgen had, prior to joining SPD, been associated with Strategic Planning Associates, a New York-based environmental planning organization.

in order for the Task Force to be able eventually to allocate resources among the several divisions.

Following this initial meeting the "shepherds," working in pairs, began the task of working with each general manager to draw up strategic plans for the respective divisions. The major responsibility for drawing up plans rested with each general manager. The "shepherd's" role was viewed as that of occasional counselor and external consultant.

RELIANCE INSTRUMENT COMPANY

Mr. Guy Converse and Mr. Alan Fayerweather made two trips to Madison, Wisconsin in response to requests from Mr. John Wayne, Reliance's general manager.

The first trip on May 16, 1975 started with a brief walk around the manufacturing plant and adjacent warehousing facility and then adjourned to Mr. Wayne's office. Mr. Wayne, who had been hired by Speer in 1974, explained that he viewed his role as one of restoring the firm to profitability through better production and inventory controls. He stated:

> Dealers are getting more sophisticated, especially the six large dealers who account for 70 percent of our volume. They are reducing inventories and beginning to cherry pick from our line. We are particularly vulnerable because, in many cases, dealers carry two or three times greater dollar inventories of our products than those of our narrower line competitors. Our current plan is to try to provide better delivery to dealers from our own warehouse so that they, in turn, can reduce some of their investment. But we are not going to increase our total inventories. Actually, we plan to decrease work-in-process and raw materials, and use our new computer controlled inventory system to manage finished goods better.

Mr. Wayne was questioned by the shepherds as to whether he believed one alternative strategy was to substantially increase finished goods inventory over and above the levels already envisioned under the new inventory control system, and whether the improved availability might have a favorable impact on sales. His reply was emphatic:

> The corporate controller's office has been on my back to reduce inventories ever since I arrived here eighteen months ago—there is no possibility that we could get additional working capital for such an undertaking. Even if we lowered the dealer discount to pay for it they wouldn't let me do it.

Mr. Wayne went on to emphasize his two major concerns with the strategic planning undertaking:

Strategic planning is all very well and good but there is no one here other than me who can do it. Secondly, I'm damned if I am going to come up with a set of projections which later turn out to be 'quotas'."

After considerable discussion of the intent of the planning exercise, it was agreed that the planning should proceed in three stages, starting with plans for the existing businesses. These steps were identified as:

Stage 1—Existing Business
1. Treat the two businesses (laboratory equipment and nuclear instrumentation) separately;
2. Estimate the total market (domestic U.S.) for each of the five major laboratory product lines;
3. Estimate total market growth in the next three years;
4. Articulate *current* Reliance strategy;
5. Identify any major competitive moves or new technologies which might upset these relationships;
6. Estimate Reliance's market share by product category for the next three years;
7. Project sales for 1976, 1977, 1978;
8. Project a P&L statement using a 55 percent contribution rate (materials 35 percent, labor 9 percent, variable overhead 1 percent), and any changes foreseeable in overheads or investment.

Stage 2—To the above base, add sales and contribution expected from international.

Stage 3—To the above base, add sales and contribution expected from new products.

Mr. Wayne submitted his draft plan, based on this outline, on October 16, 1975 (see Appendix A). At that time Mr. Converse's report on the instrumentation industry was not yet complete and had not been circulated to the Task Force members.

By the time the draft arrived, planning at SPD, Inc. had resulted in the development of a planning format which Mr. Alan Fayerweather believed might be helpful to all three other divisions. A letter, summarizing this format (see Appendix B), was drafted but, after consultation with Mr. Guy Converse, never sent. Both Mr. Fayerweather and Mr. Converse felt it might be better to present the planning outline orally to Mr. Wayne on their next visit scheduled for December 10, rather than to respond to Mr. Wayne's draft with a written request for yet more detailed information.

At Mr. Wayne's request the December 10th meeting in Madison was devoted primarily to possible new product areas in which Reliance might engage in the future. Mr. Wayne had organized a general meeting of his key executives in which each was asked to present his views of possible future product markets for Reliance. Four new areas were identified:

1. a line of products targeted specifically at clinical laboratories;
2. lower-priced water pollution measuring instruments;
3. private label manufacture for distributors who used their own brands;
4. a very low-priced gas chromatograph ($1,000–$2,000 range).

The general opinion of Reliance executives was that any of these new areas could be developed, using the existing dealer network. Since little was known about the potential of such activities, however, Mr. Wayne reiterated his belief that no detailed plans for any of these areas could be included in the division's strategic plan. Instead, he stated his intention to budget approximately $50,000 in total for market research into each area.

The final half-hour of the December 10th meeting was spent discussing Mr. Wayne's recently submitted draft plan. Mr. Guy Converse questioned whether the formula of "better delivery," "more aggressive sales promotion," "out-innovate," and "premium price" applied equally well to all the major products in the Reliance line. Mr. Wayne assured Mr. Converse that this was indeed the case.

In parting, Mr. Wayne did offer some opinions about the other divisions, particularly SPD, Inc. and Brite.

> SPD's manufacturing makes we weep. It wouldn't even fill the corner of our plant. I put them into contact with one of our distributors who wanted a low-price water quality device but they haven't followed up on it. As for Brite, it's hopeless them trying to compete with Beckman, Varian and others. They'll never make it. They have one-tenth of the market share and less than one-tenth of the sales coverage. I'd tell those guys to get the costs of their G16 unit way down as a first step. They are far too high.

BRITE INSTRUMENT COMPANY

The first meeting with executives from Brite was held on May 27, 1975 in Houston, Texas. Subsequent meetings were held on November 10th and again on January 16, 1976.

At the May 27, 1975 meeting, discussion revolved primarily around the relative roles of the existing high-quality gas chromatograph system and newer G16 lower-priced chromatograph. Further substantial R&D investment in the high-quality chromatograph product line was felt to be unjustified. On the other hand, there was concern expressed that Brite should not relinquish its dominant market position in the very specialized applications for which it was particularly suited.

With respect to the newer G16 line two divergent opinions were expressed. The sales manager believed it was necessary to increase the selling effort to reach many accounts on which Brite currently did not call. He expressed the opinion that this was the only way that Brite could ever capitalize on its current technological leadership and eventually achieve its goal of a 10 percent share of market by 1980 (current market share was approximately 1 percent of a total market of $60,000,000). The head of R&D, Mr. Roger Trent, disagreed. He believed a "pay-as-you-go" approach with continuous R&D investments to stay ahead of competition would allow Brite to reach its eventual goal.

Mr. Poensgen and Mr. Fayerweather counselled the group of Brite executives present to explore the pros and cons of each approach both qualitatively and quantitatively before reaching any firm decision. It was agreed that a plan exploring each alternative would be drafted and discussed at the next meeting.

As it turned out, the next meeting was not held until November 10, 1975. It was called by Mr. Otto Poensgen, general manager of SPD, Inc., who believed that, in comparison to his own planning activities at SPD, Brite was falling behind. It quickly became apparent, in fact, that no written plan had been prepared and that little progress had been made since the May meeting.

Having recently drawn up quite detailed plans for SPD, Mr. Poensgen and Mr. Fayerweather were determined to arrive at a draft plan for at least the new G16 line before the day was out. Armed with a flip chart, felt pens, and the budget outline drafted by Mr. Fayerweather for use at Reliance, the assembled group set to work to map out a plan and budget. Four hours later, after considerable discussion, a set of numbers had been produced (see Exhibit 2).

The impact of these numbers on the three Brite executives present was one of shock. Mr. Brite, Mr. Trent, and Brite's sales manager looked with disbelief at the projected net income and cash flow implications of their strategy to achieve a 10 percent market share by 1980. Heated discussion ensued. Selected comments follow:

Mr. Alvin Brite

We will have to rework all the numbers to see if we can make it look better. But we have to grow at all costs even beyond 1980—that's the name of the game. If we can't do that we had better give up.

Mr. Alan Fayerweather

Is 10 percent market share, by 1980, a realistic goal? You are trying to "come from behind" in a mature price-sensitive market. What do you think Perkin Elmer and Beckman's numbers look alike? Can you compete head-on with them? Should you be in this business at all unless you can imitate the efficiencies of the major competitors?

Mr. Otto Poensgen

What will happen to gross margins if there is price competition? What about a segmentation approach? Is there any way to segment this market to achieve the sort of efficiencies necessary for success?

Mr. Joe Small (Sales Manager)

Right now our advertising is "general purpose" and in many different media.

Mr. Alvin Brite

Let's look at history. When we purchased this product from the Britton Company they had targeted primarily the education market. Then, because our salesmen traditionally called on highly sophisticated university research, government, and hospital and clinical laboratories. Each of we are missing the bulk of the market.

Mr. Joe Small

Really, there are several segments: university education, university research, industrial quality control, industrial process control, industrial research, government, and hospitals and clinical laboratories. Each of these has somewhat different needs. University research labs, for example, don't want a computer attached to it; they can do it cheaper with a graduate student.

Mr. Roger Trent

The instrument we currently have is a compromise. It has something for everybody. If we made it specifically for industrial process control we could probably knock out a lot of the features.

Mr. Joe Small

The problem is that, in a university, you just walk in—no appointment necessary. But, for industrial sales, you have to get appointments to see the purchasing agent, etc. It's much harder. Why don't we concentrate on one or two industries—and run ads showing our ability to do specific tests.

The meeting concluded with an agreement that, in drawing up their final plan, Brite would consider two broad alternatives for the new G16 line:

1. a lower market share objective in the region of 3–5 percent, and
2. a segmented approach to the market.

The final meeting with Brite executives, in Houston, was held on January 16, 1976. The meeting was relatively short and confined to the discussion of several alternatives for the high-quality chromatograph line, as well as further review of the major alternatives for the G16. On the former, a concensus was reached that the market was probably stable or shrinking and that competition was increasingly active. Mr. Alvin Brite favored thinning the line to the three major instruments and cutting back on R&D. Costs, he believed, could be cut substantially once the G16 was in volume production, through a sharing of certain major components.

As the meeting broke up, Mr. Trent took Mr. Fayerweather aside and commented:

> You know we will have these strategic plans ready on time, but what worries me is whether this whole exercise doesn't focus us far too much on what we are *currently* doing. What I believe we should be working on is deciding in which key areas Speer should grow in the future. If we want to be a Hewlett Packard ten years from now—and I believe that should be our goal—worrying about all these details isn't really going to help us.

INTRON, INC.

Mr. Poensgen and Mr. Fayerweather met with Mr. Robert McNaulty, president and general manager of Intron, Inc., on one occasion, November 11, 1975, the day following their second trip to Brite Instrument Company in Houston.

Mr. McNaulty assured them that his plan would be ready by year's end. He explained that his chief accountant was currently refining the budget estimates according to the budget format provided earlier by Mr. Poensgen. According to Mr. McNaulty, his plan would consider four major alternatives.

1. Keep ahead of electron microscope trends and technology. As new applications were generated, develop accessories and modifications to accommodate users. The objective would be to match the projected annual market growth rate of 10–25 percent with a similar growth in Intron sales.
2. Cost reduce the present system without the expenditure of the large R&D funds contemplated in 1) above.
3. Provide an electron microscope at relatively low cost (in comparison to the current instrument). Feasibility studies had already been undertaken, several years previously, to develop a low-cost

instrument and a "breadboard model" assembled. These had been discontinued pending further developments in the marketplace.

4. Offer a broader line of microscopic instrumentation. This was seen as a way to expand sales coverage and increase the number of product specialists from two to five or six persons.

Perceiving that Mr. McNaulty preferred to have his plan in final form before going into detail about its content, the two shepherds agreed to await its completion by January 1, 1976.

SPD, INC.

Mr. Alan Fayerweather visited Mr. Otto Poensgen in Newark, New Jersey on August 11, 1975. Mr. Poensgen had invited his sales manager, Mr. David Channing, to join the discussion in the expectation that he would be closely involved in the draft of a final document.

The meeting focused on the various future strategic options open to SPD and the ways in which these might be presented in a future strategic plan. After considerable discussion it was agreed that SPD really confronted fifteen distinct "market classifications." This was represented by the matrix depicted below.

	MARKET CLASSIFICATION		
FUNCTIONS PERFORMED	INDUSTRIAL EFFLUENT MONITORING	'OPEN' WATER QUALITY MEASUREMENT	PROCESS CONTROL
• Concentration/purity measurement	H	H	M
• Concentration + particulate counting	H	M	L
• Concentration + counting + screening for 3–4 major pollutants	H	H	L
• Concentration + counting + screening + chemical analysis	H	H	L
• Complete water pollutant monitoring and measurement systems— all foreseeable functions	H	H	M

H = high desirability

M = medium desirability

L = low desirability

Current products were defined as being in the top two left-hand boxes of the matrix. Providing other functions would require the development of new products based on different technologies than those currently used by SPD. The various opportunities were ranked as "high," "medium," or "low," depending on a) the ease with which SPD could acquire or develop the technologies needed, b) the competitive environment existing for each type of instrument. Nine of the fifteen options were described to be of "high growth potential for Speer," and, as such, would be analyzed further in the development of a strategic plan.

It was agreed that the final SPD plan would consider each of the fundamental options incrementally for each of the two major segments, i.e., industrial effluent monitoring and 'open' water measurement. Budgets would be prepared to show the incremental impact of adding new technologies and products on a projected contribution and cash flow statement for each market segment. One such budget was prepared during the meeting as a demonstration of the way in which each alternative would ultimately be evaluated (see Exhibit 3).

OTHER DEVELOPMENTS

On January 10, 1976 Mr. James Young, chairman of the Special Task Force, called each of the shepherds to inform them that Speer's president, Mr. Paul Berger, was impatient to have in hand the final recommendations of the Task Force. He wondered whether a firm deadline should be set for the submission of each division's strategic plan and whether the plans were likely to answer the questions that Mr. Berger had originally posed.

On January 21, 1976 Mr. Berger called together Mr. James Young and Mr. Alan Fayerweather to discuss the progress of the Task Force to date. At that meeting Mr. Berger disclosed that he was considering a possible reorganization of Speer's scientific instrumentation activities. He questioned whether the strategic planning activities ordered by the Task Force might influence such a reorganization, and what the final recommendations of the Task Force were likely to be.

Exhibit 1
SPEER INDUSTRIES, INC. [C]
Budget Format

	1975	1976	1977	1978	1979	1980
PROFIT AND LOSS						
Sales						
Cost of sales	___	___	___	___	___	___
1) labor						
2) material						
3) overhead						
Gross margin						
R&D costs						
Sales costs						
Advertising & promotion	___	___	___	___	___	___
Contribution	___	___	___	___	___	___
Corporate assessment	___	___	___	___	___	___
Corporate G&A						
Net contribution	___	___	___	___	___	___
Depreciation						
Cash from operations						
CAPITAL BUDGET						
ΔWorking capital						
ΔPlant and equipment	___	___	___	___	___	___
ΔCash flow						
TOTAL CASH FLOW						
ACQUISITION COST (IF ANY)						

Exhibit 2

SPEER INDUSTRIES, INC. [C]

G16 Preliminary Marketing Plan*

	1975	1976	1977	1978	1979	1980
TOTAL MARKET	$60,000,000	$54,000,000	$55,500,000	$57,000,000	$58,500,000	$60,000,000
P&L						
Sales	$900,000	$1,650,000	$2,550,000	$3,300,000	$4,500,000	$6,000,000
COGS	585,000	900,000	1,400,000	1,815,000	2,475,000	3,300,000
Gross margin	315,000	750,000	1,150,000	1,485,000	2,025,000	2,700,000
R&D	265,000	240,000	330,000	300,000	390,000	420,000
Sales expense	495,000	555,000	675,000	750,000	900,000	1,050,000
Advertising and promotion	105,000	110,000	120,000	130,000	135,000	140,000
Gross contribution	(550,000)	(155,000)	55,000	245,000	600,000	1,090,000
Division G&A	180,000	150,000	175,000	185,000	270,000	360,000
Corporate G&A	30,000	90,000	120,000	150,000	185,000	225,000
Corporate assessment	45,000	55,000	65,000	75,000	90,000	120,000
Net contribution	(805,000)	(450,000)	(305,000)	(165,000)	55,000	385,000
Depreciation	15,000	10,000	10,000	10,000	10,000	10,000
Cash flow from ops.	(790,000)	(440,000)	(295,000)	(155,000)	65,000	395,000
CAPITAL BUDGET						
ΔWorking capital	300,000	565,000	600,000	375,000	600,000	750,000
ΔPlant and equipment	30,000	30,000	30,000	30,000	30,000	30,000
Net cash flow	(1,120,000)	(1,035,000)	(925,000)	(560,000)	(565,000)	(385,000)

*See footnote on p. 480 for assumptions underlying this marketing plan.

479

1. Ten percent market share by 1980.
2. Total market levelling at $60 million after recovery from recession (all at current prices).
3. G16 is "better piece of equipment at the same price than competition."
4. Cost of goods sold will be in 1975: 65 percent; 1976 and beyond: 55 percent.
5. R&D levelling out at about 7 percent of sales.
6. New products in 1977 and 1980.
7. Add new leased warehouse in 1977, move to new leased space in 1978 (all included in COGS).
8. Working capital additions at 75 percent of sales increment until 1977; 50 percent of increment thereafter.

Exhibit 3
SPEER INDUSTRIES, INC. [C]

SPD Projections of Current Instrumentation Sales
[WP100 & WP 2000] to the Industrial Effluent Market [$000]

	1975	1976	1977	1978	1979	1980
PROFIT AND LOSS						
Sales	427	505	580	660	720	760
Cost of sales	243	252	300	330	360	380
Gross margin	184	253	280	330	360	380
R&D costs	31	32	10	10	10	10
Sales costs	33	35	35	35	35	35
Advertising and promotion	65	58	50	50	50	50
Divisional G&A	0	0	0	0	0	0
Contribution	55	128	185	235	265	285
Corporate G&A	16	17	19	20	20	20
Corporate use charge	8	7	6	6	6	6
Net contribution	31	104	160	209	239	259
Depreciation	16	15	14	13	12	11
Cash from operations	47	119	174	222	251	270
CAPITAL BUDGET						
ΔWorking capital						
ΔPlant and equipment			Not available			
ΔCash flow						
Total cash flow						

Appendix A

Speer Industries, Inc. [C]

To: Mr. James Young
From: John Wayne, Reliance Instrumentation Company
Subject: Strategic Planning Task Force

This is in reply to your memorandum of October 3. Enclosed is the following information:

1. A revised statement of the current strategy for each business of Reliance.
2. A three-year forecast of sales for each business.

As to the next steps, I suggest that we first indentify the market segments most likely to achieve the largest growth rates—say, in the next ten years. And, that we also assess the capabilities of Speer as they might be utilized in entering and/or expanding in these markets.

The Task Force members from each division could be asked to act as a subcommittee to prepare nominations which should include:

A. The reasons why the market segment is expected to grow at that rate.
B. The capabilities of Speer that could be utilized in these markets.
C. The capabilities of competitors or likely competitors in these markets.

These nominations could then be reviewed by the entire committee to pick the most likely candidates in light of Speer available resources. In-depth studies of the most likely candidates could then be commissioned under the direction and control of the Task Force.

Assuming some favorable recommendations would be indicated by the in-depth studies, detailed plans of alternatives could then be prepared for final decision by top management.

Plans for the existing business follow:

LABORATORY PRODUCTS

The primary strategy for increasing orders for laboratory products is to give better delivery than our competitors. Our dealers tell us that we lose many orders because of competitors' material being available when our material is not available. The fact that distributors continue to order from us in spite of *average* delivery, recently as high as five months, attests to the market acceptance of our product and gives credence to the contention that orders can be increased by giving better delivery.

Our second strategy is to conduct a more aggressive sales promotion campaign than our competitors. Laboratory products dealers primarily take orders as opposed to active selling. This means that we can increase orders by persuading the end user to specify our product by name. Our principle thrust is through personal contact by our own field sales force of fifteen people working with dealer field men as well as directly with end users. This is supplemented by sales clinics for dealer salespeople, space and direct mail advertising, exhibits at industry and dealer shows, and sales literature and catalogues.

Our third strategy is to offer products of the best design and highest quality to "out-innovate" our competitors. Our new products manager works in conjunction with our field salespeople to determine customer wants and needs. These are matched with products available to be licensed. Product improvements are usually made by our own staff of nine product design engineers.

With respect to price, our strategy is to be equal to or higher than competition. We will charge what we think the market will bear.

Sales to international markets, by necessity, have not been actively promoted. This is due to our inability to make delivery in a reasonable time. It is believed that international markets offer opportunity for substantial sales as soon as our delivery is satisfactory.

A market study is currently being made to determine the demand for a low-cost gas chromatograph to be sold through laboratory products dealers.

NUCLEAR INSTRUMENTATION

The basic strategy is to license nuclear instrumentation designed by manufacturers for their own use, modify the designs to our high standards of quality and dependability, and offer the monitors to other manufacturers and contractors throughout the world.

Our sales strategy is to give superior attention to our customer needs. We do this by selling direct as opposed to using manufacturer's agents, and by constantly improving our products.

Our pricing strategy is to charge what the market will bear. Annual return on investment to the user is sometimes several times the cost of the monitor. Since there are direct competitors as well as other ways to monitor the processes, however, pricing is not unrestrained. Current policy is to increase prices by 20 percent per year.

RELIANCE INSTRUMENT COMPANY

Net Incoming Order Forecast [$000]

	FISCAL YEAR 1976	FISCAL YEAR 1977	FISCAL YEAR 1978
LABORATORY PRODUCTS			
Base (from previous year)	22,350 (est.)	25,584	33,079
Market growth	(90)	1,335	(966)
Added penetration	1,429	3,622	3,460
New product lines	0	0	1,500
Price increases	1,895	2,538	2,917
Subtotal	25,584	33,079	39,990
Percent increase	14.5%	28.0%	19.2%
NUCLEAR INSTRUMENTATION			
Base (from previous year)	1,870 (est.)	2,358	3,308
Market growth and penetration	(168)	(121)	393
New products	262	847	1,135
Price increases	394	224	265
Subtotal	2,358	3,308	5,101
Percent increase	26%	40.2%	57.7%

Appendix B
Speer Industries, Inc. [C]

Mr. John Wayne
Reliance Instrument Company
Madison, Wisconsin

Dear John:

Jim Young passed to Guy Converse and me the materials you sent him on October 16th. I thought it might be helpful if I responded briefly since I am the only "shepherd" who has been involved with progress on all four businesses in the "Scientific Products" group.

First, on your suggestion that we should set up a subcommittee to look at "new" areas, i.e., areas in which Speer is not involved at all currently; I think we have to do this before the project is complete but my impression, from working with the groups at SPD, Intron, and Brite, is that their plate is full, now, just trying to draft the strategic plans for their own businesses. As you know it has turned out to be a very substantial job. I think we have to wait at least until this round is complete. There may be additional advantages to delaying this activity until we see how many opportunities there are stemming from existing activities and how these might be integrated into some new directions for Speer.

As far as your own strategic plan for each business is concerned, I'd like to pass on to you some of the ideas that have come up from our work in the other three divisions. Since we last saw you in Madison, Otto Poensgen and I have had the chance to work in detail through the plans for these divisions and have agreed on a way to present the final plan for them. This is roughly as follows:

1.0 *Division Activities, Past and Present*
A qualitative assessment of the role of the division in its marketplace (markets, products, sales, R&D, and production history and current capabilities).

2.0 *Definition and Qualitative Analysis of Major Strategic Options Available to Division*
e.g., lab products
nuclear instrumentation
This discussion should present the overall rationale for selecting the strategic planning alternatives to be discussed in subsequent sections of their report.

3.0 *Analysis of Strategic Options for Each Business or Sub-business*

3.1 *Laboratory Products*

3.11 The market past, present and future—sales, buying behavior, major segments.

3.12 Division current market position—including discussion of competitors' approaches and their position in the marketplace.

3.13 Strategic analyses—growth potential—projections of market needs in the future for our specific products and logical outgrowths.

3.14 Major *alternative* strategies (if there are more than one) for achieving this potential, described in terms of:
- R&D needs
- marketing/sales needs
- production and facility needs
- working capital needs
- *budget*(s) reflecting the above
- relationship, if any, to other businesses or divisions
- conclusions and recommended actions.

3.2 *Nuclear Instrumentation*
Ditto for content and organization.

3.3 New business activities not falling within any of the above (your $1,500,000 in year 3, for example).

4.0 *Integrated Conclusions and Recommended Actions*
By integrating the results of the analyses conducted under 3.0, above, a recommended action plan in both qualitative and quantitative terms can be developed. This provides specific recommendations for implementation as well as a schedule for their implementation.

Our hope is to have the above format followed approximately by each division for each business. For some "businesses" there may be more than one major strategic alternative, in which case each would be represented by a plan and budget.

John, when you read this, you will probably groan and say, "No, not another draft of my plan," but, to be consistent with what the others are doing, it does seem to me that some additions and reformatting are necessary. In particular:

1. Some overall statements about the division's overall span of activities and future strategic options corresponding to my outline points 1.0 and 2.0.

2. Inclusion of some data about market trends, buying behavior, current marketing position, competitors, etc. *for each major business* (my outline point 3.0).

3. Should we break down the plan by major product areas in the laboratory products line? For example, can we "out-innovate" in every line? Or should we take a back seat in some?

4. A translation of these overall plans into some *specific* statements of R&D, marketing, facilities, working capital needs, etc.

5. A *budget* drawn up for each business (or segment) along the lines above. It must show both 1) contribution to profit and 2) cash flow.

6. An overall summary and conclusion bringing this all together again (my outline point 4).

Sorry to be placing yet additional suggestions for improvement and consistency before you. Frankly, we are all learning as we go along and the best help I can give is to pass on to you some of these ideas and lessons we are getting from working with the other divisions.

Sincerely,
(Alan Fayerweather)

DISCUSSION QUESTIONS

1. Is the industry study useful? If there are shortcomings, what is still needed?
2. What implications can you draw from the industry study in its current state?
3. What problems do you see with the way strategic plans were constructed?
4. Evaluate each of the plans and the planning.
5. How should Mr. Berger be answered? What next steps are appropriate?

SPEER INDUSTRIES, INC. [D][6]

Following discussions with the president of Speer Industries, Inc., Mr. Paul Berger, and with Speer's external consultant, Mr. Alan Fayerweather, Mr. James Young, chairman of the Task Force on Scientific Instrumentation, set February 1, 1976 as the final date for submission of strategic plans for each of the four Speer divisions involved.

SPD's plan arrived on January 15, 1976 (see Appendix A); plans from the remaining three divisions arrived the following week, all within a few days of each other (see Appendices B, C, and D). After reviewing the various submissions, Mr. Young circulated the four plans, together with Mr. Converse's report on "The Scientific Instrumentation Industry" [see Speer Industries, Inc. (B)], to all members of the Task Force. March 1st was set as the date of the next Task Force meeting, in Houston, to review all the material so far collected, and to address the questions originally raised by Mr. Berger, namely: the Task Force should:

1. Form a summary description of the scientific instrumentation market(s), including a discussion of key business, government, and technology trends, as well as the identification of key growth areas;
2. Recommend market areas and types of products Speer should be active in; and
3. Determine the major resource commitments and organization strategies to gain a significant position in these areas.

In his accompanying memorandum to the Task Force members, Mr. Young requested that each member familiarize himself thoroughly with the individual plans and industry material, and be prepared to make whatever analyses and recommendations he believed were appropriate. It was Mr. Young's belief that however complete or incomplete the data now was, Mr. Berger expected to have a clear statement of the Task Force's findings soon after the meeting. Mr. Berger had already indicated that he had his own ideas about the directions that should be taken, and that with or without the group's recommendations he was soon going to act.

---

[6]This case was prepared by Derek F. Abell.

Appendix A

Speer Industries, Inc. [D]

SPD, Inc.—Strategic Plan

1.0 SPD INSTRUMENTATION OVERVIEW

SPD is relatively new to the water pollutant monitoring field in that we initiated our efforts in this area only five years ago. Currently, our product line consists of two industrial plant effluent monitoring devices, the WP1000 and WP2000, and one 'open' water quality monitoring device, the AWP10, sold to federal, state, and local government environmental agencies.

Instrument development, fabrication and marketing functions are performed at SPD's facilities in Newark, New Jersey. Recently completed expansion of the facility will handle the increase in these functions as the requirements are projected over the next two years. Because of the portable nature of most instruments now in the field, servicing is successfully handled by shipping units back to Newark. Introduction of the AWP10 may require a significant increase in field servicing, however. Current marketing strategy is to use direct sales in geographic areas with high immediate sales potential. Currently, two direct sales persons operating out of the home office, together with three manufacturers' representative groups, handle domestic sales. Foreign sales are handled by a combination of exclusive distributors and direct sales. This sales effort is supported by advertising, direct mail, and trade-show programs.

2.0 DEFINITION AND QUALITATIVE ANALYSIS OF MAJOR STRATEGIC OPTIONS OPEN TO SPD

Discussion has revealed three broad areas for extending the base of SPD's products and activities.

1. *Industrial/Commercial Effluent Monitoring and Measurement*
   SPD is already involved in this market with its WP1000 and WP2000 products.
2. *'Government' Markets—'Open' Water Quality Measurement*
   SPD's new AWP10 instrument is aimed at this market.

3. *Process Control Instrumentation*

Many of the technologies (and instruments) which are used to monitor and/or analyze water quality for environmental purposes have applications in industrial process control areas also. This includes not only environmental process control but process control for a variety of chemical and related manufacturing activities. If we actively enter this market, then numerous other opportunities exist for expansion of our product line utilizing primarily in-house technology.

As indicated earlier, the two areas which appear to offer the greatest immediate growth opportunities for SPD (with the minimum investment expense) are the industrial effluent market and the government market. Thus, the following text places primary emphasis on these two areas.

The development of new instrumentation in *both* the industrial and government markets makes sense in terms of:

- SPD's technological strength in both market areas
- compatability of new technological developments in both markets
- government's role in setting requirements in both markets
- our understanding of both of these markets as a result of our previous environmental services experience.

Consequently, the continuation of product planning and development activities for both market segments is recommended.

We conclude that the strategic options that are open to us relate, therefore, to the degree to which we expand our product line to solve a broad variety of monitoring and measurement problems in each market.

- We can restrict our activities to the measurement of water purity using the current radiation technology.
- We can expand our product line to include particulate counting utilizing other sensing techniques. We are, in effect, already pursuing this option with the development of prototype instruments in our R&D laboratory.
- Our technological capabilities also include expertise in screening techniques. Thus we could add additional instruments designed to provide this function.
- While not an inevitable extension of the preceding options, it appears reasonable to conclude, from a marketing point of view, that an organization that has defined the water pollution area as a major focus of its activities, should consider the analysis of the

chemical composition of the pollutants as a reasonable extension of the product line. Such analytical instruments could be directed at both market areas. Accordingly, we include this option in the strategic analyses reported in this document.

- In the event that any combination of the preceding options is successfully implemented, we will have established a technological and marketing base which can be readily utilized for the development of complete water pollution monitoring systems. The potential benefits to be gained by its inclusion into SPD's "bag of tricks" warrants its inclusion in the strategic planning study.

Each of the above options was qualitatively analyzed in terms of our current and projected strengths and weaknesses. This report presents quantitative analysis of a number of these options and, in those cases where quantitative analyses have not been completed as yet, more extensive qualitative evaluations.

3.0 ANALYSIS OF STRATEGIC OPTIONS

3.1. WATER PURITY MEASUREMENT ONLY —USING CURRENT TECHNOLOGY

All of our current products can be considered to be "overhead items" in that they are not directly involved in a manufacturing or profit-making operation. As part of the regulations promulgated under various government acts, measurement instrumentation for determination of compliance have been specified. Although our instruments are not specified as compliance instruments (as they were not available when the regulations were promulgated), they have been evaluated and approved by the appropriate governmental agencies for use by industry to meet industrial monitoring requirements. In addition, they are currently being sold to federal and state regulatory agencies as a time-saving adjunct to their compliance monitoring equipment.

3.1.1. SPD's Current Marketing Position

Both the degree and rate of penetration is significantly influenced by economic factors and by both the levels of enforcement by regulatory agencies and levels of acceptance of SPD's instruments by governmental agencies. In addition, competition is commonly a significant factor. To date, most of our sales history has been with the two effluent monitoring devices (models WP1000 and WP2000) which have commanded a unique position in the marketplace. Consequently, direct competition has not been a major factor deterring market penetration. This unique situation is expected to change in the future, however, and will be further discussed in a subsequent section.

Data on our rate and degree of penetration of the market through FY-75 shows that approximately 6.4% of the total U.S. market and an estimated 4.2% of the world market has been realized. The rate of market penetration within the U.S. over this four-year period has averaged slightly more than 1% per year, with the last two years holding constant at an annual penetration rate of 1.4%.

3.1.2.1. Competition—Industrial Effluent Market

Although there has been no direct competition to the line of effluent instrumentation, the primary alternative to these units is the use of manual sampling monitors. The description of these manual devices has been well documented in earlier memoranda and will not be further belabored here. There are two major suppliers of such monitoring units. Both utilize independent stocking distributors as their primary sales force. Neither is believed to be a major threat to offer automated instrumentation which will compete with SPD's existing or proposed product line.

In early FY-76, a portable reading effluent monitor was introduced by Aqua-Science, Inc. of Cleveland, Ohio to compete with SPD's WP1000 monitor. It is selling for $3,750, approximately the same price as SPD's model WP1000. Aqua-Science sells their products through a small direct sales staff located at their home office in a manner almost identical to the sales approach which we utilize. Although there are many technical factors which indicate that our instrument is superior to theirs for industrial use, we are now faced with direct competition for the first time, and our marketing strategy is being changed to reflect this fact.

3.1.2.2. Competition—Government Market

Manual devices are the predominant systems currently employed for open water quality monitoring. These are manufactured by numerous companies including Reliance Instrumentation Company. Competition from other automated systems comes from two instruments manufactured in Europe and marketed in the United States by other manufacturers. These systems are technically less advanced but cost the same or more than the AWP10. Both companies, however, currently have a distinct advantage in size of sales force and availability of demo units. We hope to offset this advantage through an active advertising program and successful initial demos to key governmental and commercial customers —word-of-mouth information, both pro and con, spreads very fast in the water pollution fields. Competition in Europe is mainly from a German instrument.

3.1.3. Quantitative Analysis

Growth Potential—The projections of sales for WP instrumentation and the AWP Monitor through 1980 are presented in Figure 1. The three models (WP1000, WP2000 and AWP10) included in this figure are the primary instrumentation based on the radiation technology that will be offered by SPD through FY-80.

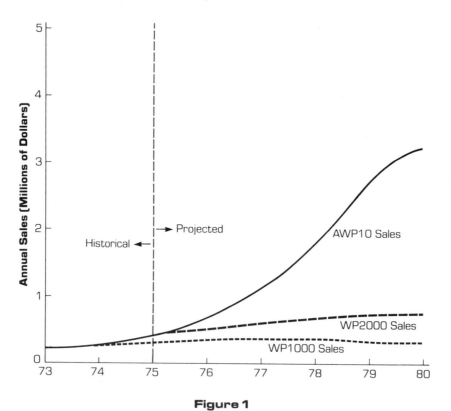

Figure 1

Summation of Projected Sales of Instrumentation Based on Radiation Technology through 1980.

R&D Requirements—The major R&D costs required to achieve the above-stated growth potential are already behind us. All three instruments are currently production units with minimal R&D expenditures forecast for the future. The AWP unit is now in the production engineering phase and the first production units will be available for shipment late in the second quarter of FY-76.

Marketing Requirements—We are of the opinion that the growth potential shown in Figure 1 can be achieved through a modest growth in our current sales and promotional program. We plan to continue to utilize direct sales in the United States and Canada as our primary method of sales, and expand our network of overseas distributors. The direct sales staff is expected to reach eight members in 1980.

In addition to direct sales, we plan to continue to rely on advertising, trade shows and selected direct mailings as our primary promotional techniques. Currently, the budget for these sales and promotional activities is about 21 percent of sales or $90,000. Although the annual expenditures for sales, advertising and promotion are expected to rise significantly over the next five years, these expenditures as a percentage of sales will decrease to an estimated 14 percent by 1980.

Production and Facility Requirements—Our current manufacturing facilities are adequate to handle the projected production requirements through 1977. To accommodate the sharp increase in expected AWP10 sales in 1978, we anticipate that we will expand our current facility into the east wing of the front building, which is currently leased by Windmere Corporation. This would provide sufficient space for production activites at least through 1980 as the production activity within the facility will be labor intensive; i.e., wiring, assembly, calibration and quality control. Our existing machine shop is believed to be adequate in size to handle the expanded production requirements through 1980, with augmentation by outside vendors. The costs associated with this expansion are included in the plant and equipment capital requirements commencing in 1978.

Budgetary Data—The cash flows resulting from our projected sales of instrumentation are shown in Tables 1 and 2, respectively. These tables further quantify the discussion of sales and costs discussed above.

Table 1

CASH FLOW OF WP1000 AND WP2000 INSTRUMENTATION
TO THE INDUSTRIAL EFFLUENT MARKET [$000]

	1975	1976	1977	1978	1979	1980
PROFIT AND LOSS						
Sales	427	501	580	660	720	760
Cost of goods sold	243	252	300	328	360	380
Gross margin	184	249	280	332	360	380
R&D costs	31	32	8	8	8	8
Sales, advertising and promotion	91	86	76	76	76	76
Divisional G&A	0	0	0	0	0	0
Contribution	62	131	196	248	276	296
Corporate G&A	18	17	19	20	19	18
Corporate use charge	7	6	6	6	6	6
Net contribution	37	108	171	222	251	272
Depreciation	14	13	13	12	11	10
Cash from operations	51	121	184	234	262	282
CAPITAL BUDGET						
ΔWorking capital	(42)	(36)	(20)	(20)	(16)	(12)
ΔPlant and equipment	(4)	(4)	(4)	(4)	(4)	(4)
ΔCash flow	(46)	(40)	(24)	(24)	(20)	(16)
TOTAL CASH FLOW	5	81	160	210	242	266
ACQUISITION COST	—	—	—	—	—	—

3.2. PARTICLE COUNTING USING FLUID FLOW TECHNIQUES

3.2.1. The Market—Past, Present, and Future

SPD is currently pursuing a novel concept which utilizes fluid flow techniques to selectively monitor and "count" the concentration of pollutants.

The presently used methods of measurement are based on the collection of samples and their subsequent analysis by means of a variety of methods, the most advanced of which employs a combination of scanning electron microscopy and computerized data processing. In general, however, the laborious procedure of counting and sizing particles under the microscope by trained personnel represents the prevalent techniques. Such an instrument would be directed to the industrial effluent market only.

Table 2

CASH FLOW OF AWP10 INSTRUMENTATION
TO THE GOVERNMENT MARKET [$000]

	1975	1976	1977	1978	1979	1980
PROFIT AND LOSS						
Sales	0	180	560	1120	2000	2400
Cost of goods sold	5	130	336	672	1200	1440
Gross margin	(5)	50	224	448	800	960
R&D costs	59	72	32	24	24	24
Sales, advertising and promotion	0	31	80	160	200	240
Divisional G&A	0	0	0	0	0	0
Contribution	(64)	(53)	112	264	576	696
Corporate G&A	0	9	22	44	80	96
Corporate use charge	0	4	8	15	27	32
Net contribution	(64)	(66)	82	205	469	568
Depreciation	0	4	12	16	15	14
Cash from operations	(64)	(62)	94	221	484	582
CAPITAL BUDGET						
ΔWorking capital	(0)	(80)	(80)	(80)	(80)	(80)
ΔPlant and equipment	(0)	(16)	(8)	(16)	(16)	(16)
ΔCash flow	(0)	(96)	(88)	(96)	(96)	(96)
TOTAL CASH FLOW	(64)	(158)	6	125	388	486
ACQUISITION COST	—	—	—	—	—	—

3.2.2. SPD's Current Marketing Position

Since the new instruments will not be commercially available until FY-77, and no alternative instrument is currently being sold, there has been no penetration of this potential market by either SPD or other instrument manufacturers. There is a projected total market of about 800 units within the U.S. representing a dollar volume of $4,000,000 (assuming a unit cost of $5,000). Using the same assumption for estimating the international market for the radiation instruments, i.e., international market potential is approximately equal to that of the U.S., then the worldwide market potential for this unit is about 1,600 units or $8,000,000.

3.2.3. Competition

As mentioned above, no competitive instrument currently exists. There are, however, several companies in the U.S. who would have the expertise to develop an instrument utilizing our measurement concept. Since there appears to be minimal opportunity for SPD to obtain a protective patent (as was the case with the WP1000, WP2000 and AWP10) it seems likely that some competition will develop in the future.

3.2.4. Quantitative Analysis

Growth Potential—Although no detailed assessment of future sales has been performed, and there is no historical data from which to extrapolate, preliminary sales volumes have been projected through FY-80 as indicated in Table 3 below. The prototype unit is estimated to be completed early in calendar 1977 with production engineering completed and the first commercial units available late in calendar 1977.

Table 3

Preliminary Sales Projections for SPD's "Counter"

| | FISCAL YEAR | | | | | |
	1975	1976	1977	1978	1979	1980
Sales (# of units)	—	—	10	25	50	100
Sales ($'s)	—	—	50,000	125,000	250,000	500,000
Percent of worldwide market capture (cumulative)	—	—	0.6%	2.21%	5.3%	11.5%

R&D Requirements—We anticipate that the majority of R&D costs for development of the prototype unit will be covered under government contracts. The production engineering costs required to commercialize the unit are estimated to be approximately $90,000 and these will be incurred by SPD during FY-77.

Marketing Requirements—The new monitor will be sold to the same market as the WP1000 and WP2000 instruments and, consequently, the same marketing channels will be utilized, i.e., a combination of direct sales and representatives domestically and direct sales and distributors internationally. Table 4, which projects the cash flows for the combined WP1000, and WP2000 and new "counter," includes the incremental marketing costs estimated for the new instrument.

Production and Facility Requirements—The anticipated expansion of SPD's floor space in FY-78 to include the area currently subleased by Windmere Corporation should provide adequate facilities to handle the production requirements of the new instrument. Because this additional facility will be rented, no major capital expenditures are anticipated.

3.2.5. Relationship to Other Speer Divisions

The technologies and markets associated with the new instruments are significantly different than those associated with the products of other Speer divisions. Consequently, there is very little apparent benefit in relating SPD's activities with sales, manufacturing and engineering programs of the other divisions within Speer.

Table 4
Cash Flow of WP1000, WP2000 **Plus** New "Counter" to the Industrial Effluent Market [$000]

	1975	1976	1977	1978	1979	1980
PROFIT AND LOSS						
Sales	427	502	620	760	920	1160
Cost of goods sold	243	252	326	400	492	620
Gross margin	184	250	294	360	428	540
R&D costs	31	32	80	56	24	15
Sales, advertising and promotion	91	86	82	90	124	124
Divisional G&A	0	0	0	0	0	0
Contribution	62	132	132	214	280	401
Corporate G&A	17	16	23	24	23	21
Corporate use charge	7	5	8	8	8	8
Net contribution	38	111	101	182	249	372
Depreciation	14	14	13	12	11	10
Cash from operations	52	125	114	194	260	382
CAPITAL BUDGET						
ΔWorking capital	(42)	(36)	(24)	(24)	(20)	(24)
ΔPlant and equipment	(4)	(4)	(4)	(4)	(8)	(12)
ΔCash flow	(46)	(40)	(28)	(28)	(28)	(36)
TOTAL CASH FLOW	6	85	86	166	232	346
ACQUISITION COST	—	—	—	—	—	—

3.3. Screening Techniques

Initial market research indicates that the potential U.S. market for such a product might be about 800 units or $12,000,000 (assuming a reasonable selling price of $15,000 per unit). These units would be sold to both the industrial effluent market and the government market.

Little is yet known about possible competition for such devices but as far as can be gauged there is no comparable product to what we have in mind on the market at present.

The budgetary data associated with the introduction of such an instrument in 1977 is shown in Tables 5 and 6. It should be emphasized that we consider the sales potential of these units to be considerably larger than incorporated in the analyses presented in this section. We have taken a conservative position with regard to these estimates because of the uncertain status of federal regulations regarding compulsory screening tests on both effluent and open water.

As in the case of the strategic options discussed earlier in this report, we do not consider that the manufacture and sale of such instruments bears any significant relationship to other Speer divisions.

3.4. Chemical Analysis and Total Water Pollution Measuring Systems

While we believe that SPD will enter the market for these devices sometime prior to 1980, little data is currently available to assess either the size of the potential market or the costs involved. Once we are established in both the industrial effluent market and the government market, such data should be more readily available.

Table 5

Cash Flow of WP1000 and WP2000 **Plus** Counting Devices
Plus Screening Instrumentation to the Industrial Effluent Market [$000]

	1975	1976	1977	1978	1979	1980
PROFIT AND LOSS						
Sales	427	501	684	896	1148	1440
Cost of goods sold	243	252	342	448	574	720
Gross margin	184	249	342	448	574	720
R&D costs	31	48	84	58	26	18
Cost of sales	91	86	86	96	132	132
Divisional G&A	0	0	0	0	0	0
Contribution	62	115	172	294	416	570
Corporate G&A	18	17	25	26	25	24
Corporate use charge	7	6	9	9	9	9
Net contribution	37	92	138	259	382	537
Depreciation	14	14	13	12	11	10
Cash from operations	51	106	151	271	393	547
CAPITAL BUDGET						
ΔWorking capital	(42)	(36)	(29)	(28)	(24)	(26)
ΔPlant and equipment	(4)	(4)	(4)	(4)	(8)	(12)
ΔCash flow	(46)	(40)	(33)	(32)	(32)	(38)
TOTAL CASH FLOW	5	66	118	239	361	509
ACQUISITION COST	—	—	—	—	—	—

Table 6

Cash Flow of AWP10 **Plus** Screening Instrumentation
to the Government Market [$000]

	1975	1976	1977	1978	1979	1980
PROFIT AND LOSS						
Sales	0	181	640	1320	2400	3000
Cost of goods sold	5	130	384	792	1440	1800
Gross margin	(5)	51	256	528	960	1200
R&D costs	59	72	68	76	88	88
Cost of sales	0	31	88	192	252	304
Divisional G&A	0	0	0	0	0	0
Contribution	(64)	(52)	100	260	620	808
Corporate G&A	0	8	25	52	96	120
Corporate use charge	0	8	20	20	20	20
Net contribution	(64)	(68)	55	188	504	668
Depreciation	0	4	8	12	12	12
Cash from operations	(64)	(64)	63	200	516	680
CAPITAL BUDGET						
Working capital	(0)	(80)	(96)	(96)	(96)	(96)
Plant and equipment	(0)	(16)	(24)	(20)	(20)	(20)
Cash flow	(0)	(96)	(120)	(116)	(116)	(116)
TOTAL CASH FLOW	(64)	(160)	(57)	84	400	564
ACQUISITION COST	—	—	—	—	—	—

Appendix B

Speer Industries, Inc. [D]

Intron, Inc.—Strategic Plan

Intron introduced commercial electron microscopes approximately
four years ago. The users of this instrumentation are sophisticated
government, university and industrial research laboratory scientists
who demand extensive applications and performance proof prior to
purchasing the equipment.

Intron's U.S. marketing and sales strategy is centered around
direct selling by highly qualified sales persons operating out of Dallas
headquarters. This is backed up by the aid and cooperation of the R&D
department. A modest and conservative advertising and trade show
program has been instituted in support of this direct sales program. All

servicing is handled from the Dallas facility and this has resulted in some sales resistance in that some customers are hesitant to purchase sophisticated instrumentation from other than a company possessing a nationwide or worldwide service network.

The worldwide 1975 market for electron microscopes has been estimated to be in excess of $18,000,000 of which Intron's share was approximately 6 percent (six systems at $190,000 each, for $1,140,000). The present market growth is difficult to determine, but the best estimate available to Intron personnel places it between 10 percent and 25 percent per year.

Intron's instrument is designed for the highest performance and greatest versatility of any existing equipment. Fully automated, it will outperform all competition at any price or in any application. All Intron users praise the equipment and are excellent sources of reference for us. The reliability of the product is very high as born out by virtually no need for service beyond installation.

The competition has adopted the following sales strategies.

— employ specialist salesmen of exceptional technical expertise
— utilize a sales approach which emphasizes the size and dependability of the company
— employ professional market and sales promotional techniques
— underprice the competition
— maintain an application lab to give customers an opportunity to work out the "economics" before they buy

MARKET TRENDS AND BUYER BEHAVIOR

The following five major market trends have been identified:

— rapidly changing areas of application constantly require new accessories and some instrument redesign
— market appearing to change from fundamental research (academic) to applied research (industry)
— proof of high performance and specific problem solving has been and will continue to be necessary to generate sales
— electron microscopy technology becoming more widely known and more widely accepted
— potential requirement sometime in the future for a less flexible and lower cost system for routine analysis

FUTURE OBJECTIVES, PLANS AND RECOMMENDATIONS

The following specific projected R&D efforts have been identified:

— as new areas of applications are generated, develop accessories and modifications to accommodate the users
— simplify and cost reduce applied instrumentation

No near-term or long-range objectives or plans for this business area have been defined for the Scientific Products Strategic Planning Task Force except the general objective of matching the projected 10 percent to 25 percent market growth, with a similar growth in Intron's sales.

A market study should be made to assist in forecasting the electron microscope market trends; and, based on the best guess, one of the following alternatives should be implemented:

1. Provide an instrument at a relatively low cost ($30,000 to $40,000) and attempt to enlarge the market by making it accessible to more budgets.
2. Cost reduce the present instrument without the expenditure of large R&D funds. This could probably allow us to drop our selling price by $30,000 but keep the same percent for cost of goods manufactured. The yield from this approach would give us a more attractive instrument from the price angle and could increase our sales by 2 to 4 instruments per year. So far, our marketing group has encouraged investing in this approach; but with a changing marketplace it is currently being reconsidered.
3. Expand our team of product specialists from two to three or four. This would give us more "muscle," but would it make us more competitive?

There are some questions outstanding with regards to the Intron product line. While it is true that we could make money on the sale of 10 to 15 instruments per year, is this a meaningful long-term goal? The electron microscope is not an "easy" product to market. It requires significant investment in staff to support the sales effort (this would include items such as applications and demonstrations lab). It is a "high-ticket" item with low unit sales. When the national economy slows down, the expensive items are the first things to be cut from budgets. Also, in a market with only a few manufacturers and total sales of 200 to 250 per year, each time a purchase is made, it is a traumatic experience, to say the least. Further, the possibility of price cutting is something we must be aware of.

Intron, Inc.
Long-Range Plan [$000]

	FY-75	FY-76	FY-77	FY-78	FY-79	FY-80
P&L						
Sales	1,200	2,000	2,400	3,500	4,600	5,500
COGS (M, L, OH)	550	900	1,080	1,580	2,100	2,600
Gross Proft	650	1,100	1,320	1,920	2,500	2,900
R&D	120	100	90	120	250	400
Selling expense	170	270	330	400	450	450
Advertising	60	70	120	150	200	250
Total	350	400	540	670	900	1,100
Contribution	300	660	780	1,250	1,600	1,800
General and administrative—incurred	80	100	120	160	220	270
General and administrative—assessed	50	100	120	170	210	250
Corporate use charge	40	40	50	60	80	100
Net contribution	130	420	490	860	1,090	1,180
Add-back depreciation	20	10	20	20	20	30
Cash from operations	150	430	510	880	1,110	1,210
CAPITAL REQUIREMENTS						
Working capital	(60)	(425)	(200)	(625)	(625)	(450)
Property and equipment	(10)	(20)	(120)	(60)	(80)	(140)
Net cash flow	80	(15)	190	195	405	620

Appendix C

Speer Industries, Inc. [D]

Brite Instrument Company—Strategic Plan

1.0. BRITE INSTRUMENT COMPANY, PAST AND PRESENT

All of our instrument and component development experience at Brite Instrument has been restricted to the moderate to very high-priced, low-volume markets. Chromatograph items are typically in the 10- to 100-thousand-dollar category. Even the G16 line (a high volume to us) is relatively expensive in its class.

There exists a definite lack of production engineering talent and know-how to design for "value" or volume. The acquisition of such personnel could have significant impact on new analytical system profitability where moderate to large volume sales would be realized. In competitive areas such as a low-cost chromatograph, value engineering with production cost savings are a must.

1.1. Manufacturing

Brite Instrument has traditionally been a precision, high quality, almost custom house. The foundation of the company has been, in the past, the ability to machine and assemble large physical-mechanical devices to high tolerances.

Within the past few years, the demand for instrumentation systems and automation has forced us to add electronics manufacturing capability beyond the rather simple electronics initially produced.

1.2. Sales and Marketing

All products are sold directly (U.S.) with our own salesmen. Most experience has been in selling to government and university laboratories with little exposure to industry or the medical fields. The wide selling price of our systems (approximately $5,000 to $150,000 each) and variations of user sophistication may be a handicap.

Most of the salesmen are technically oriented and probably quite versatile in coping with different instrumentation principles.

2.0. STRATEGIC OPTIONS AVAILABLE

Utilizing present Brite Instrument assets and acquiring some skills or experienced personnel in certain areas, several alternatives are worth evaluation with respect to a long-range business plan:

a. *Expansion and Continuation of the Two Present Product Lines: High-Quality Chromatograph and the G16*
Until a different business plan is adopted, we will assume that for the near future, this will be implemented. Modifications and details of continuation of the two lines are covered later in this report. R&D expenditures have been based on a percentage of sales projected for the active fiscal year and amount to between 6 percent and 7 percent. The total amount allotted for R&D is to be divided among the two product lines per the attached cost sheets.

b. *Discontinuing One of the Two Present Lines and Concentrating on the Remaining*
This would not appear to be too attractive since the justification for increasing our product lines was to improve the overall growth and profitability of Brite Instrument.

c. *Add a New Product Line by Acquisition or Internal R&D*
This could replace one or more existing Brite lines with the intent of adding a product with a better market potential than present Brite instruments. Utilizing the basic assets of Brite, two possibilities are evident:

1. *Introduce a new sophisticated analytical product*—that would, for a while, experience little or no competition, but would require considerable "customer educating." Selling price and Brite Instrument markup could be quite high. Sales volume would be low and slow.

   Historically, R&D costs run from $250,000 to over $500,000 to complete a project of this type. To implement such a program at Brite would mean the reallocation of present R&D dollars from the existing two lines to the new project or the procurement of additional funds from other sources.

2. *Develop a dedicated or simplified analytical instrument* utilizing an accepted technique, but a technique presently employed only in large, expensive instrumentation. The availability of R&D funds as described in (1), above, applies equally to this alternative although the overall project costs should be about one-half of that above.

3. *Concentrate on instrumentation designed for a specific application.* An example of such equipment might be a clinical analyzer such as a "centrifugal fast analyzer." Development costs could range from $200,000 to $1,000,000 depending on the complexity of the instrument, degree of testing and certification required and the amount of applications back-up data and procedures necessary.

3.0. ANALYSIS OF STRATEGIC OPTIONS

3.1. High-Quality Chromatographs

The 1975 market for instruments covering the range of capabilities possessed by the Brite line is approximately $9,000,000. Brite's share of the market in calendar 1975 was 65 percent to 75 percent. The projected market growth is 5 percent to 10 percent per year and current projections indicate that Brite will lose some of its share of the market.

The competition has been minimal until quite recently. At the present time, there are two major U.S. competitors and one major foreign competitor.

Brite instrumentation has been based on the highest quality. The result is an expensive piece of equipment with much of the quality not evident to the casual observer. The competition can and has increasingly met our specifications at a lower cost, thereby underbidding us and taking the sale. Cost reduction of Brite equipment through "value" engineering will be required.

It is difficult to conceive of any major technological breakthroughs in such chromatographs to put one manufacturer "out front." Therefore, cost/performance factors will be a strong factor in who makes the sale. Brite's reputation should help to keep us the dominant supplier.

3.1.1. Market Trends and Buyer Behavior. Three major market trends have been identified to date:

— a decided interest on the part of the research laboratories for research instrument systems as opposed to separate specialized instruments;
— an interest on the part of the using research laboratories for systems compatible with digital computer data processing;
— an interest on the part of the using laboratories for high performance to cost, in view of the increased availability of instruments capable of performing the same or similar measurements (i.e., more competition from manufacturers of similar equipment and competition from competing instrument approaches)

3.1.2. Future Objectives, Plans and Recommendations. Few R&D efforts have been applied to the high quality line during the past few years, especially to the basic instruments.

A major improvement in systems concept and cost reduction planned is to incorporate the G16 electronics into this line. This involves an engineering investment of approximately $20,000. The result will be a substantial edge over the competition.

A market study of the instruments now in existence and those desired by users should be made with the intention of selecting a few models and redesigning these for major cost savings.

In the meantime, we see declining sales in this line. Sales are likely to recover only after we reallocate our R&D efforts from the G16 to this line in fiscal 1977 (see attached budget).

Brite Instrument Company: High Quality Chromatographs*

	FY-75 $	FY-75 %	FY-76 $	FY-76 %	FY-77 $	FY-77 %	FY-78 $	FY-78 %	FY-79 $	FY-79 %	FY-80 $	FY-80 %
P&L												
Sales	6,090	100	4,300	100	4,470	100	5,630	100	6,620	100	6,620	100
COGS	2,895	47.6	2,050	47.7	2,120	47.4	2,680	47.6	3,145	47.5	3,170	48.0
Gross profit	3,195	52.4	2,250	52.3	2,350	52.6	2,950	52.4	3,475	52.5	3,450	52.0
R&D	35		50		300		200		400		350	
Selling expense	700		450		550		700		750		850	
Advertising	200		140		200		250		350		350	
Contribution	2,260		1,610		1,300		1,800		1,975		1,900	
General & admin.—incurred	250		250		275		350		420		450	
General & admin.—assessed	250		200		200		270		300		380	
Corporate use charge	130		130		140		150		150		150	
Variances	70		70		20		40		20		40	
Net contribution	1,560		960		665		990		1,085		880	
Depreciation	50		50		50		50		70		70	
Cash from operations	1,610		1,010		715		1,040		1,155		950	
CAPITAL REQUIREMENTS												
Working capital	—		850		(85)		(590)		(500)		—	
Property and equipment	(70)		(100)		(100)		(150)		(100)		(150)	
Cash flow	1,540		1,760		530		300		555		800	

*Dollar amounts are in $1,000's.

3.2. G16 Model

3.2.1. What is Brite in G16 Line Instrumentation?—The G16 line instrumentation consists of relatively inexpensive laboratory instruments and systems for applied scientific research, university science teaching laboratories, and industrial laboratories. The instruments sell in the price range between $3,000 and $7,000.

The G16 chromatograph systems have been extensively redesigned in the electronics section from those originally purchased from the Britton Corporation. Instrument concept and computer compatibility at the present time is ahead of all other similar chromatographs now on the market and will probably retain this lead for at least another year. Close association with the original developers of the G16 system, Dr. Rinze and Menck, should provide Brite with close proximity to the end user, applications experience, and a testing and proving ground for the equipment. New instrumentation and adaptations of the present system should be constantly coming in from Rinze and Menck's group.

3.2.2. Present Market Position—The 1976 market for instruments covering the range of capabilities possessed by the Brite G16 line is estimated to be $60,000,000, with the Brite share estimated to be approximately $1,900,000. The overall market is considered to be relatively stable with annual growth at about 2 to 3 percent. Brite has set its goal on significantly penetrating this market so that our market share reaches 10 percent by 1980.

The G16 system does not offer a price advantage over most of the competition but does offer considerable flexibility, automation, and some technical features above and beyond competitive lines. Our weaknesses include:

1. little or no reputation;
2. small sales force (17 versus 200 for competition);
3. no nationwide service;
4. the instrumentation which we sell has significant user benefits, but buyers have a reluctance to stray from the known.

Experience with the G16 line has provided Brite with valuable education in the last two years. To increase our market penetration, we must increase our sales force. For new products in the moderate to low-cost category, where much larger volume production is required, Brite would have to add a production-engineering capability currently lacking. This capability would have a positive influence on new products of Brite in all price ranges.

The competition is intense both in the United States and overseas with price, service, and performance being the primary determinants (in that order) of sales.

3.2.3. Market Trends and Buyer Behavior. The following major market trends have been noted:

— simplified operation with preprogrammed controls;
— greater demand for equipment tailored to the clinical-biomedical field;
— adaptation of chromatographs for compatibility with other analytical systems such as mass spectrometry, and liquid chromatography, ATR, etc.

According to the Converse report, university spending is leveling off and that portion of the market is relatively mature. This part of the market is the most accessible (no plant guards, security, etc.) to Brite and the least demanding for service, etc. Further, our instrument is well suited for this market. In addition, our sales force (due to the high quality of this instrument) are most familiar with this market. Realizing that the real growth and largest absolute size of the overall market is *industrial* will call for some new considerations.

The marketing trends in the area with regards to channels of distribution seem to fall about an arbitrary price break of $4,000 to $5,000. Under this figure, sales are through dealers; over this figure, sales are direct. There are two reasons for this. First, dealer salesmen are not perceived by the buyer to have the know-how to sell sophisticated instruments (over $5,000). Second, it is difficult to justify the expense of the number of sales calls necessary to sell a low-cost chromatograph without some other products to help defray the expense. To some extent, this second factor is also true of the more expensive equipment. All of the major manufacturers attempt (to a greater or lesser degree) to satisfy all of the instrumentation requirements of the laboratory, not just chromatographic.

The overall market seems to be growing at about 2 to 3 percent per year (1975 was an exception and showed a decrease with the national economy). The equipment being built is tending more and more toward automation and price degradation. By price degradation, I speak of it in terms of more value per dollar spent. The customers are unwilling to spend for features not needed. They are extremely price conscious and only rarely buy extravagantly. Money is becoming harder to get, and purchases must be justified against the task to be performed.

Brite Instrument Company: G16 Line
[$000]

	FY-75	FY-76	FY-77	FY-78	FY-79	FY-80
TOTAL MARKET	60,000	54,000	55,500	57,500	58,500	60,000
P&L						
Sales	1,200	1,950	2,850	3,750	5,100	6,600
COGS	850	1,170	1,570	2,065	2,660	3,430
Gross profit	350	780	1,280	1,685	2,440	3,170
R&D	360	315	270	420	375	450
Selling expenses	415	510	540	600	750	785
Advertising	150	200	190	225	375	410
Contribution	(575)	(245)	280	440	940	1,525
General & admin.						
incurred	260	215	240	275	315	335
assessed	50	100	140	185	225	240
Corporate use charge	125	135	155	165	165	185
Variances	300	45	30	90	30	30
Net contribution	(1,310)	(740)	(285)	(275)	205	735
Depreciation	10	25	25	40	45	45
Cash from operations	(1,300)	(715)	(260)	(235)	250	780
CAPITAL REQUIREMENTS						
Working capital	(375)	(450)	(450)	(470)	(525)	(450)
Property & equipment	(15)	(50)	(50)	(75)	(45)	(50)
Net cash flow	(1,690)	(1,215)	(760)	(780)	(320)	280

3.2.4. Future Objectives, Plans and Recommendations. At present, our plans for the G16 through 1980 are to continue to develop the necessary accessories to remain competitive and to develop a new G16 for introduction in or about 1978 (see attached budget). This instrument would be heavily dependent on the use of microprocessors.

One strategy which has been suggested is to target the G16 for a specific application in the industrial marketplace. In other words, become a significant factor in a unique part of the market not yet dominated by the major manufacturers. To do this will require some market research to define the requirement and design a strategy to take advantage of it. This has not yet been done.

Depending on the results of a market study and evaluation of where Brite intends to strengthen its efforts in the chromatography field, one or more of the following alternatives might be desirable:

1. *Moderate-Priced, High-Performance Instrument*
   Due to rapidly changing technology, it is our feeling that more value can be built into a lower-priced instrument. Further, such

an instrument can have significantly greater specifications without raising the price unduly. We are considering the development of a moderately-priced instrument ($4,000 to $5,500) which would have better specifications than the G16 now has and with built-in computer capability for data manipulation and automation. This would be a routine instrument for use in quality control labs, etc. (market unknown at present). We also envision a more expensive ($10,000 to $11,000) research-type instrument with great sample flexibility and higher specifications (market unknown at present). This instrument would require a significant amount of R&D ($100,000 to $150,000). Further, the overall market for the research (higher priced) chromatograph is relatively mature. The advantage of this approach is more volume (2 product categories) to defray marketing and selling costs, and economies of scale in manufacturing.

2. *Specialize for Defined Applications*

This alternative could be useful for both the short and the long term. In the short run, we might be able to target the marketing and selling of the G16 to quality control laboratories in industry. The G16 calculator combination would appear to represent important benefits to this market. Some market research would be necessary to find out where we could impact this market the best, and how. We would attempt to find an application that is not dominated by a large manufacturer.

3. *Clinical Analyzer*

At present, Brite has no significant impact on the clinical market. Our sales force does not regularly call on this market, nor do we target our advertising and promotion to reach it. Our people are just beginning to gain an appreciation of the specific requirements of this market segment. Further, the government is beginning to have a large influence in this market. At this time, guidelines and regulations are not fixed firmly. This is a fast-growing market and one which we would ultimately like to be part of.

To some degree, specialization of the existing G16 chromatograph would be required, or even a new instrument of lower-cost and simplified design. R&D plus engineering could exceed $350,000 for such an instrument.

4. *Introduce a "Low-Cost" Chromotograph*

Initial studies indicate that there may be a market for another "me too," low-cost ($3,000 list), chromatograph to be sold through a distributor. This would be followed by a more expensive ($5,000) instrument, again with the idea of dealership distribution.

To bring this instrument to the manufacturing stage within one year of initialization, it is proposed to simply copy the best features of instruments currently on the market and carefully engineer the chromatograph for low cost. The following summarizes the best information to date:

Engineering Costs	$	200,000 (3 man years exp. over one year)
Materials Cost	$	25,000 (includes prototype)
Tooling Costs	$	20,000
Marketing Support Costs	$	75,000 (exp. over three years)
Total Three-Year Sales		1,000 units (April 77–80)
Brite Price to Dealer	$	1,950/unit
Total Brite Sales (Three Years)	$1,950,000	

At present, a market survey is being conducted to estimate sales of the proposed instrument. Initial negotiations are underway with a possible distributor.

Funding for this project must be obtained from a source outside Brite if reasonable support to the present lines is to be retained. It will furthermore require special staffing of up to three professionals prior to actually starting the design work.

Possible benefits to Brite include:

— rapid, wide exposure of the Brite name in chromatography;
— an entry into a new market through dealer distribution;
— the foundation of an ongoing program to compete in the low-to-moderate-priced, high-volume instrument market;
— a staff with experience in designing lower cost, higher production volume instrumentation;

Reasons for rejecting this alternative include:

— a high risk investment due to:
   a. A new "team" will have to be recruited for production engineering and design.
   b. Entry into a highly competitive area with a "me too" instrument—assumes there will be no significant instrument improvements until 1980.
   c. Speer has no experience in the very low-cost chromotography manufacturing field.
   d. Market potential is based on single, quick and dirty study.
   e. Proposed distributor has no sales experience in chromatography.
   f. Profit margin is, at best, very low.

— other investment alternatives may prove to be more profitable;

— the only distributor selected and possibly available to us to date may not commit to a Speer exclusive on a product yet to be developed.

Appendix D

Speer Industries, Inc. [D]

Reliance Instrumentation Company: Strategic Plan

1. LABORATORY PRODUCTS

The primary strategy for increasing orders for laboratory products is to give better delivery than our competitors. Our dealers tell us that we lose many orders because of competitors' materials being available when our material is not available. The fact that distributors continue to order from us in spite of *average* delivery, recently as high as five months, attests to the market acceptance of our product and gives credence to the contention that orders can be increased by giving better delivery.

Our second strategy is to conduct a more aggressive sales promotion campaign than our competitors. Laboratory products dealers primarily take orders as opposed to active selling. This means that we can increase orders by persuading the end user to specify our product by name. Our principle thrust is through personal contact by our own field sales force of fifteen people working with dealer field men as well as directly with end users. This is supplemented by sales clinics for dealer sales people, space and direct mail advertising, exhibits at industry and dealer shows, and sales literature and catalogues.

Our third strategy is to offer products of the best design and highest quality and to "out-innovate" our competitors. Our new products manager works in conjunction with our field salespeople to determine customer wants and needs. These are matched with products available to be licensed. Product improvements are usually made by our own staff of nine product design engineers.

With respect to price, our strategy is to be equal to or higher than competition. We will charge what we think the market will bear.

Sales to international markets, by necessity, have not been actively promoted. This is due to our inability to make delivery in a reasonable time. It is believed that international markets offer opportunity for substantial sales as soon as our delivery is satisfactory.

A market study is currently being made to determine the demand for a low-cost chromatograph to be sold through laboratory products dealers.

2. NUCLEAR INSTRUMENTATION

The basic strategy is to license products designed by nuclear manufacturers for their own use, modify the designs to our high standards of quality and dependability, and offer the monitors to utilities and construction contractors throughout the world.

Our sales strategy is to give superior attention to our customer needs. We do this by selling direct as opposed to manufacturer's agents, and by constantly improving our products.

Our pricing strategy is to charge what the market will bear. Annual return on investment to the user is sometimes several times the cost of the monitor. Since there are direct competitors, as well as other ways to monitor the processes, however, pricing is not unrestrained. Current policy is to increase prices by 20 percent per year.

Fiscal Year Cash Flow (by Product Line) 1976
($000)

	LABORATORY PRODUCTS	NUCLEAR	TOTAL
Profit and loss			
Sales	26,000	2,190	28,190
Cost of sales	16,488	890	17,378
Gross profit	9,512	1,300	10,812
Product development	220	62	282
State taxes	48	10	58
Other costs	1,380	260	1,640
Total other cost	1,648	332	1,980
Gross profit after other cost	7,864	968	8,832
Selling expense	2,080	268	2,348
G & A expense	2,152	180	2,332
G & A assessed	1,028	86	1,114
Use charge	1,000	84	1,084
Other costs	188	16	204
Profit from operations	1,416	334	1,750
Depreciation	346	30	376
Cash from operations	1,762	364	2,126
Net current asset liability change			(200)
Plant and equipment			(1,000)
Increase/decrease working capital before deferred taxes			926

Fiscal Year Cash Flow [by Product Line] 1977
[$000]

	LABORATORY PRODUCTS	NUCLEAR	TOTAL
Profit and loss			
Sales	29,800	2,860	32,660
Cost of sales	18,960	1,182	20,142
Gross profit	10,840	1,678	12,518
Product development	260	74	334
State taxes	112	28	140
Other costs	1,600	300	1,900
Total other cost	1,972	402	2,374
Gross profit after other cost	8,868	1,276	10,144
Selling expense	2,400	308	2,708
G & A expense	2,468	238	2,706
G & A expense	1,020	98	1,118
Use charge	1,004	96	1,100
Other costs	218	18	236
Profit from operations	1,758	518	2,276
Depreciation	348	32	380
Cash from operations	2,106	550	2,656
Net current asset liability change			(200)
Plant and equipment			(1,000)
Increase/decrease working capital before deferred taxes			1,456

Fiscal Year Cash Flow [by Product Line] 1978
[$000]

	LABORATORY PRODUCTS	NUCLEAR	TOTAL
Profit and loss			
Sales	35,510	4,506	40,016
Cost of sales	22,932	1,830	24,762
Gross profit	12,578	2,676	15,254
Product development	316	88	404
State taxes	152	76	228
Other costs	1,936	364	2,300
Total other cost	2,404	528	2,932
Gross profit after other cost	10,174	2,148	12,322
Selling expense	2,764	356	3,120
G & A expense	2,762	350	3,112
G & A assessed	1,004	128	1,132
Use charge	1,004	128	1,132
Other costs	226	24	250
Profit from operations	2,414	1,162	3,576
Depreciation	348	32	380
Cash from operations	2,762	1,194	3,956
Net current asset liability change			(500)
Plant and equipment			(1,000)
Increase/decrease working capital before deferred taxes			2,456

Fiscal Year Cash Flow (by Product Line) 1979
($000)

	LABORATORY PRODUCTS	NUCLEAR	TOTAL
Profit and loss			
Sales	42,330	5,810	48,140
Cost of sales	27,494	2,358	29,852
Gross profit	14,836	3,452	18,288
Product development	370	106	476
State taxes	204	106	310
Other costs	2,308	434	2,742
Total other cost	2,882	646	3,528
Gross profit after other cost	11,954	2,806	14,760
Selling expense	3,224	414	3,638
G & A expense	3,184	438	3,622
G & A assessed	1,006	138	1,144
Use charge	1,022	140	1,162
Other costs	322	28	350
Profit from operations	3,196	1,648	4,844
Depreciation	358	32	390
Cash from operations	3,554	1,680	5,234
Net current asset liability change			(800)
Plant and equipment			(1,000)
Increase/decrease working capital before deferred taxes			3,434

DISCUSSION QUESTIONS

SPEER INDUSTRIES, INC. [D]

1. Evaluate individual product line strategies and plans.
2. What are the implications for resource allocation?
3. What is the impact on overall cash flow?
4. What should now be done?

Index of Text